D0260849

The Optimists

The Optimists

THEMES AND PERSONALITIES IN VICTORIAN LIBERALISM

Ian Bradley

FABER AND FABER
London · Boston

First published in 1980
by Faber and Faber Limited
3 Queen Square London WC1N 3AU
Printed in Great Britain by
Latimer Trend & Company Ltd Plymouth
All rights reserved

British Library Cataloguing in Publication Data

Bradley, Ian, b. 1950
The optimists.
1. Liberalism—Great Britain—History—
19th century
I. Title
320.5'1'0941   JN216

ISBN 0-571-11495-4

For Caroline,
a true optimist

Contents

Acknowledgements		*page* 9
Preface		11
1	The Liberal Awakening	17
2	The Creed of the Up-and-Coming	49
3	The Love of Liberty	73
4	The Nonconformist Conscience	99
5	Non-Intervention and Self-Determination	123
6	Trust the People	149
7	Lib–Labism	169
8	The Voluntary Principle	182
9	The Passion for Improvement	200
10	The Waning of Optimism	222
	Chronology	261
	The Optimists—Biographical Notes	265
	Notes	277
	Index	295

Acknowledgements

Someone whose father, like his father before him, bears the proud Christian names William Ewart and whose mother recalls her mother walking eight miles to cast her Liberal vote in an election rather than accept a lift from a Conservative car could hardly help but be fascinated from an early age by Victorian Liberalism. My parents are not only indirectly responsible for my interest in the subject of this book; they have directly assisted me in writing it by reading the manuscript.

On the historical side, Dr. Edward Royle of the University of York and Dr. Clyde Binfield of the University of Sheffield have between them read most of the chapters in the book and have made numerous useful suggestions and corrections. Dr. Paul Hayes of Keble College, Oxford, read through and commented on Chapter Five, although I fear that he will still feel that I am too kind to Mr. Gladstone. Dr. Rhodes Boyson, M.P., shared with me his stimulating thoughts on Cobden and kindly directed me to his fascinating study of the Ashworth family. To all of them I would like to express my grateful thanks and would only add that I alone am responsible for any remaining errors.

I hope that this book proves rather easier to read than it was to write. It was largely researched in university and public libraries throughout the length of Britain while I was on peripatetic assignments with the B.B.C. From the librarians at all the places where I have worked, I have received unfailing help and courtesy. My present employers, Times Newspapers Ltd., kindly gave me a month's unpaid leave at a critical stage in the book's gestation. They were also considerate enough to suspend publication of *The Times* just when I needed a few clear weeks to complete it.

I. C. B.
February 1979

Preface

In an interesting passage in his famous *Apologia Pro Vita Sua* of 1864, John Henry Newman traced the development of the spirit of liberalism which he saw pervading his own age and against which he battled for much of his life. He recalled that he had first come across the word 'liberal' as a boy in the 1810s in the title of a rather scandalous periodical set up by Lord Byron and others. Later it had become the name of a particular school of theology opposed to the tradition and authority of Roman Catholicism. 'Now', he reflected sadly, 'it is scarcely a party; it is the educated lay world.'[1]

Liberalism was, indeed, the prevailing ideology of the Victorians, or at least of most of those intelligent enough to have ideas. In marked contrast to our own pluralistic culture, most educated people in the second half of the nineteenth century shared a common system of values. They believed in the virtue of toleration and the power of reason. They had a sincere if somewhat vague commitment to the ideal of political liberty and an unwavering faith in Parliamentary institutions. In the economic sphere, they were inclined to the view that all things worked together for the good of those who helped themselves, and to favour free trade and the free market unencumbered by protection and restriction by the state. They generally favoured peace and non-intervention overseas, while manifesting sympathy for small nations fighting off tyrants and oppressors. On the whole, they believed in the inevitability of progress and agreed that all change was for the better.

It was clear, however, that some were more liberal than others. Although nearly all Victorians may have shared the same basic outlook on life, they divided sharply in their political allegiances. Well might Private Willis reflect in Gilbert and Sullivan's *Iolanthe* how comical it was how Nature always contrived that every child should be born either a little Liberal or else a little Conservative. During the second half of the nineteenth century there were few educated Englishmen who were not firmly in one camp or the other. Liberals and Conservatives formed two distinct and mutually exclusive societies, each with its own clubs and its own daily newspapers. So separate were their worlds, indeed, that they even had their own architects and favoured styles of building. George Devey, whose sponsor Sir William James was a personal friend of W. E. Gladstone, worked almost exclusively for Liberal clients and often built temples to house busts of the Liberal leader in the gardens of the homes he designed for them. While Conservatives tended to prefer their buildings to be romantically Gothic, Liberals followed the Whig tradition of severe classicism, whether for factories, free trade halls or simple dwellings.

This book is about Liberalism in its narrower, party sense rather than about the general liberalism of the Victorians which has been brilliantly analysed in such books as Walter Houghton's *The Victorian Frame of Mind* (1957) and George Watson's *The English Ideology* (1973).* Obviously, there can be no hard and fast distinction between the two. It is, none the less, possible to distinguish those Victorians like Matthew Arnold or Charles Kingsley who were undeniably liberal in their outlook without being supporters of the Liberal party from those who were both liberal and Liberals, and who form the subject of this book, among them such eminent literary men as Anthony Trollope, George Meredith and William Makepeace Thackeray, as well as the more obvious philosophers and politicians like John Stuart Mill, Lord Acton, Richard Cobden, John Bright and, of course, W. E. Gladstone.

The thoughts and actions of Gladstone must inevitably dominate any book about Victorian Liberalism. As the great Italian historian, Guido de Ruggiero, noted in his *History of European Liberalism* (1927), from the 1860s the word 'Liberal' took on a precise and specialized meaning in Britain very different from its more general application on the Continent: 'It came to mean purely and simply a member of Mr. Gladstone's party.' The subject of this book is really Gladstonianism, that distinct and dominant set of beliefs and values which effectively *was* Liberalism for most Victorians, whether they subscribed to it or not. Those other creeds, heresies one might almost call them, such as Whiggism, Liberal Unionism, Liberal Imperialism, advanced Radicalism and New Liberalism, which found favour among certain smaller groups of Liberals in the second half of the nineteenth century, do not receive much attention in the following pages.

---

* In this book, in accordance with normal usage, the term 'Liberal' is used in the party sense, and 'liberal' in the more general sense.

Gladstonian Liberalism is, rather conveniently, a wholly Victorian phenomenon, just as much as Mudie's Circulating Library or Parliamentary trains. It developed in the first thirty years of the Queen's reign and died at much the same time as she did. It flowered in that glorious and extended high noon of Victorianism which lasted from the mid-1850s to the mid-1880s. Liberal governments under Gladstone were in power from 1868 to 1874, from 1880 to 1885, in 1886, and from 1892 to 1894. This period of Liberal dominance naturally dictates the main time scale of this book, although there are frequent glances back to the 1830s and 1840s and forward to the early twentieth century.

It is important to stress that this book is about Liberalism and not about the Liberal party. Its subject is ideas and there is very little in it about political tactics and organization. Most recent published work on Victorian Liberalism has tended to stress the party and organizational aspects, following the lead given by Professor John Vincent in *The Formation of the British Liberal Party 1857–1868* (1966), a book which the present author freely confesses to having plundered both for its formidable research and its stimulating analysis. Apart from the work of Professor Vincent, which includes the microcosmic study with Dr. A. B. Cooke of a single year of Gladstonian agonizing over Ireland in *The Governing Passion* (1974), the best recent studies of Victorian Liberalism have been those by Professor David Hamer in his books *Liberal Politics in the Age of Gladstone and Rosebery* (1972) and *The Politics of Electoral Pressure* (1977), which deal respectively with high politics and with grass-roots pressure groups. The approach of both Professor Vincent and Professor Hamer is almost aggressively anti-ideological. Indeed, the latter explicitly states in his introduction to *Liberal Politics* that his interest is in studying the form of Liberal policy rather than its content and in 'eliminating conviction and conscience from the range of influences that affect political conduct'.

This book has a very different approach. It starts from the premise that ideas, emanating from conviction and conscience, were central to Victorian Liberalism. Interestingly, this premise is shared by several historians who have recently written about the Liberal 'heresies'. Dr. Colin Matthew in *The Liberal Imperialists* (1973), Dr. Michael Freeden in *The New Liberalism* (1978) and Dr. Peter Clarke in *Liberals and Social Democrats* (1978), all stress the primacy of the ideological element in Gladstonian Liberalism. I cannot hope to compete with Professors Vincent and Hamer in their depth of scholarship or originality of analysis, but I hope that I can perhaps help to correct a distortion which

I fear may have resulted from their concentration on purely organizational and tactical factors. This book will argue that Liberalism was first
and foremost a set of ideas and can only be understood as such. It will
also suggest that it was no accident that Liberalism flourished during
the half century between the first and third great Reform Acts when
there had ceased to be a narrow franchise but was not yet a mass
electorate, and when Britain came nearest in its history to banishing
vested interest and class from determining its politics and establishing
the rule of ideas and principle instead.

There is a danger in a study such as this that Liberalism will appear to
be a coherent and unified body of doctrine, when in fact it was a mass
of separate and often contradictory strands which appealed to particular
individuals and groups for widely differing reasons. By isolating these
different strands and appeals, I hope I have avoided this danger. Each
facet of Gladstonian Liberalism is given a separate chapter. As this
makes for a thematic rather than a chronological approach, I have
added appendices to establish a chronological framework and to give
biographical details of those mentioned in the text.

Although there were always tensions and contradictions within
Liberalism, it is possible to discern an overall set of principles and
assumptions which united Nonconformists, manufacturers, intellectuals, artisans and professional men in a single political movement.
Matthew Arnold, who was the most perceptive and one of the fiercest
critics of what he called 'the great middle-class Liberalism', identified
its cardinal points of belief as 'the Reform Bill of 1832, and local self-
government, in politics; in the social sphere, free trade, unrestricted
competition, and the making of large individual fortunes; in the
religious sphere, the Dissidence of Dissent, and the Protestantism of
the Protestant religion'.[2] One might also add to these points a conviction that international affairs should be conducted on the basis of
morality rather than national interest and pride; and, perhaps above
all, a strong preference for promoting the general welfare of society
through individual voluntary action, and ideally through self-help,
rather than through the compulsory activity of the state.

Perhaps the single characteristic which most clearly united all those
who espoused Gladstonian Liberalism was their all-pervasive optimism.
It was certainly a feature of Gladstone himself which considerably
impressed both his contemporaries and later historians. Lord Salisbury,
a fierce political opponent, confessed his admiration for the Liberal
leader's 'gorgeous reckless optimism'.[3] For G. M. Trevelyan Gladstone

was 'at once the most optimistic and the most Christian of statesmen', while the American historian, Robert Kelley, noted that 'he possessed that most distinguishing mark of the Liberal mind, a fundamental optimism about life in its larger aspects.'[4]

Gladstonian optimism showed itself in the belief that, once given political power, people would use it to promote high ideals rather than to further their own immediate material interests; in the faith that the dealings between the nations of the world could be conducted on the basis of rational discussion and regulated by international arbitration; and in the conviction that employers would naturally look after their workers' welfare, in bad times as well as good times, thereby obviating the need for state protection and intervention. The Liberal principles of self-government, internationalism, free trade and voluntaryism only make sense in the context of a fundamental faith in the goodness and rationality of man and the reality of progress.

Optimism is not a very dominant motif in the outlook of our own age. Two world wars and the proliferation of nuclear weapons have somewhat shaken our faith in the capacity of nations to settle their affairs by agreement and arbitration. The advent of mass democracy in the West, far from increasing interest in high ideals and principles, seems rather to have led to the politics of bribery with parties competing for votes by promises of immediate material rewards. The growing role of the state as provider of welfare and social benefits of all kinds has considerably diminished both the expectation and the possibility of individual charity and self-help.

Yet the values of Victorian Liberalism are enjoying something of a renaissance in late twentieth-century Britain. As faith in social democracy wanes, people are turning back to the ideology which it supplanted at the beginning of the twentieth century as the dominant source of values about politics and society. In the last few years there has been a revival of the concept of voluntaryism and a growing questioning of the idea that the state is necessarily the best provider of all social welfare. The principles of self-help in the community and economy in government are once again being preached by politicians. There has been a revival of interest in the idea of home rule for the constituent parts of the United Kingdom, in electoral reform to secure proportional representation, and in a closer political and economic relationship between the countries of Europe. This book is written in the conviction that the Victorian Liberals still have much to offer us today, not least in their refreshing and inspiring optimism.

Chapter 1

The Liberal Awakening

Probably 1832 is as good a date as any to take as a starting point in tracing the development of Victorian Liberalism, although there are good grounds for going back to the 1790s to find the origins of a distinctive Liberal position in British politics. Benjamin Disraeli took the year of the Reform Act as marking the advent of Liberalism in Britain when he spoke to a large Conservative audience at the Crystal Palace in 1872, while John Bright noted in his diary in 1880 that 'the Government from that time has been, with the exception of about twelve years, Liberal in name, and has steadily become more and more Liberal to the great advantage of the nation.'[1] As Matthew Arnold observed, the 1832 Reform Act had a hallowed place in the Liberal creed. It created the middle-class electorate and the expectation of reform that made Gladstonianism possible. It was to be another thirty-five years, however, before the Liberal awakening in Britain was completed.

Liberalism was not, of course, something peculiar to Britain. It had been born overseas with the demand for government by consent and the securing of individual rights in the American colonists' Declaration of Independence in 1776, and the attack on absolutist rule and on aristocratic and clerical privileges made by the leaders of the French Revolution in 1789. The use of the word 'liberal' as a political term was French in origin. It seems first to have been employed around 1807 to describe those like Madame de Staël and Chateaubriand who opposed the dictatorship of Napoleon I. In 1811 the word was used in Spain to describe reformers who championed ideas of popular sovereignty, freedom of the press and individual liberty, enshrined in the constitution of 1812 which became a model for many European liberals. The first recorded use of the term in England was in 1816 when Robert Southey, the poet, referred in the *Quarterly Review* to 'the British "liberales"'. Ten years later, Sir Walter Scott wrote in his journal of 'a mitigated party of liberaux'. It was not until the 1830s that the word came to be used in Britain in an anglicized form.

Even if the word itself was not in regular usage until the 1830s, there were recognizably liberal forces at work in British politics from the end of the eighteenth century. For much of the 1780s and 1790s the great Whig aristocrats who had held virtually unchallenged sway for most of the century found themselves out of power. This unaccustomed state of opposition, which continued for the first three decades of the nineteenth century, brought the Whigs into alliance with radicals and prompted them to develop policies and principles which took on the nature of a political ideology. Under the leadership of Charles James Fox, the Whigs committed themselves to the political emancipation of Roman Catholics and Dissenters, the abolition of the slave trade and to the extension of the franchise. They also developed a commitment to general liberal reforms exemplified in such measures as Fox's own Libel Act of 1792 which considerably eased restrictions on the press.

This enlightened Whiggism continued to develop in the first three decades of the nineteenth century. Fox's ideas were kept alive and passed on to a new generation in the great Whig salons like Holland House and in the pages of the *Edinburgh Review*. Eventually they came to fruition with the emancipation of Dissenters and Catholics in 1828 and 1829 and with the passing of the Great Reform Act in 1832. Although they were undeniably aristocratic and exclusive, the Whigs yet held firm to liberal principles of government. They were well defined by Francis Baring in 1830 as 'a body of men connected with high rank and property, bound together by hereditary feeling and party ties, as well as higher motives, who in bad times keep alive the sacred name of freedom'.[2] There is considerable justice in the claim of the French historian Elié Halévy that the years 1815 to 1830 saw the 'Liberal Awakening' in Britain.

Both on the Continent and in Britain the dawning of the 1830s seemed to give dramatic evidence of a new liberal awakening. In France the July Revolution of 1830, led by Adolphe Thiers, François Guizot and Jacques Laffitte in opposition to the ultra-conservative government of Charles X, had established a constitutional monarchy and appeared to usher in the rule of the bourgeoisie which had been urged by liberal political theorists like Henri Constant during the 1820s. Belgium had successfully won its independence from both France and the Netherlands and looked set on a secure course of constitutional government and middle-class rule. There were definite stirrings of liberalism in Italy, where thousands were flocking to join the Young Italy movement set up by Joseph Mazzini, who from his exile in Marseilles called for constitutional reform as a precondition of securing the independence and reunification of the country.

At home, the administration which came to power after the first election under the new reformed system was unmistakably Whig. Although it was narrowly oligarchic and showed little sympathy with the middle-class merchants and manufacturers who were trying to find their way into the House of Commons after 1832, it was at least made up of those men who had clung tenaciously to the principles of political reform and civil rights through the dark days of Tory rule. The Whig governments of the 1830s, led by the 2nd Earl Grey and the 2nd Viscount Melbourne, promoted an impressive catalogue of liberal measures, including the abolition of slavery throughout the British Dominions, the first annual government grant for education, the Municipal Reform Act, which established that most members of town councils should be elected rather than self-appointed, and the Marriage Act, which allowed Dissenters to be married in their own chapels. In addition, tithes, the tenth part of all produce of the land compulsorily given to the Church, were commuted to a single money rent, and the stamp duty on newspapers was reduced from fourpence to one penny.

These reforms were not, however, enough to satisfy the expectations that had been raised in 1832 among the Philosophic Radicals, a small group who formed a tiny but distinct body in Parliament and who were, in some ways, the forerunners of Victorian Liberalism. There had, of course, been Radical M.P.s in the House of Commons since the late eighteenth century who championed such causes as parliamentary reform and the mitigation of the severe criminal code. They were generally isolated, however, and lacked any overall political philosophy. In the early 1830s, Joseph Hume, a veteran Radical and zealous advocate of free trade and political reform, was joined in the Commons by Charles Buller, John Arthur Roebuck, George Grote and William Molesworth. All were ardent disciples of Jeremy Bentham whose utilitarian philosophy urged the claims of social utility and efficiency against those of antiquity and custom. The Philosophic Radicals, who were themselves middle-class bankers, lawyers and civil servants, saw the unreformed institutions and aristocratic government of the Whigs preventing essential reforms like the introduction of the secret ballot and the further extension of the franchise, the granting of self-government to the colonies, and the freeing of trade.

The reforms introduced by the Whigs in the 1830s also failed to satisfy the demands of three important communities in the country who were beginning to organize themselves into articulate and vocal pressure groups. The religious Dissenters, or Nonconformists as they were coming to be known, had at last, with the repeal of the Test and Corporation Acts in 1828, obtained the right to hold state or municipal office which they had been denied in theory, and often in practice, since the late seventeenth century, but they were still subject to numerous disadvantages that followed from the privileged position of the Church of England as the established Church. The merchants and manufacturers who were responsible for Britain's commercial and industrial supremacy in the world found it extremely irksome that national economic policy was determined by an overwhelmingly landowning Parliament and sought a way of achieving political power commensurate with their considerable economic importance in the community. The growing body of middle-class professional people objected to the aristocratic hold on government and institutions which denied them appointments and advancement.

It was the fusion of these forces, the Philosophic Radicals in Parliament and the discontented Nonconformists, manufacturers and professional middle classes outside it, that brought about the Liberal awakening in Britain. The Radicals provided a parliamentary base, however small, and, in the opinion of John Stuart Mill, the son of one of their leading lights and himself the foremost philosopher of Victorian Liberalism, they also gave 'principle and philosophy to the Liberalism which was growing in importance'.[3] The discontented groups in the country built up national organizations and gained widespread support for their campaigns of reform. They also provided the man who perhaps has more claim than any other to be regarded as the first Liberal M.P., Edward Baines, a Congregationalist and proprietor of a Leeds newspaper and printing business. When he was elected M.P. for Leeds in 1834, as successor to that great apologist for Whiggism, Thomas Babington Macaulay, the Philosophic Radicals believed he would join them. Although he agreed with them on most issues, Baines's Nonconformity and his provincial background could never quite accommodate itself to the rationalism and metropolitan urbanity of the Radicals and he ploughed a lone furrow in Parliament until his defeat in 1841.

It was also from the ranks of the discontented groups in the country, in this case the manufacturers, that a distinctively Liberal programme was first put forward in Britain. In the election that followed the accession of Queen Victoria to the throne in 1837 Richard Cobden, a

33-year-old calico printer from Lancashire, stood as reform candidate for Stockport. His platform included the disestablishment of both the Irish Church and the Church of England, the extension of the Parliamentary franchise to all households, the establishment of triennial Parliaments and a secret ballot, a national education system, the repeal of the corn laws, the abandonment of the colonies, the reform of the House of Lords to include representation of manufacturing interests, equality of treatment by the law for rich and poor, and the replacement of patronage in the Civil Service and Armed Forces by appointment on merit.

Two years after Cobden's unsuccessful contest at Stockport, John Stuart Mill, also aged thirty-three, wrote an article on 'The Reorganization of the Reform Party' in the *London and Westminster Review*, which had been founded in 1823 by his father, James Mill, as the organ of the Philosophic Radicals. Mill saw that the Reform Act had created a new situation in British politics in which parties must represent distinct communities of interest and not remain clans based primarily on family loyalty and tradition. His article called for the creation of a new party of reform, based on the existing Radical group in Parliament, but drawing its support from many other sections of the community. 'The modern Radicals are in possession of a part of the ground on which it is necessary that the combination should be built,' he wrote, 'but we well know that the new Reform party . . . cannot be Radical in any narrow or sectarian sense. There may be many coteries in a country, but there can only be two parties. What we must have to oppose the great Conservative party is the whole Liberal party . . . a phalanx stretching from the Whig-Radicals at one extremity to the ultra-Radicals and the working classes at the other.'[4]

Mill saw this new Liberal party deriving its support from the unprivileged and aggrieved classes in the community, while the Conservative party would find its natural constituency among the privileged and the satisfied. He enumerated the main sources of Conservative strength as the landed interest, the rich, the protected trades, such as the shipping interest, the timber interest and the West India interest, and 'the professions which partake of aristocracy, the army, the navy, the bar and the Church of England clergy'. The new Liberal party, he predicted, would gain the support of the manufacturing and mercantile classes, who 'feel that they do not have justice done to them by existing institutions', Nonconformists, small proprietors, and 'the skilled employments, those which require talent and education, but confer no rank—what may be called the non-aristocratic professions', like teaching, medicine, engineering and journalism. 'In addition to all these classes', he wrote, 'must be included among the natural Radicals nearly all Scotland and Ireland; and last but not the least, the whole effective political strength of the working classes.'

The working classes were, in fact, demonstrating their political strength as Mill was writing his article. They too were frustrated at the end of the 1830s, and disappointed at the Whigs' refusal to contemplate any further extension of the franchise after 1832. In the month when Mill's article was published, July 1839, the Grand Convention of the Industrious Classes, composed of working-class representatives elected from all over the country, presented a petition to Parliament calling for reforms even more radical than those proposed by Cobden. Their demands, which had first been published in the People's Charter, included manhood suffrage, voting by ballot, annual Parliaments, abolition of the property qualification for M.P.s, payment of M.P.s and equal electoral districts. Parliament's refusal even to consider the petition led the Chartists, as the working-class protesters had become known, into a heated debate as to whether or not they should use violence to back their demands. Serious riots in several towns later in the year seemed to suggest that the advocates of 'physical force', led by a fiery Irish demagogue, Feargus O'Connor, had won the day.

Mill did not specifically mention the Chartists in his article but he left his readers in no doubt of his lack of sympathy for them. Although he spoke grandly of the need for weight to be added 'to the two elements of Numbers and Intelligence and taken away from privilege', he seemed principally interested in increasing the power of the educated middle classes and noticeably unconcerned about the masses. He argued that the new Liberal party should advocate middle-class rather than universal suffrage, and wrote, 'the motto of a radical politician should be government by means of the middle for the working classes.' The working classes were not yet well enough educated or informed to receive the vote. Mill was confident that every year would see an advancement in their 'good sense' and 'good conduct' and that they would ultimately prove themselves worthy of being entrusted with political power. To hasten that day, he suggested that labourers be encouraged to become capitalists, by investing money in enterprises and dividing the profit among themselves, and that working men's associations 'continue to inculcate temperance, economy, kindness, every household virtue, and every rational and intellectual pursuit, among their members . . . and systematically discountenance all appeals to violence'. Mill went on to promise that since 'discussion is rapidly doing its work in cultivating the intelligence of the working classes, the appreciation of that intelligence will necessarily follow.' Meanwhile, they should be given just enough political power to keep the middle classes in 'salutary awe' of them.

The idea that the working classes would happily submit to middle-class government and should be given power only when they had proved themselves intellectually and morally fit for it was one of the strongest convictions of Victorian Liberalism. Initially, it helped to delay the Liberal awakening. Far from preaching the virtues of capitalism and moderation as Mill had urged, many working-class leaders continued to involve themselves in the Chartist movement during the 1840s. Several of them advocated a proto-communist economic order along the lines of that developed by Robert Owen, the socialist pioneer, and a campaign of organized disruption and violent protest. They demanded political power for the masses immediately, and not after they had satisfied a rigorous set of middle-class criteria such as those laid down by Edward Baines the younger when he set against the six points of the Charter six demands of his own for education, religion, virtue, industry, sobriety and frugality. As the hungry forties gave way to the prosperous decades of the 1850s and 1860s, however, the working classes came to see that the values being urged on them by Liberals like Mill and Baines were, in fact, beneficial to themselves.

Mill was also rather over-optimistic in his article about the new Liberal party's chances of finding a leader and winning adherents in Parliament. He pinned his hopes on the leadership of the Earl of Durham, a keen Radical who had resigned from Grey's Cabinet in 1834 to go on a tour of the North of England in which he advocated household suffrage, the ballot and triennial Parliaments. Durham then went as Governor General to Canada, where he drew up a report recommending responsible self-government for the colony. When he returned home in 1838, however, he declined all offers to lead a new Radical party and two years later he died at the age of forty-eight.

Durham's death effectively dashed the hopes of Mill and other Radicals for the early creation of a new reform party in Parliament. The Philosophic Radicals disintegrated at the end of the 1830s, disillusioned that the political hold of the aristocracy was as strong as when they had first attacked it more than ten years earlier. From the mid-1830s until the mid-1860s the Whig Party was dominated by Melbourne and Palmerston, neither of whom had any desire to create a new reforming party. The only middle-class and liberal political leader in Parliament was the Conservative, Sir Robert Peel, who was hamstrung at the head of a party representing the landed interest until he took both himself and the Tories into the political wilderness when he abolished the corn laws in 1846.

The gradual development of Liberalism during the 1840s took place almost entirely outside Parliament as a result of growing agitation by the dissatisfied and unprivileged groups in the community whom Mill had identified in his article as forming the main elements of a new Liberal party. They organized themselves into pressure groups to campaign for many of the specific reforms that Cobden had linked together in his programme to the electors of Stockport in 1837. Slowly, the various groups looked beyond their own immediate sectional interests and realized that they had in common a general outlook that could be defined as Liberalism. This realization was helped by the involvement of many of the leaders of particular campaigns in other struggles and by the overlapping membership of the dissatisfied groups. Many manufacturers, for example, were also Nonconformists and were equally concerned with the campaigns for free trade and disestablishment. Within Parliament, the agitators had a focus in Cobden, who was elected M.P. for Stockport in 1841, and John Bright, a Quaker cotton spinner from Rochdale who was elected M.P. for Durham two years later. Throughout the 1840s they effectively constituted a two-man party which was the nucleus of the Victorian Liberal Party.

The Nonconformists were in many ways the best organized and the most vociferous of the dissatisfied groups of the 1840s. Since the mid-1830s they had been agitating locally against the compulsory church rates which had to be paid by all, regardless of their own denomination, to keep up the Church of England. In 1840 John Bright led a success-ful campaign against church rates in Rochdale. In the following year Edward Miall, a Congregational minister, founded a weekly paper, the *Nonconformist*, to 'uphold the Dissidence of Dissent and the Protestantism of the Protestant Religion' and to campaign for the abolition of church rates, the disestablishment of the Anglican Church in England, Ireland and Wales, and the ending of government sup-port for education which went exclusively to Anglican schools.[5] In 1844, Miall and others set up the Anti-State Church Association to campaign for disestablishment. Soon afterwards the Voluntary School Association was founded with another Congregationalist, Henry Richard, as its secretary, to fight against the government's support of Anglican schools. From 1847 its campaign, which not all Nonconformists supported, was led by Edward Baines the younger, who was later to follow his father as M.P. for Leeds. The Nonconformists rapidly came to see that their cause would be best advanced by having their own representatives in Parliament and in 1847 they established a Dissenters' Parliamentary Committee to work for the election of Nonconformist M.P.s.

For a short time at the beginning of the 1840s it looked as though the working classes might be fulfilling Mill's hopes and co-operating with middle-class Radicals in a campaign for moderate and peaceful reform. In 1841 Joseph Sturge, a Quaker corn dealer from Birmingham, brought together five Chartist leaders, Henry Vincent, Arthur O'Neill, William Lovett, Bronterre O'Brien and John Collins, to found the Complete Suffrage Union. Although the Union accepted all six of the Chartists' main demands, it made clear that the campaign for them should be gradual and non-violent. Miall enthusiastically ran a series in the *Nonconformist* under the heading, 'Reconciliation between the Middle and Labouring Classes'. Co-operation on the suffrage issue was short-lived, however. The Union was soon divided as to whether its demands should be called a Charter, or a Bill of Rights. When its conference at the end of 1842 voted for the former, middle-class delegates walked out and the Union effectively collapsed. The more ardent spirits among the working classes turned again to the physical-force Chartism of O'Connor, while others, encouraged by the economic recovery that started in the mid-1840s, joined in the agitation for free trade and repeal of the corn laws which was being led by manufacturers.

The Anti-Corn Law League was the most immediately successful of the pressure groups set up by dissatisfied elements in the community in the 1840s. It had a single simple object: to secure the abolition of the high duties on the import of foreign grain which had originally been introduced to protect English agriculture in the aftermath of the Napoleonic wars. The continued maintenance of the corn laws caused particular resentment among manufacturers involved in exporting. They claimed that the corn laws denied the wheat-growing lands of eastern and southern Europe free access to the English market and so restricted the ability of those countries to take manufactured goods from Britain. In 1837 Dr. John Bowring, a former secretary to

Bentham, told an audience in Manchester that Germany and other grain-producing countries were beginning to manufacture their own cotton goods because the corn laws prevented them from exchanging their produce for English textiles. Cotton goods were Britain's largest export, and it was not surprising that cotton manufacturers should take a lead in the campaign against the corn laws, nor that the centre of the cotton industry, Manchester, should be the headquarters of the League which was set up in 1839 to press for their abolition. Led by Cobden and Bright, the League used hired lecturers, public meetings, pamphlets and direct electoral pressure to push its message home, and in 1846 its aim was achieved when Peel repealed the corn laws.

The repeal of the corn laws was a significant milestone in the evolution of Liberalism. It was represented as the first great triumph of one of the dissatisfied groups in the country and as a spectacular victory for the manufacturing and mercantile middle classes led by Cobden and Bright, whom Disraeli dubbed 'the Manchester Party', over the landed interest that still predominated in Parliament. It helped to hasten the formation of the Victorian Liberal party by pushing the more conservative Whigs into alliance with the protectionist majority of the Conservative party. In his novel, *Beauchamp's Career*, George Meredith talked of 'the Manchester flood, before which time Whigs were, since when they have walked like spectral antediluvians, or floated as dead, canine bodies that are sucked away on the ebb tides'.[6] The arguments used in the campaign against the corn laws were developed by theorists like Herbert Spencer, from 1846 a journalist on the *Economist*, to form a coherent doctrine of economic liberalism.

Repeal also isolated Peel and his fellow liberals from the main body of the Conservative party. There was considerable hope that Peel might now agree to lead a new Liberal party. A few days after his resignation as Tory leader, he received a letter from Cobden pointing out that 'there are no substantial lines of demarcation betwixt the Peelites and the so-called Whig or Liberal party' and calling on him to put himself at the head of the middle classes, now clearly established as the governing class in the country.[7] Peel could not be persuaded to take up the challenge, however, and the Liberals had to wait nearly twenty years before they found a leader in the brightest of his lieutenants, William Ewart Gladstone.

In 1848, the year of revolution in Europe, it seemed as though Britain was being left behind, as it had been in the early 1830s, in the triumphant progress of liberalism across the Continent. France became a republic, the Hungarians and Bohemians broke away from the Habsburg Empire and the Poles rose against their Russian masters. Metternich, the most active representative of reaction in Europe, was forced to flee from Vienna in the face of a popular rising. In Italy, the Milanese drove out Austrian troops, Venice was in arms for liberty, and Charles Albert, the King of Piedmont, had put himself at the head of a national struggle against Austria on the plains of Lombardy. The fact that the forces of authority and tradition were subsequently to reassert their power in every single case did not detract from the feeling of English Radicals at the time that their country was in some way missing out.

Cobden and Bright had hoped that the repeal of the corn laws would usher in a new era of political and administrative reform in Britain. In 1849 they set up the Parliamentary and Administrative Reform Association to advocate a programme of tax reduction and franchise extension. Bright co-operated with Hume, Roebuck and the veteran radical Francis Place in promoting a 'Little Charter' which called for household suffrage, a secret ballot and triennial Parliaments. He hoped to unite middle-class and working-class radicals behind a common programme. Cobden campaigned vigorously for a foreign policy based on the principle of non-intervention and for a reduction of Britain's naval and military establishments, both on economical and humanitarian grounds. He was actively involved in the Peace Society, which took on a new lease of life in 1848 with the election of Henry Richard, a Welsh Congregational minister, as secretary and organized annual peace congresses in European cities. The Manchester Party were putting forward the policy of 'peace, retrenchment and reform' which was to become the favourite cry of Gladstonian Liberalism.

The optimism of the late 1840s soon wore off, however. The Whig Government which came to power after the repeal of the corn laws showed no enthusiasm for further Parliamentary or administrative reforms and was distinguished chiefly for the alacrity with which Palmerston, as Foreign Secretary, embarked on costly entanglements abroad. The attempt to create an alliance between working-class and middle-class reformers failed when working-class leaders demanded something more than household suffrage and returned to the Chartist struggle. There was not even much unanimity within the small Liberal ranks as to what they should do. Bright was for concentrating on Parliamentary reform while Cobden preferred to campaign for cuts in expenditure through reductions in the military establishment and in involvement abroad. Both felt that the increasingly strident campaign being mounted by Baines and Miall, who became an M.P. in 1852, against government-supported education hindered rather than helped the cause of reform. Neither had any sympathy with the support that Radicals like J. A. Roebuck gave to the Government's policy of going to war against Russia to defend the integrity of the Ottoman Empire. In November 1853 Bright wrote to Cobden about the lack of liberal policy and prospects: 'In calling for Reform of Parliament, the Radical Party have no policy to offer as the promised fruits of another Reform Bill. When the Whigs heeded the former cry in 1830, they promised retrenchment, peace, non-intervention and all kinds of practical benefits . . . now the Radicals (I speak of those who are anything better than Whigs, and yet not of the Manchester School) have contrived to identify themselves with an absurd policy which actually precludes the possibility of any appreciable reduction in expenditure (because of their keenness for British intervention in the Eastern question). . . . Add to this, that Mr. Baines and a very large part of Dissenters, the very salt of liberalism, have managed to snatch away from us more than half of our old cry of "National Education", and you see what a mess we are in for want of a Radical policy to inspire the great supine public with some hopes of advantage from a further reform of Parliament.'[8]

It is interesting that Bright still spoke in his letter of a Radical rather than a Liberal party, while at the same time distinguishing Radicals from those, like himself, in the Manchester School. The word Liberal was only slowly coming to be used to describe a political group. In 1850 Leigh Hunt noted that 'newer and more thorough-going Whigs were first known by the name of Radicals, and have since been called . . . Liberals.'[9] There were, however, as Bright pointed out, distinct differences between Radicals like Hume and Roebuck and members of his own Manchester Party. These came out particularly strongly in the early 1850s in debates over Palmerston's aggressive and interventionist foreign policy, which was applauded by the Radicals as championing the cause of liberty abroad and condemned by Cobden and Bright as being fundamentally inimical to the principles of peace and retrenchment. Both strains were to be assimilated into Victorian Liberalism.

1855 was a bleak year for Liberalism both in Britain and abroad. In Europe, Louis Napoleon was firmly entrenched after the *coup d'état* which had set up a centralized despotism in France, while the Concordat signed by Pius IX with the Austrian Government establishing church control over all education marked the crowning political achievement of the Papal counter-revolution against the advance of liberal opinions. At home, Palmerston, the arch-enemy of reform and retrenchment, was Prime Minister, and the country was plunged deep into the Crimean War. Cobden and Bright were galled by the popular enthusiasm for the war, compared to the lack of public interest in their own proposals for reform.

In fact, the Crimean War hastened the Liberal awakening in Britain. The incompetence and corruption with which it was managed by the aristocracy aroused the anger of the talented and educated among the middle classes, whom Mill had rightly seen as forming an important element in a new Liberal party. In 1855 a group of business and professional men under the chairmanship of Samuel Morley, a Midlands hosiery manufacturer and prominent Nonconformist, set up the Administrative Reform Association to protest against the incompetence and jobbery that came from the aristocratic hold on government and to champion management by the middle classes. The Association campaigned for appointments to the Civil Service to be made on the basis of merit, tested by competitive examination, rather than by patronage. Its call for the opening of careers to talent and for government by the able was to become one of the great sustaining principles of Victorian Liberalism.

The aims of the Administrative Reform Association appealed particularly to the more intellectual members of the middle classes. The Association attracted the active support of both Charles Dickens and William Makepeace Thackeray. The two novelists both had strong reforming sympathies. Dickens had been asked to stand as Liberal candidate for Reading in 1841, but he declined. He made his first public speech on a political subject at the Administrative Reform Association's second public meeting. He was never an active Liberal, however, and subsequently became highly critical of the party for its middle-class manufacturing bias and its opposition to social reform. Thackeray, on the other hand, was a committed Liberal. As a young man he had advocated universal suffrage and the ballot, and in 1836 he had helped to found a periodical, *The Constitutional*, in an effort to bolster the waning fortunes of the Philosophic Radicals in Parliament. In articles for *Punch* in 1846 and 1847 he lampooned the corruption and archaism of British institutions. His horror at the consequences of aristocratic rule as revealed in the management of the Crimean War led him to become an active Liberal politician. In 1857 he stood unsuccessfully against a Whig opponent in the election for a second M.P. for Oxford on a platform which included the ballot, the extension of the franchise and the establishment of middle-class rather than aristocratic predominance in government.

Another event of 1855, the abolition of stamp duty on newspapers, helped to hasten the Liberal awakening. Stamp duties had been maintained by governments in the early nineteenth century not so much to raise revenue as to limit the circulation of radical literature. They were abolished by Gladstone, as Chancellor of the Exchequer in Lord Aberdeen's Coalition Government, in response to pressure from the Association for the Abolition of Taxes on Knowledge, an organization of ex-Chartists, Radicals and secularists set up in 1851 under the chairmanship of Thomas Milner Gibson, M.P. for Manchester, and with Cobden and Bright on its General Committee. The abolition of stamp duty, which was followed in 1861 by the ending of the tax on paper, led to the emergence of a popular national and provincial press, overwhelmingly Liberal in its politics. In 1855 the first mass-circulation daily paper was born when the *Daily Telegraph* merged with the Peelite *Morning Chronicle*. It was staunchly Liberal and had a circulation of 150,000 by 1860. Its main rival, the *Daily News*, which had been started by Dickens in 1846, was also Liberal and was the main Nonconformist paper. In 1868, under Samuel Morley's ownership, it took over the *Morning Star*, the paper of Cobden and Bright's Manchester School.

The provincial press which developed as a result of the abolition of stamp duty was, if anything, even more attached to the emerging Liberal cause. It was pre-eminently the voice of the middle-class, manufacturing, Nonconformist communities of the North and the Midlands, preaching reform and free trade. In 1855 both the *Manchester Guardian*, which had been started in 1819 by the Radical John Edward Taylor, and the *Liverpool Daily Post* (previously the *Liverpool Times*) became penny dailies. Two years later, the *Birmingham Daily Post* was started as an off-shoot of the *Birmingham Journal* which had been set up by Parliamentary reformers in the city. The circulation of these papers far outstripped that of their Conservative and working-class rivals. In Lancashire, there were over forty Liberal papers and less than twenty Conservative ones. In neighbouring Yorkshire, the *Leeds Mercury* was selling over ten thousand copies a day in the late 1850s under the editorship of Edward Baines the younger. Baines was at the centre of a remarkable dynasty of Nonconformist Liberal newspaper editors. The *Leeds Mercury* was continuously edited by Baineses from 1801, when his father bought it, to 1870, when his son handed it over to T. Wemyss Reid. His brother Thomas was editor of the *Liverpool Times*, and his mother's cousin Robert Leader bought and edited the *Sheffield Independent*. All were fervent supporters of the Liberal cause.

The development of a mass-circulation press to cater for the rising bourgeoisie was a feature of the Liberal awakening throughout the industrialized world in the mid-nineteenth century. In Germany *Die Gartenlaube*, founded in 1853 by an ex-Radical, Ernst Keil, was selling 160,000 copies by 1863, and *Die Frankfurter Zeitung* established itself as the leading paper for businessmen soon after its foundation in 1856. In France, the liberal *Le Figaro*, begun as a weekly paper in 1854, became a daily in 1866 and easily outsold its conservative, imperialist rival, *Le Constitutionnel*. Two papers, *La Lanterne* and *La Marseillaise*, started in the late 1860s by the Republican Henri de Rochefort opposing Napoleon's authoritarianism, each had circulations well over 100,000. In America, the *New York Tribune*, founded by the Liberal Whig Horace Greeley in 1841, sold 200,000 copies daily, with the rival *New York Times*, started in 1851, not far behind.

By the end of the 1850s Liberalism had made significant headway in Parliament. The general election of April 1859 brought several leading Liberals to Westminster, including a formidable trio from Yorkshire, Edward Baines the younger as M.P. for Leeds, Titus Salt, who owned worsted mills, as M.P. for Bradford, and James Stansfeld, an ally of Sturge in the Complete Suffrage Union and an enthusiastic supporter of Continental liberalism, as M.P. for Halifax. The previous M.P. for Halifax, Francis Crossley, a carpet manufacturer, was returned for the West Riding. The election gave the Conservatives under Lord Derby a slight majority over the Whigs, with Radicals, Peelites and the Manchester Party holding the balance. At a meeting on 6 June in Willis's Rooms, a suite of assembly rooms in St. James's, the minority groups agreed to combine with the Whigs to bring the Conservatives down. Four days later Derby was defeated on a vote in the House of Commons and Palmerston became Prime Minister as leader of a coalition of the groups that were to make up the Victorian Liberal party in Parliament. Gladstone, who had voted for the Conservatives in the crucial division, crossed the floor of the House to take office as Chancellor of the Exchequer in the new ministry. Palmerston even offered a seat in the Cabinet to Cobden. Bright told the Commons that 'since the fall of the government of Sir Robert Peel there has been no good handling of the liberal party in the House: the cabinet has been exclusive, the policy has been sometimes wholly wrong, and generally feeble and faltering', and predicted enthusiastically that 'in the new government there should be found men . . . grappling with the abuses that were admitted to exist, and relying upon . . . the general sympathy of the people of England for improvement in our legislation.'[10]

The meeting in Willis's Rooms in June 1859 is often taken to mark the formation of the British Liberal party. The Liberal Registration Association, set up in 1860, acted as a party headquarters, interviewing candidates, co-ordinating election strategy and putting life into dormant constituencies. It was not until the mid-1860s, however, that the Liberal party emerged fully fledged in Parliament. Palmerston's administration was still essentially Whig, even though it depended on the support of Radicals, Peelites and the Manchester Party. Even when he died in 1865, the Liberals did not at once gain the upper hand. He was succeeded as Prime Minister by Lord John Russell, aptly described by Sir William Harcourt as 'the last Doge of Whiggism', with Gladstone as leader of the House of Commons.[11] Significantly, it was in the country rather than in Parliament that Liberals first became established as a major political party. During the 1860s Liberal Associations sprang up around the country, particularly in the manufacturing areas of the Midlands and the North, replacing old Whig Registration Associations and Reform Leagues. Manchester had a Liberal Association in 1862, Birmingham in 1865 and Leeds soon after. Nonconformists, manufacturers and working-class radicals were finding a single political focus for their own particular interests and grievances.

While the establishment of Liberal Associations in the provinces provided one element in the combination of 'Numbers and Intelligence' which Mill had seen as forming a new Liberal party, an equally important movement among the intelligentsia in London and the ancient universities was providing the other. A significant number of leading intellectuals and academics were attracted to Liberalism in the 1860s, among them some of the most brilliant minds of the day. During the decade Liberal representation in Parliament included two philosophers, John (later Lord) Acton, M.P. for Carlow from 1859 to 1865, and J. S. Mill, M.P. for Westminster 1865 to 1868; a historian, Alexander Kinglake, the author of *Eothen* and of the standard history of the Crimean War, who sat for Bridgwater from 1857 to 1868; and a leading novelist, Thomas Hughes, the author of *Tom Brown's Schooldays*, who was M.P. for Lambeth from 1865 to 1868. There was nearly a second novelist Liberal M.P. in Anthony Trollope who contested

Beverley in Yorkshire in the 1868 election. He did not enjoy the experience, being annoyed to be told that he would lose much of his support if he went out hunting, and that it was useless going to the splendid Minster on Sundays since those who worshipped there were, as staunch Anglicans, bound to support the Tories. Trollope did not take to the political life. He wrote, 'From morning to evening every day I was taken round the lanes and byways of that uninteresting town, canvassing every voter, exposed to the rain, up to my knees in slush, and utterly unable to assume that air of triumphant joy with which a jolly, successful candidate should be invested . . . it was the most wretched fortnight of my manhood.'[12] He was not elected.

Trollope was one of a group of distinguished men and women of letters who came together in 1865 to set up a new periodical, the *Fortnightly Review*. The others included George Eliot, George Meredith, who based his novel *Beauchamp's Career* on his own experience of helping the Liberal candidate for Southampton in the 1868 election, and Frederic Harrison, the Positivist philosopher. The first issue of the *Fortnightly Review* announced that the new journal would be closely tied to the Liberal party which, it said, 'has already converted the country from what it was in the dark days of the Prince Regent and Fourth George to what it has become in the days of Queen Victoria'.[13] From 1867 the editor was John Morley, a brilliant young journalist who quickly established it as the leading political review of the day with a circulation of 25,000 by 1872. Another influential periodical, the *Economist*, was strongly Liberal under its editor, Walter Bagehot, and in 1865 the old-established political weekly, the *Spectator*, espoused the Liberal cause.

Several of the young academics attracted to Liberalism in the 1860s fought Parliamentary elections. From Cambridge, Henry Fawcett, fellow of Trinity Hall, contested Southwark in 1860 and was elected Liberal M.P. for Brighton in 1865 despite the fact that he was totally blind as the result of a shooting accident, and George Otto Trevelyan, who had come down from Trinity College with a brilliant first in classics, became Liberal M.P. for Tynemouth in 1865. Henry Sidgwick, fellow in moral philosophy at Trinity College, Leslie Stephen, fellow of Trinity Hall, and his brother James Fitzjames Stephen, who contested Harwich in 1865, were also keen Cambridge Liberals. The young Liberal academics at Oxford included A. V. Dicey, fellow of Trinity College, James Bryce, fellow of Oriel College, the Hon. G. C. Brodrick, fellow of Merton College who contested Woodstock in

1868, and T. H. Green, fellow of Balliol College. All four were members of the Old Mortality Society, the leading essay club in Oxford, which became infatuated with Liberalism in the 1860s. Three older Oxford academics, James Thorold Rogers, Professor of Political Economy, Goldwin Smith, Regius Professor of Modern History, and Edward Freeman, fellow of Trinity College and later Regius Professor of Modern History, also became active Liberals, and Benjamin Jowett, Regius Professor of Greek, was strongly sympathetic.

Literary men and intellectuals were attracted to the emerging Liberal party in the 1860s because it represented the best hope for achieving reforms that they wanted to see. Just as manufacturers wanted free trade, Nonconformists the end of religious disabilities, and the professional middle classes careers open to talent, so they had a particular aim, the creation of a tolerant and open society which encouraged free speech and free inquiry. The writers and philosophers who set up the *Fortnightly Review* were disturbed by the dogmatism and narrow conventionality of Victorian thought and morals. The young Liberal academics were passionately committed to reforming the higher education system which they felt to be narrow and exclusive. Many of them came to Liberalism through their participation in the agitation throughout the 1860s to abolish the religious tests for admission to fellowships at Oxford and Cambridge and their involvement in the University Extension Movement.

Intellectuals were also attracted to the new Liberal party for more self-interested reasons. Just as Cobden and Bright saw it as ushering in rule by manufacturers, Miall and Baines, rule by Nonconformists, and Samuel Morley and his colleagues in the Administrative Reform Association, rule by the professional middle classes, so Mill and John Morley believed Liberalism would lead to rule by intellectuals. Against the prevailing claim of property to govern, they set the counter-claim of intellect. John Morley wrote in the *Fortnightly Review* that social and political progress would be achieved 'only on condition of enlightened and strenuous effort on the part of persons of superior character and opportunity'. He saw himself and other intellectuals providing the enlightened leadership which alone could solve the crucial problem of modern democracy, 'how the rule of numbers is to be reconciled with the rule of sage judgment'.[14] Mill went even further in his advocacy of a ruling élite of intellectuals. He called on the government to provide 'by means of endowments or salaries for the maintenance of what has been called a learned class'.[15]

This movement of writers and intellectuals into the Liberal fold in the 1860s contributed to the general awakening of Liberalism in Britain. 'In those days', James Bryce wrote later of the decade, 'literary men were mostly Liberals.'[16] The fact that the Liberals had a virtual monopoly of the political allegiance of the intelligentsia had a powerful influence on the popular mind. The general spread of education and literacy in the first half of the nineteenth century, together with such reforms as the abolition of stamp duty on newspapers, had created a much more informed and politically aware public. It had also changed the nature of those who were looked to for leadership and guidance, as Thomas Carlyle had first observed in *Past and Present* (1843), when he contrasted 'the ancient guides of nations, prophets, priests or whatever their name' with 'the modern guides of nations, who also go under a great variety of names, journalists, political economists, politicians, pamphleteers'.[17]

The Victorian Liberal party was to be particularly rich in these 'modern guides'. It was able to secure the active services of several of the leading thinkers and writers of the time in a way that would be impossible today because of the pressures of political life and the specialization of academic life. Victorian Liberalism provides some delightful examples of the successful marriage of the speculative and the practical life: Mill wrestling with his logic at the same time as preparing a Bill on contraception, T. H. Green going straight from the poll where he had been elected a Liberal town councillor to lecture on Kant's *Critique of Pure Reason*, John Morley being summoned by the Prime Minister to be offered the Chief Secretaryship of Ireland when he was in the middle of writing a leader for the *Manchester Guardian*, and not least, Gladstone himself translating Horace or the Old Testament in between writing his speeches in the study at Hawarden.

The 1860s was the decade when Liberalism finally awoke, both in Britain and overseas. In Europe a series of victories for the principles of constitutional rule and political emancipation regained what had seemed lost in the false starts of 1832 and 1848. Tsar Alexander II liberated the Russian serfs. Napoleon III's edict of 1860 allowing Parliament to debate its reply to the speech from the throne was the first in a series of reforms in French government and society which culminated in the proclamation of *L'Empire liberal* and enabled the development of a strong Liberal opposition led by Thiers and Gambetta. Italy was at last unified by Garibaldi and Cavour with a constitution modelled on that of Britain after the 1832 Reform Act. Belgium was under the enlightened rule of the Liberal Charles Rogier. Elections to the Prussian *Landtag* in 1861 and 1862 returned liberal majorities, and Bismarck, the arch-conservative who became Premier in 1862, was obliged to consult Bennigsen, the Liberal leader, on policy with the result that free trade and freedom of the press were established and labour unions legalized. In the Habsburg lands Anton von Schmerling introduced a federal system of government and the new constitution of 1867 was accompanied by the installation of a bourgeois ministry of liberal complexion.

Liberalism was also advancing on the American continent. In Canada, George Brown, the founder of the *Toronto Globe*, created in the 1860s a Liberal party committed to abolishing privilege, championing voluntaryism and self-reliance and providing free secular education. In the United States the Democratic party had grown steadily since its creation by Andrew Jackson in the 1840s along remarkably similar lines to the British Liberal party, deriving its main support from dissatisfied and excluded groups in society, economic free traders, religious dissenters and the ethnic minorities. Like the British Liberals, the Democrats were strong in both brains and numbers. They attracted the support of East Coast intellectuals, the 'Brahmins' of Boston, like the Adams family, the Wendell Holmeses, J. R. Lowell and C. E. Norton, while their heartland was New York, the Manchester of America.

The triumphs of Liberalism overseas had a powerful influence in encouraging Liberals in Britain. In particular, the victory of the North in the American Civil War, interpreted as a victory both for humanity and democracy, played a crucial role in strengthening and unifying the various disparate groups who came together under Gladstone's leadership to form the Liberal party in the late 1860s. According to John Morley, the North's victory was 'the force that made English Liberalism powerful enough to enfranchise the workmen, depose official Christianity, and deal a first blow at the landlords'.[18]

The war was initially a divisive rather than a unifying force among British Liberals. Some, like Mill, Thomas Hughes and John Bright, saw the struggle as one of democracy against aristocracy and freedom against bondage, and threw their support behind the North. Others, like Cobden, Acton and Gladstone, supported the South which they saw as seeking independence from an over-mighty Union and championing free trade against the protectionist North. Mill was horrified by what he called 'the rush of nearly the whole upper and middle classes of my own country, even those who passed for Liberals, into a furious pro-Southern partisanship' and wrote an article in *Frazer's Magazine* in January 1862 'to encourage those Liberals who had felt overborne by the tide of illiberal opinion'.[19] Bright was even more furious when Gladstone made a speech in Newcastle in October praising the South for making a nation. However, Liberal opinion united behind the North in 1863. Abraham Lincoln's Emancipation Proclamation of September 1862, which established that the overriding issue in the war was slavery and not the maintenance of the Union, brought over those who had previously been doubtful, and created what most Liberals, including Gladstone, took to be a great popular movement for justice and freedom.

Support for the North in the American Civil War brought on to the same platform and into active political collaboration for the first time representatives of the different groups who had felt separately the pull of Liberalism over the past twenty years. It led Cobden and Bright to make contact with intellectuals like Mill and Thomas Hughes. Goldwin Smith spoke regularly at Nonconformist rallies and became a close friend of Edward Miall. Henry Fawcett invited Nonconformists and northern manufacturers to Trinity Hall, Cambridge, to meet University Liberals. The co-operation was even more marked in 1865 over the *cause célèbre* of Edward Eyre, the governor of Jamaica who had suppressed a revolt by negroes on the island with excessive cruelty. A committee which included John Stuart Mill, Thomas Hughes, Herbert Spencer, Goldwin Smith, John Bright, Samuel Morley, Titus Salt, Edward Baines and Edward Miall was set up to press for Eyre's prosecution in a criminal court. Those who defended Eyre included Carlyle, Kingsley, Palmerston, Derby and *The Times*. As in the case of the American Civil War, Nonconformists, manufacturers and intellectuals were mostly on one side, Socialists, Whigs, Tories, and the Establishment on the other. The battle lines were being drawn between the friends and enemies of Liberalism.

The Liberal awakening in Britain had started with an extension of the franchise in 1832 and it was completed with another in 1867. There was a renewed demand for the vote by the unenfranchised working classes in the 1860s. This was inspired partly by the progress of liberalism across the Atlantic and on the Continent and partly by the growing confidence and political consciousness of the 'labour aristocracy' of skilled workers active in the New Model Unions which had been set up in such trades as engineering and carpentry. In 1859 a Non-Electors'

Reform Association was formed in Rochdale to press for an extension of the franchise. Workers in other northern towns followed suit and in 1861 the Leeds Working Men's Parliamentary Reform Committee called the first of a series of conferences of working-class and middle-class reformers which resulted in the setting up of a national Reform Union in Manchester in 1864. The following year a group of ex-Chartists, trade unionists and middle-class sympathizers led by Samuel Morley and Edmund Beales, a barrister, set up the more radical Reform League. Many of them had been directly inspired by the visit to England in 1864 of Garibaldi, the hero of the Italian Risorgimento, and by the victory of the North in the American Civil War.

The growing demand for Parliamentary reform was taken up by Liberals in Parliament. In 1864 Edward Baines introduced a Bill to reduce the borough franchise qualification to a £6 annual rental. During the debate on this Bill, Gladstone finally and irrevocably nailed his colours to the Liberal mast by committing himself to a substantial extension of the franchise, much to the dismay of Palmerston and the Queen. Two years later, with Palmerston's death having removed the greatest obstacle to further reform, Gladstone and Russell introduced a Bill to lower the borough franchise qualification to a £7 rental, and extend the county franchise to those paying an annual rent of £14 or more. The measure failed and Russell resigned, leaving Gladstone as leader of the Liberals.

Unlike in the 1840s, the agitation for Parliamentary reform in the 1860s united working-class and middle-class reformers. It brought together artisans, professional politicians and academics. In the spring of 1867 a group of recent graduates from Oxford and Cambridge, which included Dicey, Brodrick, Bryce, Frederic Harrison, Goldwin Smith, Thorold Rogers and Leslie Stephen, brought out a volume of *Essays On Reform* which argued in intellectual terms the case that John Bright had been putting over rather more simply in town halls across the country.

When Parliamentary reform finally came in August 1867 it was at the hands of a Conservative government and in a far more sweeping form than most Liberals had ever contemplated. Disraeli's Reform Act established household suffrage and almost doubled the electorate from about 1,430,000 to 2,470,000 voters. The major groups to which it gave the vote, the shopkeepers, craftsmen and 'respectable' artisans wealthy or provident enough to have their own homes, were predominantly Liberal in their politics. Under a deal worked out by one of their leaders, George Howell, the votes of many of these 'aristocrats' of labour were pledged to the Liberal party in 1868 in return for financial help for the Reform League. The most immediate and important consequence of the 1867 Reform Act was, therefore, to secure the election in 1868 of the first truly Liberal administration in Britain, and incidentally, the first government with a clear Parliamentary majority since 1831. From being a mere element within the Whig fold, the Liberals became the major political party in the country in their own right.

The party which Gladstone led to victory in 1868 was a coalition of the various groups which had been agitating for change and reform during the previous twenty-five or more years. Gladstone was at the head not so much of a political party as a movement of manufacturers, Nonconformists, and reformers of all kinds who had gradually found a common political expression for their particular sectional interests. In a sense, the Liberal party was a super pressure group which took up all the causes for which people had been campaigning through their own specific societies and associations. It always remained a collection of disparate, and even conflicting, communities and interests, each with its own pet 'fad'. Sir William Harcourt rejoiced that 'like the Kingdom of Heaven, the Liberal Party is a house of many mansions.'[20] Queen Victoria described it to Disraeli as a 'shamefully heterogeneous union' and lived in the hope that it would one day break up into its component parts.[21] To Dr. Shrapnel in *Beauchamp's Career*, the Liberals were an ill-assorted collection of 'stranded Whigs; crotchety manufacturers; dissentient religionists; the half-minded and the hare-hearted'.[22]

Of all the groups that made up the Liberal coalition, the 'stranded Whigs' were the most anomalous. Whiggism did not suddenly disappear in the late 1860s. The great Whig families like the Russells, the Cavendishes, the Campbells of Argyll, the Grosvenors, the Leveson-Gowers, and the Fitzmaurices remained firmly within the Liberal fold. It was true that in the House of Commons their influence waned rapidly. Only twenty-seven M.P.s from historic Whig families sat in the three Parliaments from 1859 to 1874. In the upper house, however, they remained an extremely powerful force. Whig peers dominated Gladstone's Cabinets until most of them finally left the party over the issue of Irish Home Rule in 1886. Gladstone favoured aristocrats as party whips and private secretaries as well as for high government positions. The resulting Whig hold over both the administration and the Parliamentary party is one of the great paradoxes of Victorian

Liberalism. As Trollope observed in *Phineas Redux* (1873), 'there is probably more of the flavour of political aristocracy to be found still remaining among our Liberal leading statesmen than among their opponents.'[23]

Outside Parliament, in the Liberal movement as opposed to the Liberal party, the eclipse of Whiggism was much more evident. It is summed up in Gladstone's definition of the essential difference between the Whig and the Liberal: 'a man not born a Liberal may become a Liberal, but to be a Whig he must be a born Whig.'[24] The most striking fact about those who had come together as Liberals in the mid-nineteenth century was that they were bound by common background and parallel interests, not by family ties. As Trollope again remarked in *Phineas Redux*, they were not 'uncles, brothers-in-law, or cousins to each other' as 'in former days, when there were Whigs instead of Liberals'.[25]

Perhaps the most obvious unifying feature among those various groups which made up the Liberal movement, and the one that distinguished them most sharply from the Whigs, was their common middle-class background. Of all those groups catalogued by Mill in 1839 as forming essential components of a new reform party, the working classes had probably played the least active role in the creation of the Liberal party, even though their votes were vital to its success. It is true that many ex-Chartists had forsaken physical force and moved to Liberalism in the 1850s through their involvement in reform movements. Their arrival certainly helped to radicalize the Liberal movement. Yet the fact remains that Liberalism as it had developed between the early 1830s and the late 1860s, was a predominantly middle-class movement. Cobden's remarks about the struggle against the corn laws could equally well have been applied to any of the campaigns by Nonconformists, manufacturers and reforming pressure groups in the 1840s and 1850s: 'Most of us entered upon the struggle with the belief that we had a distinct class interest in the question . . . it has eminently been a middle-class agitation. We have carried it on by those means by which the middle class usually carries on its movements. We have had our meetings of dissenting ministers; we have obtained the co-operation of the ladies; we have resorted to tea parties.'[26]

Critics of Victorian Liberalism made much of the class interest which they saw as holding it together. In *Culture and Anarchy* (1869) Matthew Arnold described the Liberal ideal as 'the legislation of middle-class parliaments . . . the local self-government of middle-class vestries . . .

the unrestricted competition of middle-class industrialists ... the dissidence of middle-class Dissent and the Protestantism of middle-class Protestant religion'.[27] Interestingly, the same point was made by Continental critics of Liberalism. The German Radical Julius Froebel regarded Liberalism as 'a system in the interest of quite specific elements of society which are assembled in the commercial and industrial middle class'.[28] William Morris, the Socialist artist and poet, was particularly scathing about the class bias of Liberalism. In his lecture on 'The Signs of Change' in 1885 he noted how, following the collapse of Chartism and the waning of revolutionary sentiment among the working classes in the prosperous 1850s and 1860s, 'the Liberal Party, a nondescript and flaccid creation of bourgeois supremacy, a party without principles or definition, but a thoroughly adequate expression of English middle-class hypocrisy, cowardice, and short-sightedness, engrossed the whole of the politically progressive movement in England, and dragged the working classes along with it, blind as they were to their own interests and the solidarity of labour.'[29]

Morris's picture of the Liberal party was only half true. Ideas as much as class interest united those who came together to form the Liberal movement. The reforming pressure groups of the 1840s and 1850s had based their campaigns around such abstract principles as voluntaryism, free trade, meritocracy and democracy. Perhaps the best definition of the difference between Whiggism and Liberalism was Lord Acton's: 'the Whig governed by compromise; the Liberal begins the reign of ideas.'[30] Liberalism was infinitely more ideological, and ideologically demanding, than either Whiggism or Conservatism. The Conservatives deserved the sobriquet of 'the stupid party' which stuck to them for more than twenty years after it was first applied by Mill in 1861. In the 1860s, as James Fitzjames Stephen put it, 'to be a Conservative meant to be opposed to pretty well all the main intellectual movements of the time.'[31] Henry Lunn, the founder of the travel firm that still bears his name, used as a young man 'to calculate the number of Liberals present at a political meeting by looking at the hats on the pegs outside. The big hats belonged to Liberals, because Liberals had big brains; the small hats to the unintelligent Tories.'[32]

Victorian Liberalism rested on the assumption that ideas played an important role in politics, and that people voted for principles and not just according to class or sectional interest. Mill held that 'one person with a belief is a social power equal to ninety-nine who have only interests.'[33] In common with Acton and several Continental liberal theorists, he believed that ideas were themselves the main motive power in history, and not the mere effects of social circumstances. 'The order of human progression in all respects', he wrote, 'will mainly depend on the order of progression in the intellectual convictions of mankind.'[34] It followed that the way to achieve social, political and economic improvement was by gaining possession 'of the intellects and dispositions of the public' rather than by simply appealing to their immediate self-interest by government provision of welfare services.[35]

The Liberals' confidence that they could take politics out of the realm of interest and into the realms of morality and philosophy was initially well founded. During the late 1860s and the 1870s many of the electorate moved from near subsistence level to an awareness of progress and the reality of freedom. With a rise in real wages of 40 per cent, people could afford to vote for ideas without too much concern for their own personal benefit. The economic decline that began in the early 1880s ended this luxury and brought politics back for most people to the level of narrow self-interest. Changes in the franchise reinforced the effect of the economic situation. Before 1867 a small electorate voted largely according to family tradition and sectional interest. After 1885 a mass electorate voted largely according to class. In the intervening period an electorate that was for the most part reasonably educated and informed voted perhaps more than at any other time in British history for ideas and principles. It was no coincidence that Liberalism flowered during those years.

The central idea around which Liberals rallied was that of emancipation. Contemplating the final awakening of British Liberalism in 1867, John Morley echoed Mill's prediction of nearly thirty years earlier. The new Liberal party, he wrote in the *Fortnightly Review*, 'is likely to have on its side a great portion of the most highly cultivated intellect in the nation, and the contest will be between brains and numbers on the one side, and wealth, rank, vested interest, possession in short, on the other'.[36] Liberals sought the removal of all unnatural and unfair advantages in society, whether of corn grower over manufacturer, of Anglican over Nonconformist, or of the idle aristocratic place-hunter over the diligent middle-class professional. They wanted to do away with the external impediments to individual moral, social, political and economic advancement which were created by privileges of rank, wealth or custom and by the restrictive activities of the government. They were motivated by their own feelings of exclusion and by a more radical dissatisfaction with the existing state of things and a vision of a new kind of society. 'You are a Liberal,' the Duke of Omnium told Phineas Finn in Trollope's *The Prime Minister*, 'because you know that it is not as it ought to be, and because you would still march on to some nearer approach to equality.'[37]

Liberals were spurred on to advocate reform and change not so much by their dissatisfaction with the present as by their hopes for the future. In his final article for the *Fortnightly Review* John Morley replied to a critic who had accused him of writing as though he believed everything to be bad, 'Nay, but I do believe everything could be better.'[38] Samuel Morley defined the Liberals as 'a party of progress, a party whose desire it is to keep pace with the times and with the requirements of the nation—not seeking change for the sake of change, but for improvement'.[39] The twin ideas of progress and improvement lay at the heart of Victorian Liberalism. 'We have no thread through the enormous intricacy of modern politics', wrote Acton, 'except the idea of progress towards more perfect and assured freedom and the divine right of free men.'[40] Joseph Chamberlain replied to the question as to why he was a Liberal, 'progress is the law of the world; and Liberalism is the expression of this law in politics.'[41]

Faith in progress was not, of course, a peculiarity of Liberals in the first three decades of Queen Victoria's reign. It was the common theme of Carlyle's modern prophets, the popular poets, historians and philosophers of the day. Alfred Tennyson, perhaps the most popular and representative poet of the age, wrote in *Locksley Hall*, published in 1842:

For I dipt into the future, far as human eye could see,
Saw the vision of the world, and all the wonder that would be;
Saw the heavens fill with commerce, argosies of magic sails,
Pilots of the purple twilight, dropping down with costly bales;
Heard the heavens fill with shouting, and there rain'd a ghastly dew
From the nations' airy navies grappling in the central blue;
Far along the world-wide whisper of the south wind rushing warm,
With the standards of the peoples plunging through the thunder storm;
Till the war-drum throbb'd no longer, and the battle-flags were furl'd
In the Parliament of man, the Federation of the world . . .
Not in vain the distance beacons. Forward, forward, let us range,
Let the great world spin for ever down the ringing grooves of change.

Macaulay's *History of England*, the great literary monument to Whiggism and the most widely read history book of the age, which was published in 1846, was a catalogue of the improvements that made contemporary life better in every respect than it had ever been before. In 1851 the popular versifier Martin Tupper joined in the general hymn of praise to progress with reflections on more recent improvements:

> *These twenty years—how full of gain to us,*
> *To common humble multitudinous man;*
> *How swiftly Providence advances thus*
> *Our flag of progress flaming in the van.*

At a more intellectual level, Henry Buckle in his *History of Civilisation in England*, which first appeared in 1857, attempted to prove human advancement empirically and proclaimed, 'the progress of every people is regulated by principles . . . as certain as those which govern the physical world.'[42]

Only a few lone voices sounded a discordant note in this general chorus of complacency and optimism. Carlyle, Ruskin, Newman and Arnold suggested in their different ways that things might not necessarily be better than ever before and questioned the prevailing gospel of progress. They were not saying what their contemporaries wanted to hear, however. 'We do not put very much faith in Mr. Carlyle, nor in Mr. Ruskin and his other followers,' Trollope wrote at the end of his *Autobiography*, 'the loudness and extravagance of their lamentations, the wailing and gnashing of teeth which comes from them, over a world which is supposed to have gone altogether shoddywards, are so contrary to the convictions of men who cannot but see how comfort has been increased, how health has been improved, and education extended.'[43] Arnold might complain that the English faith in human and institutional progress was 'like our reliance on freedom, on muscular Christianity, on population, on coal, on wealth—mere belief in machinery and unfruitful'. He was forced to admit, however, that 'the country is profoundly Liberal; that is, it is profoundly convinced that a great course of growth and transformation lies before it.'[44]

As Arnold's remark suggests, the belief in progress which characterized the early part of Victoria's reign was in many ways a triumph for the Liberal view. Liberals carried the general optimism of the period into a quasi-religious belief in the possibility of perfectibility in every sphere of life, including man himself. John Morley noted in his *Recollections* that for his generation, which grew to manhood in the 1860s, 'belief in progress had become the basis of social thought, and had even taken the place of religion as the inspiring, guiding, and testing power over social action.'[45] There was virtually nothing young Liberals felt could not be achieved by appealing to man's reason and creating the social environment in which his essential goodness could function freely. Mill wrote confidently in 1863: 'Most of the great positive evils of the world are in themselves removable, and will, if human affairs continue to improve, be in the end reduced to within narrow limits. Poverty, in any sense implying suffering, may be completely extinguished by the wisdom of society, combined with the good sense and providence of individuals. Even that most intractable of enemies, disease, may be indefinitely reduced in dimensions by good physical and moral education, and proper control of noxious influences, while the progress of science holds out a promise for the future of still more direct conquests over this detestable foe. .... As for vicissitudes of fortune, and other disappointments connected with worldly circumstances, these are principally the effect either of gross imprudence, or ill-regulated desires, or of bad or imperfect social institutions. All the grand sources, in short, of human suffering are in a great degree, many of them almost entirely, conquerable by human care and effort.'[46]

While Mill represented one strand of the Liberal optimism of the 1860s with his faith in scientific and intellectual progress, John Bright exemplified another with his no less certain belief in the benefits that would accrue from specific political reforms. He told a gathering of workmen in Edinburgh in 1868: 'If Government were just, if schools were as prominent institutions in our landscapes and in our great towns as prisons and workhouses now are, I suspect that we should find people gradually gaining more self-respect; that they would have much hope of improvement of themselves and their families, that they would rise above, in thousands of cases, all temptations to intemperance, and that they would become generally—I say almost universally— more virtuous and more like what the subjects of a free state ought to be.'[47]

The exuberant, almost millenarian quality of Liberal optimism in the 1860s is well brought out in two of the leading novels of the decade. In *Tom Brown at Oxford* (1861) Thomas Hughes has his hero speculate that 'that state of the world which this universal democracy was to bring about, and which was coming no man could say how soon, was to be in fact that age of peace and goodwill which men had dreamt of in all times, when the lion should lie down with the kid, and nation should not vex nation any more.'[48] In a more detached vein, George Eliot's *Felix Holt the Radical* (1866), although set in 1832, reflects much more closely the spirit of the year in which it was written: 'At that time . . . faith in the efficacy of political change was at fever-heat in ardent Reformers. . . . Crying abuses—"bloated paupers", "bloated pluralists", and other corruptions hindering men from being wise and happy—had to be fought against and slain . . . hope was mighty . . . the speakers at Reform banquets were exuberant in congratulation and promise. . . . Some dwelt on the abolition of all abuses, and on millenial blessedness generally; others, whose imaginations were less suffused with exhalations of the dawn, insisted chiefly on the ballot box.'[49]

Twenty years later, when the reforms that Liberals had clamoured for had failed to produce greater wisdom and happiness and man seemed no more rational or good, it was easy to dismiss this optimism as misplaced and hopelessly naive. A Tory pamphlet complained in 1885: 'Liberalism is a policy of noble sentiments, of superfine professions, of exalted motives, of plausible platitudes. It appeals to the ear alone; it professes to believe that the world is better than it is, and that we are better than the world.'[50] In the 1860s, however, it was less easy to mock the Liberals' faith in progress. In America and across Europe, freedom seemed in the ascendant. Britain was on the verge of becoming a democracy. 'I feel certain that the fort of selfishness and monopoly cannot be held for ever,' John Bright wrote in 1865, 'and that the walls of privilege cannot through all time resist the multitude that are gathering to the assault. In all the nations of the world of this day, I believe the powers of good are gaining steadily on the powers of evil. I think it is eminently so in this country.'[51]

Liberals did not believe that progress and improvement came inevitably and automatically. John Morley wrote: 'Progress is very far from being of the nature of an automaton. It wants human agents to keep it at work.' He criticized the doctrine of evolution for its tendency 'to place individual robustness and initiative in the light of superfluities'.[52] The Liberals' belief in progress depended on their faith in man's capacity to change his world. Mill once imagined himself in a debate with an Owenite Socialist, who held that man's character was entirely influenced by circumstances and social forces. Against him, Mill maintained that man himself created social forces and that 'the Norman Conquest was as much the act of a single man as the writing of a newspaper article.'[53]

It is significant that when Victorian Liberals stressed man's capacity to influence his world, it was almost entirely in terms of individuals rather than groups or classes that they thought. As James Stansfeld put it: 'Liberalism believes in individuality, in the capacity for liberty and progress of the individual man. There is no Liberalism without this as the basis of its faith.'[54] Intense individualism was a characteristic of nineteenth-century Liberalism throughout Europe. 'Individualism,' Georg Gervinus, the leading German liberal theorist, wrote in his *History of the Nineteenth Century* (1856), 'the self-awareness of the personality, has become so powerful in men that it will modify political concepts and institutions; it will dissolve the closed corporations, the states within the state; it will eliminate all caste and class divisions.'[55]

It was no coincidence that the novels of the period should produce a group of intensely individualistic Liberal heroes. Colonel Thomas Newcome in Thackeray's *The Newcomes*, Harold Transome in George Eliot's *Felix Holt the Radical*, Plantagenet Palliser in Trollope's Palliser novels, and Nevil Beauchamp in Meredith's *Beauchamp's Career* had much in common. They were all high-minded and earnest reformers who stood for Parliament confident that they could change and improve the world. They had the heroic quality of the ideal Liberal as described by Andrew Reid, a journalist who collected confessions of faith from leading Liberals in the 1880s for publication in a best-selling booklet, *Why I Am A Liberal*: 'He is a man of indestructible, illimitable, and indomitable faith. . . . He has no idea of finality. He refuses to listen to the voice of the darkness—"Thus far shalt thou come and no further." To the challenge of the sentinel of the night "Who goes there?", he gives the password "Light!" . . . Over impassable mountains and through adamantine frontiers, into dark continents and black forests he plunges; and while the Tory-hearted, ancient-minded, and feeble-kneed are crying out "Impossible!", "Dreadful", he emerges on the other side, amid the ringing cheers of the people, with his hands full of glorious discoveries.'[56]

As they surveyed the onward march of freedom across Europe and America and contemplated their own ascent to power in the late 1860s, Liberals felt certain of their ability to carry out their great mission of emancipation. They were confident of continuing progress and improvement in every sphere of life and saw every reason to look forward to the future. Liberalism, said James Stansfeld, was 'robust and hopeful. It represents the natural mental attitude and condition of manly educated intelligence in youth and manhood.'[57] Mill wrote in 1865: 'A Liberal is he who looks forward for his principles of government, a Tory looks backward.'[58] In *Culture and Anarchy* published in

1869, Matthew Arnold summed up nicely the spirit which prevailed with the completion of the Liberal awakening in Britain. 'The heroes of middle-class Liberalism', he wrote, 'speak with a kind of prophetic anticipation of the great destiny which awaits them, and as if the future was clearly theirs.'[59] They were certain that it was.

Chapter 2

The Creed of the Up-and-Coming

Liberalism was the creed of the up-and-coming. It appealed particularly to the young, the active, the ambitious and the restless. George Meredith described it as 'the thing of the present and its urgencies'.[1] To Gladstone Liberalism embodied the principle of action which characterized Greek art, while Conservatism represented the principle of repose found in the work of the Egyptians. R. W. Dale, a Birmingham Congregational minister who was a close associate of Joseph Chamberlain, believed that 'the very function of Liberalism is to discover and settle new political territory. We are always on the frontiers.'[2] Disraeli portrayed Liberals as restless and excited in his novel *Sybil* (1845) where Lady St. Julians asks, 'Men who breakfast out are generally Liberals. Have you not observed that? I wonder why?' and Lady Firebrace replies, 'It shows a restless, revolutionary mind that can settle to nothing, but must be running after gossip the moment they are awake.'[3]

In his article in the *Westminster Review*, Mill had predicted that the new reform party would have the support of the talented and ambitious members of society who saw their way blocked by the old and stupid incumbents of the *ancien régime*. 'The men of active and aspiring talent', he wrote, 'in all classes except the highest, are Radicals everywhere, for what is Radicalism, but the claim of pre-eminence for personal qualities above conventional or accidental advantages? And what more certain than that a man of talent, compelled to serve men of no talent, and taught by daily experience that, even if fortune favours him, he can scarcely by the labours of a life raise his head to a level with their feet, will be, by a natural tendency, something of a leveller?'[4]

It is significant that Mill saw the new party representing the disqualified against the privileged and not the poor against the rich, or the weak against the strong. The various groups which made up the Victorian Liberal movement were disadvantaged only in that they were excluded from offices and privileges enjoyed by the aristocracy and the Establishment. In all other respects, they were highly successful and self-confident. Indeed, it was partly their consciousness of the disparity between their own success and value to the community and their political and social status as second-class citizens that made them Liberals.

Matthew Arnold created a caricature of the up-and-coming Liberal in Mr. Bottles, the hero of *Friendship's Garland* (1870). 'One of our self-made middle-class men', Bottles had made an immense fortune and, since leaving school, had 'with a sturdy self-reliance thoroughly English, left his mind wholly to itself, his daily newspaper and his Particular Baptist wife'. He was a firm believer in progress, and supported all measures advocated by the Manchester School, the *Daily Telegraph* and the Liberal party. 'He was one of the earliest free traders; he has always gone as straight as an arrow about Reform; he is an ardent voluntary in every possible line . . . and he paid the whole expenses of a most important church rate contest out of his own pocket. And, finally, he looks forward to marrying his deceased wife's sister. Table the whole Liberal creed, and in not a single point of it will you find Bottles tripping.'⁵

There were undoubtedly many men like Mr. Bottles in the Liberal movement, just as there were also many representatives of that familiar breed in Victorian fiction, the earnest young men from humble origins who worked their own way up through society to make a respectable professional career or establish their own successful business. Such figures were not just the fanciful creations of literary men. The mid-nineteenth century, when the national income was increasing by twenty per cent a decade, was a time of unparalleled upward social mobility in Britain. The development of a fragmented, sub-contracting economy of small independent businesses enabled many men to become their own masters. Those who found themselves for the first time calling no man master, providing for their own families and able to have their own religion and politics, were naturally drawn to the Liberal philosophy of independence and self-help.

The leading representatives of the up-and-coming classes in Parliament and the architects of their distinctive strain of Liberalism, Richard Cobden and John Bright, were themselves self-made men who had achieved wealth and success through their own efforts rather than through birth and inheritance. Cobden left his native Sussex to work first as a clerk and then as a salesman in the cloth trade in London. In 1828 with two friends he borrowed £1,000 to sell goods for calico printers. Three years later they set up their own calico-printing factory near Burnley in Lancashire. John Bright rose at 5 a.m. every morning to study for three hours before breakfast in a room over the counting house in his father's cotton mill. Even more impressive examples of progress from rags to riches are to be found among the ranks of leading provincial Liberals. Samuel Morley joined his father's small hosiery firm as a boy of sixteen in 1825 and rose to become head of the largest commercial enterprise in Victorian Britain with seven factories directly employing three thousand workers. Archie Scarr, whose father was a bankrupt grocer from Burnley, started selling vegetables from a market stall in Leeds in the 1840s. By the 1880s he had twelve shops employing thirty assistants and was mayor of Leeds, having entered public life through the local Liberal Association as a temperance orator preaching the virtues of hard work and thrift.

Within the working classes, Liberalism had very little support among labourers in the mines, the docks and in large factories, who saw little chance of rising in the social scale. It appealed rather to those with initiative and skill, craftsmen, retailers and small producers, for whom upward social mobility was a distinct possibility. These latter groups made up a high proportion of the new electorate enfranchised in 1867. Their expectation that they would themselves rise in society in part explains why they were so ready to put their votes behind a party whose policies were manifestly in the interest of the middle classes and did not have any immediate appeal to them. It was because they fervently hoped that they, or at least their children, would one day become professional people or businessmen that the skilled artisans and small shopkeepers of mid-Victorian Britain strenuously supported the Liberals' call for a Civil Service open to talent and for cheap government and free trade.

It was, however, from the ranks of the rising middle classes that Victorian Liberalism derived its greatest strength. Mill's 'men of active and aspiring talent' were to be found chiefly among the merchants, manufacturers and members of the learned professions who rose in number and importance in the aftermath of the Industrial Revolution. As early as 1824, in the very first number of the *Westminster Review*, Mill's father James had pointed out that within the middle class 'are the hands that invent, and the hands that execute; the enterprise that projects, and the capital by which these projects are carried into operation . . . in this country at least, it is this class which gives the nation its character'.[6] Since then the emerging Liberalism had been inextricably bound up with the growing consciousness of the bourgeoisie. Liberal orators and journalists lost no opportunity to shower praises on the middle classes and back their growing demand to govern the country. Edward Baines described them in the *Leeds Mercury* in 1842 as 'the most virtuous, the most attached to well-regulated liberty, the most interested in freedom of trade, and therefore the best depositories of political power'.[7]

Cobden and Bright, through their anti-corn law campaign in the 1840s, mobilized and focused the growing consciousness of the middle classes. Contemporaries were in no doubt about their ultimate objective. A Halifax manufacturer wrote: 'The Cobden and Bright party are striving for power. Their object is to form a middle-class administration in contradistinction to the aristocratic element which has hitherto predominated in the government of this country.'[8] Bright's speeches constantly attacked the ruling aristocracy as a moribund social caste and called for their removal by an alliance of the middle and working classes. Cobden told a meeting in 1849 that his object, now that the corn laws were repealed and the first victory against the *ancien régime* won, was to 'place as much political power as he could in the hands of the middle and industrious classes'.[9] He clearly regarded the two as synonymous.

Up-and-coming Liberals argued that educational and industrial advances had created a new natural governing class of intelligent, successful, independent men. The only qualification they lacked was the noble background and ownership of land which Whigs and Tories still insisted were the essential requirements for political power. Cobden and Bright pointed to the anomalous position of Britain as the most intellectually and technically advanced nation in the world which yet retained a political and social system based on birth and land. They believed that once this anomaly was put right, the exclusive privileges and obstacles against which they fought would crumble away. 'If we survey the entire field of political action,' John Morley wrote in the *Fortnightly Review* of September 1867, 'we shall find that progress, wherever it is stayed, is stayed by the untimely relics of territorialism, and that in removing them we at once find ourselves led on to the true conditions by taking the policy of industry for our foundation.'[10]

For a party dedicated to the overthrow of territorialism, the Liberals had an embarrassingly large number of its relics among their Parliamentary supporters. It has been calculated that of the 456 Liberal M.P.s who represented English constituencies between 1859 and 1874 nearly half were either large landowners or their sons, and 113 were relatives of peers.[11] In terms of their representation at Westminster, the Liberals were emphatically not a middle-class party, and reflected rather the predominance of those aristocratic and landed elements favoured by Gladstone and Trollope. It was outside Parliament, in the Liberal movement in the country, that there existed the middle-class predominance extolled and represented in the House of Commons by Cobden and Bright.

The most powerful economically and the most vocal of the rising middle classes in the mid-nineteenth century were the manufacturers and merchants, and it was not surprising that they should constitute a dominant and distinctive element within the Liberal movement. Cobden wrote in 1862: 'Our mercantile classes and manufacturing classes as represented in the Chambers of Commerce are after all the only power in the State possessed of wealth and political influence sufficient to counteract in some degree the feudal governing class of this country.' Three years later Bright observed that 'merchants and manufacturers are gradually becoming much more important in the world than warriors or statesmen.'[12]

Liberalism attracted the support of two distinct groups from the world of commerce and industry. The first was made up of those who were not themselves manufacturers, but who were either financiers in the City of London, or owners of enterprises in the country, and whose background and education put them firmly in the upper middle classes. It included members of such well-known banking houses as the Rothschilds and the Gurneys, and of trading companies like Jardine, Matheson & Co., four of whose directors sat as Liberal M.P.s. Five members of this group sat in Liberal Cabinets: Edward Cardwell, who came like Gladstone from a wealthy Liverpool merchant family; George Goschen, the financier son of a German merchant, who wrote a widely selling work on *The Theory of Foreign Exchanges* in 1863; Hugh E. Childers, the son of a Yorkshire clergyman, who was chairman of an English bank and an Indian railway company, deputy chairman of an Australian bank and director of several English railway companies; the 2nd Earl Granville who was a Staffordshire ironmaster; and Henry Bruce, a South Wales mine owner and ironmaster. As befitted their membership of the financial and business 'establishment' these men tended to be fairly conservative in their outlook, and to be drawn to Liberalism because of its administrative and economic policies, rather than its social complexion.

The other group of Liberal businessmen were more provincial in their background and more radical in attitude. They were in fact more representative of the up-and-coming elements in British society, being almost all Dissenters from solidly middle-class or even working-class families. They included many of the most famous names in Victorian manufacturing: Samuel Morley, the hosiery and knitwear king; Jeremiah Colman, the Norwich mustard maker; George Palmer, the Reading biscuit manufacturer; Sir Henry Doulton, the porcelain manufacturer; Titus Salt, the Yorkshire woollen magnate; M. T. Bass, head of the Burton-on-Trent brewery which still bears his name; Peter Taylor, a partner in Courtaulds; William Rathbone, a successful Liverpool merchant; Henry Ashworth, whose two cotton mills employed a thousand workers; and Sir Francis Crossley, whose Halifax carpet works was the largest single factory in the world.

Liberalism gave these new manufacturers a feeling of status and self-confidence by stressing their value to the community and championing their claim to run the country against that of the landed aristocracy. Liberal politicians encouraged manufacturers to take a higher view of themselves and publicly extolled their virtues. Edward Baines wrote a series of pamphlets in the 1840s to defend manufacturers against the accusation that they neglected their own education and the well-being of their workers in their thirst for profit. Henry Ashworth complained that critical reports by the factory inspectors disparaged 'a class of men who are . . . entitled to consideration for their respectability, intelligence, benevolence, and propriety of feelings.'[13] Samuel Morley proclaimed that 'the true secret of England's greatness, and the best guarantee for the maintenance and extension of the liberties we enjoy are found in the intelligence, the perseverance, and, above all, the integrity which is found in the great mercantile and trading transactions of this country.'[14] 'How I wish I could inspire the mercantile and manufacturing community with a little more self-respect,' Cobden wrote in 1862, 'the future of England must depend on them . . . and yet how little a share this all-important interest claims in the government of the country.'[15]

In championing manufacturers against landowners, Liberalism inevitably stood for the industrial Midlands and North of England against the predominantly agricultural South. In itself, this involved backing the disqualified against the privileged. The Reform Act of 1832 left the North grossly under-represented in Parliament. Ten southern counties with a quarter of the population of England had a third of the total representation. The North was 'naturally' Liberal, just as Mill had predicted Scotland and Wales would be. It was the stronghold of

Dissent, the home of the self-made man, and in economic terms the powerhouse of the nation. The North scored its first victory over the South with the repeal of the corn laws. Speaking in Manchester after repeal, Bright said: 'It is to this and a neighbouring county that the great element of power in this country is henceforth to be found. Lancashire, the cotton district, and the West Riding of Yorkshire, must govern England. I don't mean that they must of themselves assert a superiority over other parts of the kingdom, like that which the rural and agricultural counties have asserted over us in times past; but I say that the vast population of those counties, with their interests, their morality, their union, that all these must exercise an immense influence upon all future legislation in this kingdom.'[16]

Victorian Liberalism had a distinctly pro-northern and anti-southern flavour. Several leading Liberals came from Lancashire and Yorkshire: Gladstone, Cardwell and Rathbone from Liverpool, Bright from Rochdale, John Morley from Blackburn, Titus Salt and Edward Baines from Leeds. Their pamphlets and speeches consciously promoted and defended northern ruggedness against the smooth ways of the South. Baines wrote *The Manufacturing Areas Vindicated* (1843) to counter the prevailing impression that Lancashire and Yorkshire were heathen lands without culture or enlightenment. Bright told an Anti-Corn Law League meeting in London that 'the provinces had acted as well as spoken . . . and done that which was the duty of the people of London.'[17] Much later, when W. T. Stead, the crusading editor of the Darlington newspaper the *Northern Echo*, was waging war on London's clubland, he appealed for support to 'the sober, hard-working, intelligent men who in North and Central England constitute the saving strength of our land'.[18]

The quality of 'Northern-ness' almost attained the status of a cult for Liberals who had been unlucky enough to be born south of the Trent. Cobden's reversal of the usual route to fame and fortune in leaving his native Sussex for Lancashire was repeated by W. E. Forster, the Secretary for Education in Gladstone's first Ministry, originally from Dorset, who gave up a career at the bar for a post in a worsted factory near Bradford. He was subsequently M.P. for Bradford for twenty-five years and became the only Victorian apart from the Queen to have a railway station named after him—Bradford, Forster Square. The rough individualism and moral integrity of the North particularly appealed to Liberal intellectuals. When he left Oxford, T. H. Green nearly went to teach at Owen's College, Manchester, which attracted him by its

northern Nonconformist tradition. Goldwin Smith found that 'the
Liberal manufacturers of the North ... enlarged my political experience. In Bradford I learned much that no books could have taught
me.'[19] G. C. Brodrick told the inaugural meeting of the Manchester
Reform Club in 1867 that reforms like the abolition of university
religious tests would only be accomplished 'with the aid of that motive
power which Lancashire, above all places, could supply'.[20] James Bryce
took a more detached view of his fellow intellectuals' worship of
northern grit. 'People sick of a southern squirearchy admire far off
these Lancashire politicians,' he wrote in 1866, 'Near at hand, the
roughness and dirt can be seen.'[21]

Gladstone epitomized both the genuine and the cultivated Northern-
ness of Victorian Liberalism. As a High Anglican and a former Conservative M.P. for Oxford University, where he had completed his own
education after Eton, he could hardly have been further removed from
the world of provincial Nonconformity from which he was to draw
his greatest strength as Liberal leader. Yet when he delivered his great
free trade budget in 1860, an old Whig who heartily disapproved of it
muttered, 'Ah, Oxford on the surface, but Liverpool below.' In his
Biographical Studies, Bagehot quoted the remark and reflected: 'Mr.
Gladstone has carried into other pursuits the eagerness, the industry—
we are loth to say the rashness, but the boldness—which Liverpool
men apply to the business of Liverpool. Underneath the scholastic polish
of his Oxford education, he has the speculative hardihood, the eager
industry of a Lancashire merchant.'[22]

It was, perhaps, a recognition of these qualities that led eight thousand
electors in South Lancashire to ask Gladstone to be their member in the
1861 election, the first since his final break with the Conservatives in
1859. He turned down their request, feeling that his ties with Oxford
were too strong. Four years later, however, the University rejected him
at the polls, alarmed by his increasing identification with Liberalism.
Symbolically, perhaps, on the day of his defeat the Bible fell from the
hands of James I's statue in the Bodleian Library quadrangle. Gladstone
quit the city of High Anglicanism and Toryism and hurried to South
Lancashire where there was still time to stand because of the drawn-out
nature of nineteenth-century elections. He announced at the opening
meeting of his campaign in the Free Trade Hall, Manchester, 'I am
come among you, and I am come among you unmuzzled.' Later, in
Liverpool, no doubt with as much calculation as conviction, he took
the North as standing for all that was best and most exciting about the

emerging Liberal creed: 'I come into South Lancashire and I find the development of industry. I find the growth of enterprise. I find the progress of social philanthropy. I find the prevalence of toleration. I find an ardent desire for freedom.'[23]

When he first met W. T. Stead in 1877, Gladstone praised the distinctive qualities found in the North of England. 'Yes Mr. Gladstone,' Stead replied, 'You have always done justice to the North.'[24] The Liberal leader's undoubted appeal in the North was not simply a result of his panegyrics on the qualities of its inhabitants delivered at appropriate moments. Gladstone was admired there for the same reasons that he was worshipped by the electors of Scotland and Wales, who delivered massive Liberal majorities throughout his time as leader. What appealed to them all were his moral earnestness, his stress on freedom and his ideal of self-help.

Victorian Liberalism was essentially an urban movement. It is no coincidence that many leading Liberal M.P.s represented the new and expanding towns of the age. Cobden sat for Stockport and Rochdale, Bright for Manchester and Birmingham, John Morley for Newcastle-on-Tyne, Edward Miall, Titus Salt and W. E. Forster for Bradford, Edward Baines for Leeds, and A. J. Mundella, a hosiery manufacturer of Italian parentage, for Sheffield. The growth of provincial Liberalism in the 1840s and 1850s had been closely bound up with the struggle of new towns to achieve self-government and with the incursion of urban candidates and issues into rural seats. Cobden first achieved political fame and influence as leader of the campaign to incorporate Manchester under the terms of the 1835 Municipal Corporations Act and so give the city an elected local government to replace the old manorial court leet which still persisted from medieval times. When a free trade candidate was elected for the West Riding of Yorkshire in 1846, the Conservative local paper complained that the rural electorate had been 'unresistingly scoured by the Manchester moneybags... and trampled upon by supercilious and ambitious cotton lords'.[25]

The two largest provincial cities in England, Manchester and Birmingham, played distinctive and important roles in the development of Liberalism. Manchester made its contribution first, in the 1840s, as a result of its position as centre of the cotton trade and its concentration of large manufacturers. The economic doctrines of free trade and free competition were first promulgated there by the Anti-Corn Law Leaguers, and it was not surprising that they became known as 'the

Manchester School'. Where other cities had a cathedral as their crowning architectural glory and focal point, Manchester had the Free Trade Hall, designed by Edward Walters, the architect of the Manchester Liberals, in 1853. Bright, who was M.P. for the city from 1847 to 1857, and Cobden, M.P. for neighbouring Stockport from 1841 to 1847, made the demands of the Manchester manufacturers the policies of their embryo Liberal party.

The closeness of Liberalism's identification with Manchester became something of an embarrassment. Cobden explained the problem to Baines in the early stages of the agitation against the corn laws: 'Our enemies are trying hard to make the corn laws a mere question between the millowners of Manchester and the landowners. This is, as they well know, putting the case on the narrowest and least popular basis. A prejudice has been got up against cotton spinners and Manchester capitalists and this they seek very craftily to affix in the anti-corn law agitation.'[26] Manchester's particular concentration of large capitalists was not something with which Liberals wished to be identified too closely, nor was its reputation as a refuge for people like Timothy Turbot, the hack Liberal orator from Ireland in *Beauchamp's Career* who lent his talents indiscriminately to 'Corn Law campaigns, Reform agitations, and all manifestly popular movements requiring the heaven-endowed man of speech, an interpreter of multitudes, and a prompter . . . and rejoiced in the happy circumstances which had expelled him from the shores of his native isle to find refuge and a vocation in Manchester.'[27]

It was perhaps just as well that the geographical focus of the emerging Liberal movement shifted southwards in the 1850s. With the battle for free trade won, the struggle for a further extension of the franchise became the dominant Liberal preoccupation. Birmingham was the natural centre for this agitation, just as Manchester had been the natural centre of the campaign for free trade. The Midland city had a tradition of campaigning for Parliamentary reform that went back to Thomas Attwood's Birmingham Political Union of 1832 and Joseph Sturge's Complete Suffrage Union of 1841. Bright's election as M.P. for Birmingham in 1857 after he had been thrown out by the electors of Manchester for moving from economic to political Liberalism, heralded a new epoch in the making of the Liberal party. Cobden wrote that it confirmed his opinion 'that the social and political state of that town is far more healthy than that of Manchester; and it arises from the fact that the industry of the hardware district is carried on by

small manufacturers, employing a few men and boys each . . . whilst
the great capitalists in Manchester form an aristocracy, individual
members of which wield an influence over sometimes two thousand
persons. There is a freer intercourse between all classes than in the
Lancashire town. . . . The great capitalist class formed an excellent basis
for the Anti-Corn Law Movement . . . but I very much doubt whether
such a state of society is favourable to a democratic political
movement.'[28]

Bright's first speech in Birmingham as M.P., delivered to an audience
of 5,000 in the Town Hall in October 1858, marked the start of the
Liberals' campaign to reform Parliament by extending the franchise,
introducing the ballot and curbing the power of the House of Lords.
He made much of the venue from which he was launching his call for
democracy: 'Am I not in the town of Birmingham—England's central
capital; and do not these eyes look upon the sons of those who, not
thirty years ago, shook the fabric of privilege to its base?'[29] Bright
made Birmingham the centre of his campaign through the 1860s for
Parliamentary reform. In the following decade it was the scene of
Joseph Chamberlain's experiments in social reform and played an
equally important role in influencing and moulding Liberalism.

Britain's new industrial cities like Manchester and Birmingham
excited and fascinated the up-and-coming Liberals. While Dickens,
Carlyle and Arnold saw them only as living testaments to man's
cruelty and depravity, they saw them as visible monuments to his
enterprise and progress. As a young man, Cobden journeyed round the
manufacturing areas of the country eagerly noting the facts of industrial change, as, for example, that 'between the date of Waterloo
and the date of the Reform Act, the power looms in Manchester had
increased from 2,000 to 80,000 and the population of Birmingham had
grown from 90,000 to 150,000.'[30] After gazing on Lake Lucerne and
the mountains surrounding it, R. W. Dale wrote: 'There is nothing in
this magnificent view which makes me feel half the thrill I have sometimes felt when I have looked down on the smoky streets of Birmingham
from the railway as I have returned to work from a holiday.'[31]

Liberal idolization of the industrial landscape was part of a more
general enthusiasm for everything new. Bright rhapsodized over the
railway system and the daily press. Gladstone enthused over the
development of sewage-treatment plants in London which he believed
would produce enough gas to light the homes of the inhabitants and
disperse the smog hanging over the capital. Cobden wrote to the

veteran Radical, Francis Place, a few days after the repeal of the corn laws: 'Bless yourself that you live in times when Reform Bills, steamboats, railroads, penny postage and free trade, to say nothing of the ratification of civil and religious liberties, have been possible facts.'[32]

Worship of the new led naturally to Liberal admiration for America. The United States was regarded as a shining example of all that was best in modern civilization. Cobden visited America in 1835 and 1859, Rathbone in 1841, Henry Ashworth in 1857, John Morley in 1867, Bryce and Mundella in 1870, and Forster in 1874. They all came away excited and enthusiastic about what Cobden described as 'the vitality, force, and velocity of progress of that people, and their inborn aptitude for self-government'.[33] They returned determined to introduce into Britain the institutions and practices which they saw working for enlightenment and emancipation across the Atlantic.

The United States impressed Cobden first and foremost because its government was carried out in the interests of manufacturers and businessmen. After his first visit he published a pamphlet, *England, Ireland and America* warning that America was fast overtaking Britain as a commercial and industrial power. While British laws and governments put obstacles and restrictions in the way of industrialists at every turn, everything in America was designed to smooth their way. One only needed to compare the difficulties in getting railways built over land here with the ease with which the railroad network was extended there. The United States had free trade, cheap government, and a policy of non-intervention abroad. Its navy and army were respectively seven and twelve times smaller than those of Britain. It was, in short, a model of how to run a country to achieve maximum prosperity.

Cobden was also much impressed by the Americans' system of universal, secular education provided at public expense. He commended it strongly in speeches in the House of Commons and told a meeting at the Mechanics' Institute in Barnsley in 1853 that it had put an end to unemployment and destitution. The American school system became a model for Liberal educational reformers in Britain. In 1868 Jesse Collings, a Birmingham businessman, published an *Outline of the American Schools System* which led directly to the formation of the National Education League, with Collings as its secretary, to campaign for universal secular education in Britain financed out of the rates. Forster's Education Act of 1870, establishing a national system of elementary education paid for out of public funds, owed much to the American example.

The American Constitution, with its universal manhood suffrage and fully democratic institutions, had appealed to English radicals ever since its adoption. So great was his admiration of it that Jeremy Bentham described himself to Andrew Jackson as 'more of a United Statesman than an Englishman'. The American experience was held up as a model by Liberals calling for Parliamentary reform. In 1857 Ashworth wrote to Cobden from New York that, 'universal suffrage and the Ballot are the soundest foundations for a great country.'[34] In 1866 the *Fortnightly Review* argued that the wealth and moderation of the United States showed that 'universal suffrage and the freest institutions are compatible with a well-ordered state, where life and property are secure.'[35] Bright told an audience in Rochdale in 1863 of the democratic delights awaiting the English working man who emigrated to America: 'He does not find that he belongs to what are called the "lower classes"; he is not shut out from any of the rights of citizenship; he is admitted to the full enjoyment of all political privileges.' He also found, Bright continued, 'a free church, a free school, free land, a free vote, and a free career for the child of the humblest born in the land'.[36] In his book *The American Commonwealth* (1888), Bryce described the United States Constitution as the best yet devised by the human race.

The openness and classlessness of American society particularly impressed British Liberals. Mundella noted after visiting a school in Boston: 'There side by side sit the child of the governor of the state, the child of the Irish immigrant, the young gentleman with his gold watch and chain, and the child of the negro, all receiving the same education.'[37] Cobden regarded the social mobility found in the United States as the main reason for the self-respect and lack of servility among its inhabitants. He wrote to Bright from America in 1859: 'It is this universal hope of rising in the social scale which is the key to much of the superiority that is visible in this country.'[38] For Bright the most impressive feature of the United States was its humanity and tolerance, shown in its abolition of capital punishment, its religious freedom and its liberal attitude towards immigrants. It was, he told his Birmingham constituents in 1862, 'the home of freedom and a refuge for the oppressed of every race and of every clime'.[39]

There was particular admiration among Liberals for the American style of politics. After reading a characteristically pro-American article by Mill in 1866 Lord Stanley observed that 'the Americans seem to be to modern Liberals what the French were seventy years ago, the type and pattern of political excellence.'[40] Cobden was deeply impressed by the vigour with which the leaders of the Democratic party dismantled the tariff system and he consciously modelled the meetings of the Anti-Corn Law League on Democratic rallies that he had seen during his visits to the United States. Joseph Chamberlain set up the National Liberal Federation, which was designed to bring grass-roots opinion to bear on Liberal policy-making, in imitation of the American party organizations which he admired for their fully democratic and participatory nature. Abraham Lincoln was a hero for most Liberals, not least for John Bright who solemnly exchanged busts with him. Bright was himself invited to take part in the centenary celebration of the framing of the American Constitution and there was even a suggestion among some Democrats that he should be a candidate for the American Presidency, despite the fact he had never set foot in the United States.

British Conservatives, on the other hand, saw American politics as corrupt, vulgar and demagogic, and accused Liberals of wanting to introduce them into Britain. Cobden and Bright were contemptuously dubbed 'the two Members for the United States' and Disraeli complained in 1866 that Gladstone's Reform Bill would lead to 'an American constitution'. Chamberlain was accused of seeking to import the worst features of American political life in establishing the National Liberal Federation. The Tory press predicted that it would introduce the corruption of machine politics and the rule of the party boss and Disraeli told the Queen after the 1880 election, 'the Liberals have worked on that American system called caucus, originated by the great Radical, Mr. Chamberlain.'[41]

At times the Liberals were perhaps a little uncritical in their worship of everything across the Atlantic and shared the 'almost idolatrous admiration for all political movements in America' that characterized Turnbull, the radical Liberal M.P. in Trollope's *Phineas Finn*.[42] But for many of them the United States represented the promised land of Liberalism. It was self-reliant, acquisitive and individualistic, and yet at the same time open, tolerant and free. It was the country of the future, bold, imaginative and exciting. When John Morley visited America in 1867, George Meredith wrote in the *Fortnightly Review* of:

> *The strange experimental land*
> *Where men continually dare take*
> *Niagara leaps;—unshatter'd stand*
> *'Twixt fall and fall; for conscience sake*

Meredith concluded his 'Lines to A Friend Visiting America':

> *Adieu! bring back a braver dawn*
> *To England, and to me, my friend.*[43]

In contrast to America's boldness and readiness to put new ideas into practice, Liberals saw Britain as timid and wedded to the old and traditional. Cobden deplored the classical bias of English education, protesting that more time and energy was devoted by the best brains at Oxford to finding the location of ancient Greek rivers than to analysing the success of Chicago. Everywhere he found antiquity and custom being worshipped and being held up as a defence for manifestly bad practices. This was why landowners still dominated government, the Church of England had a privileged position, and administrative appointments were made on the basis of birth and not ability. The English constitution, he wrote, was 'a thing of monopolies, and Church-craft, and sinecures, armorial hocus-pocus, primogeniture and pageantry'.[44] It was not surprising that Palmerston complained of Cobden and Bright in 1864: 'They have run amuck against everything that the British Nation respects and values—Crown, Aristocracy, Established Church, Nobility, Gentry, Landowners.'[45]

Liberals found particularly lacking in Britain the American spirit of individualism and pioneering which encouraged those with ambition and talent to rise, regardless of their social position. There were too many obstacles created by birth, precedent, tradition, too much privilege and protection. Liberals wanted to see competition, the great enemy of the privileged and the great friend of the up-and-coming, introduced into every department of English life. They wanted it brought into government, the armed services, the universities and into the running of the economy. Competition was obviously in their own interest, but it was also a matter of principle. 'No one', wrote Mill in his *Lectures on Political Economy*, 'can foresee the time when it will not be indispensable to progress.'[46]

Lord Acton regarded the open competitive examination for entry into the Civil Service, introduced in 1870 by Gladstone following the recommendations of the famous report by Sir Charles Trevelyan and Sir Stafford Northcote and the agitation of the Administrative Reform Association in the mid-1850s, as the most characteristic invention of nineteenth-century Liberalism. Certainly it had all the right ingredients. It was a frontal attack on the aristocratic hold over government and the system of patronage and nepotism that denied entry to the Civil

Service to the talented and ambitious members of the middle classes. It firmly established the claims of intelligence and merit to govern the country. It also involved bringing the values of business and commerce into government. The campaign mounted by the Administrative Reform Association was very much a businessmen's agitation. The first official paper issued by the Association declared that 'the whole system of Government office is such as in any private business would lead to inevitable ruin.'[47]

Mill felt that the members of the Administrative Reform Association were rather too optimistic in 'their assumption that the middle classes of this country possess the eminent qualities which are wanting in the higher'.[48] He was, nonetheless, unqualified in his support of the principle of competitive examination. He commended its introduction into the Civil Service for 'the extraordinary stimulus which would be given to mental cultivation in its most important branches . . . by the effect of the national recognition of it as the exclusive title to participation in the conduct of so large and conspicuous a portion of the national affairs' and looked forward to 'the great and salutary moral revolution, descending to the lowest classes, which would follow the knowledge that Government would henceforth bestow its gifts according to merit, and not to favour'.[49]

The overwhelming justification for introducing competition into government was the Benthamite one of efficiency and public good. Mill regarded the Civil Service reforms proposed in 1855 as offering 'to liberals the realisation of the principal object which any reformer desires to effect by political changes, namely, that the administration of public affairs should be in the most competent hands'.[50] The Administrative Reform Association's motto, 'The Right Man in The Right Place', lay equally at the root of Cardwell's efforts to abolish the purchase of commissions in the Army and of the Liberal academics' crusade to abolish religious tests for entry to fellowships at Oxford and Cambridge, both of which reforms were enacted by Gladstone's Government in 1871. Whether it was a matter of civil servants, army officers or dons, the Liberals' object was to make sure that those in the job were there because they were the best people to do it, and for no other reason.

Efficiency and competence were obsessions of the Victorian Liberal mind. They particularly appealed to the financiers and to the former followers of Sir Robert Peel who sat in the Liberal Cabinets. The Liberal party inherited from the Peelites both a commitment to

administrative excellence and a particularly talented group of administrators, led by Gladstone, Cardwell and the 8th Duke of Argyll. This
legacy was undoubtedly one main reason why for much of the second
half of the nineteenth century the Liberals tended to be the natural
party of government, and to be better than the Tories at organizing
the administration and managing the economy. Equally important was
the high premium that they put on intellectual and business talents
and the richness of expertise they could draw on from among their members. In 1867 John Morley called for a transference into government of
'those virtues which few Englishmen lack in the conduct of great
commercial undertakings, to infuse into the legislature a love of good
government as strong as the love for vigorous and large enterprise,
promptitude, and order, which presides over the management of any
great private business'.[51] Gladstone's first Cabinet in 1868 contained
two prominent City financiers, Goschen and Childers, and his second
in 1880 included two former industrialists, Lord Granville and Joseph
Chamberlain, who had made his fortune manufacturing screws in
Birmingham.

The activities of the leading members of the first Liberal Government
clearly displayed the Liberals' passion for ordering and systematizing
things and for governing by experts rather than aristocratic amateurs.
Gladstone himself established Parliamentary Counsel attached to the
Treasury to draft Bills, very much along the lines suggested by Mill in
his *Considerations on Representative Government*, which had called for a
legislative commission, composed of legal experts, to draft Bills under
Parliament's surveillance. Cardwell's Army Regulation Act (1871)
abolished the purchase of commissions and completely reorganized the
Army. Lord Selborne's Judicature Act (1873) fused the common law
and equity systems and united the seven existing courts to form one
High Court with divisions. The other great reformer in the first
Gladstone administration, Robert Lowe, the Chancellor of the Exchequer, had already shown his passion for efficiency in the system of
'payment by results' which he had incorporated in his Revised Code
on education in 1861 and which ensured that public grants were given
only to those pupils who performed satisfactorily in tests.

Several Liberal back-benchers had pet schemes of administrative
reform which they championed. Peter Rylands, for example, spent
much of his eleven years as M.P. for Warrington, where he owned a
wire-making business, in fighting for the reform of the Diplomatic
Service. Rathbone took a particular interest in the reform of the

bankruptcy laws. Henry James, a distinguished barrister who entered the House of Commons in 1869, brought forward several measures to secure greater purity in the conduct of elections. In 1883, as Attorney General in Gladstone's second administration, he drafted and carried through the Corrupt Practices Act which remains the basis of modern electoral law. Trollope's Plantagenet Palliser, with his lifelong devotion to the cause of decimalizing the currency, epitomized exactly the Liberals' commitment to administrative tidiness and efficiency.

There was only one quality in government that Liberals prized more highly than efficiency. That was economy. Businessmen and industrialists called for low public spending, and therefore low rates and taxes. Nonconformists felt excessive spending to be extravagant and therefore immoral, while for administrators it offended against the utilitarian canons of efficiency. In both local and central government Liberals raised the cry of economy wherever they saw waste. Cobden and Bright were horrified in 1853 when Manchester Corporation decided to adopt scarlet gowns and hold civic junketings in imitation of the City of London. In the same year Gladstone began his lifelong commitment to the cause of reducing public expenditure when he announced in his first budget his proposals for the phasing out of income tax.

As a Treasury minister for a total of twenty-four years and the author of thirteen budgets between 1853 and 1882, Gladstone virtually took on the Liberals' commitment to economical government single-handed and had no lack of opportunity to put into practice his belief that excessive public expenditure was 'not only a pecuniary waste, but a great political, and above all, a great moral evil'.[52] It was chiefly thanks to him that between 1853 and 1882, when annual government spending tripled in the rest of Europe, it fell in Britain from sixteen and a half per cent to nine per cent of the gross national product. His cardinal principle, inherited from Peel, was to balance budgets at the lowest possible figure, and finance public spending out of taxation rather than borrowing, so that no debt was ever carried over from one year to another. He relied on the income tax, but hoped it could eventually be abolished as he regarded it as a standing temptation to governments to spend too much. It was important, Gladstone believed, for the Government to keep out of costly social commitments and not to become involved in the management of industry.

The single biggest item of expenditure for nineteenth-century governments was defence. Liberals had campaigned to reduce it ever since Cobden had argued in 1835 that America's very low level of spending on defence made its economy so healthy. The heavy cost of the Crimean War forced Gladstone to raise income tax to 1s 4d in the £, a level which he regarded as totally unacceptable. During the more peaceful 1860s he was able to reduce annual government spending from £73 million to £66 million and by 1874 he had brought income tax down to 2d in the £. In that year he went to the polls on a platform of abolishing income tax, but the electorate was unhappy about his plans for vastly reduced naval and military establishments. In Gladstone's last budget, in 1882, income tax was still only 4d in the £. Significantly his resignation from the premiership in 1894 was caused by his opposition to the high naval estimates proposed to meet the threat posed by German rearmament.

Gladstone's pursuit of economy in government was unceasing. In 1861 he established the Public Accounts Committee of the House of Commons, which remains to this day Parliament's watchdog on public expenditure. He ruthlessly eliminated unnecessary public offices. When he heard a clerk in the National Debt Office was dying, he sent an urgent note to the Prime Minister saying that there was no need to replace him. In 1871 he somewhat tactlessly began a speech at Greenwich by announcing that he had just sacked 1,463 superfluous clerks and workmen from the Dockyards and amalgamated two jobs in the Board of Customs. He constantly reduced the salaries of government officials and even tried to persuade Secretaries of State and High Court judges to take a cut in pay. He believed small savings to be as important as big ones, regarding it as 'the mark of a chicken-hearted Chancellor when he shrinks from upholding economy in detail, when because it is a question of only £2,000 or £3,000 he says that it is no matter. He is not worth his salt if he is not ready to save what are meant by candle ends and cheese parings in the cause of economy.'[53] True to his word, Gladstone ordered the Foreign Office to use single rather than double sheets of foolscap for its dispatches and insisted on reusing the labels on diplomatic bags. He scrupulously paid for the headed notepaper which he used for private letters during his time at No. 10 Downing Street. Not even expenditure on the monarchy escaped his censure if he regarded it as excessive. On visits to Balmoral and Windsor he invariably complained to his wife about his 'hatred of the fine sheets'.[54]

Second only to public economy, Gladstone's budgets were dominated by the theme of free trade. As Chancellor of the Exchequer in the 1850s, he completed the work begun in the 1820s by Huskisson of dismantling the mass of important duties and taxes which stood in the way of free trade with foreign producers and markets. In 1852 there were still more than a thousand dutiable articles in the British tariff. After Gladstone's 1860 budget only sixteen remained. Free trade had by then become a national rather than a narrowly Liberal obsession. *The Times* described it in 1859 as 'like parliamentary representation or ministerial responsibility, not so much a prevalent opinion as an article of national faith' and when President Grover Cleveland tried to reduce tariffs in the United States in 1867, the Republicans accused him of 'a direct attempt to fasten upon this country the British policy of free foreign trade'.[55] For Liberals, however, free trade had a special sanctity and importance. They had pioneered it in the 1830s and 1840s against the protectionist Tories and they clung on to it in the 1880s and 1890s long after it had ceased to be in the obvious interest of Britain and when other countries were building up high tariff barriers. Indeed, Liberalism became more closely identified with free trade as the Conservatives espoused protectionism at the turn of the twentieth century. 'We are Liberals,' Henry Campbell-Bannerman told a meeting in Bolton in 1903, 'We believe in free trade because we believe in the capacity of our countrymen.'[56]

The doctrine of free trade was the supreme expression of the Liberalism of the up-and-coming. It sought to erode protection and monopoly and open up all markets to perfect competition. It derived from a position of economic strength. Its original architect, the eight-eenth-century Scottish economist Adam Smith, had made the point that the country with the largest volume of trade in the world would necessarily derive most benefit from the establishment of free markets. Until the 1880s Britain was that country, with the power to out-produce and out-sell all its competitors. Free trade was also pre-eminently a manufacturers' and businessmen's cause. Its greatest popular exponent, Cobden, had realized very early on in his travels across the country that Britain, with a huge population and without the resources to feed it, would only survive on its ability to manufacture and sell goods to the rest of the world. He had led his agitation against the corn laws because they prevented food reaching Britain and manufactured goods leaving it at the cheapest possible prices. They denied the foreigner a market for his raw materials and the English manufacturer a market for his goods. Free trade might have the incidental benefits of making the working man's food cheaper and his job in the factory or mill more secure, but essentially it was something that helped manufacturers and businessmen. Goldwin Smith noted in his *Reminiscences* that, for all Cobden and Bright's high-flown moral rhetoric, most manufacturers were not 'universal philanthropists' and supported free trade out of pure self-interest.

To its critics, this naked self-interest was the greatest weakness of the Liberalism of Cobden and Bright. In *Culture and Anarchy* Matthew Arnold attacked 'the spurious Hellenism of our free-trading Liberal friends, mechanically worshipping their fetish of the production of wealth and of the increase of manufacturers and population, and looking neither to right nor left so long as this increase goes on . . . to this idea of glory and greatness the free trade which our Liberal friends extol so solemnly and devoutly has served . . . and for this it is prized. Therefore the untaxing of the poor man's bread has, with this view of national happiness, been used not so much to make the existing poor man's bread cheaper, or more abundant, but rather to create more poor men to eat it.'[57] Newman criticized Liberals for worshipping mere material progress and arguing that 'education, periodical literature, railroad travelling, ventilation and drainage' were all that was necessary to make a people moral and happy.[58] Thomas Carlyle dismissed the free trade movement as mere mammon worship, while the 7th Earl of Shaftesbury complained that his efforts to promote factory legislation in the interests of the workers were frustrated by 'a body of Capitalists, the wealthiest, the most united, the most selfish, the most determined'.[59] Even Mazzini, the Italian liberal leader, attacked English Liberals for being ruthlessly individualistic and acquisitive.

Victorian Liberalism had an undeniably thrusting, go-getting quality. It was the creed of strong men who believed in standing on their own feet and who did not want protection or interference from the Government. The Liberal manufacturers and mill owners opposed efforts to reduce hours worked in factories and regulate conditions of work not just because they would interfere with their profits, but also because they represented a paternalistic approach which they abhorred. Cobden asked the electors of Stockport in 1836: 'Am I told that the industrious classes in Lancashire are incapable of protecting themselves from oppression unless by the shield of the legislature? . . . Mine is that masculine species of charity, which would lead me to inculcate in the minds of the labouring classes the love of independence, the privilege of self-respect, the disdain of being patronized or petted, the desire to accumulate, and the ambition to rise. I know it has been found easier to please the people by holding out flattering and delusive prospects of cheap benefits to be derived from Parliament rather than by urging them to a course of self-reliance; but, while I will not be the sycophant of the great, I cannot become the parasite of the poor.'[60]

It is certainly true as well that the Liberal manufacturers and mill owners disliked anything which got in the way of their money-making. But their self-interest was enlightened. They believed that their own pursuit of profit was the best guarantee of raising the general level of prosperity and welfare in the country. To reduce the hours of factory work as Tory paternalists wanted to do would, they believed, only diminish their capital and so lower wages, increase unemployment, and limit their own capacity to help their workers in times of trouble. They resisted government interference in their activities not just because it threatened their own direct interests but because they felt it was against the interests of the community as a whole. 'Private enterprise has done much for this country—much more than the Government or the Executive had ever done,' Bright said in a speech in 1844 opposing state plans to purchase railways. 'There was a wholesome absence of interference on the part of the Government in this country in all these matters, which experience showed might be wisely, safely and benefi-cially left to private individuals, stimulated by the love of gain and the desire to administer to the wants and comforts of their fellow men.'[61]

The rising professional men and manufacturers to whom Liberalism appealed were also fiercely competitive and individualistic. But that was largely because many of them had risen by their own efforts. It was not surprising that someone like Samuel Morley believed that 'life is really a continued competitive examination.'[62] If Liberals did not seem to care too much about those who failed the competition, then that was partly because they felt that their fate would be worse in a less competitive society. 'Whoever succeeds in an overcrowded profession, or in a competitive examination,' wrote Mill, 'whoever is preferred to another in any contest for an object which both desire, reaps benefit from the loss of others . . . but it is, by common admission, better for the general interest of mankind, that persons should pursue their objects undeterred by this sort of consequence.'[63] In championing merit, enterprise and drive, Liberalism sanctified success, and almost implied that might was right. Herbert Spencer saw all men starting with equal advantages and justified inequalities of wealth and social status as indices of virtue. Cobden once commented, 'it is certain that in this world the virtues and the forces go together, and the vices and the weaknesses are inseparable.'[64]

There was also an undeniably philistine quality to the Liberalism of the up-and-coming, exemplified by Dale's preference for the view of Birmingham to the vista of the Italian lakes, and Cobden's remark that there was more to be learned from *The Times* than from Thucydides. It was part of their excitement with the new and their impatience with the old. When Edward Baines made a tour of Europe as a young man he was far more interested in the latest factories and industrial techniques than in the art of the countries he visited. Arnold was not being unfair when he observed that 'your "earnest Liberal" in England thinks culture all moonshine' and when he wrote in *Culture and Anarchy*: 'Mr. Bright, when he wishes to give the working class a true sense of what makes glory and greatness, tells it to look at the cities it has built, the railroads it has made, the manufactures it has produced. . . .What an unsound habit of mind it must be which makes us talk of things like coal or iron as constituting the greatness of England. . . . If England were swallowed up by the sea tomorrow, which of the two, a hundred years hence, would most excite the love, interest and admiration of mankind, the England of the last twenty years, or the England of Elizabeth, of a time of great spiritual effort, but when our coal, and our industrial operations, were very little developed?'[65]

If the Liberal manufacturers and mill owners had something of the ruthlessness and philistinism of the *parvenu*, they also had a conspicuous lack of the airs and pretension often associated with that type. They generally followed a simple, even austere, life-style, and shared Bright's dislike of 'society, smart people, hot rooms, elaborate meals, and ceremonious observances'.[66] Many were Nonconformists and totally abstained from the use of alcohol. They also remained physically close to the working people from whose ranks many of them had come. Not for them the lavish country estates of later entrepreneurs. A survey of 1849 showed that only 29 of the 904 owners of cotton mills in Lancashire and Cheshire did not live in the same town as their mills, and of those 29, 17 lived in Manchester to supervise warehouses and sales. They were close to their workers in other respects as well, often devoting a large amount of their time and money to philanthropic activity among their employees. Samuel Morley personally paid all his workers every week so that he could maintain contact with them until his business became so large that this proved physically impossible. Titus Salt provided his employees at Saltaire with houses, chapels, schools, almshouses, infirmary, club, library, laboratory, games room and gymnasium. They did not believe in shuffling off on to personnel managers and welfare departments the responsibilities that went with ownership and capitalism.

The competitiveness and philistinism of the up-and-coming Northern manufacturers was, anyway, only one element in Victorian Liberalism. Trollope, who heartily despised the mentality of the Manchester mill owners, underlined a very different element when he wrote in his autobiography that the Liberal 'is ever willing to help the many ascend the ladder a little, though he knows, as they come up towards him, he must go down to meet them'.[67] Bagehot once commented that he often felt 'that deep and irrational hatred for the strong and successful, that love for the weak over whom the strong have climbed to success, which is perhaps the surest mark of the Liberal temperament'.[68] They represented another side to Victorian Liberalism which was just as much concerned with diffusing culture and light as was Matthew Arnold.

Chapter 3

The Love of Liberty

It was as a philosophy with deep roots in both British and European traditions of thought, and not as a convenient creed for the up-and-coming middle classes, that Liberalism appealed to writers and intellectuals like Thackeray, Meredith, John Morley and T. H. Green. The philosophy of Liberalism directly inspired such noble literary works as the Brownings' poems on Italian freedom, Mill's essay *On Liberty*, and the monumental *History of Liberty* for which Lord Acton spent his life collecting material and which remained largely unwritten at his death.

A single common theme underlay the Brownings' poems, Mill's essay and Acton's projected history. They were celebrations of human freedom. 'The basis of my Liberalism is this,' Gladstone told an audience in Norwich in 1860, 'I am a lover of liberty, and that liberty which I value for myself, I value for every human being in proportion to his means and opportunities.'[1] At root, the philosophy of Victorian Liberalism was a passionate attachment to the ideal of freedom. The attachment was both rational and sentimental, with the happy result, as John Morley observed, that 'the rational prevented the sentimental from falling into pure emotional.'[2]

The most recent, and most rational, of the British philosophical traditions on which Victorian Liberalism drew were those of political economy and philosophic radicalism. Behind them lay the tradition of enlightened Whiggism exemplified in the *Edinburgh Review*. In the notes for his history, Acton made much of the Whigs' championship of the ideas of toleration and the sovereignty of the individual conscience which had first been promoted by Milton and other Puritans in the mid-seventeenth century and subsequently developed by John Locke. The Whigs, Acton acknowledged, had made themselves an aristocratic party of liberty. However, he regarded their achievements between the Glorious Revolution of 1688 and the Reform Act of 1832 as severely limited. The true fathers of modern Liberalism, he argued, were those two rebel Whigs, Adam Smith and Jeremy Bentham, who initiated 'the reign of ideas'.

Adam Smith and the classical economists of the late eighteenth century argued for full and complete freedom in all economic dealings between individuals and nations. Bentham and the Philosophic Radicals extended this call for liberty into other areas of life. Their creed was well summed up in Mill's description of the utilitarian faith in which he was brought up by his father: 'In politics, an almost unbounded confidence in the efficacy of two things: representative government, and complete freedom of discussion. So complete was my father's reliance on the influence of reason over the minds of mankind . . . that he felt as if all would be gained if the whole population were taught to read, if all sorts of opinions were allowed to be addressed to them, and if by means of the suffrage they could nominate a legislature to give effect to the opinions they adopted. He thought that when the legislature no longer represented a class interest, it would aim at the general interest . . . accordingly, aristocratic rule . . . was the object of his sternest disapprobation, and a democratic suffrage the principal article of his political faith. . . .

'Next to aristocracy, an established church, or corporation of priests, as being by position the great depravers of religion, and interested in opposing the progress of the human mind, was the object of his greatest detestation. . . . In ethics, his moral feelings were energetic and rigid on all points which he deemed important to human well-being, while he was supremely indifferent in opinion to all those doctrines of the common morality, which he thought had no foundation but in asceticism and priestcraft. . . . In psychology, his fundamental doctrine was the formation of all human character by circumstances, through the universal Principle of Association, and the consequent unlimited possibility of improving the moral and intellectual condition of mankind by education. Of all his doctrines, none was more important than this.'[3]

That statement shows clearly the belief in human perfectibility and the attack on all forms of authority which were the Utilitarians' greatest contributions to the development of the philosophy of Liberalism. Equally important was a very different, and much more sentimental, literary tradition of extolling freedom which went back to Wordsworth's 'flood of British freedom',

> *Which to the open sea*
> *Of the world's praise from dark antiquity*
> *Hath flowed, 'with pomp of waters unwithstood',*

and to Shelley's vision of man, in *Prometheus Unbound*, as 'sceptreless, free, uncircumscribed, equal, unclassed, tribeless and nationless'.[4] The idolization of liberty by the English romantic poets in the early nineteenth century helped to create the cultural climate in which Liberalism thrived. Byron had even called the periodical which he produced with Leigh Hunt in 1821 *The Liberal*. The poems which he and Shelley wrote on the Greek struggle for independence first inspired many Liberals with the commitment to the self-determination of small states that was to become a cardinal article of Gladstonian foreign policy. Even Mill, the arch-rationalist, was deeply affected by their romantic and sentimental approach. Lady Amberley, Bertrand Russell's mother, recalled him in his last years reading Shelley's *Ode to Liberty* to her: 'He got quite excited and moved over it, rocking backwards and forwards and nearly choking with emotion, and murmuring, "it is almost too much for one".'[5]

The legacy passed on to Liberals by enlightened Whigs, classical economists, Philosophic Radicals and romantic poets was a fervent commitment to liberty in all areas of life. This commitment had perhaps reached its fullest expression in the abolition of slavery in the British Empire in 1833. Abolition had long been urged by economists and utilitarians as well as by evangelicals and humanitarians. When it came, at the hands of the first Whig Government after the Reform Act, the emancipation of the negro slaves was heralded by poets and philosophers as a great triumph for the principle of liberty. Carlyle sourly attributed it to 'that unhappy wedlock of philanthropic Liberalism and the Dismal Science of political economy' which he saw taking hold of the country.[6] He was right. The abolition of slavery was the first great characteristic act of the emerging liberal consensus in Britain.

Last, but by no means least, of the native influences which helped to shape the philosophy of Victorian Liberalism was the tradition of rationalism and free thought established in John Locke's *The Reasonableness of Christianity* and developed in Thomas Paine's *The Age of Reason*. For many people in the nineteenth century 'liberalism' meant a sceptical approach to religion rather than a political creed. In his *Apologia Pro Vita Sua*, J. H. Newman wrote: 'By liberalism I mean the anti-dogmatic principle and its developments.' As described by Newman, religious liberalism developed along remarkably similar lines to political liberalism. He dated its emergence as a serious force in the religious world to the early 1830s, when it became the cry of church and university reformers at Oxford. Before then there had prevailed the less threatening latitudinarianism and deism, similar to Whiggism in its unideological character and its lack of any cutting edge. By 1864, when he wrote the *Apologia*, liberalism had become a 'deep, plausible scepticism' which affected the entire country.[7]

There were, in fact, even closer parallels between the development of free thought and the development of Liberalism in the mid-nineteenth century. In the 1830s and 1840s religious liberalism was largely subsumed in more general economic and political radicalism and was little more than an adjunct to Owenism and Chartism. It was only with the failure of these working-class movements in the 1850s that George Holyoake, a Birmingham whitesmith, created a distinct and 'respectable' secular movement, which was given organizational form by Charles Bradlaugh, who founded the National Secular Society in 1866. Secularism was in many ways the intellectual counterpart to political Liberalism. Holyoake developed it as a philosophy which sought to promote secular improvement while avoiding theological controversy. He was always careful to distinguish it from mere atheism. His three leading principles—that the lives of men were improved by material means; that science, natural and social, was the source of the most reliable assistance to man; and that the greatest good was service to mankind—were those of enlightened Liberalism. 'A Liberal', he once wrote, 'is one who seeks to secure for everyone the same rights political, social or religious, which he claims for himself.'[8]

Secularist religious views often went hand in hand with Liberalism in politics. W. J. Fox, a Unitarian minister who was at the centre of an important free-thinking circle, became M.P. for Oldham in 1847 and was a strong ally of the Manchester Party in the House of Commons. In 1879 G. W. Foote, a leading secularist and journalist, founded a periodical, *The Liberal*, to promote 'progress' and 'liberal ideas on all subjects—political, social and religious'. Charles Cattell, who became a well-known free-thinker, was converted simultaneously from Tory Anglicanism to Liberalism and to secularism while preparing lessons for a Sunday school class as a young man. The two leaders of the Victorian secularist movement participated actively in Liberal politics. Holyoake was a strong advocate of Parliamentary and administrative reform in the 1840s and 1850s and was on the governing council of the Reform League. He was put up as an 'advanced' Liberal candidate for Tower Hamlets in the election of 1857, but withdrew in favour of a Liberally inclined Whig, 'to keep in sight the interests of the Liberal cause'.[9] In

1868 he stood in Birmingham as a Liberal advocating working-class representation. Bradlaugh was also on the council of the Reform League. In 1860 he founded the *National Reformer* as a journal of 'advanced Liberal opinion', and he was four times elected Liberal M.P. for Northampton between 1880 and 1886.

Secularism never really penetrated the Victorian Liberal party, however. British Liberals did not display the anti-clericalism and the commitment to free thought that distinguished liberal parties abroad. In the United States, the Democrats were known as 'the free thought party' and the free-thinkers called themselves Liberals. Rogier's Belgian Liberal party made the protection of individual liberty against attacks from the Church one of the main planks of its policy. The close association of the British Liberal party with Nonconformity, and the fact that it operated in a Protestant rather than a Catholic country, tended to weaken and isolate its free-thinking elements. Fox, Foote, Holyoake and Bradlaugh were all in the Radical wing of the party and their main contacts were with those 'advanced' Liberals who shared their republicanism and concern for civil rights.

But if Victorian Liberalism could not really be described as a movement of free-thinkers, it was none the less true that there was a strong rationalist strain at least among its more intellectual adherents. Herbert Spencer and Leslie Stephen were leading apostles of free thought. So were Mill, whom Gladstone dubbed 'the Saint of Rationalism', and John Morley, who scandalized his contemporaries by insisting in the *Fortnightly Review* on spelling God with a small 'g'.[10] Liberalism was a philosophical refuge for several of those eminent Victorians who experienced severe crises of faith. T. H. Green, Leslie Stephen and John Morley had all been brought up in strict evangelical households and had subsequently lost their Christian beliefs. The earnestness and high-mindedness which they brought from their religious upbringings were characteristic features of intellectual Liberalism. There were many like Dr. Skinner, the learned public school master in *The Way of All Flesh*, whose most distinguishing feature was 'the simple-minded and child-like earnestness of his character, an earnestness which might be perceived by the solemnity with which he spoke even about trifles. It is hardly necessary to say he was on the Liberal side in politics.'[11]

This high-mindedness was not just confined to those Liberals who had evangelical backgrounds. No one was more earnest than Mill, whose utilitarian upbringing had filled him with as much seriousness of purpose as if he had been taught to walk in fear of a judging God. He

was appalled by the cynicism and flippancy of many of his contemporaries and noted in his diary in 1854: 'A Philosophy of Life, in harmony
with the noblest feelings and cleared of superstition, is the great want
of these times. There has always been talent enough in the world when
there was earnestness enough, and always earnestness enough when
there were strong convictions. There seems to be so little talent
now, only because there is universal uncertainty about the great
questions.'[12]

Most Liberal intellectuals shared Mill's desire for a new secular and
humanist faith. Having lost their religious convictions, they sought a
guiding set of beliefs and values, and fought passionately against
cynicism and relativism. John Morley's great essay *On Compromise*
(1877) was a fierce tirade against half truths and hypocrisy and a plea
for moral steadfastness in a generation which lacked the religious
convictions of its predecessors. For many who had experienced doubt,
Liberalism was itself a kind of substitute religion. Morley wrote of
Cobden that 'his whole mind was possessed by the high needs and
great opportunities of society, as the minds of some other men have
been possessed by the aspirations of religion', while Newman saw only
two directions that a man could take in the mid-nineteenth century,
'the way to Rome, and the way to Atheism. Anglicanism is the halfway
house on the one side, and Liberalism is the halfway house on the
other.'[13]

Matthew Arnold accused Victorian Liberalism of being narrow and
insular in its outlook. It was perhaps an understandable criticism of the
provincial Nonconformist element which was the particular target of
his attack, but it was anything but true of the intellectuals, who were
deeply influenced by Continental ideas. Disraeli persistently complained, indeed, that Liberalism was too cosmopolitan in outlook and
too determined by Continental rather than native traditions. Although
British Liberalism was very different in character from Continental
Liberalism, being less romantic and nationalistic, it was equally influenced by the general European currents of philosophy which flowed
from the Enlightenment.

Several Liberal intellectuals traced their attachment to liberty back
to classical ideas. Ancient Greece was an important democratic symbol
in mid-nineteenth-century Britain. George Grote's *History of Greece*,
published between 1854 and 1856, helped to foster the image of the
country as the birthplace of freedom. Reviewing Grote, Mill commented that Marathon was a more important battle for the English than

Hastings. Gladstone, as an accomplished classical scholar, found much in the ancient world to confirm and strengthen his Liberalism. In the Parliamentary recess at the end of 1867 he composed his fourth study of Homer's poems with a view to elucidating their modern relevance. The principles he found expressed in them could well be taken as the keynotes of his own first administration which began the following year: 'the power of opinion and persuasion as opposed to force; the sense of responsibility in governing men; the hatred, not only of tyranny, but of all unlimited power; the love and the habit of public in preference to secret action; the reconciliation and harmony between the spirit of freedom on the one hand, the spirit of order and reverence on the other; and a practical belief in right as relative, and in duty as reciprocal.'[14]

Gladstone's deep consciousness of the classical and Christian foundations of Western civilization gave him a European perspective that was perhaps wider than that of any other Liberal. In 1866 he visited the Italian monastery of Monte Cassino, the first home of the Benedictine Order. He subsequently took up the defence of the monastery which was threatened with closure by the Italian Government. 'If it should be asked why Englishmen should speak and feel on this Italian subject,' he wrote to a friend, 'my answer would be this: that the foundation and history of Monte Cassino have the interest for us which the Americans of the States feel in Alfred, in Edward III, in Henry V. They are part of the great current of Italian civilisation which has been diffused and distributed over all European lands.'[15] Gladstone's conception of Europe as a moral and cultural entity, deriving from its classical and Christian roots, was an important element in his foreign policy, lying at the heart of his concept of a Concert of Europe asserting the public law and the conscience of the Continent.

Other Liberal intellectuals went less far back in finding the roots of European Liberalism. Both Acton and John Morley complained that Gladstone overrated the part played by Christianity and underrated the role of the French Enlightenment in civilizing and humanizing Europe. In shunning the ideas of the French *philosophes*, Gladstone was in the company of most of his countrymen, who shared his distaste for their atheism and associated them with the slaughter of the French Revolution. Most rank-and-file Liberals would have agreed with his remarks on Garibaldi in 1864, 'as to his Goddess Reason, I understand by it simply an adoption of what are called on the continent the principles of the French Revolution. These we neither want nor warmly relish in

England.'[16] For an important group of Liberal intellectuals, however, the ideas of the French *philosophes* were fundamental.

John Morley was the most devoted of all Victorian Liberals to the ideas of the French Enlightenment. Indeed in his books on Rousseau, Voltaire, Diderot and Montesquieu, he put them back on the British intellectual map from which they had disappeared in 1789. He also gave Victorian Liberalism a European pedigree by identifying the French *encyclopédistes* as its pioneers. They had established, he said, 'that human nature is good, that the world is capable of being made a desirable abiding place, and that the evil of the world is the fruit of bad education and bad institutions'.[17] Morley felt, in company with other Liberal intellectuals like Herbert Spencer, that the world had at last reached the stage predicted by the *encyclopédistes* in which scientific and intellectual progress had banished superstition and erected reason as the only authority to be obeyed by man.

Positivism, the philosophy developed by Auguste Comte which followed on from the notions of secular progress of the French Enlightenment, had a considerable influence on several Liberal intellectuals. In marked contrast to most Continental philosophers, Comte had more of a following in England than at home. It was only because of Mill's financial support that he was able to go on working after he had been thrown out of the École polytechnique for his unorthodox opinions. Both Mill and Morley were attracted to Comte's proposal for an ethical system independent of Christianity and divine sanctions, and deriving from the progress of science and the rationality of man. Comte offered a creed for the agnostic, demanding a belief in nothing that could not be verified by empirical observation. It was also a creed for optimists. Comte's 'religion of humanity' rested on the assumption that as men became more intelligent, they also became more moral and saw that a life of unselfishness led to satisfaction and happiness. Positivism combined a faith in science with active humanitarianism.

It was no coincidence that Comte's leading English disciples were Liberals. Mill was dubious about the notion of a religion of humanity but in his *Logic* he used Positivist arguments to prove that things could not be known to the mind independent of observation and experience, and therefore that there was no defence for manifestly bad institutions. Morley was a more enthusiastic adherent to Comte's religion of humanity, being convinced that a new movement was about to sweep the world based on 'undivided love of our fellows, steadfast search after justice, firm aspiration towards improvement, and generous contentment in the hope that others may reap whatever reward may be'.[18] The leader of the Positivist movement in Britain, Frederic Harrison, who conducted austere ceremonies in honour of humanity, personified by a reproduction of the Sistine Madonna, at the movement's headquarters in Newton Hall, London, saw the Liberal party as the best available vehicle for bringing in the new era.

While Positivism was the Continental philosophy which most influenced British Liberal intellectuals, the idealism of Kant and Hegel also had an important effect on the development of Liberal philosophy towards the end of the nineteenth century. T. H. Green was strongly influenced by its conception of reality as something more than the mere sensually perceived facts that the Positivists and Utilitarians took it to be. Idealism led Green to develop a theory of moral obligation, deriving from the consciousness of perfection to be attained, and a sense of the organic nature of society which produced a political philosophy very different from the individualistic Liberalism of Mill.

On a less rarified plane, the ideas of Continental political theorists played a part in shaping the philosophy of Victorian Liberalism. The French Liberal theorists of the 1820s and 1830s, Guizot, Constant and de Tocqueville, evoked a considerably more sympathetic response in Britain than had their predecessors during the Revolutionary period. This was because they stressed civil rights rather than natural rights, and individuals rather than communities. They were also more complimentary about British liberties, which the Revolutionaries had dismissed as being mere privileges enjoyed by a minority to the detriment of the community as a whole. De Tocqueville was almost certainly the greatest influence on British Liberals. His *Democracy in America* (1835) convinced Mill that the American system of a universal franchise and free institutions was successful and that, provided there were certain safeguards to avoid the tyranny of the majority, democracy was the most desirable political system for Europe. Gladstone was impressed by de Tocqueville's argument that Britain had been conspicuously more successful than France in founding colonies and impressing her traditions on America because of her freer institutions at home.

The work of German Liberal theorists also played a part in encouraging the development of philosophic Liberalism in Britain. Ironically, in a country where Liberalism was to lead to extreme nationalism and the growth of the state, it was as an individualistic and anti-authoritarian ideology that German Liberal theory had most influence abroad. Kant's argument that while the state controlled the sphere of legality, it had

nothing to do with the sphere of morality, and that its role was limited
to ensuring conditions for the ordered co-existence of individuals,
clearly influenced Mill. Mill was also much influenced by the Prussian
political theorist, Wilhelm Von Humboldt, whose *Essay On The Limits
of the Action of the State*, published posthumously in 1852, argued that
the function of the state should be restricted to security and that
individuals should be left to act freely and spontaneously. Significantly,
Mill took as the motto for his own essay *On Liberty* Von Humboldt's
statement that 'the grand, leading principle, towards which every
argument in these pages directly converges, is the absolute and essential
importance of human development in its richest variety.' The works of
Georg Gervinus, the German historian, also helped to give British
Liberals a sense that they were involved in a great European movement.
For him, the nineteenth century was the century of liberation. 'The
emancipation of all the oppressed and suffering', he wrote, 'such is the
call of the century.'[19]

The Continental Liberals who had most influence on the development
of British Liberalism, however, were undoubtedly the leaders of the
Italian Risorgimento. Cavour, Mazzini and Garibaldi were not only
theorists, they were also active politicians. Of all the struggles for
freedom being waged in the mid-nineteenth century, by Greeks,
Belgians, Magyars, Rumanians, Bulgarians, Bohemians and Poles, it
was the Italians' battle to unify their country and free it from Papal and
Habsburg domination that most inspired and impressed British Liberals.
It was not difficult to see why. Because of its classical past, Italy had a
fascination for intellectuals and poets. James Bryce recalled that the
Old Mortality Society at Oxford discussed the Risorgimento more than
any other subject in the 1860s. The romance of Italian reunification
moved Meredith, Swinburne, Landor and the Brownings to compose
some of their finest poems. Secularists, free-thinkers and Nonconformists warmed to the struggle against the very heart of Catholic bigotry
and idolatry. The leaders of the Risorgimento were men of intense
charisma who made a deep impression on all who loved liberty. John
Morley embarked towards the end of his life on a biography of Cavour
which, with his works on Gladstone and Cobden, he intended would
form a trilogy on Liberalism. Mazzini inspired James Stansfeld to found
the People's International League, later the Friends of Italy, by telling
him that Britain should play a leading role on behalf of 'right and
liberty'. Garibaldi's visit to England in 1864 provoked spectacular
popular demonstrations of support from working-class Radicals and

ex–Chartists. As John Morley put it, 'the Italian revolution of 1860 gave new vitality to the popular side in England.'[20]

No one was more influenced by the Italian Risorgimento than Gladstone. John Morley observed in his biography: 'Italy it was that first drew him by the native ardour of his humanity, unconsciously and involuntarily, into that great European stream of liberalism which was destined to carry him so far.'[21] Gladstone was first affected by Italian liberalism when on a family holiday to Naples in 1850 he attended the trial of Carlo Poerio, a former minister who had tried to work a constitution which had been wrung from King Ferdinand in the 1848 revolution and subsequently repudiated. Having seen Poerio sentenced to twenty-four years' imprisonment in chains, Gladstone visited the gaol where he was confined and was appalled to discover that about 20,000 political prisoners were being kept in conditions of terrible filth and cruelty in Italy. He returned to England seething with indignation and wrote an open letter describing what was going on in Italy as 'the negation of God erected into a system of Government'.[22] It was the first of Gladstone's many public outbursts on moral questions. He helped Italian political prisoners throughout the 1850s, and in the spring of 1859, on the way back from his mission to devise a constitution for the Ionian Islands, he went again to Italy where the struggle for reunification and liberation from Austria was now on in earnest. Gladstone's discussions with Cavour convinced him of the rightness and nobility of the Risorgimento and he returned to England persuaded, in Morley's words, that 'the resurrection of Italy could only be vindicated on principles of liberty and the right of a nation to choose its own rulers.'[23] He also returned to find Lord Derby's Conservative administration firmly opposed to that view and committed to supporting Austrian rule over Italy. It was his opposition to that policy which finally took Gladstone into the Liberal party.

The Italian Risorgimento impressed Liberals as being a moral crusade led by visionaries rather than just a narrow bid for power by a group of calculating politicians. For this Mazzini was largely responsible. His idealistic assertion that politics was about morality and his fashioning of democratic nationalism into something approaching a religion had a considerable impact on British Liberals. Hugh Price Hughes, a leading Methodist minister and preacher, admired Mazzini more than any other man who had ever lived, and that despite his atheism. His daughter wrote that the Italian's 'sublime and highly religious conceptions of Democracy fired him with a passion unspeakable'.[24] As John Morley put it: 'Of all the democratic gospellers of that epoch between 1848 and 1870 . . . it was Mazzini who went nearest to the heart and true significance of democracy. He had a moral glow, and the light of large historic and literary comprehension, that stretched it into the minds of men with social imagination enough to look for new ideals, and courage enough to resist the sluggard's dread of new illusions.'[25]

One of the reasons why Mazzini made such an impact on Liberals in Britain was his presence in the country throughout the 1840s and for much of the 1850s. Britain was the refuge of liberal exiles from the Continent in the mid-nineteenth century in the same way that it was the home of Socialist refugees in the 1880s. In addition to Mazzini, the colony of European liberals in London in the 1850s included Alexander Herzin, a Russian revolutionary, Lajos Kossuth, the leader of the 1848 Hungarian rising against Austrian rule, Francis Pulszky, another leading Hungarian Liberal, Louis Blanc, the French Socialist, and a large number of Italians including Gabriele Rossetti, father of the Pre-Raphaelite poet. Victor Hugo spent the 1850s and 1860s in the Channel Islands, having fled from France because of his liberal views. These refugees mixed freely with Radical Liberals like Stansfeld and Holyoake who had strong Republican sympathies. They also had a romantic appeal, particularly to Liberal intellectuals, as men who had carried the torch of liberty and had suffered for it. As John Morley put it in his *Recollections*: 'Foreign ideas reached us of that generation in glorious mould. England was the refuge of two famous exiles between 1849 and 1871, a great Italian and a great Frenchman, voices of the most energetic and imaginative genius since Byron and Shelley. Mazzini and Victor Hugo imparted activity, elevation, and generous breadth of cosmopolitan outlook to the most ardent spirits of the new time in our own island. . . . If we seek a word for the significance of it all, it is not hard to find. Alike with those who adore and those who detest it, the dominating force in the living mind of Europe for a long generation after the overthrow of the French monarchy in 1830 has been that marked way of looking at things, feeling them, handling them, judging main actors in them, for which, with a hundred kaleidoscopic turns, the accepted name is Liberalism.'[26]

From these varied philosophical and cultural roots, Victorian Liberals took the simple idea of liberty. Gladstone found it in Greek civilization and Christian Europe; John Morley in the ideals of the French Enlightenment; Mill in his father's philosophic radicalism and Comte's Positivism; Acton in the Puritan Whig tradition of tolerance;

Green in his evangelical upbringing and the idealist philosophy of Hegel; Bryce and Stansfeld in the democratic fervour of Mazzini and the Italian freedom fighters. Liberty was the theme of the three greatest works of Liberal philosophy, Mill's essay *On Liberty*, Acton's projected *History of Liberty* and John Morley's essay *On Compromise*.

For the British Liberal, much more than for his Continental counterparts, liberty meant first and foremost freedom from externally imposed restrictions. It was a negative freedom rather than a positive freedom to pursue certain ends, as in France where it meant primarily liberty to participate in national affairs, or Germany where it came to mean nationalism. The Victorian Liberals' attachment to liberty was accompanied by a detestation of all externally imposed authority, whether represented by state, public opinion, religion, or custom. Indeed, dislike of authority might be a better description of the Liberal position than love of liberty. Mill saw it as the essential difference between Conservatives and Liberals. Toryism, he wrote 'is *tout bonnement* a reverence for government in the abstract. It means . . . it is good for man to be ruled; to submit both his body and mind to the guidance of a high intelligence and virtue. It is, therefore, the direct antithesis of Liberalism, which is for making every man his own guide and sovereign master, and letting him think for himself, and do exactly as he judges best for himself, giving other men leave to persuade him if they can by evidence, forbidding him to give way to authority; and still less allowing them to constrain him more than the existence and tolerable necessity of every man's person and property renders indispensably necessary.'[27]

The Liberals' dislike of submitting to authority and their insistence that men should follow their own lights followed equally from the Christian, free-thinking and Positivist traditions in which they stood. However different these philosophies, they all three led to the central conclusion that it was better to let the individual decide and judge his own fate than have anyone else impose it on him. On this the Roman Catholic Acton, the rationalist Morley and the Positivist Mill were agreed. Acton defined liberty for his projected history as 'the assurance that every man shall be protected in doing what he believes his duty against the influence of authority and majorities, custom and opinion'.[28] Mill declared the object of his essay *On Liberty* as being 'to assert one very simple principle, as entitled to govern absolutely the dealings of society with the individual in the way of compulsion and control . . . that principle is, that the sole end for which mankind are warranted, individually or collectively, in interfering with the liberty of action of any of their number, is self-protection'.[29] Morley ended *On Compromise*: 'Our main text has been that men should refuse to sacrifice their opinions and ways of living out of regard for the status quo, or the prejudices of others.'[30]

Three main threats to liberty were identified by Liberal philosophers, and dealt with most clearly by Mill in his essay *On Liberty*. The first was interference with free thought and opinion. In practice, such interference traditionally came from churches and religious establishments. As Mill put it, 'it has been on this [religious] battlefield, almost solely, that the rights of the individual against society have been asserted on broad grounds of principle, and the claim of society to exercise authority over dissentients, openly controverted. The great writers to whom the world owes what liberty it possesses, have mostly asserted freedom of conscience as an indefeasible right, and denied absolutely that a human being is accountable to others for his religious belief.'[31] The Liberal philosophers saw themselves as standing in the great Protestant and humanist tradition of tolerating all shades of opinion and conceding to every man the right to private judgement. They opposed all manifestations of religious dogmatism and authoritarianism and called for a free market in opinions. Significantly, Acton became the main Catholic protagonist against the doctrine of Papal infallibility promulgated by Pius IX in 1870. Liberals wanted to see a secular state where no one creed was given a favoured position over another and where men were allowed to make up their own minds on everything. It was hardly surprising that the greatest opposition to philosophical Liberalism should come from the ardent Catholic, Newman. 'By Liberalism', he wrote, 'I mean false liberty of thought, or the exercise of thought upon matters, in which, from the constitution of the human mind, thought cannot be brought to any successful issue and therefore is out of place. . . . Liberalism is the mistake of supposing that there is a right of private judgement, that is, that there is no existing authority on earth competent to interfere with the liberty of individuals in reasoning and judging for themselves.'[32]

The second threat to liberty perceived by Liberal intellectuals was posed by the activities of the state as the single most important source of temporal authority. Liberals were naturally hostile to government interference, because of their preference for voluntary action and their dislike of bureaucracy. In *Culture and Anarchy*, Matthew Arnold noted the tendency of 'our Liberal friends' to 'preach the right of an Englishman to be left to do as far as possible what he likes, and the duty of his government to indulge him and connive as much as possible and abstain from all harshness and repression'.[33] Mill gave three major objections to government interference in *On Liberty*: first, that generally speaking, those personally interested in any business were the best people to manage it, and therefore government should not, for example, interfere 'with the ordinary processes of industry'; secondly, that even where something could not necessarily be handled better by individuals than the government, it was none the less preferable it should be done by them 'as a means to their own mental education'; and thirdly and most importantly, that 'every function superadded to those already exercised by the government causes its influence over hopes and fears to be more widely diffused, and converts, more and more, the active and ambitious part of the public into hangers-on of the government.'[34]

Proposing counters to the authority of the state was a major theme of Victorian Liberal philosophers. Acton was particularly enthusiastic about having rival centres of power, local corporations, voluntary groups, commerical and professional interests and religious sects which stood between the nakedness of the individual and the omnipotence of the state. He saw the number and diversity of these groups as the great guarantor of British liberties. Mill and Morley concentrated on attacking what they called respectively authoritative intervention and repressive legislation which prohibited people from doing certain things and compelled them to do other things. Mill advocated instead 'another kind of intervention which is not authoritative: when a government, instead of issuing a command and enforcing it by penalties adopts the course so seldom resorted to by governments, and of which such important use might be made, that of giving advice, and promulgating information'.[35] Morley called for 'more effective, humane, and durable kinds of preventive legislation' and suggested that instead of passing a law outlawing drunkenness, the Government should 'apply itself to improving the dwellings of the more drunken class and provide amusements that might compete with the ale house'.[36]

The third threat to liberty identified by the Liberal philosophers came from the authority of public opinion and social custom. Mill, in particular, saw this as a much greater danger to freedom than the activities of the state. Only four pages of *On Liberty* were devoted to the theme of government interference, as against one hundred and ten on society's interference with individuals. The fact was that in Victorian Britain, as Mill said, 'the yoke of public opinion is perhaps heavier, and that of the law is lighter, than in most other countries of Europe'.[37] Government as yet impinged upon people's lives very little in comparison with the domination of notions of propriety and respectability derived from prevailing public opinion and from the propaganda of particular pressure groups. As instances of the latter Mill cited the temperance movement in Britain which could well achieve the same results as the prohibitionists in America, and the Sabbatarian movement which had successfully imposed the drab rigours of a Puritan Sunday on the entire population. Mill's cry was against the Victorians' slavery to the idea of 'proper' behaviour. 'In our own times,' he wrote, 'from the highest class of society down to the lowest, everyone lives as under the eye of a hostile and dreaded censorship. Not only in what concerns others, but in what concerns only themselves, the individual or the family do not ask themselves what do I prefer? or what would suit my character or disposition?, or what would allow the best and highest in me to have fair play, and enable it to grow and thrive? They ask themselves, what is suitable to my position? What is usually done by persons of my station and pecuniary circumstances? or (worse still) what is usually done by persons of a station and circumstances superior to mine?'[38]

Mill was appalled at the extent to which prevailing whims in society could assert authority over an individual's way of life. As an example, he speculated that if there was 'a considerable diffusion of socialist opinions, it may become infamous in the eyes of the majority to possess more property than some very small amount, or any income not earned by manual labour'.[39] *On Liberty* was written to make clear that the individual should not be accountable to anyone but himself for his actions, words or thoughts. 'The only freedom which deserves the name', he wrote, 'is that of pursuing our own good in our own way.'[40]

Critics of Victorian Liberalism saw the development of this idea of liberty as a recipe for anarchy and permissiveness. With the authority of religion, the state and social custom removed, liberty seemed to mean licence. Newman described Liberalism as the offspring of the spirit of lawlessness which had come in with the Reformation. Arnold wrote in *Culture and Anarchy*, 'our prevalent and most important notion is that it is a most happy and important thing for a man merely to be able to do as he likes. On what he is thus free to do as he likes, we do not lay so much stress.'[41] In fact, his criticism was unfair, because for none of the Liberal philosophers did liberty mean licence. They regarded it rather as a moral property, and a quality of life which would enable the full personality to develop. They thought of duties rather than rights and advocated liberty not so much for its own sake as for its effect in enabling man to fulfil his highest obligations.

Mill came nearest to making liberty an end in itself. To a certain extent his essay *On Liberty* was a hymn in praise of nonconformity and eccentricity for its own sake, and a plea for the individual's right to dissent from the ways and opinions of his fellows. Essentially, however, Mill advocated liberty because he thought it was indispensable to the pursuit of truth and to the achievement of progress. He defended freedom of thought and speech on the grounds that the opinion being suppressed might be true, that if it were erroneous it might contain a portion of the truth, and that even if it were completely wrong, its free statement prevented truth becoming a mere profession. Only from the interplay of completely free minds did Mill see truth emerging in the shape of new ideas and insights. It followed also that, since improvement came through innovation, liberty was essential to progress. 'The despotism of custom', he wrote, 'is everywhere the standing hindrance to human advancement, being in unceasing antagonism to that disposition to aim at something better than customary, which is called, according to circumstances, the spirit of liberty, or that of progress or improvement . . . the only unfailing and permanent source of improvement is liberty, since by it there are as many possible independent centres of improvement as there are individuals.'[42]

Like Mill, Acton saw liberty as a means to a higher end. He explicitly rejected the idea that it constituted mere licence. 'Liberty is not the power of doing what we like,' he wrote, 'but the right of doing what we ought.'[43] In contrast to Mill, his notion of liberty derived from Christianity and embodied a distinct moral duty. He regarded it as the freeing of man from external authority which enabled him to follow the dictates of his conscience, enlightened by the totality of knowledge. 'The more perfect and assured freedom' to which he felt mankind was progressing was 'the divine right of free men' to be guided by God and themselves alone. 'Liberalism', he wrote, 'is ultimately founded on the idea of conscience. A man must live by the light within and prefer God's voice to man's.'[44]

John Morley's advocacy of liberty also rested on the belief that free men would live by the light within, in his case by 'the lamp of loyalty to Reason'. Liberalism, he wrote, 'stands for the subjection to human judgement of all claims of external authority, whether in an organised Church, or in more loosely gathered societies of believers or in books held sacred'.[45] He believed that man had the reasoning power and the sense of responsibility to make judgements for himself. Like Mill and Acton he looked forward to liberty producing superior moral characters who thought for themselves and lived by their own lights.

The notion of liberty propounded by Mill, Acton and Morley was an intensely individualistic one. They saw men as entirely autonomous units, pitted against society and the state rather than as dependent members of a community sharing opinions with others. They had no conception of the General Will as developed by Burke, Rousseau and Hegel. They were interested in the individual will, and in encouraging it to develop as a counter to the prevailing opinion of the masses. Their great enemy was the dull uniformity of thought and action that came from unthinking adherence to the values and beliefs of society or the state. Mill's great fear of communism was that it would leave no asylum for individuality of character.

This stress on the importance of individual nonconformity and independence led the Liberal theorists to adopt a somewhat élitist position. Mill wrote: 'When the opinions of masses of merely average men are everywhere become or becoming the dominant power, the counterpoise and corrective to that tendency would be the more and more pronounced individuality of those who stand on the higher eminences of thought.'[46] It was to provide this corrective that Mill advocated the establishment of a new 'clerisy', an intellectual élite who would educate the masses in their political responsibilities and free them from their habitual enslavement to custom and arbitrariness. Morley had much the same idea. Progress, he wrote, would only come with 'the multiplication and elevation of types of virtuous character, and the practical acceptance of these types by the general sentiment'.[47] He wrote his own biographies of the heroes of the French Enlightenment and the European liberal awakening as instruments of moral training to encourage other men to follow their shining example. Paradoxically, the notion of liberty developed by the great Liberal philosophers was in a sense highly authoritarian, resting as it did on the premise that people must obey their consciences or reasons and follow the lead given by their intellectual and moral superiors.

The paradox is in part explained by the uncompromisingly intellectual approach adopted by Mill, Morley and Acton. Mill assumed naturally that all men were interested as he was in indulging in endless speculations and in searching for truth, Morley that they were motivated primarily by reason, and not by prejudice, habit, instinct or mere whim, Acton that they would obey their consciences before they gave way to their baser natures. All three shared an extremely optimistic and exalted view of human nature which was summed up in Morley's affirmation to Gladstone: 'I have faith in mankind, placed under free institutions.'[48] They believed that, once freed from external authority and taught how to use their liberty, men would respond to the call of duty, the lamp of reason or the voice of conscience. Critics of Victorian Liberalism found this belief in the goodness and rationality of man one of its most disturbing features. Newman deplored it for running completely counter to the Christian doctrine of Original Sin. Arnold and Carlyle saw it leading only to political anarchy and moral confusion and called for the authoritarian rule of the cultured minority or of commanding heroes as the only corrective to the irrationality and moral fickleness of the mob. In fact Mill and Morley were suggesting much the same thing. They differed from their critics in believing that the élite could rule by reason and consent rather than by force and in confidently predicting that the masses would themselves be raised up by the influence of those diffusing culture and light.

The most trenchant critic of the Liberal philosophers' theory of liberty was James Fitzjames Stephen, the distinguished lawyer who had been an ardent Liberal himself in his younger days. Stephen's political outlook was transformed by his experiences as legal member of the Viceroy's commission in India between 1868 and 1872. He saw that the natives had to be coerced and that autocratic government, unhampered by a legislature or a franchise, was far more efficient than democracy. 'India', he wrote to the Viceroy on his departure, 'is the best corrective in existence to the fundamental fallacies of Liberalism.'[49] On the boat home, Stephen wrote his book, *Liberty, Equality, Fraternity*, in which he bitterly attacked Mill's doctrine of liberty. His argument was essentially a political version of Newman's. Mill's great defect, Stephen suggested, was that 'he has formed too favourable an estimate of human nature.' The majority of people would always be 'stupid, selfish, frivolous, idle, absolutely commonplace and wrapped up in the smallest routine'. The 'freest of free discussion' would not help them at all.[50] They needed a consensus of shared opinions on standards and values which rested on some external authority, rather than a mass of moral positions individually thought out. Compulsion and restraint, based on force if necessary, were more efficient and more constructive than freedom.

Perceptively, Stephen saw that the faith in liberty of Mill, Acton and

Morley was the product of an exceptional period in British history
when reason did actually seem to prevail over force and political
problems could be solved by counting heads rather than breaking
them. During the 1860s and 1870s the Liberals' conviction that private
discipline would render large areas of public discipline unnecessary
gained a wide measure of acceptance. What they saw around them
tended to confirm the mid-Victorians in their faith in human nature
and their love of liberty.

Love of liberty was not just a detached intellectual attitude. For
many Liberals it was a vital principle which demanded and inspired
action, and which could be put into practice both at home and abroad.
Several actively assisted struggles for liberty on the Continent. There
was a strong tradition of British involvement in liberal movements
abroad which went back to Byron's enlistment in the Carbonari in
1821 and his election to the Greek Revolutionary Committee in 1823.
In 1830 Tennyson had gone to Spain with two fellow Cambridge
students to assist in an unsuccessful liberal rising from which they were
lucky to escape alive. Several Liberals actively assisted the Italians in
the struggle to reunify their country. Joseph Cowen, a Newcastle
manufacturer and journalist, concealed Mazzini's pamphlets in bricks
and sent them to Italy where they were proscribed. Bryce volunteered
unsuccessfully to join Garibaldi's thousand redshirts in 1860. Holyoake
appealed for money to buy 1,000 rifles for the first Italian province to
rise and was secretary of a committee which recruited a volunteer
British legion of 850 men to serve under Garibaldi.

The Italian Risorgimento was only one of several nineteenth-century
movements for liberation which Liberals supported. Their attachment
to the ideal of liberty led them to champion the continuing fight for
independence by Greece and the risings of the Bulgarians and the
Armenians against Turkish rule. It was, in fact, one of the inspirations
of Gladstonian foreign policy which stressed the right to self-determination of the small states and peoples of Europe. 'The foreign policy of
England', Gladstone told the electors of Midlothian, 'should always be
inspired by the love of freedom.'[51]

Many Liberals carried their love of liberty into active support for
the European refugees who congregated in London in the middle years
of the nineteenth century. As well as forming friendships with the
Continental exiles, they championed their right to enjoy asylum in
Britain when it was challenged. In 1857, following an attempt on the
life of Napoleon III by an Italian patriot named Orsini who had used a

bomb made in England, Palmerston introduced a Conspiracy to Murder Bill which would have made it a felony to plot in Britain the death of someone abroad, and given the government power to eject political refugees. It was strongly opposed by Bright in Parliament and by Stansfeld and Holyoake outside and was defeated when Disraeli saw it as a way of bringing down Palmerston's administration. In 1866 Liberals led by Mill defeated an Extradition Bill which would have authorized the surrender of political refugees charged with attempts at insurrection, to be dealt with in the criminal courts of the countries against which they were accused of acting. Mill considered that the Bill would have made 'the British Government an accomplice in the vengeance of foreign despotisms'. As a result of Liberal pressure, a new measure was introduced, and passed, which allowed any refugee whose extradition was demanded to be heard before a British court. Mill wrote triumphantly, 'the cause of European freedom has thus been saved.'[52] In 1871 Gladstone's Government refused a French request to extradite refugees from the Paris Commune.

Inspired partly by their contact with political refugees from the Continent, a few Liberals carried their support for republican principles into domestic politics. Republicanism was strong among secularists in the 1860s and it briefly became more widespread in the Liberal movement in the early 1870s, largely as a result of frustration over the Queen's protracted and almost total withdrawal from public life following the death of Prince Albert. More than fifty Republican Clubs were established, including one at Cambridge set up by Henry Fawcett and another at Birmingham founded by Charles Cattell and patronized by Chamberlain. In 1870 Goldwin Smith wrote to George Howell suggesting the formation of an English Republican Party and Chamberlain declared that 'I do not feel any great horror at the idea of the possible establishment of a Republic in this country. I am quite certain that sooner or later it will come.'[53] An application in 1871 for substantial allowances for two young members of the Royal Family provoked considerable opposition in Parliament and strongly republican speeches from Henry Fawcett, Peter Taylor and Sir Charles Dilke, a radical barrister. By the following year, however, republican fervour had died down and only two M.P.s, Dilke and Auberon Herbert, a libertarian political philosopher, voted in favour of a motion to enquire into the Civil List. Although Dilke and a few others with radical and secularist sympathies continued to adhere to Republicanism, Liberals as a whole showed no further interest. It had appealed to them, if at all, more as a matter of cheap government than as a matter of fundamental principle.

Campaigns for the extension of civil liberties attracted the support of several Victorian Liberals, especially those with secularist and libertarian sympathies. Mill was particularly active in this field, campaigning for birth control, women's rights, abolition of the blasphemy laws and the repeal of legislation restricting activities on Sundays, as well as making the general case for individual freedom in his writings. In an important rebuttal of Carlyle's notorious *Discourse on the Nigger Question* (1849) Mill powerfully argued the case for racial equality. John Morley commented that 'in the sovereign field of tolerance, his victory has been complete. Only those who can recall the social odium that surrounded heretical opinions before Mill began to achieve popularity are able rightly to appreciate the battle in which he was in so many ways the protagonist.'[54]

Although the extension of personal liberty was never a party cause as such, much was achieved in that area by successive Liberal governments. Gladstone's first Ministry passed an impressive list of civil rights measures including the abolition of church rates, the ending of religious tests for admission to fellowships at Oxford and Cambridge Universities, the repeal of laws demanding from newspapers securities against blasphemy and sedition, the liberalization of Sabbatarian legislation, the granting of the municipal franchise to women and the 1869 Evidence Amendment Act which allowed atheists to make an affirmation instead of taking an oath in courts of law. During his second period in government he saw on to the Statute Book the Married Women's Property Act and forwarded those two *causes célèbres* of Victorian progressives, the right to make an affirmation instead of an oath in the House of Commons and the right to marry a deceased wife's sister.

Gladstone himself was instrumental in removing an important barrier to the freedom of the press. His abolition of stamp duties on newspapers in 1855 had done much to clear the way for a free and critical press. A serious obstacle to the expression of radical opinion still existed, however, in the system of securities which were required to be paid by printers and publishers of newspapers costing less than 6d as a surety against blasphemy and sedition. Disraeli's first Government demanded substantial securities from Bradlaugh's *National Reformer* and provoked an outcry from secularists. In 1869, after some initial hesitation, Gladstone decided to end this last remaining financial restriction on the press.

The cause of free speech generally was one dear to many Liberals and they actively championed it against efforts at censorship and suppression. Bradlaugh's election manifesto in 1880 called for the abolition of all penalties on opinion and Liberal free-thinkers campaigned for the repeal of the blasphemy laws. The attempted suppression of unorthodox political and religious opinions generally provoked a Liberal outcry. When the Clerkenwell public house which was the regular meeting place of the notorious republican and atheistic Patriotic Club had its licence taken away, Mill sent a cheque from Avignon, 'in aid of the subscription to provide a place for political lectures and discussions, independent of coerced tavern-keepers and licensing magistrates'.[55] Samuel Morley also made a generous contribution, as did the local Liberal M.P., Alderman Lusk.

Individual Liberals also gave strong support to what was perhaps the single most important civil rights cause in the Victorian period, the movement for the emancipation of women. W. T. Stead declared 'The Independence of Woman' to be the second article of his 'Gospel according to the *Pall Mall Gazette*'. Mill was an ardent advocate of female suffrage and put it in his manifesto to the electors of Westminster in 1865. His essay, *The Subjection of Women*, published in 1869, became the Bible of the feminist movement not just in Britain but throughout Europe. In it, he linked female emancipation to current Liberal social and political ideas, pointing out that women alone among all sections of the population were not allowed to rise above the station to which they were born. He called for the removal of all legal and social restraints on them, 'their recognition as the equal of men in all that belongs to citizenship, the opening of all honourable employments and of the training and education which qualifies for those employments, and the removal of the excessive authority which the law gives to husbands over their wives'.[56]

Although like many Liberals, Gladstone had no sympathy with the demand for female suffrage, he promoted two major pieces of legislation which contributed considerably to improving the lot of women. The Married Women's Property Act of 1882, which had been drafted by Richard Pankhurst, husband of Emmeline, the suffragette leader, established for the first time the right of women to keep their own property after marriage. The repeal of the Contagious Diseases Acts four years later in response to the agitation led by Josephine Butler ended a system of blatant double standards whereby innocent women and girls had been subjected to degrading medical examinations in the interest of providing 'clean' prostitutes for the benefit of soldiers and sailors. James Stansfeld had given up a promising political career in 1874 to devote himself to ending the system of licensed prostitution which the Acts introduced in garrison towns. At first Gladstone held that prostitution could only be curbed by individual voluntary missionary work but he later came to favour repeal of the Acts in the face of mounting Liberal pressure.

The campaigns led by Victorian secularists to promote birth control and easier divorce were too advanced and tinged with irreligion to find much support from all but the most free-thinking Liberals. Holyoake sold contraceptives in his shop in London and, as a youth of seventeen, Mill was sentenced to a fortnight's imprisonment for distributing literature on the subject to members of the working classes. When *The Times* reported this episode shortly after Mill's death Gladstone promptly cancelled his subscription to a national memorial. Gladstone had also vehemently opposed the major effort at liberalizing divorce law in the nineteenth century, the Matrimonial Causes Act of 1857 which abolished the matrimonial jurisdiction of the ecclesiastical courts and established the Divorce Court, thus for the first time making it possible in England to obtain divorce by an action in a court of law rather than through a costly private Act of Parliament. Liberals were not active in moves to bring divorce within reach of the working classes, or to remedy the obvious injustice in the Act whereby husbands could divorce wives on grounds of adultery but wives could only divorce husbands on grounds of proved rape, sodomy or bestiality.

One specific movement to liberalize the marriage laws was, however, enthusiastically supported by many Liberals, including Gladstone. This was the campaign to allow a man to marry his deceased wife's sister which was led by the Marriage Law Reform Association after such a union had been included in the Church's list of prohibited marriages in 1835. The subject came up so frequently in Parliament that Gilbert's Faery Queen in *Iolanthe* could be sure of a cheer in promising that Strephon, when elected to the Commons, 'shall prick that annual blister, marriage to deceased wife's sister'. The Liberals' enthusiasm for it was made much of by Matthew Arnold who insisted that, having passed legislation on the subject, 'the Liberal party must supplement that Bill by two others: one enabling people to marry their brothers' and sisters' children, the other enabling a man to marry his brother's wife.'[57] It was not until 1907, however, that the reform was achieved.

Birth control, easier divorce, and even marriage to deceased wife's sister were all liberal reforms which were opposed by prevailing Christian morality and the dictates of the Church. Free-thinking Liberals challenged the right of the Established Church, or of any other group of Christians, to impose their moral standards on the country as a whole through legislation or moral pressure. Mill, Holyoake and George Howell were active supporters of the Sunday League, which was set up in 1855 to oppose Sabbatarianism and to press for the opening of public houses, museums and other places of entertainment and instruction on what was for many their only day of rest. Although Sunday opening of public houses did not come until 1896, the reformers won some success with the passing of the Sunday Observance Prosecution Act in 1871 which limited prosecutions for breaches of Sabbath observance to those authorized by a chief constable, two justices of the peace, or a stipendiary magistrate, and so put an end to the private prosecutions that had often been brought by Sabbatarian zealots.

The Liberal free-thinkers' determination to diminish the influence of religion and the Church on society led them to campaign with other Liberals for the abolition of compulsory church rates, the disestablishment of the Church of England and the ending of denominational schools. In 1850, on the suggestion of Mill, W. J. Fox introduced a Bill proposing a wholly secular system of education. Opposition to 'priestly control' over education continued to be a strong feature of free-thinking Liberalism throughout the 1860s and 1870s. John Morley noted that 'Liberalism in 1868' meant above all else hostility to the extension of the denominational system and a demand 'for the assumption by the nation of duties which had hitherto been left to the clergy'. 'If liberalism means anything at all beyond a budget of sounding phrases', he continued, it involved the creation of a wholly secular state.[58]

Perhaps the most celebrated aspect of this campaign to create a secular state was the struggle to de-Christianize Parliament itself. It was a battle that lasted more than forty years. A motion by Lord John Russell to delete the words 'on the true faith of a Christian' from the oath taken by all new M.P.s before they could take their seats passed the Commons in 1847, where it was supported by the young Gladstone to the consternation of his High Anglican and Tory friends, but was blocked by the Lords. In 1858 the Oaths Act allowed each House of Parliament to determine the form of oath to be administered to a Jew

D

and in 1866 the Parliamentary Oaths Act introduced a simplified form of oath similar to that proposed by Russell.

The campaign to have an affirmation accepted for admission as an M.P., and therefore by implication to show that Parliament was not a Christian assembly, began with Charles Bradlaugh's victory at the poll for Northampton in the General Election of 1880. Bradlaugh claimed that the Liberals' 1869 Evidence Amendment Act gave him a right to affirm rather than take an oath to be allowed to sit in the Commons. A Select Committee ruled otherwise and when he subsequently took the oath, having publicly declared he did not believe in it, his right to sit as an M.P. was successfully challenged by the Tories. Gladstone supported Bradlaugh's claim, which he saw as a matter of fundamental freedom of opinion, and introduced an Affirmation Bill in 1882. It was supported by all but nine Liberal M.P.s but opposed by the Tories and Irish Nationalists and was eventually lost by three votes. In 1885 the Court of Appeal ruled that Bradlaugh could validly take the oath and the following year he was finally allowed to take his seat in Parliament, having been re-elected three times by the voters of Northampton since first being debarred. In 1888 he himself successfully piloted an Affirmation Act through Parliament. As he lay on his deathbed three years later, the Commons carried a motion expunging from the Records of the House the Resolution of 1880 which had deprived him of his seat.

In their fight against conventional morality on such issues as birth control and divorce, the free-thinkers and secularists stood isolated and alone within the Liberal movement. In their battle against the Church and their struggle to create a secular state, however, they fought side by side with another element within Liberalism, itself deeply religious, but with an equally strong interest in the disestablishment of the Church, the abolition of church rates and university tests and the secularization of schools. On the Continent, where there was often no effective religious alternative to Catholicism, Liberalism tended to be wholly atheistic. In Britain, however, the official Christianity of the Established Church was balanced by a powerful and lively body of Nonconformists. While one element in Victorian Liberalism was undeniably secularist and free-thinking, another much larger element was deeply religious.

Chapter 4

The Nonconformist Conscience

'Nonconformity', Gladstone observed in 1877, 'supplies the backbone of English Liberalism.'[1] His view was shared by both the champions and the critics of Victorian Dissent. The influential inter-denominational Nonconformist paper, the *British Weekly*, proudly proclaimed: 'We do not know what the Liberal Party is, if it is not a Nonconformist party.'[2] James Fitzjames Stephen complained in 1879 that Liberalism had come to mean 'the small dissenter way of looking at all national and international affairs'.[3] Matthew Arnold objected to the predominance of 'the Puritan and Nonconformist cause which, in this country, Liberals are always tempted to think themselves safe in supporting'.[4] Nonconformists were as important an element in the Victorian Liberal movement as manufacturers or free-thinkers. There were many like Henry Lunn, the Methodist travel agent, who 'derived their Liberalism not from Manchester but from Nazareth'.[5]

Nonconformity made a deep mark on Victorian Liberalism. It pushed issues like disestablishment and temperance reform to the front of the Liberal party programme. It brought disciplined supporters and an atmosphere of moral crusading that were vital to the Liberals' electoral success. The relationship between Nonconformists and Liberals was not always an easy one. Just as Stephen and Arnold felt that Liberalism had been made puritanical and provincial, so there were Nonconformists who felt that their religion had been compromised and subordinated to the demands of politicians. Ultimately, however, Nonconformists and Liberals were tied to each other by mutual need and by a certain mutual respect.

Nonconformist religion played as powerful a part in making men active Liberals as support for free trade or love of freedom. Edward Miall, Edward Baines, Samuel Morley and W. T. Stead derived their attachment to Liberal politics from their Congregationalism. Miall rejoiced in being the first Nonconformist minister to sit in the House of Commons since the days of Praise God Barebones. Joseph Chamberlain's active espousal of Liberalism owed much to his

Unitarianism. John Bright first came into political prominence when he led the Dissenters of Rochdale against church rates in 1840. Twenty-eight years later he became the first English Nonconformist ever to sit in the Cabinet.

Many Nonconformist ministers made no secret of their support for the Liberal cause. Lloyd George remembered from his childhood an old Welsh Baptist minister praying for deliverance from Disraeli, 'Kill him, O Lord, kill him. We cannot kill him without being hanged ourselves, but Thou canst kill him.'[6] Hugh Price Hughes's daughter recalled that the announcement of every election result was liable to move him to deep emotion: 'the return of a Liberal meant fresh strains of exultation . . . the return of a Conservative meant silence and gloom, and sometimes tears.'[7]

Nonconformist ministers often exerted a considerable influence over the political behaviour of their congregations. The Liberalism of Mr. Bottles in *Friendship's Garland*, Matthew Arnold suggested, was the result of his having left his mind 'wholly to itself, his daily newspaper and the Particular Baptist minister under whom he sat'.[8] In *Felix Holt*, the Revd. Rufus Lyon, minister of the Independent Chapel in Treby Magna, possessed no vote, but 'had considerable influence over Liberal electors', and was a most important ally to be won by Harold Transome as he prepared to stand as Liberal candidate in North Loamshire.[9] A group of Nonconformist ministers in Birmingham directly contributed to the Liberal awakening of the 1860s by preaching active political involvement to their congregations. George Dawson, the minister at Mount Zion Baptist Chapel and subsequently at the independent Church of the Saviour; Charles Vince, Dawson's successor at Mount Zion; R. W. Dale, Pastor at Carr's Lane Congregational Chapel; and later H. W. Crosskey, minister at the Unitarian Church of the Messiah, inspired the commitment to municipal reform which characterized the city's Liberalism and found its fullest expression in the career of Chamberlain. At its root was their call from the pulpit for Christian involvement in public life and their solemn warning, delivered most persuasively by Dale in numerous sermons and pamphlets throughout the 1860s, that 'those who decline to use their political power are guilty of treachery both to God and to man.'[10]

Why, though, should Dale have called his flock only to political activity on the Liberal side, as he did, and Lloyd George's Welsh preacher have cursed Disraeli and not the High Anglican Gladstone? It was because, like the manufacturers, the professional classes and the respectable artisans in whose ranks they were generally to be found, Nonconformists felt themselves to be disqualified and underprivileged. The national census of religion taken in 1851 showed that Nonconformity had almost as many active adherents as the Established Church of England, yet in few other respects were the denominations equal. Nonconformists were denied the use of their own burial service if their chapels lacked a graveyard, and they had to make do with the local churchyard. They were barred from taking a degree or holding a fellowship at Oxford or Cambridge. They were obliged to pay church rates where these were levied for the upkeep of the local Anglican Church, already heavily supported by endowments and tithe income, and to see their taxes being used to support Anglican schools when their own educational efforts rested almost entirely on voluntary funding.

It was the favoured position accorded to Anglicans as members of the Established Church of the country to which Nonconformists objected. They were constantly reminded of the inferiority of their own position by a succession of incidents, comparatively trivial in themselves but which, taken together, indicated their official status as second-class citizens. In 1868, Samuel Morley was dismayed to learn that the London and North Western Railway Company were giving half-price tickets to passengers attending the Church Congress in Manchester but were offering no similar concession to those going to the Congregational Assembly in Liverpool. In 1874 Chamberlain was shocked when a tea party organized for miners' families following a colliery explosion in Derbyshire was cancelled because the local vicar objected to Dissenters being invited. In the face of such manifest unfairness, Nonconformists were moved to political action.

Nonconformist antipathy to the position of the Church of England was not motivated simply by the 'jealousy of the Establishment' that Matthew Arnold noted in *Culture and Anarchy*.[11] It derived also from more positive moral and religious considerations. The object of the *Nonconformist* newspaper started by Miall was to show that 'a National Establishment of religion is essentially vicious in its constitution, philosophically, politically, and religiously.'[12] 'I object to the alliance of Church and State most of all,' Dale wrote in his *Churchmen and Dissenters* (1862), 'not because of the unjust superiority it gives to one Christian denomination . . . but because by it the religious character of the Church is corrupted, her spiritual freedom almost destroyed, the efficiency of her true work seriously diminished.'[13] Nonconformists regarded the Established Church as an essentially irreligious institution,

supported by endowments and taxes rather than the voluntary gifts of
believers, its bishops appointed by government ministers who might be
atheists, its Prayer Book dependent on the deliberations of Parliament
'where men of every religion and none sit side by side'.[14]

The existence of an Established Church was seen by Nonconformists
as a positive hindrance to the spread of Christianity in Britain. In his
first speech against church rates in Rochdale in 1840, John Bright
catalogued the failures of the Church of England to Christianize the
people and went on, 'I would that that venerable fabric were the
representative of a really reformed church—of a church separate from
her foul connexion with the state—of a church depending upon her own
resources, upon the zeal of her people, on the truthfulness of her
principles. Then would the Church really be free from her old vices.
Then would she unite heart and hand with her sister churches in this
kingdom, in the great and glorious work of evangelising the people of
this great Empire.'[15]

Nonconformists had further political and religious objections to the
Established Church which they shared with other Liberal groups. Like
the free-thinkers, many of them were strongly anti-clerical and disliked the way that the Church of England parson was able by virtue of
his favoured position to influence so many areas of life. They also
shared the Radicals' view of the Anglican Church as a bastion of aristocratic and landed influence. So long as the tithe system and the rights
of private presentation to livings remained, the Church was as much a
piece of property as a religious institution. 'Our present object', an
early number of the *Nonconformist* declared, 'is simply to exhibit the
Church as a piece of political machinery, plied by the aristocracy for
their selfish purposes.'[16]

The demand for parity of treatment with Anglicans and for the
abolition of the Established Church lay at the root of Nonconformist
involvement in politics in the mid-nineteenth century. The first signs
of that involvement were the setting up in the 1840s of the Anti-State
Church Association (after 1853 the Society for the Liberation of
Religion from State Patronage and Control) and the Dissenters'
Parliamentary Committee to secure the election of Nonconformist
M.P.s. It was natural and inevitable that Nonconformists should choose
the Liberal rather than the Conservative side in deciding the direction
of their political involvement. Toryism was historically tied to Angli-
canism and the maintenance of the Established Church, Whiggism to
Dissent. Already the Whigs had begun the process of Nonconformist

emancipation by fighting for the repeal of the Test and Corporation Acts, commuting tithes and legalizing Nonconformist marriages in the 1830s. Lord Aberdeen's Government had continued it in 1854 by abolishing religious tests before matriculation and before a degree could be taken at Oxford and Cambridge. The best chance of completing their emancipation lay in Nonconformists joining those other disqualified groups in the Liberal movement that had taken over from Whiggism as the progressive force in British politics.

Historical consciousness was another factor in turning Nonconformists to Liberalism. In the *Memoir* of his youth, John Bright wrote: 'I could not be otherwise than a Liberal. I was, as I now am, a member of the Society of Friends. I knew something of their history and of the persecutions they had endured, and of their principles of equality and justice. I knew that I came from the stock of martyrs, that one of my ancestors had been in prison for several years because he preferred to worship in the humble meeting-house of his own sect rather than in the church of the law-favoured sect.'[17] Memories of persecution at the hands of Anglicans and Tories bound Nonconformists to the Liberal cause. Their heroes were Cromwell, Vane and Milton, a distinctively English group in a very different mould from the philosophers of the Continental Enlightenment worshipped by Liberal free-thinkers.

Under the influence of Nonconformity, the leaders of the Puritan Revolution came to play a major role in the mythology of Victorian Liberalism. Bright told audiences of working men that Milton was the greatest name in English political history. W. T. Stead dreamed of writing a great work on Cromwell until he realized that his motive was rather to make a name for himself than to do justice to his hero. He abandoned the project, but wrote an essay on Cromwell which led to him being invited to submit articles for the *Pall Mall Gazette*, the paper which he later made into the leading example of crusading Liberal journalism. Cardinal Manning once commented, 'When I read the *Pall Mall* it seems to me as if Cromwell had come to life.'[18] The adulation of the Puritan fathers was not confined to Nonconformist Liberals. T. H. Green, who was himself a distant descendant of Cromwell, described the Protectorate as 'the great spring of political life in England' and said that the spirit of Independency which inspired Sir Harry Vane had 'more than any other ennobled the plebeian elements of English life'.[19] Even John Morley paid tribute to the Puritan leaders of the seventeenth century, although he deplored their fanaticism and their theology: 'They sought truth and ensued it, not thinking of the practicable nor cautiously counting majorities and minorities.'[20]

Nonconformists found in Liberalism the Puritan virtues which they admired. It stood for freedom of thought and the sovereignty of the individual conscience against the claims of some externally imposed authority. It championed self-help, thrift and voluntary charity and condemned indiscriminate state aid for the indolent. It stressed moral progress, peace and justice. Edward Miall's son Arthur saw Gladstone's second administration as 'the strongest reforming Government this country has seen since the Commonwealth'.[21] Liberal politicians generally behaved in a purer and less corrupt way than Conservatives. Many Nonconformists would have echoed William Rathbone's impression of the first election that he took part in: 'there was a large amount of treating going on, a great number of small bribes in the form of payments of 5/- as a day's wage to everyone who chose to claim it for voting Conservative; the Liberal side were absolutely pure, not a penny or a glass of beer being given.'[22]

It is not too much to say that many Nonconformists supported the Liberal party in the second half of the nineteenth century because they believed it to be the party of Christ. The justification for their involvement in party politics, according to one Nonconformist minister, was that 'the Liberal policy makes for the establishment of the Kingdom of God.'[23] 'Britain has had some inspiring visions of the Kingdom of justice one day to be established among men,' the *Nonconformist* noted in 1880. 'The Liberal Party has striven to follow the fiery pillar of conscience into this promised land. It has striven to be the party of moral principle as against that of selfish and corrupt interests, the party of peace as against that of violence, the party of popular improvement and reform as against that of resistance to progress, the party of justice as against that of despotic force or social disorder. The backbone of this party has been the religious Protestantism and Puritanism of England for a very good reason, because a party whose object it is to rule men's action by a moral principle in legislation and government derives its force from conscience.'[24]

Nonconformist commitment to Liberalism was founded on a sense of deep emotional and spiritual affinity as well as on pragmatic political calculation. To a large extent it rested also on a remarkable personal devotion to Gladstone. It is at first sight difficult to see how the Liberal leader with his High Anglican faith and his cosmopolitan outlook could possibly appeal to the narrow and provincial minds of English

Nonconformity as portrayed by Matthew Arnold. They were attracted
by those deeper features of Gladstone's character which derived from his
Lancashire background and evangelical upbringing, and impressed by
the intensity of his religious belief and the strength of his moral feelings.
When Hugh Price Hughes was asked by his children who Mr.
Gladstone was, he replied simply, 'a man who says his prayers every
morning'.[25] Samuel Morley attributed his unswerving loyalty to the
Liberal leader to the fact that 'he always looked at the moral side of
things.'[26]

It was Gladstone's insistence that Christian principles should always
govern political behaviour and his enthusiasm for leading national
crusades on great moral issues that most appealed to Nonconformists.
Shortly after the start of the famous Bulgarian atrocities campaign of
1876 a Baptist minister promised that Gladstone would 'find his
warmest friends and best disciplined troops, in the descendants of
Cromwell's Ironsides, the Nonconformists of England'.[27] He was not
to be disappointed. Nonconformists proved to be the staunchest supporters of Gladstone's tactic of fighting elections on appeals to the
conscience of the nation.

If Gladstone was never to be disappointed by the Nonconformists,
then they were to become very disillusioned with him. Increasingly, as
his ministries passed without their most important demands being met,
Nonconformist voices were heard questioning the adulation bestowed
on the Liberal leader. A correspondent felt compelled to remind the
more fervent Gladstone worshippers among the readers of the
Nonconformist in 1885 that 'not yet has it been made an article in our
unwritten creed that a man must have unbounded faith in Mr.
Gladstone which, unless he possesses, he shall without doubt perish
everlastingly.'[28] Gladstone had started off well in remedying Nonconformist grievances. The abolition of church rates was one of the
first measures of his first government in 1868. Religious tests for entry
to fellowships to Oxford and Cambridge were abolished in 1871. A
Burials Bill allowing burial in churchyards with any form of Christian
service or with no religious service at all was introduced in 1872
although it did not become law until 1880. Over their more fundamental demands on education and disestablishment, however, Nonconformists were to find the Liberals, and Gladstone in particular, less
than enthusiastic.

Nonconformists radically changed their views on education during
the Victorian period. At first, they tended to champion the continued

existence of voluntary schools, most of which were run by the Anglican National Society and the Nonconformist-dominated British and Foreign Schools Society, and opposed government support for education. They were not a little influenced by the fact that where the state did support schools, it was nearly always those run by the Established Church. In 1850, for example, eighty per cent of government grants for education had gone to National Society Schools. Opposition to state provision of education was one of the strongest rallying cries of Nonconformists in the 1840s and 1850s. The Anti-State Church Association was born out of successful Nonconformist opposition to the educational clauses of the 1843 Factory Bill which had proposed setting up factory schools under the charge of Anglican clergymen and schoolmasters. Miall and Baines campaigned vigorously against subsequent Whig proposals for a system of schools funded out of the rates. Meanwhile, between 1841 and 1851, Nonconformists built 364 schools and a teacher-training college at Homerton without any assistance from the state.

During the 1860s, however, most Nonconformists came to see that a voluntary system could never provide an adequate education for all children in Britain. The Newcastle Commission of 1861 revealed that many areas were without any schools, and surveys in Manchester and Birmingham showed that many parents could not afford school fees. By the late 1860s nearly all Nonconformists, including Miall, had abandoned voluntaryism in favour of a national system of secular, undenominational free schools funded out of the rates, although Baines preferred a system of state-supported denominational schools. In 1869 Chamberlain, with the active support of Dale and Crosskey, set up the National Education League as a largely Nonconformist pressure group to campaign for free, undenominational state education. Its hopes were pinned on W. E. Forster, an ex-Quaker whom Gladstone had made Vice-President of the Council with responsibility for education.

In fact, Forster's Education Act of 1870 was a bitter blow to Nonconformist hopes. It was too voluntaryist for the new mood of Dissent in its proposal for undenominational Board Schools only where existing denominational schools, four-fifths of which were Anglican, were inadequate. A clause which empowered school boards to pay from the rates the fees of indigent children attending denominational schools was regarded as a sell-out to the Church. More than two-thirds of the Nonconformist ministers in England and Wales signed a petition against the Act. Dale announced that it 'relieves Nonconformists from their old allegiance to the Liberal Party' and Nonconformist defections were widely blamed for the Liberals' defeat at the polls in 1874.[29]

The Nonconformists' call for disestablishment found a more ready response within the Liberal party. Gladstone made the disestablishment of the Church of Ireland the focal point of the General Election campaign in 1868, to the despair of Matthew Arnold who saw it as a departure from the noble Liberal ideal in favour of the narrow prejudices of Dissent. As conceived by Gladstone, disestablishment in Ireland was a matter of civil justice, since less than one-seventh of the population were Anglicans. Disestablishment was sought not just by Nonconformists, but also by Roman Catholics, who formed the majority of the population, and by radical nationalists for whom the Established Church symbolized the hated English presence in the country. The case for disestablishment in Ireland was overwhelming and the legislation which brought it about in 1869 met with unanimous Liberal support in Parliament.

Disestablishment in Scotland and Wales was keenly canvassed by many Liberals from 1868 onwards. The case for disestablishment in Wales was almost as strong as it had been in Ireland. Nonconformists outnumbered Anglicans by seven to one in the Principality. There was less obvious reason for disestablishment in Scotland where the established church was based on the voluntary principle, being supported out of gifts from congregations rather than endowments, and commanded the allegiance of the majority of the population. In 1877 Gladstone admitted the justice of disestablishment in both Scotland and Wales and promised that disestablishment would be the 'great work' for the Liberal party once the Eastern Question was resolved.[30] He refused, however, to give it priority over Irish Home Rule and so effectively blocked it from 1885 until 1893 when his Government finally drew up Church Suspensory Bills for Scotland and Wales. The Scottish Bill was dropped, but in 1895 H. H. Asquith, the Home Secretary in Rosebery's administration, introduced a Bill for disestablishing the Church of Wales. The measure was not, however, finally passed until 1914 and it did not become effective until 1920.

Disestablishment of the Church of England was first proposed in Parliament in 1870 by Edward Miall. He used the standard Nonconformist arguments that the Church of England would be much stronger if it was supported by the voluntary contributions of its members rather than by endowments, and that its disestablishment would enable cooperation between Anglicans and Nonconformists in vital evangelistic and philanthropic work. Miall saw disestablishment in England as the logical sequel to the abolition of church rates and to disestablishment in Ireland. 'Religious equality', he told his fellow Liberal M.P.s in moving for disestablishment in 1873, 'is in strict keeping with the entire framework of Liberal policy which they have helped by past legislation to construct.'[31] Still smarting from the blows inflicted by the 1870 Education Act, Dale wrote in the *Liberator* in 1871 that if the Liberals failed soon to introduce a measure proposing the disestablishment of the Church of England, it was time for the Nonconformists to split with them. The Liberation Society resolved at its conference following the 1874 Election that 'it should become impossible to reconstruct the now shattered Liberal Party except on a basis which would make religious equality a necessary condition of its existence.'[32]

By no means all Nonconformists were happy about this uncompromising line on disestablishment. Jeremiah Colman was worried that Miall's motions would split the Liberal party. 'I am a Nonconformist,' he wrote, 'but I am a Liberal too, and I fear that the latter will lose more than the former will gain.'[33] Samuel Morley had resigned from the Executive Committee of the Liberation Society as early as 1868 because he disapproved of the way in which it was trying to force disestablishment in England prematurely. Edward Baines was worried that the Society's resolution in 1874 would separate Nonconformists 'from the great Liberal Statesmen and the Liberal Churchmen by whose aid every reform of modern times, from the repeal of the Corporation and Test Act down to the opening of the Universities has been carried'.[34] Even Miall began to have doubts about the wisdom of pursuing disestablishment too vigorously.

During the mid-1870s the campaign for disestablishment of the Church of England within the Liberal movement dramatically changed its nature. From being an exclusively Nonconformist concern it became rather more a cry of free-thinkers and radicals. Many Nonconformists questioned the need to pursue disestablishment now that so many of their grievances had been remedied. The new protagonists of disestablishment were John Morley, who conceived it as the goal of a great secular crusade with meetings 'with only one clergyman and not a word to be said about the freedom which is in Christ Jesus', and Joseph Chamberlain, who was more interested in its economic and political than its religious aspects.[35] Morley sought disestablishment for the same reason that he supported a national scheme of secular education, because it would lessen the clergy's control over the country.

Chamberlain proposed in the *Fortnightly Review* of October 1874 that the Liberals should make disestablishment their main policy for wholly secular reasons. It would facilitate philanthropic activity, education and social improvement generally, and be of direct material benefit to the nation by releasing the £90 million endowments of the Church of England and ending its control of property which rightly belonged to the country as a whole. In addition, he appealed to the traditional radical cry of anti-clericalism and portrayed the Church as an instrument perpetuating aristocratic privilege and obscurantism.

John Morley and Chamberlain stressed disendowment more than disestablishment, since they saw the released revenues of the Church paying for a free national system of elementary education. The *Radical Programme* which Chamberlain issued in 1885 contained a chapter on disestablishment written by John Morley and incorporating the ideas of the Liberation Society. It refused to acknowledge the corporate existence of the Church of England and envisaged a fragmentation occurring after disestablishment. All churches and cathedrals built before 1818 were to be regarded as national property and shared between different denominations or turned over to secular use.

Any chance that Gladstone might have responded to the call for disestablishment of the Church of England when presented as a religious cause by Nonconformists was scotched by its transformation into a secular issue centring on a campaign for disendowment. Gladstone could never have countenanced the secularization of British cathedrals, nor indeed could Nonconformists like Samuel Morley. The champions of disestablishment were convinced that Gladstone deliberately took up other issues on the two occasions when pressure for disestablishment was at its height and might have been successful with a little help from the Government. Both Dale and J. Guinness Rogers, a London Congregational minister, thought that he had raised the subject of the Bulgarian atrocities to divert Nonconformist attention from disestablishment in 1877. There was also suspicion that he had introduced Irish Home Rule in 1885 to forestall the pressure for disestablishment that had mounted with the enfranchisement of numerous working men. Chamberlain later told R. W. Perks, a leading Wesleyan Methodist and Liberal M.P., that 'When Mr. Gladstone suddenly sprang his Irish policy upon the country, it was not so much to satisfy Ireland that he did so, as to prevent me placing the Disestablishment of the Church of England in the forefront of the Liberal Programme. . . . You Nonconformists have got nothing—nothing.'[36] Guinness Rogers complained, 'Gladstone seems ready to do anything for the Irish. What is he going to do for his best friends, the English Nonconformists?'[37]

For Matthew Arnold, Nonconformity's most unforgivable contribution to Victorian Liberalism was to put it against the civilizing and Christian principle of an Established Church. In fact, that was only a small part of the Nonconformist legacy. 'It is too commonly believed', Guinness Rogers complained in 1879, 'that "political Dissent" means nothing more nor less than antagonism to the Establishment. It really means the subordination of politics to Christian principles. One result of this would, in the judgement of Nonconformists, be the removal of all invidious distinctions resting on the ground of religious opinion, but the principle is of much wider application.'[38]

The Nonconformists' insistence that politics should always be subordinated to Christian principles led them to censure Liberals for occasional moral lapses. Gladstone was doubly damned in Nonconformist eyes in the 1874 election. Not only had his Education Act favoured Anglicans, but he had also gone to the country on the materialistic and ignoble issue of repealing income tax. Dale sternly reminded the electors of Birmingham: 'the Liberal Party does not exist for the repeal of the income tax. Such a bribe discredits the ministers who offer it and the electors who take it.'[39] Several Nonconformists objected to Gladstone's support for Bradlaugh's atheistic principles although others backed his stand for freedom of conscience. Those few Liberal politicians who fell short of the high moral standards generally prevailing in the party found themselves the object of considerable righteous indignation. Nonconformist pressure played a part in keeping Sir Charles Dilke out of the Cabinet in 1886 after he had been cited as co-respondent in a divorce case.

This moral pressure was perhaps most spectacularly and successfully exerted on the Liberal party in helping to force Charles Parnell's removal from the leadership of the Irish Nationalists after he had been found guilty of adultery in 1890. Hugh Price Hughes and John Clifford, the leading Baptist minister in the country, thundered from their pulpits, 'Parnell must go.' The *Methodist Times* threatened that no Methodist would vote for the Liberals again if they allowed an adulterer to remain at the head of a political party. Colman warned Gladstone that Parnell's continuation as leader of the Irish party would cost the Liberals five seats in East Anglia alone. At a private meeting Hughes and W. T. Stead told the Liberal front bench that it would no longer receive Nonconformist support unless Parnell went. 'The minimum demand of the great Nonconformist party is the abdication of Mr. Parnell,' a correspondent wrote to *The Times*, 'Nothing less will satisfy the Nonconformist Conscience now.'[40] He had coined a phrase to describe one of the most powerful forces at work in late Victorian politics and society.

The Nonconformist Conscience confirmed Liberalism as the moral crusading movement which Gladstone conceived it to be. The strong Nonconformist presence in the party encouraged the belief that, as Sir Wilfrid Lawson, an ardent Congregationalist and M.P. for Carlisle, put it, 'politics is not a pastime, but . . . a perpetual contest with wrong.'[41] Nonconformity gave Liberalism the quality of a religious crusade both by influencing many of its leading politicians and by creating expectations among its electorate. Many of the voters of 1867 to 1885 were members of Bagehot's 'second order of English Society which, from their habits of reading and non-reading, may be called *par excellence* the scriptural classes'.[42] The Nonconformist manufacturers and artisans who were the backbone of Liberal support looked for high moral principles and religious commitment from their elected representatives. Liberal politicians ignored the Nonconformist Conscience at their peril. Felix Holt failed to secure the votes of the Dissenters of Treby because he did not involve himself in 'some great struggle in which he was distinctly the champion of Dissent and Liberalism'.[43] Few real-life Liberal politicians made the same mistake. Most of them couched their political campaigns in moral terms and gave them the aura of religious crusades. As Sidney Webb observed, 'a Liberal reform is never simply a social means to a social end, but a struggle of good against evil.'[44]

The Nonconformist Conscience was first and most successfully harnessed to a Liberal political movement in Cobden and Bright's direction of the Anti-Corn Law campaign. The two leaders presented it as a moral crusade and gave it a heavily Biblical basis which assured solid Nonconformist support. Cobden told audiences around the country that repeal involved 'carrying out to the fullest extent the Christian doctrine of "Doing to all men as ye would they should do unto you" '.[45] Bright told a meeting after repeal had been secured, 'You find it in Holy Writ that the Earth is the Lord's, and the fulness thereof. We have put Holy Writ into an Act of Parliament.'[46]

Cobden and Bright had different motives for couching their demands for the repeal of the corn laws in religious language. Bright, as a convinced Quaker, genuinely saw repeal as a righteous cause of God.

He told one gathering: 'I consider when I stand upon a platform, as I do now, that I am engaged in as solemn a labour as Mr. Dale when he addresses his congregation. It is not only upon the affairs of the other world that men must be true to themselves and to their consciences.'[47] Cobden's appeal to religion was more conscious and contrived. He saw the considerable gains to be made by enlisting Nonconformist opinion in support of repeal. He had been deeply impressed by the way in which the campaign for the abolition of slavery had successfully appealed to the religious and moral feelings of the public. He was determined that a similar appeal could be made over the corn laws. 'It appears to me', he wrote to a friend in 1840, 'that a moral and even a religious spirit may be infused into the topic and if agitated in the same manner that the question of slavery has been, it will be irresistible.'[48] In August 1841 he organized a conference of over 600 ministers of religion to forge a link between Christianity and repeal. 'Henceforth we will grapple with the religious feelings of the people,' he wrote, 'Their veneration for God shall be our leverage to upset their reverence for the aristocracy.'[49] After repeal, Cobden wrote to another friend: 'It is fortunate for me that I have the religious sympathy which enables me to co-operate with men of exclusively religious sentiment. I mean it is fortunate for my powers of usefulness in this my day and generation. To this circumstance I am greatly indebted for the success of the great Free Trade Struggle, which has been more indebted to the organ of veneration for its success, than is generally known.'[50]

Cobden and Bright's successful prosecution of the Anti-Corn Law campaign as a quasi-religious crusade had an effect on both Nonconformists and Liberals. For Hugh Price Hughes it reconciled and attracted him to Liberalism. As his daughter put it, 'the Liberal and Democratic movement which originated with the French Revolution and which the religious had been taught to fear and to condemn, had now assumed quite another character. It was no longer lawless and anti-Christian. Cobden and Bright, in their humane campaign against the Corn Laws, had infused into it a new and religious spirit.'[51] To Liberal politicians, and to none more than Gladstone, it showed the success and the votes to be gained from turning political campaigns into moral crusades and making frequent allusions to Scripture.

In his campaigns of the 1840s and 1850s, Bright harnessed Nonconformity to the emergent Liberal movement. In oratorical style and solemnity of purpose, he resembled a revivalist preacher and appealed as such. After attending Bright's first public meeting as M.P. for

Birmingham, Dale commented, 'Surely the Lord is in this place and I knew it not.'[52] More than any other single figure, Bright gave Victorian Liberalism its distinctive moral rhetoric and fervour. Palmerston hated him for it, calling him 'the Honourable and religious gentleman' and accusing him of introducing cant and humbug into Parliamentary debate. Gladstone, on the other hand, admired him as a truly religious politician. With Bright, the language of British politics began its transformation from the witty classical tags of the Regency period to the 'lofty maxims and sacred names' of the high Victorian age.[53]

One of the most interesting expressions of the crusading atmosphere which Nonconformity gave to Liberalism was the 'New Journalism' created by W. T. Stead in the 1880s. The son of a Northumberland Congregational minister, Stead showed himself as a young boy to have a well-developed Nonconformist conscience. At the age of eleven he knocked down another boy who had stared rudely at a girl tying up her garter. When even younger, he had declared, 'I wish that God would give me a big whip that I could go round the world and whip the wicked out of it.'[54] The whip that Stead was to wield against evil in later life was the press. As editor of the *Northern Echo* from 1871 to 1883 and then as John Morley's successor at the *Pall Mall Gazette*, he developed a new sensational style of campaigning journalism which powerfully assisted the Liberal cause.

The feeling that the world could be changed through a campaigning press attracted many Liberals to journalism. Mill saw it as the modern equivalent of oratory in Greece and Rome and wrote in *The Westminster Review* in 1836: 'There are now, in this country, but two modes left in which an individual mind can hope to produce much direct effect upon the minds and destinies of his countrymen generally; as a member of parliament, or an editor of a London newspaper. In both these capacities much may still be done by an individual.'[55] John Morley followed Mill in writing for the reviews where their views on proportional representation or birth control might not reach many people but would at least be read by the decision-makers. At the other end of the journalistic spectrum the provincial Nonconformist newspaper dynasties like the Baineses of Leeds, the Byleses of Bradford and the Leaders of Sheffield campaigned vigorously on such issues as church rates and disestablishment.

By the end of the nineteenth century these two strands of journalism had been fused by a talented group of Liberal editors who ran large-circulation national papers, which were broad and cosmopolitan in scope and yet campaigning and crusading in style. The leading members of this group were C. P. Scott of the *Manchester Guardian*, H. W. Massingham of the *Daily Chronicle*, A. G. Gardiner of the *Daily News* and J. A. Spender of the *Westminster Gazette*. They established a tradition of Liberal journalism which reached its apogee in the Edwardian era in the hands of such talented writers as Hilaire Belloc, C. F. G. Masterman, J. L. Hammond and L. T. Hobhouse. All were deeply influenced by Stead.

Stead started to develop his crusading and fiercely partisan style of journalism on the *Northern Echo*. As editor, he later wrote: 'I was a thorough-going Gladstonian of a very stalwart fighting kind, with a wholesome conviction that Tories were children of the Devil, and that the supreme duty of a Liberal journalist was to win as many seats as possible for the Liberal Party.'[56] In 1876 he launched his first great journalistic crusade when he used the *Northern Echo* to start the national agitation over the Bulgarian atrocities. Four years later he moved to London to become John Morley's assistant on the *Pall Mall Gazette*. 'He was invaluable,' Morley later wrote, 'abounding in journalistic resource, eager in conviction, infinitely bold, candid, laborious.'[57] In 1883 Stead became editor. Within two years he had pushed the *Gazette*'s circulation up from 8,360 to 12,250 by introducing features wholly new to the English press like interviews, gossip columns, dramatic headlines across several columns and racy, investigative stories.

Matthew Arnold christened the style of the *Pall Mall Gazette* 'the New Journalism' and described it as 'full of ability, novelty, variety, sensation, sympathy, and generous instincts'.[58] Stead's methods were soon copied by George Newnes, who incorporated them in his *Titbits* magazine, and Alfred Harmsworth, who started *Answers to Correspondents* in 1888. Those two periodicals were the forerunners of the mass-circulation tabloid papers of the twentieth century. While Newnes and Harmsworth used racy style and sensation simply to make money, however, Stead used them to popularize his Liberal crusades. It was a sad comment on the coming times that while Harmsworth's empire went from strength to strength in the 1890s with the setting up of the *Evening News* and the *Daily Mail*, the *Pall Mall Gazette* collapsed in 1892 when its staff walked out rather than submit to a new American owner who wanted to turn it into a Conservative paper.

During his time as editor of the *Pall Mall Gazette*, Stead was, in

John Morley's words, 'the most powerful journalist in the island'.[59] The ill-fated expedition to relieve General Gordon in Khartoum, the vital re-equipment of the Navy in 1884 and the dropping from Gladstone's Home Rule Bill of 1886 of the clause excluding Irish M.P.s from the House of Commons all resulted from campaigns initiated by the paper. Stead's serialization of *The Bitter Cry of Outcast London*, an exposé of the capital's slums by a Congregational minister, led to the setting up in 1884 of a Royal Commission on Housing the Working Classes and eventually to the Artisans' Dwelling Act of 1890. Not unreasonably, he noted: 'I have been more useful, more powerful, than half a dozen ordinary M.P.s, and a Parliamentary career offers few attractions compared with those of a journalist.'[60]

Stead's success led him to develop an exalted concept of the role of the press. During the three months' imprisonment that he endured in 1885 as a result of his most daring crusade, against the international traffic in girl prostitutes, he wrote: 'I have been thinking long and deeply about the ideal of Government by Journalism. I think that there I have grasped a great idea: to organise a secular Church with a journal as preacher and all readers congregation.'[61] In 1890 he noted in his diary: 'the newspaper idea grows. I now see that I am called to found for the nineteenth century a City of God which will be to the age of the printing press and the steam engine what the Catholic Church was to the Europe of the tenth century ... it will be father confessor, spiritual director, moral teacher, political conscience.'[62] Stead would, one feels, be impressed with the extent to which government by journalism has gone in the twentieth century and with the role that the mass media have taken as secular guides and prophets, even if some of their preaching might not appeal to his Nonconformist conscience.

The subjects on which Stead campaigned most energetically and consistently were the causes dearest to the hearts of Nonconformist Liberals. He enumerated them as editor of the *Northern Echo* when he said he had a threefold mission: spirits, women and peace. Individual Nonconformists took up other causes, of course. Bright, for example, like other Quakers, actively campaigned for the abolition of capital punishment. None the less, drink, prostitution and foreign despotism were the subjects on which the Nonconformist Conscience had its greatest influence on the outlook and policy of Victorian Liberalism.

Temperance reform was almost certainly the most important political commitment which the Liberal party took on as a result of

Nonconformist pressure. It was not, of course, an exclusively Non-conformist interest. The idea that excessive drinking was responsible for many social ills and should be curbed appealed naturally to the individualist self-help ethic of Liberalism. Cobden was a strong advocate of temperance reform and held that 'the Temperance cause really lies at the basis of all social and political progression in this country. . . . The energy natural to the English race degenerates to savage brutality under the influence of habitual drunkenness; and one of the worst effects of intemperate habits is to destroy that self-respect which lies at the bottom of all virtuous ambition.'[63] Bright, Miall and Samuel Morley were temperance lecturers. Edward Baines, like Morley a total abstainer, was the author of a best-selling pamphlet against drink. The leaders of the temperance movement, which was dominated by the United Kingdom Alliance, were naturally attracted to Liberalism as a creed of moral reform. It has been calculated that of 123 temperance leaders between 1831 and 1871 whose political affiliations are known, 119 were Liberals.[64] At least two Nonconformist Liberal M.P.s, Sir Wilfrid Lawson and William Caine, a Baptist iron miner, devoted most of their Parliamentary careers to pressing for temperance legislation.

It took some time, however, before the main aim of the Alliance, a restriction on the sale of alcoholic drinks, became the policy of the Liberal party. Initially, the Liberal attitude to drink was dominated by the notion of free trade. In 1860 Gladstone introduced a free licensing system for liquor. Free trade in drink continued to be advocated by an important group of Liberals which included Henry Fawcett, William Rathbone, Auberon Herbert and, to a large extent, Gladstone himself. The pressure of the Alliance and a growing awareness of the extent of the drink problem were, however, pushing the Liberals towards pro-hibition in the 1860s. In 1864 Lawson, as the Alliance representative in Parliament, introduced a Permissive Bill, which provided for a system of local veto on the drink trade whereby a majority of ratepayers could prevent any licences from being granted in their locality. The Permis-sive Bill, introduced annually by Lawson until 1880, became the central feature of Liberal efforts at curbing the drink trade.

The alliance between Liberals and prohibitionists was cemented in the 1870s. In 1871 George Trevelyan, who was on a countrywide tour with Lawson, said, 'the Liberal Party must ere long become a temper-ance party.'[65] In the same year Henry Bruce, Home Secretary in Gladstone's first Government, introduced a Licensing Bill which would have reduced the number of licences issued to a particular proportion of the population, incorporated the principle of a ratepayers' veto and reduced opening hours of public houses. When finally passed in 1872 the Licensing Act had been considerably watered down, both the licence reduction and the local veto having been removed, but it was still a significant enough departure from free trade towards restriction of the drink trade to please most temperance groups and antagonize brewers and publicans. The Tories lost no time in castigating the Liberals as an anti-drink party and in wooing the considerable drink interest that had previously backed them. Opposition to the Licensing Act undoubtedly played a part in the Liberals' disastrous defeat in the 1874 election. The Revd. W. Arthur, a Wesleyan Methodist minister, attributed Edward Baines's defeat in Leeds to 'the enmity of the publicans. This has been the fulcrum for the Tory-democratic lever and has told immensely.' Baines's uncle was even more emphatic in his diagnosis of the defeat: 'the Leeds constituency, after receiving its original assistance from the hands of the party of Progress . . . has on this occasion thought fit to float downwards on the tide of beer and bribery.'[66]

The Liberal party was never wholly committed to prohibition. Libertarians like Mill opposed all attempts at temperance legislation on the grounds that individuals should judge for themselves about alcohol. Sir William Harcourt, a leading Liberal lawyer, initially agreed with that view. Even among those who believed in promoting temperance there was not unanimity as to the desirability of the system of an optional local veto. Stead opposed it, as did Bright who argued for municipal control over licensing. Chamberlain advocated the management of the liquor trade by companies of disinterested citizens on the model of the system adopted in Gothenburg, Sweden. None the less, the principle of prohibition through the local veto gradually gained ground among Liberals. Among its foremost proponents were T. H. Green, John Morley and, eventually, Harcourt who was converted when, as Home Secretary in Gladstone's 1880 Government, 'I had cognisance of those causes of crime which led many a man, aye, and many a woman, to the loss of liberty and life, and brought them shameful death.'[67]

During the 1880s temperance became a dominant theme of Liberal party policy. Three important measures were enacted in Gladstone's second Government: the ending of the system whereby wages were paid in public houses, the prohibition of the use of public houses as committee rooms for elections, and Sunday closing in Wales. The local veto was included in the programme of the National Liberal Federation in 1889 and the Newcastle Programme of the following year. Several leading Liberals saw prohibition as a cause which would unite the party after its splits over Home Rule. Lawson wrote: 'My recipe for getting the Liberals back to power is for them to declare a crusade against drinking and fighting . . . and counter the Tory arguments in favour of gin and glory.'[68] Harcourt believed that temperance reform should be the main Liberal call to the electorate. He advocated prohibition of the drink trade by local veto, with no compensation given to publicans who lost their licences. In 1893 and 1895 he introduced as government measures Bills providing that polls should be taken on the request of one-tenth of the electors. If two-thirds of those who voted called for an end to licensing, all licensed premises in the town or area would be closed. It was the high point of the Liberals' commitment to temperance and, as in 1874, many blamed the defeat in the 1895 election on the party's attack on drink.

It is easy to over-state the extent to which the Liberal party was taken over by Nonconformist ideas on drink. Gladstone remained solidly opposed to prohibition of the drink trade, and to the promotion of total abstinence. None the less, the United Kingdom Alliance regarded the Liberals as 'the Temperance party', and so did the publicans. Liberals and temperance reformers were bound by mutual need as well as by sympathy. The temperance movement provided highly disciplined troops for the Liberals. 'When the others are smoking and drinking in public-houses and clubs' one temperance zealot wrote in 1898, 'the teetotallers are hard at work canvassing and winning the election.'[69] Lloyd George reckoned that 'the best fighting men in the ranks of the Liberal army were the Temperance men.'[70]

This close identification with the temperance movement illustrates well the strengths and weaknesses of the Liberals' connection with Nonconformity. Chapels and temperance societies provided a ready-made source of local membership and organization for the party, but they also committed Liberals to particular forms of social and political activity. There could be no possibility of competing with the Conservatives' 'bread and circuses' approach to wooing the electorate by providing working-men's clubs with cheap drink and subsidized entertainments. George Howell, the trade union leader, told William Rathbone in 1870 that 'everywhere there is less of geniality and bonhomie in the treatment of the working classes by the Liberals than by the Conservatives.'[71] It was all very well for local Liberal associations to wear an austere puritanical face while there were still plenty of Nonconformist votes to be won. As Nonconformity declined, however, the Liberals suffered from their killjoy image. Harcourt was hardly courting electoral success when he wrote to John Morley in 1888: 'Temperance is the backbone of the Liberal Party *vice* Nonconformity retired.'[72] If Nonconformity had retired, then so had temperance.

After drink, the Nonconformist Conscience was probably most offended by sexual irregularity. Nonconformist sexual ethics reinforced already strong Liberal feelings about prostitution. It was no coincidence that three of the best-known efforts to curb prostitution in Victorian England were carried out by Liberals: Gladstone's celebrated solo attempts to redeem fallen women whom he met on his nocturnal prowls through London; the crusade led by Josephine Butler and Sir James Stansfeld against the Contagious Diseases Acts and the principle of licensed prostitution that they involved; and W. T. Stead's campaign against the international trade in child prostitutes. All were individual rather than party campaigns, but they received strong support from Liberal Nonconformists.

Stead's campaign was the most dramatic and his target the most vile; the regular shipping to the Continent of young British girls, lured to London by advertisements for maids, and the return traffic of Continental girls. Several attempts had been made in the early 1880s by Liberal M.P.s to raise the age of consent from thirteen (where it had been fixed in 1875) to sixteen and give magistrates power to search places where girls were being detained for immoral purposes. They received no support from the Government, however. Strongly encouraged by Josephine Butler, Gladstone and Bramwell Booth of the Salvation Army, Stead decided to expose the trade in children in the hope of shocking the nation into ending it forever. He visited places where he found girls aged between three and seven being chloroformed before they were violated by old men. Stead set out to prove how easy it was to buy a child in Britain for immoral purposes and ship her to the Continent. With the aid of a reformed procuress, he bought a thirteen-year-old girl, Eliza Armstrong, from her parents and took her to Paris. Stead told the story in a series of sensational articles in the *Pall Mall Gazette* in July 1885 under the title 'A Maiden's Tribute to Modern Babylon'.

The effect of Stead's articles was a vindication of his belief in the power of journalism and an example of the strength of the Nonconformist Conscience. They provoked an immediate outcry in the country and in Parliament where a month later the age of consent was raised to sixteen, and magistrates were given power to stop the trade. Unfortunately, because Eliza's father had not been informed of her abduction, criminal charges were brought against Stead and the female Salvation Army officer who took her to Paris. She was sentenced to a year's imprisonment and he to three months.

The crusades against drink and prostitution were typical products of the Nonconformist influence on Liberalism. They appealed to religious and moral feelings and even free-thinking Liberals saw them as ennobling. John Morley told Liberal audiences that the temperance crusade was 'the greatest and deepest moral movement in this country since the anti-slavery agitation'.[73] For many Liberals drunkenness and prostitution were the sources of social problems like homelessness and disease. Others, less influenced by Nonconformist concern with personal sin, suggested that they might rather be symptoms of bad physical conditions and poverty. Such was Disraeli's argument in the 1870s and the early Socialists' case in the 1880s. It was a point of view that did not much appeal to Nonconformist Liberals with their belief in individual moral choice and responsibility, but even among them it gradually began to gain currency. Hugh Price Hughes reflected that Stead's revelations about the trade in prostitutes had shown 'that we cannot touch any point in this hideous vice . . . without also touching a thousand points in our ordinary life in which lie concealed the evil which has produced these hideous fruits . . . we have seen how the whole thing hangs together and therefore . . . that it will be impossible to do anything in furthering morality by the law of the land without also touching the economical relations of society.'[74] The Nonconformist Conscience was beginning to send some Liberals in a new direction.

The atmosphere of religious revivalism extended into the field of foreign affairs. Nonconformists had a strong commitment to morality in international relations which went back to the formation of the Peace Society by Quakers and evangelicals in 1816. During the 1840s and 1850s the Society, led by Henry Vincent and Edward Miall, lent powerful support to Cobden and Bright's attack on Palmerstonian foreign policy. In the 1860s Nonconformists were prominent on the Liberal side in the two great issues which shaped the Liberal awakening, the American Civil War and the case of Governor Eyre. T. H. Green noted excitedly over the latter: 'It's a great thing when the religious public, as seldom happens, really gets stirred up in the right direction.'[75]

Probably the single event that roused the Nonconformist Conscience more than any other in the nineteenth century was the savage suppression by the Turks of a revolt by their Bulgarian subjects in 1876 which involved the massacre of 12,000 men, women and children. The storm of indignation provoked by this brutality was exacerbated by Disraeli's refusal as Prime Minister to condemn it. Seeking to maintain Palmerston's policy of supporting a strong Ottoman presence in the east Mediterranean as a counter to Russian ambitions there, he leant over backwards to avoid offending Turkey and even seriously contemplated going to war on its behalf against Russia. It mattered not to British interests, Disraeli insisted, whether it was 10,000 or 20,000 who perished in the suppression of the Bulgarian rising. Appalled by this insistence that national interest should override the claims of morality and by the prospect of an imminent war, Nonconformists determined to mobilize the country in the cause of justice and peace.

The national agitation over the Bulgarian atrocities was started by Stead. At the end of August 1876, he began a campaign in the *Northern Echo* and organized a series of protest meetings throughout the northeast of England. Within a month, the whole country was reading the Darlington paper and forty-seven meetings had been held. Stead likened the massacre of the Christian Bulgarians by the heathen Turks to the massacre of the Protestants of Piedmont which had provoked Cromwell's intervention in the mid-seventeenth century. He appealed for a national day of mourning and humiliation and called on Gladstone to assume Cromwell's mantle as Protector of the persecuted Christians. Gladstone was at first reluctant. He had resigned from the Liberal leadership in January 1875 after the electoral defeat of 1874 which he took to be a betrayal of his trust in the people. What brought him back into active politics, and to the leadership of his party once again, was his conviction that the state of public feeling over the Bulgarian atrocities provided a basis for another great moral crusade on which he could lead the Liberals to victory at the next election.

In August 1876 Gladstone wrote to Lord Granville: 'Good ends can rarely be attained in politics without passion: and there is now, the first time for a good many years, a virtuous passion.'[76] He gave up the theological speculations of his retirement and pencilled on a sheaf of notes headed 'Future Retribution': 'from this I was called away to write on Bulgaria.'[77] The pamphlet which he wrote in September, *The Bulgarian Horrors and the Question of the East*, with its demand that the Turks should 'one and all, bag and baggage, clear out from the provinces they have desolated and profaned', sold two hundred thousand copies in a month. By becoming the champion of the Bulgarians, Gladstone put himself at the head of the Nonconformists. His part in the 1870 Education Act and his lukewarmness over disestablishment were forgotten. Henry Broadhurst, the trade union leader, recalled in his autobiography that, 'the Nonconformists of Great Britain to a man, ay, and a woman, had ranged themselves on his side. They looked upon him as the deliverer of nations, the inspired leader of peoples, as a giant of unsurpassed strength wrestling with and conquering the powers of injustice and oppression.'[78]

The agitation over the Bulgarian atrocities was the supreme achievement of the Nonconformist Conscience. G. W. E. Russell, a young Liberal journalist, noted that 'a kind of romantic and religious glamour, such as no one had ever before connected with politics seemed to surround this attack on the strongholds of Anti-Christ. The campaign became a crusade.'[79] Stead reflected after the successful conclusion of the agitation, which had effectively prevented war with Russia, that it had 'rekindled my faith in my countrymen, renewed my faith in Liberalism and strengthened my trust in God' and proved that 'life is once more brilliant as in heroic days. Our time is as capable of Divine service as Puritan times.'[80]

It was significant that Gladstone should have turned the Nonconformists' call for justice and peace into a national campaign and used their 'virtuous passion' as the basis for his return to the Liberal leadership. The Bulgarian atrocities agitation shows more clearly than any other episode why it was that the Liberal leader and the Nonconformists enjoyed so close a relationship. He needed their support to sustain his political style of appealing to the conscience of the nation just as much as they needed his power and influence to put their demands into practice. Certainly there was no doubt of their mutual admiration at the time of the campaign. J. Guinness Rogers noted: 'Mr. Gladstone is recognised by the Nonconformists as one of the very few Statesmen who feel that the law of Christ is to govern nations as well as individuals.'[81] Gladstone told an audience at Holyhead, 'I am a decided and convinced member of the Church of England, I have been there all my life, and I trust that there I shall die. But that will not prevent me from bearing an emphatic testimony to this: that the cause of justice, the cause of humanity, of mercy, of right, of truth for many millions of God's creatures in the East of Europe, has found its best, its most consistent, and its most unanimous supporters in the Nonconformist Churches of the land.'[82]

Chapter 5

Non-Intervention and Self-Determination

The foreign policy of Victorian Liberalism was dictated by its three main components: the demand for economy and free trade, the love of liberty, and the Nonconformist Conscience. On the whole, they worked together to produce a preference for peace, neutrality and internationalism and a dislike of militarism, imperialism and diplomacy. There was, however, a fundamental conflict between the absolute isolationism and non-interventionism preached by Cobden and Bright and the call by Mill and others for active support of small nations struggling to be free. Gladstone partially reconciled the conflict with his strong commitment to the ideal of a Concert of Europe embodying the collective moral strength of the great powers.

The basic principles of Liberal foreign policy were established during Palmerston's long period of rule over Britain's dealings overseas which began when he became Foreign Secretary in 1830 and did not effectively cease until he relinquished the Premiership in 1865. His support for independence movements in small states—most marked by his championship of Belgian independence in the 1830s—and his recourse to international conferences to settle disputes anticipated important strands of future Liberal policy. At the same time, the opposition of Cobden and Bright to Palmerston's balance-of-power theory, his secret diplomacy and his tendency to counter slights to British pride with a show of military force led to the development of the doctrines of non-intervention and arbitration.

The Manchester Party's advocacy of neutrality was based primarily on economic grounds. Cobden first stated its case in his essay *England, Ireland and America* (1835), in which he took as his maxim George Washington's Farewell Address to the American People: 'The great rule of conduct for us in regard to foreign nations is, in extending our commercial relations, to have with them as little political connection as possible.'[1] Cobden argued that America's economic success derived from its policy of isolationism and its consequent low spending on armaments and diplomats. It was similarly in the interests of British manufacturers and merchants that their country should keep out of all foreign entanglements. 'Our cry should be neutrality and isolation unless attacked,' he told Baines in 1848, 'this cry must be put forth . . . by the manufacturers and merchants of the country upon whom the efforts of war would fall with serious force.'[2]

Economic considerations similarly underlay Cobden and Bright's attack on Britain's colonial system. They argued with Adam Smith that history showed colonies to be a drain on the wealth of nations. 'Spain lies, at this moment, a miserable spectacle of a nation whose own national greatness has been immolated on the shrine of transatlantic ambition', Cobden warned. 'May not some future historian possibly be found recording a similar epitaph on the tomb of Britain?'[3] The notion that colonies were a source of weakness to Britain continued to be popular among Liberals. It was expressed most forcibly in Goldwin Smith's letters to the *Daily News* on the subject of 'the Empire' in 1863. Many Tories, on the other hand, accepted the argument of Sir John Seeley's *The Expansion of England*, that colonial development brought political and economic strength. 'This policy', Bright told an audience in Manchester in 1879, 'may lead to a seeming glory to the Crown, and may give scope for patronage and promotion and pay and pensions to a limited and favoured class, but to you, the people, it brings expenditure of blood and treasure, increased debt and taxes, and added risks of war in every quarter of the globe.'[4]

As Bright's remarks indicate, the Manchester Party's foreign policy had a distinct class bias. 'The middle and industrious classes of England', Cobden had written in *England, Ireland and America*, 'can have no interest apart from the preservation of peace. The honours, the fame, the emoluments of war belong not to them; the battle plain is the harvest-field of the aristocracy, watered with the blood of the people.'[5] Bright made the point even more strongly in a speech in Birmingham in 1858 when he dismissed Palmerstonian foreign policy, with its fondness for complex diplomacy and involvement overseas, as 'neither more nor less than a gigantic system of outdoor relief for the aristocracy of Great Britain'.[6]

The idea that foreign policy as traditionally pursued by secret alliance among the grandees of Europe represented an aristocratic conspiracy against the interests of the people took firm root in the Victorian Liberal mind. In 1864, during a war between Germany and Denmark, Cobden accused Palmerston of having tried to settle the destinies of the people of Schleswig and Holstein by his London Conference of

1852 without any reference to their own wishes: 'Kings, princes, emperors, were represented at that meeting, but the people had not the slightest voice or right in the matter.'[7] In 1878 Gladstone attacked Disraeli for making a compact with the Turks 'not in the light of day, but in the darkness of the night'.[8] This call for open diplomacy and for popular rather than aristocratic control over foreign policy reached its apogee in 1914 when E. D. Morel and other Liberal pacifists set up the Union of Democratic Control in an effort to end the First World War by open negotiation and democratic diplomacy. The Union played an important role in determining the attitude to foreign affairs of the infant Labour party.

In calling for Britain's foreign policy to be determined by the interests of merchants rather than diplomats, Cobden and Bright were demanding a change in the national character. During a typical episode of Palmerstonian intervention in the affairs of Spain in 1847, Cobden wrote to Bright: 'I have always had an instinctive monomania against this system of foreign interference, protocolling, diplomatising, etc., and I shall be glad if you and your other Free Trade friends . . . would try to prevent the Foreign Office from undoing the good which the Board of Trade has done to the people. But you must not disguise from yourself that the evil has its roots in the pugnacious, energetic, self-sufficient, foreigner-despising and pitying character of that noble insular creature, John Bull.'[9] It was not surprising that to patriots this Little Englander attitude seemed to be based largely on mean economic self-interest. Tennyson dismissed Cobden and Bright's opposition to war with France in 1852 in terms which left no doubt as to his opinion of them:

> *Though niggard throats of Manchester may bawl,*
> *What England was, shall her true sons forget?*
> *We are not cotton-spinners all,*
> *But some love England and her honour yet.*[10]

In fact, the Manchester Party's attack on national pride and chauvinism and on the measurement of a country's greatness by its military power and colonial possessions went beyond mere economic considerations. It brought a moral element into Liberal foreign policy which was also strongly promoted by free-thinkers and Nonconformists. No one represented this element better than the Quaker John Bright, who formulated his principles of foreign policy while sitting among the ruins of the Roman Empire: 'From her history, and indeed from all history, I learn that loud boasting, great wealth, great power, extended dominion, successive conquests, mighty fleets and armies, are not immovable foundations of national greatness. I would rely rather on an educated and moral people, and on a system of government free at home, and scrupulously moral and just in its dealings with every other government and people.'[11]

Cobden and Bright sowed the seeds of the anti-militarism which characterized Victorian Liberalism. 'We have been the most combative and aggressive community that has existed since the days of the Roman Empire', Cobden observed; 'it is displayed in our fondness for erecting monuments to warriors, even at the doors of our marts of commerce; in the frequent memorials of our battles in the names of bridges, streets and omnibuses.'[12] The pacific tendency which the Manchester Party encouraged was powerfully reinforced by Nonconformists, Radicals and free-thinkers. Under Henry Richard's secretaryship, the Nonconformist-dominated Peace Society was a significant Liberal pressure group in the 1850s and 1860s. Its second peace congress, held in Paris in 1849 with Victor Hugo as chairman, was addressed by Cobden, Miall and Henry Vincent, the ex-Chartist. John Morley's lifelong antipathy to militarism, which he considered 'the point blank opposite of Liberalism', led him to oppose Britain's entry into the First World War, while Gladstone, fired equally by zeal for economy and desire for peace, waged a continuous battle against efforts to increase spending on armaments.[13]

Manchester School principles stood similarly at the root of the Liberals' opposition to imperialism and their championship of the principle of self-government for the colonies. Britain's imperial role first came under Liberal criticism in the early 1850s when Bright took up the cause of native self-government and eventual independence for India. Characteristically, he had become interested in India as a new source of cotton for the Lancashire mills, but he soon became committed to the well-being of the people, which he felt was impossible of achievement under British rule. Cobden observed that 'the world never yet beheld such a compound of jobbing, swindling, hypocrisy, and slaughter, as goes to make up the gigantic scheme of villainy called the "British rule in India" .... The English people in Parliament have undertaken to be responsible for governing 150 millions of people, despotically in India .... I have no faith in such an undertaking being anything but a calamity and a curse to the people of England .... Is it not just possible that we may become corrupted at home by the reaction of arbitrary, political maxims in the East upon our domestic politics, just as Greece and Rome were demoralized by their contact with Asia?'[14] To Bright, British rule in India was simply a matter of 'ambition, conquest and crime'.

Cobden and Bright's anti-imperialist views did not go unchallenged. In 1878 James Fitzjames Stephen wrote to *The Times* to express his disgust at Bright's view of British rule in India. 'I deny that ambition and conquest are crimes,' wrote Stephen, 'I say that ambition is the great incentive to every manly virtue, and that conquest is the process by which every great state in the world has been built up.'[15] Evoking the memory of such heroes as Clive, Hastings and Havelock, he argued that Britain should be proud rather than apologetic about its rule over India which had brought order and justice to the people. Significantly, it was India that first caused Stephen to have doubts about Gladstonianism and to set him on a course which ultimately took him out of the Liberal party.

India continued to be a focus for Liberal attacks on British imperialism throughout the nineteenth century. Both Henry Fawcett and Charles Bradlaugh took over Bright's championship of Indian self-government. Indeed, Fawcett came to be known as 'the Member of Parliament for India'. During the 1890s the cause of Indian nationalism was powerfully argued from the Liberal benches of the House of Commons by William Wedderburn, a retired Indian civil servant, and Dadabhai Naoroji, the first coloured man to be elected a British M.P.

Cobden and Bright first seriously clashed with Palmerston over the Don Pacifico incident in 1850. Palmerston had ordered the British fleet to blockade Athens to ensure the repayment of debts owed to a Portuguese Jew who lived in Gibraltar and was therefore technically a British subject. He defended the blockade in Parliament, on the grounds that Britain should apply the principle of *civis Romanus sum* and protect its subjects wherever they were. Bright told his constituents that intervention in the affairs of other countries on such comparatively trivial issues could lead to war and involved far greater spending on armaments than was necessary. Cobden also made a strong plea in favour of the principle of non-intervention. When they forced a division in the Commons on the incident, they were opposed by Whigs, Philosophic Radicals and most Tories. They were, however, supported by Gladstone who, in a signal of things to come, made a three-hour speech on the duty of national humility and respect for the rights of others.

Six years later, Cobden and Bright succeeded in carrying a motion of censure against Palmerston over another incident involving a supposed slight to British pride. The *Arrow*, a boat registered in Hong Kong and therefore sailing under the British flag, was intercepted by the Chinese authorities and its Chinese crew arrested for piracy in the Canton River. Having been refused an apology, the governor of Hong Kong ordered a bombardment of Hong Kong which was accomplished with serious loss of life. The governor's action was fully supported by Palmerston who maintained that 'an insolent barbarian . . . had violated the British flag.'[16] Cobden's motion of no confidence in Palmerston, which led to a dissolution of Parliament, was supported by Gladstone and the Tories. It was opposed, however, by the mercantile and manufacturing community who sent messages to Palmerston congratulating him on his support for English traders abroad. The *Arrow* affair was one incident when free trade and morality did not go hand in hand. The Opium War of 1840 had been another occasion when Palmerston had been supported by merchants in his policy of fighting the Chinese because of their efforts to suppress the lucrative opium trade. Then, as later, the main spokesman for morality had been Gladstone who accused Palmerston of hoisting the British flag 'to protect an infamous contraband traffic'.[17]

Palmerston described Cobden's speech in Parliament on the *Arrow* affair as showing 'an Anti-English feeling, an abnegation of all those ties which bind men to their country and to their fellow-countrymen, which I should hardly have expected from the lips of any member of this House'.[18] The allegation that they were unpatriotic and insensitive to Britain's interest was to be continually levelled at the Liberals by their political opponents. Disraeli portrayed them as the 'cosmopolitan' party, opposed to the patriotic Tories. Cecilia Halkett maintained in *Beauchamp's Career*, 'the greatness of England has been built up by the Tories . . . . They have the honour and safety of the country at heart. They do not play disgracefully at reductions of taxes, as the Liberals do.'[19] It was true that in promoting the claims of economy and morality against those of national pride, the Liberals projected an unpatriotic image. T. H. Green once told James Bryce that he 'would rather see the flag of England trailed in the dirt than add 6d to the taxes that weigh upon the poor'.[20] Gladstone told a friend in the last year of his life that he had informed Parliament in the debates on Don Pacifico and the *Arrow*: 'The English are arrogant.'[21]

Apart from his patriotism, Palmerston's guiding principle in foreign policy was the maintenance of the balance of power. Following conventional wisdom, he saw France and Russia as the two over-mighty powers of Europe needing to be constantly kept in check to preserve the delicate equilibrium prevailing in the continent. Cobden and Bright regarded this as a misguided theory which encouraged bellicosity and brinkmanship. In 1853 a wave of Francophobia pre-cipitated by a scare of invasion from across the Channel prompted Cobden to write *1793 and 1853* in which he showed the groundless nature of the earlier panic and called on the Peace Society to lead a national movement to erase the memories of Agincourt and Waterloo from the English consciousness. He also argued that the Russian advance against Turkey should cause no fears in England. The French scare died down but not so the feeling that Russia's actions disturbed the balance of power and must be countered. In 1854 Lord Aberdeen declared war on Russia and took an enthusiastic Britain into the Crimean War.

At first, the Manchester Party stood almost alone with a few Tories in opposing the Crimean War. Bright attacked it on economic grounds, for disturbing trade and raising taxes; on political grounds, since 'war throws power into the hands of the most worthless of the class of statesmen'; on religious grounds, as it involved helping the barbarian Turks to suppress Christians; and above all out of moral principle, because of the terrible waste of life.[22] Few, however, heeded his famous warning to the Commons in February 1855: 'the Angel of Death has been abroad throughout the land; you may almost hear the beating of his wings.'[23] The mood of the country was summed up in Tennyson's poem *Maud*, which glorified war and poured contempt on those who 'prate of the blessings of Peace'. Tennyson singled out Bright for particular attack:

> *Last week came one to the county town,*
> *To preach our poor little army down,*
> *And play the game of the despot kings,*
> *Though the state has done it and thrice as well;*
> *This broad brimm'd hawker of holy things,*
> *Whose ear is cramm'd with his cotton, and rings*
> *Even in dreams to the chink of his pence.*[24]

Gradually, however, as the war dragged on others came round to Bright's point of view. The most important was Gladstone, who, prompted largely by his abhorrence of the effect of the war on the national finances, began to call for peace in the summer of 1855. The opposition of Gladstone and the Manchester Party to the Crimean

E

War marked a decisive step in the development of Liberal foreign policy. From it emerged the idea that Britain's traditional enmity towards Russia, like its hostility to France, was misplaced. The war also left several Liberals, not least Gladstone, with a strong conviction of the need for a European concert of nations. In his pamphlet, *What Next and Next* (1856), Cobden proposed the abandonment of the concept of the balance of power and the substitution instead of a federal union of European states to promote peace.

In place of Palmerston's system of secret diplomacy to maintain national interest and preserve the balance of power, Cobden and Bright had proposed a new internationalist policy based on the principles of open treaties, arbitration and free trade. Their approach was summed up in Cobden's call for 'as little intercourse as possible betwixt the *Governments*, as much connection as possible between the *Nations* of the world'.[25] Strongly backed by Nonconformists and the Peace Society, the Manchester Party argued that instead of entering into secret military alliances, Britain should make open agreements with other powers to limit armaments. Cobden proposed such an agreement with France in 1851. Two years earlier he had proposed a motion in Parliament inviting foreign powers to bind themselves to refer to external arbitrators any future misunderstanding which could not be settled by amicable negotiation.

The principle of resolving disputes by arbitration became an important article of faith for many Liberals. It was naturally held particularly dear by Nonconformists and those with pacifist tendencies. Henry Richard, as M.P. for Merthyr, succeeded in carrying through the House of Commons in 1873 a resolution calling on the Queen to enter into communication with the great powers with a view to establishing a general system of arbitration. W. T. Stead regarded as one of the great aims of his life 'establishing a High Court of Justice among the Nations, whose decrees would not merely be the recommendations of arbitrators, but would be enforced by the authority of the Court'.[26] Gladstone showed his enthusiasm for the principle by using arbitration to settle matters affecting British pride where Palmerston might rather have sent in the gunboats.

More even than arbitration, Cobden and Bright looked to free trade as the agency which would promote internationalism and end war. They believed that the extension of free trade would destroy the colonial system which had caused most of the wars in Europe over the last 150 years, and produce a sense of interdependence among the countries of the world. 'For the disbanding of great armies and the promotion of peace', wrote Bright, 'I rely on the abolition of tariffs, on the brotherhood of the nations resulting from free trade in the products of industry.'[27] Cobden felt certain that 'free trade, by perfecting the intercourse and securing the dependence of countries one upon another, must inevitably snatch the power from the governments to plunge their people into wars.'[28] He saw a key role for Britain in starting the new world order based on free trade rather than military power. 'In the present day', he had written in 1835, 'commerce is the grand panacea which, like a beneficent medical discovery, will serve to inoculate with the healthy and saving taste for civilisation all the nations of the world.'[29] Eleven years later, in the midst of the campaign against the corn laws, he wrote: 'It is because I do believe that the principle of Free Trade is calculated to alter the relations of the world for the better, in a moral point of view, that I bless God I have been allowed to take a prominent part in its advocacy.'[30] When repeal had been secured, Henry Ashworth told Cobden that he could already see a map in which the countries of Europe were but counties.

The optimism of the Manchester Party that the day was near when all peoples of the world would beat their swords into ploughshares was seen as dangerously misplaced by its critics. Palmerston told Cobden 'it would be delightful if your Utopia could be realized and if all the nations of the earth would think of nothing but peace and commerce, and would give up quarrelling and fighting altogether. But unfortunately man is a fighting and quarrelling animal; and that this is human nature is proved by the fact that republics, where the masses govern, are far more quarrelsome, and more addicted to fighting, than monarchies, which are governed by comparatively fewer persons.'[31] Tories made much of the dangers of the Liberals' naive idealism in foreign affairs which had been implanted by Cobden and Bright. In his Midlothian campaign of 1880, Gladstone felt compelled to scotch their allegation 'that what is called "the Manchester School" is to rule the destinies of this country if the Liberals come to power'. He went on: 'this Manchester School has sprung prematurely to the conclusion that wars may be considered as having closed their melancholy and miserable history, and that the affairs of the world may henceforth be conducted by methods more adapted to the dignity of man.'[32] The belief that the universal practice of free trade would bring about the end of war and the brotherhood of man was never quite as widely accepted by Victorian Liberals as the other ideas advanced by Manchester men. It none the less remained a distinctive feature of the British Liberal mind until 1914, at least, in the form of a horror of protectionism and a fundamental optimism about international relations.

In his pamphlet, *1793 and 1853*, Cobden observed that there seemed little disposition for war among his contemporaries 'with the exception of a lingering propensity to strike for the freedom of some other people'.[33] In that remark he identified what was to become the other main strand in Liberal foreign policy apart from his own Manchester principle of non-intervention. The notion that Britain should actively intervene to assist other nations and peoples struggling for freedom was a well-established principle of foreign policy by the mid-nineteenth century. It had led both Canning and Palmerston as foreign secretaries to support independence movements in Europe. The strong sympathy felt by many Englishmen for the Italian Risorgimento prompted demands for British intervention. The declared object of the People's International League, founded by Stansfeld in 1847, was 'to embody and manifest an efficient public opinion in favour of the right of every people to self-government, and the maintenance of their own nationality'.[34] The idea of Britain's role in the world as an active ally of all movements for freedom commended itself naturally to lovers of liberty, just as the principle of non-intervention appealed to manufacturers.

Not surprisingly, the leading proponent of this view was Mill. In 1849, inspired by the Italian rising against the Austrian Empire, he wrote a pamphlet, *Vindication of the French Revolution of February 1848*, in which he supported the new French Government's appeal to men everywhere who valued freedom to assist in struggles against oppression. It was the duty of every Liberal government or people, he wrote, 'to assist struggling liberalism, by mediation, by money, or by arms, wherever it can prudently do so; as every despotic government, when its aid is needed or asked for, never scruples to aid despotic governments'.[35] Mill qualified his stance somewhat in a later pamphlet, *A Few Words on Non-Intervention* (1859), in which he made it clear that he did not believe Liberals should seek to impose freedom on those who were not already struggling to establish it. Those who did not appreciate the value of free institutions were clearly not ready to govern themselves. Those, however, whose aspirations for self-government were denied by a foreign power, he reiterated, ought to receive positive assistance from other countries in resisting interference in their national affairs.

The ideal of self-government lay at the heart of Mill's thinking about foreign policy, just as it underlay his writings on domestic politics. 'The government of a people by itself has a meaning and a reality,' he wrote, 'but such a thing as government of one people by another does not and cannot exist.'[36] His demand that the principle of self-government should dominate Britain's dealings overseas led him to oppose imperialism and to advocate colonial self-rule and independence. To that extent at least, the lovers of liberty and the Manchester School were agreed. But Mill took his passion for self-government further. By their very nature, most struggles for self-determination were nationalist movements. To Mill nationalism was desirable as a means to the attainment of liberty. To Cobden that seemed a dangerous sentiment.

There was a clear conflict between Mill's call for British intervention in movements for national self-determination and Cobden's strict principles of non-interventionism and internationalism. Debate between the protagonists of these two positions was a recurrent feature of Victorian Liberalism. It first showed itself in 1851 during the visit to Britain of the Hungarian revolutionary Kossuth. Radicals and lovers of liberty like Stansfeld and Mill lauded Kossuth as the heroic leader of a great movement of national self-determination. The Peace Society, however, sought to dampen down his reception by the people which it feared would lead to a wave of anti-Russian feeling. The Crimean War provoked a similar split in the Liberal ranks. Many continued to follow Gladstone's initial view of the war as a crusade against a despotic and reactionary power rather than Cobden and Bright's strict adherence to the principle of non-intervention. The Old Mortality Society was split down the middle with Dicey supporting the war and Green opposing it.

Between them, the ideal of peace and internationalism and the principle of supporting movements for national self-determination effectively dictated the broad direction of Liberal foreign policy between 1865 and 1895. That two potentially conflicting principles were reconciled with reasonable harmony was at least partly because the direction of policy was throughout the period effectively in the hands of one man. As long as he led the party, Gladstone had a dominant influence on Liberal foreign policy. His principles were a happy amalgam of those of Cobden and Mill. He listed them conveniently, in order of priority, in his Midlothian campaign of 1879 as 'just legislation and economy at home, to preserve to the nations of the world the blessings of peace, to strive to cultivate and maintain the Concert of

Europe, avoid needless and entangling engagements, acknowledge the equal rights of all nations, and the foreign policy of England should always be inspired by the love of freedom'.[37]

Economy was perhaps the single most important consideration determining Gladstone's attitude to foreign policy. It underlay his lifelong commitment to reducing armaments. He consistently opposed Palmerston's efforts to increase the Army and Navy. When he came to power he encouraged his first Foreign Secretary, the Earl of Clarendon, to secure an international agreement limiting armaments. Throughout subsequent Liberal administrations he kept spending on defence down to what his opponents regarded as a dangerously low level. It was when his own Liberal colleagues agreed with the Tories and sought to raise spending on the Navy that he finally resigned as Premier and party leader. But economy was not the only factor which led him to oppose increases in armaments. He firmly believed that large standing armies and sabre-rattling diplomacy greatly increased the chances of war. Walter Bagehot described Gladstone as 'the most pacific of our statesmen in theory and in policy'.[38] His commitment to peace was deep, but so also was his devotion to the principle of national self-determination. If Manchester ideas predominated in his outlook, a Millite belief that Britain should help in movements for liberty was not far behind.

Very early on in his Liberal career Gladstone showed he shared the faith of Cobden and Bright in the power of trade to bring nations together. In 1860, as Chancellor of the Exchequer, he succeeded in persuading a very reluctant Cabinet to send Cobden to Paris to negotiate a commercial treaty with France. The ostensible purpose of the treaty, which had originally been proposed by Bright, was to abolish virtually all tariffs between the two countries. Cobden saw it as the first of a series of treaties with other powers which would lower all import and export duties and establish Britain as an entrepôt where Americans, Australians and Asians would come to buy European goods. The main motive for the Anglo–French treaty, however, was political rather than commercial. Both Cobden and Gladstone regarded it as a significant chance to end the traditional enmity across the Channel which had reached a new dangerous pitch as a result of the provocative behaviour of Palmerston who was convinced that the French intended to invade Britain. For Gladstone there was the added advantage that an Anglo–French alliance would help to secure the unity and freedom of Italy, which was threatened by possible hostilities over the French annexation of Nice and Savoy. The treaty represented a first step towards the European

Concert which he sought. He wrote to his wife: 'It is really a great European operation.'[39]

The Manchester School attached considerable significance to the Anglo–French commercial treaty and hoped that it would be followed by further agreements binding the two countries closer together. In a pamphlet, *The Three Panics* (1861), Cobden repeated the argument of *1793 and 1853* that Britain had greatly over-exaggerated the aggressive tendencies of the French and should now regard her as a firm friend rather than a foe. As a practical step towards closer relations, he recommended the mutual abolition of passports. Bright proposed an agreement to limit armaments. 'At least £15 million a year might be saved to the two countries,' he wrote, 'besides the increasing peril of war from those frightful preparations and this incessant military excitement.'[40] The country had not sufficiently lost its Francophobia, however, for such ventures to be remotely feasible even should they have been welcomed across the Channel.

Gladstone was equally enthusiastic about the possibilities of Britain and France drawing closer together. He was a strong supporter of a Channel Tunnel and was 'suffused with shame' when Palmerston turned down a French proposal to build one because he thought it would increase the risk of invasion. He pointed out that 'since the Norman Conquest, the English have invaded France at least ten times as often as the French have invaded England.'[41] Gladstone hoped that the commercial treaty of 1870 would lead to the eventual establishment of a European common market and political union which France and Britain would take the initiative in creating. This was a constant object of his foreign policy. Towards the end of his life a friend noted: 'Mr. Gladstone has stated publicly, not once nor twice, his well-known sympathy for France, and his belief that England and France, two national civilisations more essentially alien, more deeply internationally influential in past and present than any two others, might together perform a great worth for universal civilisation.'[42]

Gladstone also showed early in his Liberal career that he was firmly attached to the Cobdenite principle of settling disputes with other countries by negotiation or arbitration rather than by a show of military strength. In 1861 he played some part in moderating the tone of British protests about the removal by the United States authorities of two Confederate agents from a British ship, the *Trent*. Had Palmerston had his way, the *Trent* affair might have led to war with America. Instead, it was settled amicably with the two captured envoys being released. Ten years later Gladstone played a much larger part in averting what was potentially a more serious conflict when he insisted that the *Alabama* affair be dealt with by international arbitration. The *Alabama* was a British ship which had been allowed to escape from Liverpool Docks to carry on piracy on behalf of the rebel Confederate states during the American Civil War. When the United States sank the *Alabama* in 1864, the Americans demanded substantial British compensation for the damage which it had done to their commerce. British public opinion was strongly opposed to meeting the American claims which were regarded as wildly excessive, and many people felt that the 'Yankee sharpers' should be taught a severe lesson for daring to insult the British flag. Gladstone, however, was adamant that the whole matter should be settled by an international tribunal.

In September 1872 five arbitrators at Geneva awarded the Americans £3,250,000 in damages. Although he regarded the award as somewhat excessive, Gladstone instantly ordered the money to be paid and incurred considerable unpopularity as a result. The sum involved, he said, 'is dust in the balance compared with the moral value of the example set when these two great nations of England and America, which are among the most fiery and most jealous in the world with regard to anything that touches national honour, went in peace and concord before a judicial tribunal to dispose of these painful differences rather than resort to the arbitrament of the sword'.[43]

Gladstone established an important principle of Liberal foreign policy in settling by independent arbitration the disputes between the British and United States governments arising out of the American Civil War. He strongly advocated that the same method should settle the disputes between Britain and Russia which made up the perennial Eastern Question. Disraeli believed that the protection of India and the preservation of a favourable balance of power in the East demanded British aggression and intervention. His 'forward' policy in the 1870s gained much public support and was the subject of a popular music-hall song, 'We don't want to fight, but by Jingo if we do', which added the word 'jingoism' to the English language. Gladstone consistently opposed it, calling instead for the disputes between Britain and Russia to be referred to an impartial European tribunal. In 1885 he persuaded the Russians to submit their claim to occupy Afghanistan to international arbitration rather than risk the war that many in Britain were clamouring for.

In his colonial and imperial policy, Gladstone was closer to Mill than to Cobden and Bright. His guiding principle of self-government led him to eschew imperialism but at the same time to support the continued existence of the British Empire. His ideas on colonial matters were formed before he became a Liberal during his time as Parliamentary Under Secretary for the Colonies in 1835 and as Colonial Secretary in 1845–6. He came to see the granting of self-government to the colonies as the means of preserving the unity of the Empire. He was a keen admirer of what he took to be the Greek ideal of empire, a loose union of self-governing, self-defending, free-trading, democratic states bound together by affection and respect for the mother country.

Gladstone set out his imperial and colonial policy in a speech to the Mechanics' Institute in Chester in 1855. He began by making clear his belief that 'the lust and love of territory have been among the greatest curses of mankind' and by condemning colonization undertaken to increase the military, political or economic power of the mother country or for reasons of national prestige. It was none the less desirable, he maintained, for Britain to establish and maintain colonies: 'We think that our country is a country blessed with laws and a constitution that are eminently beneficial to mankind, and if so, what can be more to be desired than that we should have the means of reproducing in different portions of the globe something as like as may be to that country which we honour and revere?' Britain should not interfere with her colonies, they should be encouraged to govern themselves wherever possible, but they should be maintained as colonies all the same. British colonization, said Gladstone, should be 'the reproduction of a country in which liberty is reconciled with order, in which ancient institutions stand in harmony with popular freedom, and a full recognition of popular rights, and in which religion and law have found one of their most favoured homes'.[44]

If those remarks sounded dangerously imperialistic to Cobden, to the Tories they betokened a willingness to break up the Empire. Throughout Gladstone's leadership the Liberals were portrayed by their opponents as Little Englanders bent on destroying Britain's imperial greatness by their refusal to annex new dependencies and their haste to give self-government to existing colonies. 'If you look at the history of this country since the advent of Liberalism forty years ago,' Disraeli told his audience in the Crystal Palace in 1872, 'you will find that there has been no effort so continuous, so subtle, supported by so much energy, and carried on with so much ability and acumen, as the attempts of Liberalism to effect the disintegration of the Empire of

England.'[45] Nor was it only the Tories who felt that Gladstone was too much influenced by the Manchester School idea that Empire was a source of weakness rather than strength. In 1877 A. V. Dicey, in an article in the *Nineteenth Century* advocating the British occupation of Egypt to safeguard possession of India, argued that Britain owed its power and greatness to the fact that it was an imperial nation. Gladstone replied, in terms that would have delighted Cobden, that 'the central strength of England lies in England.'[46]

The twin themes of granting self-government to existing colonies and resisting the acquisition of new dependencies dominated the policies and actions of Gladstone's first two governments. In 1871 the Cape of Good Hope was given responsible government and in 1873 Australia and New Zealand were allowed to impose their own duties and tariffs. In a debate on Fiji in 1872 Gladstone laid down the maxim that 'Her Majesty's Government would not annex any territory, great or small, without the well understood and expressed wish of the people to be annexed, freely and generously expressed.'[47] In the event, the first Liberal Government annexed Fiji, the Malay straits and the South African diamond fields in response to the demands of traders and missionaries. This was nothing, however, to the annexations made by the Conservatives between 1874 and 1880, which were roundly condemned by Gladstone in the Midlothian campaign. During the second Liberal Government much of Disraeli's empire building was undone. British troops were withdrawn from Afghanistan, which had become a virtual British protectorate in 1879. The Transvaal, which Disraeli had annexed in 1877, was given back to the Boers in 1881, and Cyprus, another of the Tories' acquisitions, was given self-government. Gladstone surrendered Britain's imperial supremacy in South Africa by granting effective 'Home Rule' to the Afrikaners and made an important concession in the Caribbean by granting self-government to Jamaica. In India, the Viceroyalty of Lord Ripon from 1880 to 1884 marked a brief Liberal attempt to train the natives to govern themselves.

There was, however, one imperial commitment which Gladstone's second Government inherited from the Tories and which, far from shedding, it actually increased. In 1875 Disraeli had purchased shares in the Suez Canal and had established dual control with France over Egyptian finances, thus making Egypt effectively an Anglo–French protectorate. This action provoked a nationalist revolt led by Arabi Pasha which confronted Gladstone when he came to power in 1880. On his past record, Gladstone might have been expected to give in to the nationalists' demand for self-government or refer the matter to arbitration. Instead, in 1882, he took the Palmerstonian course of ordering the bombardment of Alexandria and sending out a military expedition to crush the revolt. So began a British military presence in Egypt that did not end until withdrawal from the canal zone in 1953. That was not all. In 1884 Gladstone was obliged to send a force under General Charles Gordon to the Sudan to crush a revolt led by a Muslim fanatic, the Mahdi, which threatened the stability and security of Egypt. Underestimating his opponents and overestimating his own resources, Gordon found himself cut off at Khartoum. With extreme reluctance, and after considerable delay, Gladstone sent out a relief force under Sir Garnet Wolseley. It arrived at Khartoum two days after Gordon had been killed. Gladstone found himself an object of almost universal contempt, with most of the public joining the Queen in blaming his dilatoriness for the death of a great British soldier, and the Radicals and Nonconformists cursing him for ever becoming involved in such imperial and military adventures.

There are several explanations for Gladstone's extraordinary decision to occupy Egypt and send soldiers to the Sudan. He saw the revolt led by the Mahdi as a movement of violent fanaticism rather than a manifestation of genuine nationalism. He was under extreme public pressure to take a hard line in Egypt after being accused of being too 'soft' on the Irish and the Boers. Moreover, he saw the immense strategic and economic importance of the Suez Canal. Gladstone maintained that he never regarded the British occupation as anything more than an unfortunate temporary expedient although he made preparations for a more permanent presence, sending out Baring to reconstruct the administration. The truth is that he was plagued by indecision and committed Britain without ever really knowing why. Undoubtedly he hoped for quick British withdrawal and the settlement of the Egyptian question by joint agreement between the European powers. In that hope he was frustrated by the French, who had pulled out of what should have been a joint expedition against the Mahdi, and the Germans, who were themselves bent on annexing Africa. Ultimately Gladstone fell victim to the New Imperialism and the scramble for Africa that overtook Europe in the last two decades of the nineteenth century, and which found friends among a rising group of Liberals. Some, however, felt that Gladstone was himself the instigator rather than the victim of the New Imperialism which accorded so ill with the traditions of Liberal foreign policy. When he occupied Egypt, John Bright resigned from the Cabinet convinced that his leader had abandoned one of the most sacred tenets of Liberalism.

There was, surprisingly, one important issue in the 1880s over which Bright was much more of an 'imperialist' than Gladstone. While he recognized the demand for self-government in the colonies, Bright could not understand why the Irish wanted Home Rule and were not content with full representation in the Imperial Parliament at Westminster. Gladstone, on the other hand, conceived Ireland as a colonial problem. In his first Commons speech on Home Rule, in April 1886, he declared, 'The principle that I am laying down I am not laying down exceptionally for Ireland. It is the very principle upon which, within my recollection, to the immense advantage of the country, we have not only altered, but revolutionised our method of governing the colonies . . . . England tried to pass good laws for the colonies; but the colonies said, "We do not want your good laws; we want our own." We admitted the reasonableness of that principle . . . we have to consider whether it is applicable to the case of Ireland. . . . I ask that we should practise, with firm and fearless hand, what we have so often preached, the doctrine which we have so often inculcated into others, namely, that the concession of local self-government is not the way to sap or impair, but the way to strengthen and consolidate unity.'[48]

The policy of Home Rule for Ireland was inspired by Mill's principle of national self-determination. Gladstone told Georges Clemenceau, the French Radical politician, in 1882 that, 'We are now going to produce a state of things which will make the humblest Irishman realize that he is a governing agency and that the government is to be carried on by him and for him.' He regarded the Irish demand for self-government as particularly urgent because it sprang from a powerful sense of oppression under British rule and, in his view, 'there can be no more degrading spectacle upon earth than the spectacle of oppression, or of wrong in whatever form, inflicted by deliberate act of a nation upon another nation.'[49]

Although Ireland with its exceptional problems and its strong and politically powerful nationalist movement naturally took up most attention, many Liberals were committed to extending the principle of Home Rule to Scotland and Wales as well. In 1877 Sir George Campbell, M.P. for Kirkcaldy, proposed a federal system of government for the United Kingdom with a tribunal in Edinburgh to deal with all specifically Scottish legislation. Three prominent Liberal peers, the Duke of Argyll, the Earl of Fife and Lord Rosebery, were keen advocates of devolving legislation and government to Scotland.

The main pressure for Welsh Home Rule came from the *Cymru Fydd* (Young Wales) movement, which was started in the early 1880s and led by Tom Ellis. In 1886 Ellis became Liberal M.P. for Merioneth, having put a demand for Home Rule for Wales in his election manifesto. Stuart Rendel, M.P. for Montgomeryshire and a close friend of Gladstone, was another ardent Welsh devolutionist. Nonconformity played an important part in fanning nationalist sentiment in Wales and it was significant that the first piece of legislation which treated the principality as a country rather than as a region was the Welsh Sunday Closing Act of 1881 which shut public houses on the Sabbath.

Gladstone himself was very sympathetic to demands for both Scottish and Welsh Home Rule. In 1885 he established a separate Scottish Office with a Secretary of State in the Cabinet and substantial powers over home affairs, local government and education. The following year in his *Home Rule Manifesto* he declared his support for the principle of self-government for the component nations of the United Kingdom and his belief that Home Rule could be given to Scotland and Wales without the painful controversy which was threatening its introduction in Ireland.

In fact, partly because of the overwhelming nature of the Irish problem, and partly because of apathy and resistance among English Liberals, progress towards Scottish and Welsh self-government was only made very slowly. Although in 1887 the Scottish Liberal Association adopted Home Rule as its official policy, the only substantial concession that it won from Gladstone was the establishment in 1894 of a standing committee of Scottish M.P.s to consider all legislation relating to the country. The Welsh did not achieve even that until 1907, despite the fiery nationalism of the young David Lloyd George. The establishment of a Welsh Office with a Secretary of State on the Scottish model, which was first proposed in Parliament in 1892 by Alfred Thomas, M.P. for East Glamorgan, did not come until 1964. Many Liberals retained their commitment to administrative and legislative devolution in the United Kingdom, and there were serious attempts to give self-government to Scotland and Wales on the eve of the First World War, but their proposals never reached the statute book.

The championship of national self-determination against foreign oppression was a constant theme of Gladstonian foreign policy. It had, after all, been support for Italian reunification that had finally taken

Gladstone into the Liberal party. On the outbreak of the Franco–Prussian war, he obtained agreements from both parties to respect the sovereignty and neutrality of Belgium. It was agreed that if either side violated Belgian independence Britain would co-operate with the other to restore it. After the war, Gladstone strongly opposed Prussia's proposed annexation of Alsace and Lorraine not, as Palmerston would have done, because it threatened the balance of power in Europe, but because it involved 'the transfer of the allegiance and citizenship of no small part of the heart and life of human beings from one sovereignty to another without any reference to their own consent'.[50] He tried unsuccessfully to take the Cabinet with him in proposing a plebiscite supervised by the neutral powers of Europe to establish the wishes of the people of the affected areas.

Gladstone was particularly moved by the struggles for self-determination being waged by the peoples of central and eastern Europe who were under Turkish rule. As Christians facing oppression from a barbarian imperial power, they had an obvious appeal to him. During the 1870s he canvassed the notion of giving the provinces 'local liberty and self-government' while retaining Turkey's titular sovereignty over them and maintaining the territorial integrity of the Ottoman Empire. He hoped that British influence could secure concerted European action 'for the effectual deliverance of these Provinces from oppression, but not for their transfer to any foreign domination'.[51] The other European powers, however, did not share his passionate interest in the self-determination of the Turks' subject peoples and failed to intervene when they were oppressed.

The most celebrated of the campaigns which Gladstone waged on behalf of the oppressed subject peoples in the Ottoman Empire was, of course, the agitation over the Bulgarian atrocities in 1876–8. The way that Liberals divided over this issue gives an interesting indication of the extent of the support for Gladstonian foreign policy and also provided an early warning of the serious split which was to take place later within the movement. As well as the Nonconformists, lovers of liberty like Stansfeld, Mill, Fawcett and G. O. Trevelyan, and working-class radicals like George Howell backed Gladstone's campaign, as did sensitive literary men like Trollope and William Morris. The agitation over the Bulgarian atrocities, in fact, brought Morris briefly into the Liberal movement. He became treasurer first of the Eastern Question Association, and then, in 1879, of the National Liberal League, which brought together Radicals and working-class leaders who had been actively involved in the campaign. Bright and W. E. Forster, on the other hand, although horrified by the Turkish massacres, kept out of the agitation on strict Manchester principles of non-intervention. The Positivists, led by John Morley, were uneasy about Gladstone's bias towards Christianity and his Russophilia. More significantly, a group of Liberal intellectuals led by Benjamin Jowett, James Fitzjames Stephen, A. V. Dicey and Walter Bagehot had profound doubts about the Bulgarians' capacity to benefit from self-government and saw that supporting the Balkan rising might have considerable implications in terms of attitudes to property rights and sovereignty at home and in Ireland. In their doubts as to the suitability of Gladstone's utopian international morality and unquestioning patronage of movements for national freedom in the rough conditions of the late nineteenth century lay the origins of Liberal imperialism.

Gladstone's campaigns on behalf of oppressed countries and peoples struggling for self-determination had an undeniably romantic appeal. In 1877 Tennyson was inspired after a meeting with the Liberal leader to compose his sonnet on the Montenegrins, in which he praised the struggle against the Turks of the 'smallest among peoples'. In 1892 one of the largest crowds ever gathered together in Wales stood on the windy foothills of Snowdon for several hours while Gladstone delivered a speech on 'Freedom and Small States'. The title and the venue were both appropriate. It was the struggle of the small states of Europe for independence which most appealed to Gladstone. Nowhere did he find a warmer response than in Wales, where he recognized the attributes which qualified a people for self-rule and self-determination: 'Among them are race, religion, language, history, sympathy or antipathy in character, geographical proximity, internal conformation of the country, material wants and interests, relief from internal difficulties, relations to the outer world; last, and perhaps most of all, that peculiar sentiment of nationality, which modern civilization has done so much to develop, and which almost assumes, in and for a nation, the office which conscience discharges for the individual, as the tribunal of ultimate appeal. It is not a mere sentiment of race . . . it is not simply an ambition to attain independence. In order to ascend to the honours of nationality, there must be all the necessary conditions of what may be termed collective or corporate individuality, tested by reason, and sufficiently confirmed by history.'[52]

The concept of nationality lay at the heart of Gladstone's foreign policy. When he affirmed his belief in a speech in Swansea in 1889 that

'Welsh nationality is as great a reality as English nationality', he was saying that there existed in Wales a definitive individualism, a conscience and a sense of responsibility which justified and demanded self-determination.[53] This exaltation of nationality owed much to the ideas of Mill and Mazzini. In *Considerations on Representative Government* Mill had argued that the principle of representative government could not be separated from that of national self-determination, and that 'the boundaries of governments should coincide in the main with those of nationalities.'[54] Mazzini had reconciled the incompatibility between the Utilitarian liberal call for the greatest happiness of the greatest number and its appeal to the self-regarding instinct of the individual as the basis on which society should be constructed by demanding a loyalty greater than that of mere self-interest. His idea of loyalty to the nation, conceived not simply in racial, geographical or linguistic terms but as a moral entity, made a deep impression on Gladstone.

Not all those Liberals who normally followed his views shared Gladstone's belief in nationalism. In an essay on *Nationality* (1862), Acton pointed out that it was not necessarily compatible with liberty. When fused with popular sovereignty, he suggested, it could strengthen the absolutist tendencies of modern democracy. Too often nationalist movements were accompanied by a harsh intolerance towards minority groups inhabiting the same state, as was displayed, for example, by the Magyars in Hungary. 'If we take the establishment of liberty for the realisation of moral duties to be the end of civil society,' Acton wrote in his *History of Freedom*, 'we must conclude that those states are substantially the most perfect which . . . include various distinct nationalities without oppressing them.'[55]

Acton saw clearly that the rising nationalist tide in the late nineteenth century was a movement for strength and unity rather than freedom. He wrote to Gladstone in 1888: 'I should be afraid to admit the priority of National Independence before individual liberty, of the figurative conscience before the real. We do not find that Nationalists are always Liberals, especially in Austria.'[56] Nationalist movements in the old Habsburg Empire were to lead to the First World War and to the destruction of the Liberal world order. Yet when Britain entered the war it was on the quintessentially Gladstonian issue of preserving the neutrality and independence of the small state of Belgium. National self-determination had more than one face.

It was ironic that while Acton criticized Gladstone for being too

nationalistic in his outlook, the Tories accused him of being an internationalist. They constantly complained that the Liberals determinedly
championed the national interest of almost every country in the world
except their own. Disraeli observed that Gladstone's behaviour over the
Eastern Question rested on a false belief that 'the people of this country
are deeply interested in humanitarian and philanthropic considerations',
when in fact their main interest lay 'in a determination to maintain the
Empire of England'.[57] Lord Salisbury even criticized Gladstone in the
1880s for advocating concerted action by the great powers to civilize
Turkey on the Cobdenite grounds that it was in Britain's interest to
keep out of all foreign entanglements, however noble their purpose
might appear.

The truth was that Gladstone's outlook was neither simply nationalistic nor internationalist. It was perhaps more than anything else
European. From his own deep immersion in its Christian and classical
foundations, Gladstone conceived of Europe as having a cultural, moral
and spiritual unity. After the Crimean War he developed the notion of
'a European conscience expressed by the collective guarantee and
concerted action of the European powers' to check tendencies towards
aggression or aggrandizement on the part of any one power.[58] In 1878
he declared his central faith in 'the pursuit of objects which are European, in concert with the mind of the rest of Europe and supported by
its authority'.[59] The idea of the Concert of Europe was perhaps
Victorian Liberalism's most original and important contribution in the
field of international relations.

The notion of a European Concert to guarantee collective security was
not, of course, new. Castlereagh and others had instituted the Congress
system after the Napoleonic Wars, and Palmerston regarded the formal
association of the European powers as a key element in maintaining the
balance of power. But while these earlier ventures were based on secret
diplomacy and self-interest, Gladstone's vision of the Concert of
Europe was of a family of nations brought together by a common
moral consensus to uphold principles of law and justice. 'In moral forces,
and in their growing effect upon English politics, I have a great faith,'
Gladstone wrote. 'There is but one way of maintaining permanently
what I may presume to call the great international policy and law of
Europe, but one way of keeping within bounds any one of the powers
possessed of such strength as France, England or Russia, if it be bent on
an aggressive policy, and that is, by maintaining not so much great
fleets, or other demonstrations of physical force, which I believe to be

really an insignificant part of the case, but the moral union—the effective concord of Europe.'[60]

Gladstone felt that his Concert of Europe would ensure the security of its individual members. After the Franco–Prussian War, he confidently declared: 'It is idle to pretend that [the Prussians] have before them a career of universal conquest or absolute predominance, and that the European family is not strong enough to correct the eccentricities of its peccant and obstreperous members.'[61] But the Concert was for him much more than a mere instrument for guaranteeing national security. It was the agent through which moral crusades would be channelled to settle disputes peacefully and to liberate the oppressed. 'Certain it is,' he wrote in 1870, 'that a new law of nations is gradually taking hold of the mind, and coming to sway the practice, of the world; a law which recognises independence, which frowns upon aggression, which favours the pacific, not the bloody settlement of disputes, which aims at permanent and not temporary adjustments; above all, which recognises, as a tribunal of paramount authority, the general judgement of civilised mankind.'[62] It was in the collective judgement of Europe, the home of civilization, that Gladstone felt that tribunal lay, although he was less than clear about the practical reality of how its judgement could be reached or implemented.

In this optimistic spirit, Gladstone constantly appealed to the collective moral sense of Europe to forward the progress of peace and liberty in the world. In 1856 he had called for a European guarantee of the rights of the Turks' Christian subjects in the Balkans. In 1870 he wrote about the proposed annexation of Alsace and Lorraine: 'I am much oppressed with the idea that this transfer of human beings like chattels should go forward without any voice from collective Europe.'[63] In 1877 he tried to invoke the public law of Europe to condemn the Bulgarian atrocities and attempted to secure the deliverance of the oppressed Turkish provinces at the hands of 'the great Council of Europe'. In this he had the strong support of W. T. Stead who advocated 'the use of the Allied Forces of all the European powers to compel the Turks by the use of their overwhelming force to obey the mandate of civilisation as formulated by the nearest approach to an International Court that the world has yet seen'.[64] In 1880 Gladstone secured his one and only success in obtaining concerted action from the European powers when a conference of ambassadors in Berlin produced an agreed policy on Turkish evasions of clauses in the Treaty of Berlin prescribing boundary changes in favour of the Greeks and

Montenegrins. Saburov, the Russian ambassador, remarked, 'Behold at last, the realization of the philosophers' dream. The Concert of Europe is established.'[65]

Although it was too optimistic and unrealistic ever to become established in the atmosphere of growing nationalism and militarism at the end of the nineteenth century, Gladstone's vision of a Concert of Europe became more of a reality in the twentieth century. As early as 1875 John Morley had argued that in the face of growing militarism peace in Europe would only be secured, 'if it can be secured at all, by a league of pacific powers, not afraid to wage war against the aggressor'.[66] In the years leading up to 1914, and even more in the terrible years that followed it, Morley, Sir Edward Grey, the Foreign Secretary, and other Liberals evolved the idea of a formal and institutionalized League of Nations to guarantee the collective security and peaceful development of Europe and the world.

The attitude of younger Liberals towards the First World War shows the persistence of the conflict between the principle of non-intervention and the ideal of fighting to preserve the independence of small states. While John Morley and others like Francis Hirst and J. A. Hobson adhered to a strict Cobdenite view and opposed the declaration of war with Germany, Grey, H. W. Massingham, L. T. Hobhouse and J. L. Hammond welcomed Britain's intervention on behalf of Belgium. After the war, the creation of the League of Nations helped to reconcile the conflict within Liberalism by providing a formula for both guaranteeing the sovereignty of small nations and promoting internationalism and peace. Those who supported the League in the 1920s and 1930s had no doubt as to its origins. In the dark days of 1936 Hammond wrote an essay on 'Gladstone and the League of Nations Mind' and called for the spirit of the Grand Old Man to visit Geneva where representatives of the great powers were gathered. Two years later he was horrified when Neville Chamberlain betrayed the Czechs in the Munich agreement and so contravened the principles of Gladstone.

If the League of Nations was one important legacy of Victorian Liberal foreign policy, then so also was the idea of a politically united Europe. Curiously, Gladstone himself was always reticent about giving institutional form to his concept of the Concert of Europe and had left it to other Liberals to point out the political implications of what he said. In 1876 Bright called for 'a more strict and generous and peaceable political union among the nations of Europe'.[67] The greatest advocate of European political unity was Stead, who wrote in his autobiography

apropos of Gladstone's great principal: 'I was ever anxious to aid in
the development and strengthening of the principle of the European
Concert which seemed to me the germ of the United States of Europe.'[68]

In his 'Gospel according to the *Pall Mall Gazette*', Stead wrote: 'The
old doctrine of non-intervention as opposed to the old policy of
intervention was sound. But it is not possible for England to stand
absolutely aloof from the discussion of European questions. We have
ceased to be a military power in the European sense of the word. A
state which perseveres in the system of voluntary military service
cannot enter the lists against nations whose whole manhood is drilled
in arms. We are out of the game, and it is a good thing for us that we
are. Our strength is needed otherwise . . . to labour in season and out
of season in creating a Europe which will be an organic whole, instead
of being, as at present, a more or less anarchic amorphous congeries of
States. The germ of a federated continent exists in the Concert of
Europe. To foster that germ until it attains its full development in the
establishment of the Federated United States of Europe is the special
role of English statesmanship.'[69] It is interesting to reflect that if the
Liberals had been in power in the middle of the twentieth century,
Britain would have been one of the founder nations of the European
Economic Community and perhaps the one most committed to the
establishment of a federal political union.

Chapter 6

Trust the People

'What do I understand by the Liberal principle?' Gladstone asked rhetorically in a speech in Chester in 1865. 'I understand, in the main, it is a principle of trust in the people only qualified by prudence. By the principle which is opposed to the Liberal principle, I understand mistrust of the people, only qualified by fear.'[1] In an abbreviated form, those words are carved beneath his bust in the porch of the National Liberal Club in Whitehall, an institution which itself epitomizes this central feature of Victorian Liberalism, having been set up specifically for middle-class men from the provinces rather than the usual upper-class habitués of London's clubland.

Trust in the people was the force which animated Gladstonian Liberalism and sustained its attack on the aristocracy and the traditional bastions of power. It inspired the Liberal demand for extension of the franchise and made self-government the great Liberal ideal in domestic as well as foreign policy. James Bryce described T. H. Green as 'a thorough-going Liberal, full of faith in the people, an advocate of pretty nearly every measure that tended to democratize English institutions'.[2] Millicent Garret Fawcett, the suffragette and wife of Henry Fawcett, wrote: 'I am a Liberal, because Liberalism seems to me to mean faith in the people, and confidence that they will manage their own affairs far better than those affairs are likely to be managed for them by others.'[3]

The Liberals' faith in the people was based on what they took to be the demonstrable earnestness, intelligence, political maturity and sense of responsibility of the Victorian working man. While the Tories tended to see the working classes as deferential and stupid, to be won over by appeals to their prejudices and with bread and circuses, the Liberals had an altogether less cynical and patronizing attitude. They regarded the masses possibly with less affection but with more respect, seeing in them those virtues of self-reliance and rationality which they particularly valued and which they found conspicuously lacking in the higher classes of society. Among Liberal intellectuals particularly, the moral and mental superiority of the working classes was a constant subject of comment. Mill wrote of 'the greater mental honesty, and amenability to reason' shown by the lower classes.[4] John Morley argued in the *Fortnightly Review* in 1870 that 'in foresight, cearnless, consistency, and the other elements of political capacity, the workmen have not been less but more endowed with vision [than other classes], and to get to the depths of political ignorance and conceit one must fathom the opinion . . . of the clergy, the peerage and the journalists.'[5] Gladstone, who based many of his political campaigns on appeals to the people over and against the 'upper ten thousand', told his friend Madame Novikov in 1876 that 'though virtue of splendid quality dwells in high regions with individuals, it is chiefly to be found on a large scale with the masses.'[6]

This faith in the people was not just the result of a romantic idolization of the sturdy virtues of the labourer against the effete values of the aristocrat, although there were elements of that among the Liberal intellectuals in particular. It derived principally from an awareness of recent social and political developments in Britain. During the middle years of the nineteenth century a number of different factors had combined to bring about a significant rise in the self-reliance and political maturity of a substantial section of the working class. The most important was the overall rise in national prosperity which brought large numbers of people out of poverty and into a condition where they could think beyond their immediate material needs. The development of working-men's clubs, the first of which was started in Brighton in 1848, with their attendant friendly and benefit societies, and the rise of the Co-operative movement, which is generally taken to have begun with the Rochdale Pioneers in 1844, showed an impressive commitment among the working classes to the virtues of self-help, thrift and responsibility. The same virtues were further spread by the growing popular hold of Nonconformity and the temperance movement. Higher prosperity and improved educational standards produced a rising rate of literacy, while the advent of a cheap daily press led to the development of a much more informed public opinion.

Liberals were not slow to see the implications of these developments. As early as 1836, in his essay on *The State of Society in America*, Mill had pointed out that 'high wages and universal reading are the two elements of democracy; where they co-exist, all government, except the government of public opinion, is impossible.'[7] Thirty years later Edward Baines asked the Leeds Working Men's Parliamentary Reform

Association: 'Has not the press taken a new start, and popularized all kinds of knowledge—whilst railways and the telegraph cause the pulse of mankind to beat quicker than in any former age? And can we believe that the educated and skilled workmen of England will be content to remain in ignominious exclusion from the franchise? Will ⅚ of the population, of whom a considerable proportion are readers, thinkers, members of Mechanics' Institutes, teachers in Sunday schools, and enrolled in clubs of mutual insurance or as depositors in Savings Banks, long bear to be shut out of the pale of the constitution?'[8]

The practice by at least the upper sections of the working class of the virtues of self-help and self-reliance was a major factor in developing the Liberals' commitment to extending the franchise. Bright was appalled that neither the President nor the Secretary of the Rochdale Equitable Pioneers Society had a vote even though they were entrusted by their members with handling many thousands of pounds. Gladstone seems finally to have been converted to the idea of giving working men the vote in 1864 by a deputation from the Society of Amalgamated Engineers who asked him to modify the rules of the Post Office Savings Bank that he had established so that the Society's funds could be deposited there. Such dedication to thrift could not fail to move the stern economist's heart. A year earlier he had been delighted when another trade union delegation had answered his question as to why they were so inactive over the suffrage question: 'Since the abolition of the corn laws, we have given up political agitation . . . instead of political action we tried to spend our evenings in the improvement of our minds.'[9] When in 1866 he introduced his Bill lowering the borough franchise qualification to £7, he argued that 'Rochdale has probably done more than any other town in making good to practical minds a case for some enfranchisement of the working classes.'[10]

In Liberal eyes, the working classes had grown in political responsibility and judgement as well as in self-reliance during the 1840s and 1850s. They had moved from Chartism to Liberalism. The violent hostility to the middle classes which had characterized working-class politics in the 1830s had ended. In its place there was a new co-operation between working-class and middle-class reformers, against the common aristocratic enemy. Robert Lowery, in the 1830s a leading advocate of working-class unity and a strong opponent of popular participation in middle-class movements, was by the mid-1840s a dedicated member of the Anti-Corn Law League and the Complete Suffrage Movement. Other working-class political leaders, including William Lovett, Henry

Vincent and George Howell, had also rejected Chartism and espoused the Liberal cause. They were undoubtedly influenced by the success of the middle-class agitation against the corn laws compared to the failure of purely working-class struggles. Bright felt that the activities of the Anti-Corn Law League had taught the people 'that the way to freedom is henceforward not through violence and bloodshed, and that there is in public opinion a power much greater than that residing in any particular form of government'.[11] Certainly the more politically aware members of the working class came to realize that their best hope lay in joining and seeking to influence the rising middle-class Liberal movement. G. J. Holyoake, perhaps the greatest mid-nineteenth-century advocate of working-class Liberalism, told an audience of Chartists in the 1850s that 'the enfranchisement of the working class, for which Francis Place worked so unceasingly, could not come—in the ordinary course of things English—until the middle class had succeeded in their contest with their feudal masters.'[12]

Many in the working class threw themselves in the 1840s and 1850s into the Liberal battle against the aristocracy, joining the Anti-Corn Law League and the Association for the Repeal of Taxes on Knowledge, backing the movement for economical government and Civil Service reform and supporting Cobden and Bright's attack on Palmerston's foreign policy. In the process, they found that the middle-class Liberal reformers shared many of their own aims, such as the destruction of privilege, the lowering of prices and taxes, and the promotion of peace and internationalism abroad. In particular, they found not only that Gladstone stood for those values of self-improvement and self-reliance that they themselves most cherished, but also that he brought about reforms which directly benefited them, such as the ending of duties on basic foods and the creation of a cheap press. The legend of the People's William was beginning to be born. Gladstone's trust of the people was at least partly the result of their unshakeable trust in him.

The popular acclaim which greeted Gladstone's public appearances in the early 1860s did much to confirm the Liberals' trust of the people. On the eve of a visit to Newcastle by Gladstone in 1862, Holyoake whipped up popular support with a series of adulatory articles in the local press which proclaimed him to be a unique being, 'a Chancellor of the Exchequer with a conscience'.[13] Gladstone's reception in the city was like nothing ever seen before. Holyoake wrote: 'When he went down the Tyne . . . twenty miles of banks were lined with people who came to greet him. Men stood in the blaze of chimneys; the roofs of factories were crowded; colliers came up from the mines, women held up their children on the banks that it might be said in after life that they had seen the Chancellor of the People go by.'[14] Not even Royalty normally received such treatment, while Holyoake pointedly observed that when Palmerston went to Bradford in the same year the streets were silent. Four years later, after the new Liberal leader had committed himself to giving the vote to working men, the banners carried at a reform demonstration in Hyde Park read: 'Gladstone and Liberty: An Honest Man's the Noblest Work of God.'

Perhaps no single episode did more to strengthen the Liberals' belief that the working class were now politically responsible enough to be given the vote than the support which they saw being given to the North in the American Civil War by the cotton workers of Lancashire. To the Liberals, this seemed a straight case of morality being preferred to self-interest, since the cotton trade was being ruined by the North's blockade of Southern ports. Bright, Bryce and Fawcett in particular were greatly influenced in their views on the franchise by what they took to be the noble altruism of the Lancashire cotton workers. Gladstone referred to it in the speech introducing his Reform Bill of 1866 as 'a magnificent moral spectacle . . . and a great lesson to us all'.[15] In his contribution to the 1867 *Essays on Reform* Richard Hutton, the co-proprietor of the *Spectator*, wrote that the working class had seen 'but one great idea involved in the struggle—that of freedom contending with slavery: and this decided them. Their want of culture stood them in good stead. It acted as a sieve to prevent any smaller considerations permanently influencing their minds; so that they were swayed only by what literary men characterised as "much too simple issues".' In their stand over the American Civil War, Hutton concluded, the working class had conclusively established their right to vote by showing their moral superiority to both the territorial and mercantile classes, neither of whom 'is in the habit of examining political questions by the single light of any great moral principle'.[16]

In fact, recent research suggests that the cotton workers of Lancashire were less altruistic than Liberals imagined. There were no strikes against the use of slave-grown blockade-run cotton. It is true that the Lancashire cotton workers showed genuine virtues in enduring sudden poverty and hardship without resorting to violence, but the idea that they enthusiastically supported the cause of the North seems to have been largely a myth sustained by leading Liberals. The working-class commitment to liberal movements abroad was genuine enough, witness the tremendous reception given to Garibaldi on his visit to England in 1864. None the less, it did not go quite so far against self-interest as some Liberals cared to imagine.

The tendency to romanticize the Lancashire cotton workers' attitude to the American Civil War shows the extent to which Liberal faith in the people had developed by the mid-1860s. In that particular case it reached excessive proportions, but in general it was not misplaced. The upper sections of the working class, the 'labour aristocracy', had become exemplary Liberals in nearly every respect. In their behaviour they manifested the Gladstonian virtues of thrift and self-help. In their attitude to foreign affairs they were generally far more liberal and pacific than the aristocracy. They showed commendable restraint in forwarding their own political and economic interests, preferring gradual reformism to violent revolution or industrial action. They had, indeed, become a virtual adjunct to the Liberal movement. The process was to be completed when George Howell took the Reform League, the one great distinctive working-class political organization, into alliance with the Liberals in 1867 and thereafter made it an election agency of the Liberal party.

The effect that this development had on Liberal views about the franchise is well illustrated by the changing attitude of Edward Baines. In the 1840s he had been a strong opponent of household suffrage. 'We regard the franchise as a political trust,' he wrote, 'and we regard intellectual and moral fitness, and a condition in society above mere dependence, as the qualifications for that trust. . . . Could there be a mistake more fatal than to bring down the substance and staple of the constituency from the educated to the uneducated classes? from classes, a great majority of whom possess considerable information, to classes a large proportion of whom (perhaps a majority) cannot write their own names? from classes accustomed to the management of their own businesses or professions . . . to classes who have been confined to mere manual employment, and have had no pecuniary concerns beyond their weekly or daily wages?'[17]

By 1864, however, Baines's attitude had entirely changed. In that year he introduced a Bill to reduce the borough franchise qualification to a £6 rental. He told the Commons that he was impressed by the great progress that the working class had made over the past thirty years 'in education, in habits of reading, in political knowledge, in habits of association for mutual improvement and insurance, in temperance, in providence and in attendance upon public worship'. He quoted figures to show the extent of this progress. The proportion of children attending day schools had risen from one in eleven in 1833 to one in six in 1861. The number of copies of daily newspapers sold in a year had gone up from $38\frac{1}{2}$ million in 1831 to 546 million in 1864, and the annual circulation of weekly and monthly periodicals had risen from 400,000 to over 6 million. Baines concluded: 'The very class on which we seek to confer the franchise is exactly that upon which almost all those influences to which I have referred are concentrated, viz. the better part of the working classes. . . . I believe they are a thinking, self-reliant and independent body of men.'[18]

During the debate on Baines's Bill Gladstone enumerated what he regarded as the essential qualifications for being granted the vote. They were, he said, 'self-command, self-control, respect for order, patience under suffering, confidence in the law and regard for superiors'. These qualities, he suggested, were now to be found in the working classes. He went on to make the remark that shattered Palmerston and the Whigs and committed the Victorian Liberal party to widening the franchise: 'I venture to say that every man who is not presumably incapacitated by some consideration of personal unfitness or of political danger, is morally entitled to come within the pale of the constitution.'[19] Two years later, as Liberal leader, he introduced a Bill to reduce the borough franchise qualification and told the Commons: 'Whether we take education in schools; whether we take social conduct; whether we take obedience to the law; whether we take self-command and power of endurance; whether we take avidity for knowledge and self-improvement . . . there can be no doubt at all that if the working man was in some degree fit to share in political privileges in 1832 he has, at any rate, attained some degree of additional fitness now.'[20]

The Times accused Gladstone in 1864 of using 'the language of sweeping and levelling democracy'. The *Daily News* felt rather that 'he had unfurled the old, long lost flag of the Liberal Party.'[21] It was true that Parliamentary reform had long been the rallying cry of the Whigs, keeping them together in the dark decades of Tory rule before 1832. Throughout the 1840s and 1850s a few brave spirits had kept alive the commitment to extending the franchise. After the success of the Anti-Corn Law League, Cobden and Bright considered setting up a new league in Manchester to press for Parliamentary reform. From 1854 Lord John Russell carried around in his pocket a Bill for extending the franchise which he hoped to introduce at an appropriate moment.

Bright proposed a Bill in 1858 to confer the borough franchise on all those paying poor rates and on lodgers paying a rental of £10 per annum, to reduce the qualification for the county franchise to an annual £10 rental and to introduce a secret ballot.

Those who proposed Parliamentary reform in the 1840s and 1850s realized that the time was not yet right. 'The extension of the franchise must and will come,' Cobden wrote to Bright in 1851, 'but it chills my enthusiasm upon the subject when I see so much popular error and prejudice prevailing upon such questions as the Colonies, religious freedom and the land customs of our country. I do not mean to say that these thoughts make me for an instant falter in my advocacy of the extension of the franchise, but they make me doubt whether I may not be better employed in trying to diffuse sound practical views, than in fighting for forms or theories of government which do not necessarily involve the fate of practical legislation at all.'[22] It was not only that the working classes had still to prove their moral and intellectual fitness for the franchise. They had also yet to show by responsible political agitation that they actually wanted it. During the 1850s Bright went round calling on the working classes to 'arouse themselves from the political apathy which had hitherto characterised them'.[23] Cobden wrote in 1861: 'So long as five millions of men are silent under their disabilities it is quite impossible for a few middle-class members of Parliament to give them liberty. . . . The middle class have never gained a step in the political scale without long labour and agitation out of doors, and the working people may depend on it they can only rise by similar efforts.'[24]

The organized political action by the working class in support of Parliamentary reform for which Cobden had been waiting came in the 1860s. In 1860 Bright addressed his first reform meeting which had been set up under wholly working-class auspices when he spoke to the newly formed Leeds Working Men's Parliamentary Association. Other towns soon followed suit and established their own working-class organizations to press for an extension of the franchise. The Reform League of 1865 brought together ex-Chartists and trade unionists as well as middle-class sympathizers in a national organization dedicated to the aim of securing manhood suffrage. In 1866 a mass demonstration of working men in favour of reform organized by the League trampled down the railings of Hyde Park when they were denied access. There was now no doubt that the people wanted the vote.

It was the great achievement of John Bright to bring together these two features of the 1860s, the increasing demand of the working classes

for the vote and the realization by middle-class Liberals of the legiti-
macy of that demand. In the autumn of 1866, following the defeat of
Gladstone's Bill and the election of a Tory government, Bright stumped
the country to preach the message of reform to huge working-class
audiences in the major cities of Britain. He denounced aristocratic rule
with a frenzy that delighted his hearers and terrified conservatives of all
kinds. The aristocracy, he told a meeting in Glasgow, 'revels in power
and wealth, whilst at its feet, a terrible peril for its future, lies the
multitude which it has neglected. . . . If a class has failed, let us try the
nation.'[25] To supporters and opponents alike this seemed the dangerous
advocacy of democracy and popular rule. Bright convinced the people
that the Liberals were committed to giving them power.

In fact, his real attitude to the working classes was rather different
from what it seemed from his speeches. It was significant that his attack
was always on privilege and never on poverty, his tone always anti-
aristocratic rather than pro-working class. Every remark that seemed to
hint at democracy and popular rule was qualified. 'I deny altogether
that the rich alone are qualified to legislate for the poor', he said in
Glasgow, 'any more than the poor alone would be qualified to legislate
for the rich.'[26] Bright's real object was, as it always had been, middle-
class rule. He saw that the power of the working class could be used to
help achieve this object and to break the power of the aristocracy. He
genuinely believed that the working classes and middle classes had an
identity of interests, that they both wanted free trade, low taxation,
minimal government, and no intervention abroad. An extension of the
franchise would bring these things about by enabling the middle
classes to rule with working-class support.

Matthew Arnold observed shrewdly in 1867 that 'Mr. Bright . . .
has a foot in both worlds, the world of middle-class Liberalism and the
world of democracy, but brings most of his ideas from the world of
middle-class Liberalism.'[27] Bright certainly used the working-class
agitation for reform in the 1860s to forward the progress of middle-
class Liberalism more than he used the Liberal movement to help the
cause of Parliamentary reform. As Arnold said, 'it is notorious that our
middle-class Liberals have long looked forward to this consummation,
when the working class shall join forces with them, aid them heartily to
carry forward their great works, go in a body to their tea-meetings,
and in short, enable them to bring about their millennium.'[28] The last
thing that Bright and his fellow Liberal advocates of reform wanted
was working-class domination of Parliament. There was no suggestion

that the property qualification for becoming an M.P. should be altered. At the time of his Borough Franchise Bill, Baines wrote to his brother-in-law, 'we need not fear that the Parliament will ever be composed of low class men.'[29]

The spirit of the Liberal call for the franchise to be extended to working men in the 1860s was not, then, a democratic one. The vote was conceived as a privilege rather than a right. None the less, Liberals felt that respectable working men had earned that privilege by their behaviour and their attitudes. They had shown themselves worthy of being trusted with the vote. To that extent, Liberal support for extending the franchise was based on trust of the people. It was founded even more on faith in the effect that the vote would have on those to whom it was given. The Liberals had an extremely exalted notion of the franchise. Arnold observed that Bright 'leads his disciples to believe —what the Englishman is always too ready to believe—that the having a vote, like the having a large family, or a large business, or large muscles, has in itself some edifying and perfecting effect upon human nature'.[30] T. H. Green noted after the passing of the 1867 Reform Act: 'We who were reformers from the beginning always said that the enfranchisement of the people was an end in itself. We said, and were much derided for it, that citizenship makes the moral man; that citizenship only gives that self-respect which is the true basis of respect of others, and without which there is no lasting social order or real morality.'[31]

The notion that the granting of voting power to the people would in itself effect a change in their moral and intellectual qualities underlay the Liberals' commitment to extending the franchise and encouraging self-government. As early as 1851 Edward Miall argued in *The Franchise Considered as a Means of a People's Training* that the extension of the vote would create a thirst for information and education and also lead to a new spirit of independence as people began to undertake for themselves what they had previously relied on the government to provide. The franchise was seen as conferring a sense of responsibility and political maturity. The same argument was later used by Liberals to support local government and Home Rule for Ireland, Wales and Scotland.

Nobody had a higher conception of the moral value of the vote than Mill. For him it was not a right to be used as the voter pleased, but rather a trust which carried 'an absolute moral obligation to consider the interest of the public, not his private advantage, and give his vote to the best of his judgement, exactly as he would be bound to do if he were the sole voter and the election depended upon him alone.'[32] Mill regarded the act of voting as a supreme exercise of moral choice and responsibility in which the individual 'is called upon to weigh interests not his own; to be guided, in case of conflicting claims, by another rule than his private partialities; to apply at every turn, principles and maxims which have for their reason of existence the common good'.[33]

Mill's notion of the moral and educative value of the vote led him to be the foremost exponent in the nineteenth century of the notion of representative government. His ideal was the Greek city state system where all citizens participated in the functions of administration. For this reason he passionately supported institutions like the jury system and elected local councils which involved Englishmen taking part in public duties. Representative institutions were lauded by Mill because they allowed individual citizens to make moral choices and take a hand in running their country. It was for this reason that he differed from Bright and most reforming Liberals over the secret ballot. While they saw secret voting as a safeguard against coercion of voters by employers and those with influence, he regarded an open ballot as the best way of ensuring that the exercise of the vote was seen as a solemn public duty to be performed in the public eye.

The ballot was not the only subject on which Mill differed from other Liberal reformers in the 1860s. His championship of votes for women was not shared by Bright and aroused only lukewarm Liberal support. The campaign for women's suffrage began in 1866 when Mill and Henry Fawcett presented a petition in the Commons signed by 1,499 women demanding the vote. It was led in the country by Lydia Becker, an ardent Manchester Liberal, and in Parliament by John Bright's brother Jacob. The Bill which he introduced in 1870, providing that in all acts relating to qualifications for the vote, 'wherever words occur which import the masculine gender, the same shall be held to include females', actually passed its second reading, but it was subsequently defeated, as was each successive female suffrage Bill introduced annually by Jacob Bright and others during the nineteenth century.[34] Although Liberal and Radical M.P.s contributed the majority of pro-suffrage votes in all divisions on the subject up to 1884, the Liberal leadership, and even progressive Liberals like John Morley and Chamberlain, were firmly opposed to votes for women. Gladstone felt that to give a woman the vote would be to 'trespass upon the delicacy, the purity, the refinement, the elevation of her own nature'.[35]

While Mill was unusual among Liberals in vigorously supporting

women's suffrage, he was also unusual in entertaining grave doubts as
to the desirability of a straight extension of the franchise. He was
worried that without proper safeguards, granting the vote to the masses
as advocated by Bright would lead to less rather than more enlightened
government with the predominance of the mere majority and the
virtual disenfranchisement of minorities. Strongly influenced by de
Tocqueville's unenthusiastic picture of democracy in America, and
Constant's fear of the tyranny of the crowd in France, he foresaw the
triumph of class interest and the rule of the ignorant if the reforming
Liberals' enthusiasm for extending the franchise was allowed to go
unchecked.

Mill set out the safeguards that he felt must accompany the extension
of the franchise in his essay on *Representative Government* (1861). To
prevent universal suffrage, which he admitted to be the most desirable
system of government, from degenerating into the rule of the ignorant,
he proposed two checks. First and foremost, there should be an
educational qualification for the franchise. No one should be allowed
to vote without being able to read, write, and perform a sum in the
rule of three. He admitted his own preference that 'some knowledge of
the conformation of the earth, its natural and political divisions, the
elements of general history, and of the history and institutions of their
own country' should also be required of all electors, but conceded that
those kinds of knowledge were not accessible to the whole population,
and were anyway difficult to test.[36]

As a further device to prevent ignorance from triumphing in a
democratic system, Mill proposed that any future Reform Bill lowering
the financial qualification for voting should at the same time add weight
to the intellectual qualification by giving a plurality of votes to
university graduates, those who had passed creditably through high
school, members of the professions and others who by examination had
shown themselves to have superior knowledge. Mill suggested that this
intellectual weighting should be achieved either by giving the educated
three or four votes against the ordinary man's one, or by allowing them
to register in any constituencies they liked as well as in their home. He
believed that this two-class system of voting would be both acceptable
and beneficial to the electorate: 'The Democracy, at least of this
country, are not at present jealous of personal superiority, but they are
naturally and mostly justly so of that which is grounded on mere
pecuniary circumstances. The only thing which can justify reckoning
one person's opinion as equivalent to more than one, is individual

mental superiority. . . . The distinction in favour of education, right in itself, is further and strongly recommended by its preserving the educated from the class legislation of the uneducated.'[37]

It was not only the educated that Mill feared would be swamped in a democratic system of voting, although they were undoubtedly closest to his heart. He was concerned at the way that all minorities would be under-represented. 'The pure idea of democracy', he wrote, 'is the government of the whole people by the whole people, equally represented. Democracy as commonly conceived and hitherto practised, is the government of the whole people by a mere majority of the people, exclusively represented. . . . Real equality of representation is not obtained unless any set of electors amounting to the average number of a parliamentary constituency, wherever in the country they reside, have the power of combining together to return a representative.'[38] To achieve this pure democracy, Mill advocated the system of proportional representation put forward by Thomas Hare in his book *Election of Representatives* in 1859. Hare proposed that a particular number of electors should be fixed as being entitled to have a representative in Parliament. Electors could then give their votes to any candidate in the country and all candidates receiving the agreed quota of votes would be elected. Votes cast over and above the quota would be redistributed among other candidates according to preferences expressed by the electors. By adopting Hare's scheme, Mill was confident that minorities would be represented and that no loss would result from abandoning traditional geographical constituencies: 'I cannot see why the feelings and interests which arrange men according to localities should be the only ones thought worthy of being represented; or why people who have other feelings and interests, which they value more than they do their geographical ones, should be restricted to these as the sole principle of their political classification.'[39]

It is interesting to note that both of Mill's ideas were applied in the seven university seats which returned twelve M.P.s to the House of Commons until their abolition in 1948. Graduates of the universities could vote both in their home and their university constituencies, and in 1918 proportional representation, in the form of the single transferable vote, was introduced in the four university seats which returned more than one member. This brief use of the single transferable vote has so far been the only application of proportional representation in the English electoral system. The last great Parliamentary Reform Bill, in 1918, included an experimental scheme of proportional

F

representation, but it was defeated in the Commons. The modern British Liberal party is strongly committed to proportional representation, although not on the lines advocated by Mill.

Several other leading Liberals agreed with Mill in the 1860s in stressing the need to ensure that any extension of the franchise did not lead to mob rule. In 1860 Herbert Spencer wrote an article in the *Westminster Review* on 'Parliamentary Reform: the Dangers and the Safeguards' in which he warned that giving the vote to the working classes without any check could lead to less freedom and more legislation. He observed prophetically: 'men who render up their private liberties to the despotic rulers of Trade Unions seem scarcely independent enough rightly to exercise political liberty.'[40] In 1865 George Holyoake in *The Liberal Situation: Necessity for a Qualified Franchise* argued, like Mill, for a plurality of votes to be given to the educated. 'He is not a democrat, but an anarchist,' he wrote, 'who insists that the vote of the most ignorant shall count for as much as that of the most highly educated class in the community.' Holyoake proposed a special intelligence franchise as an addition to any other extension: 'Practical mastery of some sound popular book on Political Economy and one on Constitutional History would secure the requisite intelligence. Government school examiners might attend at mechanics' institutions and give certificates of electoral fitness.'[41]

The strongest Liberal opponent of the extension of the franchise in the 1860s was Robert Lowe. Like Mill and Holyoake, he was concerned that extending the franchise would lead to less enlightened and less liberal government. Eight years in Australia and a visit to America had left him a convinced opponent of democracy. 'Venality, ignorance, drunkenness and facility for being intimidated' were found at the bottom rather than the top of society, he reminded Parliament during the debate on Baines's Borough Franchise Extension Bill in 1865. He went on: 'Because I am a Liberal and know that by pure and clear intelligence alone can the cause of true progress be promoted, I regard as one of the greatest dangers with which the country can be threatened a proposal . . . to transfer power from the hands of property and intelligence and to place it in the hands of men whose life is necessarily occupied with the daily struggle for existence.'[42] The way to elevate the working class, Lowe held, was not to bring the franchise down to their level, but to keep it as something to be earned and saved up for.

Most Liberals, however, for all their misgivings, were ultimately in favour of extending the franchise in the 1860s. Mill, Spencer and

Holyoake all supported Gladstone's 1866 Reform Bill. The opposition of a group of about forty rebel Liberal M.P.s, led by Lowe, however, effectively killed the measure. Gladstone warned them: 'You may bury the Bill that we have introduced but . . . [you] cannot fight against the future. Time is on our side. The great social forces which move onwards in their might and majesty . . . are against you.'[43] In fact, extension of the franchise was to come very much more quickly and in more drastic form than Gladstone had anticipated, and from a surprising direction. In 1867 Disraeli, motivated by a mixture of opportunism, calculation, fear of popular pressure and muddle, carried a Reform Bill introducing household suffrage in the towns and adding one million working men to the electorate.

The 1867 Reform Act inaugurated an era of Liberal rule based on the great principle of mutual trust built up between Gladstone and the people. The voters enfranchised by the Act were in the main those 'respectable' working men who felt most affinity for Gladstone and were natural Liberal voters. Disraeli might have done better to have lowered the franchise qualification even further and, as Cobden had warned that the Tories might do in 1849, 'take their chance in an appeal to the ignorance and vice of the country against the opinions of the teetotallers, nonconformist and rational Radicals, who would constitute $\frac{9}{10}$ of our phalanx of forty shilling freeholders'.[44] As it was, the Act helped the Liberals by not enfranchising the 'lumpen proletariat' who would have been most susceptible to Tory appeals to prejudice and bread and circuses. It also helped them by changing the style of politics so that popularity became of paramount importance. John Morley wrote perceptively in September, 1867: 'The new problem for statesmen will not be how the Queen's Government may be carried on, but how the National Will may be most properly executed.'[45]

Nobody was better placed to benefit from this new situation than Gladstone. His rise to power in the 1850s and 1860s had been based on popular acclaim for his budgetary and administrative measures. His political strength lay far more in the country and far less in Parliament than had that of any previous Prime Minister. Indeed, what distinguished Gladstone's Liberalism from Palmerston's Whiggism was in part its special relationship with the electorate and its appeal 'out of doors'. Gladstone constantly appealed to the people. Traditionally governments had gone to the polls on their capacity to govern. Gladstone went to the country on great issues of principle—the abolition of the income tax in 1874, the foreign policy of Disraeli in 1880, Irish Home Rule in

1886. He put himself at the head of popular movements, as over the Bulgarian atrocities. Disraeli portrayed him as a dangerous populist who told his friends that the way to influence the House of Commons was to 'address the people out of doors'.[46] Stead told him that he was 'the spokesman of the national conscience and the exponent of the sentiments which animate every man worthy of the name'.[47]

Gladstone only occasionally doubted the validity of his rapport with the masses and the wisdom of his appeal to them rather than to the upper classes. He had one such period of doubt after his defeat in 1874 but the popular outburst of 'virtuous passion' over the Bulgarian atrocities soon reconfirmed his faith in the people. In an important article in the *Nineteenth Century* in July 1878 he argued that while the higher classes might have intellectual superiority, the lower classes were generally superior in their moral sense. Looking back over the first Reform Act, the freeing of slaves, the repeal of the corn laws, cheap postage, the relief of the press from taxation, the second Reform Act, the abolition of church rates, and Irish disestablishment, he felt confident in affirming 'that the popular judgement on the great achievements of the last half-century, which have made our age a praise among the ages, has been more just and true than that of the majority of the higher orders'. Characteristically, he found Scriptural authority for his assertion: 'Did Scribes and Pharisees or did shepherds and fishermen yield the first, most and readiest converts to our Saviour and the company of His Apostles?'[48]

The appeal to the people over and against the 'upper ten thousand' reached its apogee in the first Midlothian campaign of 1879 when Gladstone showed that he had more trust and respect for obscure Scottish crofters than for the members of high society. Never before had a politician introduced himself to the electors in a series of public speeches around his constituency. Gladstone did not fill the public halls of Midlothian with promises of immediate material benefits in the manner of a twentieth-century politician. Instead he thrilled his audiences by expounding complicated issues of foreign and domestic policy and appealing to their moral and intellectual judgement. When he was met by a large gathering at Perth railway station after he had returned from giving a speech in the town, he mounted the platform and gave an impromptu but detailed account of the Eastern Question, announcing, 'I have so much reliance on your intelligence as well as upon your patience, that I am confident you will clearly understand what I want to convey to you.'[49] His reliance was not misplaced; the normally

Conservative electors of Midlothian returned him to Parliament in 1880 with a comfortable majority.

Trust in the people was not just an empty slogan of Gladstone's to win elections in an era of mass voting. It was an article of Liberal faith that expressed itself in a fervent commitment to democratizing institutions and achieving a greater degree of popular and responsible control over them. It underlay his opening of the Army and the Civil Service to talent and his insistence on greater Parliamentary and popular control over foreign affairs against Disraeli's secret diplomacy in 'the darkness of the night'.[50] It led him to champion open government and to subject the workings of the Executive to maximum scrutiny and public gaze. He once told Stead that 'publicity is the great advantage, the great security of English political life.'[51] The same inclination to throw political decision-making on to the people rather than keep it as a preserve of the aristocracy inspired Gladstone's long campaign against the power of the House of Lords which began in 1861 when, following its veto on his reduction of newspaper duty, he collected all his tax provisions into a single Bill so that the Upper House was obliged to accept or reject it in toto. This procedure, customary ever since, confirmed the supremacy of the House of Commons in finance that went unchallenged until 1909. During the 1880s the Lords' resistance to the Reform Bill and Irish Home Rule led to persistent Liberal calls for the reform of the Upper Chamber and the ending of its veto. Gladstone's last speech in Parliament in February 1894 was a vigorous attack on the power of the Lords and their ability to frustrate measures passed by the elected representatives of the people.

The principle of trusting the people infused much of the Liberal policy of the 1870s and 1880s. It lay behind devices to make elections more truly democratic and effective, like the introduction of the secret ballot in 1872 and the Corrupt Practices Act of 1883. It inspired the creation of a system of elected local government pioneered by Mundella, Chamberlain and Dilke and begun in 1870 with the establishment of school boards directly elected by ratepayers. It was at the heart of the policy of local option which was seen as a way of achieving popular control over drink. 'The key-note of all Liberalism', George Trevelyan declared in a countrywide tour advocating temperance reform in 1871, 'is the paramount and unlimited authority of popular control.'[52] Chamberlain extended the principle to the Liberal party itself when in 1877, with Gladstone's blessing, he set up the National Liberal Federation on the model of his own Birmingham Liberal Association. 'The

essential feature of the proposed Federation', he told its inaugural
meeting, 'is the principle which must henceforth govern the actions of
the Liberals as a political party, namely, the direct participation of all
members of the party in the formation and direction of policy.'[53]
Chamberlain aimed to give rank-and-file Liberals control over their
M.P.s through their local association and over national party policy
through the Federation's annual conferences. In 1883 Stead stressed the
same theme when he wrote that the leading principle of the home policy
of the *Pall Mall Gazette* during his editorship would be 'to associate
with the responsibilities of government the greatest possible number
of the governed.'[54]

The most direct expression of Liberal trust in the people was the
further significant extension of the franchise in the 1884 Reform Act
which gave the vote to some two million men, most of whom were
agricultural labourers. George Trevelyan had first called for the enfranchisement of the agricultural workers soon after the 1867 Reform
Act. Although Gladstone did not take up the cause until the late 1870s,
the strong vote of confidence that he won in 1886 reassured him that
he had been right to do so. Chamberlain told an audience that the
granting of the franchise to agricultural workers had produced the
sense of political maturity and responsibility that Liberals had predicted: 'When I was in Wiltshire the other day, a gentleman told me
that he had attended a meeting of Wiltshire labourers, and he was
surprised by the quickness and intelligence with which they followed
the speakers; and he said to the man who was standing by him, "How
is it that these labourers understand politics so well?" "Oh," said the
other, "It is because since they got the franchise they have thought of
nothing else. They talk of it by day, they dream of it by night." '
The Liberal dream, it seemed, had come true.[55]

There were, however, an increasing number of people in the 1880s
who felt that the Liberals' trust of the people and their ideas of popular
control had gone too far. Matthew Arnold was worried by Gladstone's
courting of the populace. While he accepted that 'aristocrats are not,
in general, the best guides in politics', he questioned whether 'the
political Dissenters and the Radical working men are any better guides,
or even so good. They know little and prize little beyond the one their
dissent, the other their union for trade or politics.'[56] Critics were
concerned that the Liberals were cultivating an American style of
populism and demagogy. The meetings of the Midlothian campaign
had been based on a Democratic party rally which Rosebery, Gladstone's

election manager, had attended in New York. The National Liberal Federation was modelled on the American party machine. There were considerable fears that the Liberals would bring the corrupt and unseemly practices of Tammany Hall to Britain.

The 1884 Reform Act particularly worried those who saw it opening the flood-gates to democracy. It confirmed James Fitzjames Stephen in his view that the Liberals were progressing towards universal suffrage, a condition which in his view, 'tends to invert what I should have regarded as the natural relation between wisdom and folly' by allowing the foolish to rule the wise.[57] Even staunch Gladstonians were unhappy about the Act. Goldwin Smith criticized it for enfranchising the illiterate and Goschen, who supported it with extreme reluctance, confessed, 'my party seems to breathe an atmosphere of Utopia, and feel a confidence I cannot share.'[58] Acton felt that it was only thanks to the genius of Gladstone that the Act did not lead to class war or mob rule. Even Bright, the great reformer, was worried that the advent of a mass electorate in which the working class formed so large a proportion might lead to the dominance of one sectional interest over all others.

The fact was that there had always been two very different views within the Liberal camp of what extending the franchise involved. Dicey distinguished them clearly in his contribution to *Essays on Reform* in 1867 when he pointed out that for some reformers Parliament chiefly represented classes while for others it chiefly represented individuals. Radicals in the party saw the enfranchisement of the working class as a right. They were quite happy to see the rule of the majority and the dominance of class in politics. Indeed, they wanted Liberalism to lose its traditional individualism and respond to the working-class demand for collectivist economic policies and state-provided social welfare. That outlook was anathema to Gladstonians. They believed in giving working people the vote because, as individuals, they had shown themselves worthy and deserving of exercising it. They were interested in Parliament representing individuals not classes.

The real basis of the Gladstonian trust of the people and preference for popular control was summed up in Bright's phrase that if a class had failed, it was time to try the nation. Class or sectional interest of any kind was widely regarded as the antithesis of Liberalism. Mill had defined class in *Representative Government* as 'any number of persons who have the same sinister interest, that is, whose direct and apparent interest point towards the same description of bad measures'.[59] Acton regarded Locke's great legacy to the English Liberal tradition as 'his idea that the powers of Government ought to be divided according to their nature, and not according to the division of classes'.[60] George Meredith felt the Liberals to be 'the only party that has ever taken a forward step on behalf of the country and in defiance of interested sections', while for Lowe, 'the ideal of the Liberal Party consists in a view of things undisturbed and undistorted by the promptings of interests or prejudice, in a complete independence of class interests.'[61]

During the formative years of Gladstonian Liberalism, the most powerful class interest was represented by the aristocracy. So it was the 'upper ten thousand' whom Bright had attacked in the 1860s and Gladstone had denounced in the Midlothian campaign. By the 1880s, however, a new threat was in John Morley's mind when he cried: 'Do let us try to give a national, not a class tone to English politics.'[62] Labour rather than the aristocracy now seemed in danger of becoming the dominant sectional force in politics. No one was more conscious or worried about this new trend than John Bright, the great architect of the Liberals' trust in the people. He had not hammered the aristocracy and championed the extension of the franchise merely to see another sectional interest take over. In a letter of 1887 he expressed a fear that was beginning to haunt Liberals and make them wonder if their trust in the people had perhaps been misplaced: 'I am not in favour of what is called a Labour party in Parliament. . . . A Parliamentary representative should strive to further the interests of all classes of our people, and to do justice to all. A Parliament divided into sections is less likely to be wise and just than one not so divided. . . . In years past we have had too much of legislation of classes. Landowners and farmers for a generation, from 1815 to 1846, ruled both Houses of Parliament to the great injury of the nation. Let us not return to this system, or to anything like it, under the idea that we shall advance the interests of all classes who live by and from their labour.'[63]

Chapter 7

Lib–Labism

In 1885 Chamberlain described the 'best friends' of the Liberal party as 'the respectable artisans and the Nonconformists'.[1] The 'labour aristocracy' of mid-Victorian Britain was as important an element in the Liberal movement as Nonconformity or free-thinking Radicalism. In many ways, indeed, it was a more integrated and less troublesome one. Among the craft trade union leaders of the 1860s and 1870s were to be found some of the most fervent Gladstonians in the country. George Howell put behind the Liberal party the full force of the Reform League and the Trades Union Congress, of which he was Parliamentary Secretary from 1871 to 1874. Thomas Burt, the miners' leader, became one of the first labour representatives in Parliament when he was elected Liberal M.P. for Morpeth in 1874. Henry Broadhurst, an Oxfordshire stonemason who succeeded Howell as Parliamentary Secretary of the Trades Union Congress in 1874, became the first working-class minister when he was made Under Secretary at the Home Office by Gladstone in 1886. Joseph Arch, who founded the National Agricultural Labourers' Union in 1872, held Gladstone, whom he invariably described as 'my chief', to be 'one of the mighty men of the earth'.[2]

The 'Lib–Labism' represented by trade union leaders like Burt and Arch and by the skilled artisans who followed them in the 1860s and 1870s was also reflected in the attitude and behaviour of enlightened Liberal employers. A. J. Mundella, M. T. Bass and Samuel Morley were strong supporters of trade unionism, the co-operative movement and the principle of resolving industrial disputes by arbitration. Indeed, it was largely thanks to their achievements, and to the advocacy of Mill and Thomas Hughes, that Victorian Liberalism helped to promote these three particular developments which benefited labour in the second half of the nineteenth century. During the period of the mid-Victorian economic boom, the leaders of organized labour were generally happy to work with and through the middle-class industrialists who represented them in Parliament. It was only with the coming of economic decline in the late 1870s that they seriously began to entertain thoughts of seeking separate working-class representation and creating their own labour party.

Skilled labour's identification of interest with the Liberals was based on a shared acceptance of the values of self-help and self-reliance rather than on any feeling that Liberals would promote measures specifically to help working men. Cobden and Bright very early disabused people of that idea with their solid opposition to legislation to shorten hours of work and improve conditions in factories. In 1836 Cobden wrote to a colleague: 'I have sufficient confidence in the growing intelligence of the working classes to be induced to believe that they will now be found to contain a great proportion of minds, sufficiently enlightened by experience to concur with me in the opinion that it is to themselves alone individually that they must trust for working out their own regeneration and happiness. Again I say to them, look not to Parliament, look only to yourselves.'[3] If they disliked conditions in Britain, he added, they need only save £20 to be able to go to the United States, the only market where labour had a higher value.

In the more prosperous decades that followed the hungry forties, the respectable artisans of Britain took Cobden's advice very much to heart, forsaking physical-force Chartism and collaborating in middle-class movements for economic and political reform. The middle years of the nineteenth century saw an explosion of working-class self-help through the setting up of friendly and benefit societies, co-operative ventures and 'model' trade unions. The German social scientist J. M. Baernreither believed that the development of this vast network of voluntary associations had prevented Britain from going through the violent revolution that Engels and other visitors in the 1840s had prophesied as inevitable. In a society 'so pervaded by the power of capital', the working classes had themselves become small capitalists.[4]

Liberals naturally welcomed these expressions of working-class self-help. They were particularly impressed by the co-operative movement. Cobden wrote an article in the 1861 issue of the *Co-Operator* warmly supporting the principle and practice of co-operation as it had been pioneered in his own Rochdale constituency. The first congress of the co-operative movement in 1869 was chaired by Thomas Hughes with Mundella as Vice-Chairman. By then, there were 1,300 co-operative societies with a share capital of £2 million and a trade of £8 million. Gladstone told Holyoake, who was another enthusiastic supporter, that

he 'looked to Co-operation as the new influence which should reconcile the mighty powers of capital and labour'.[5]

The greatest enthusiast in the Liberal ranks for the co-operation
movement was perhaps Mill. In his *Principles of Political Economy* (1848)
he identified the continuing growth of the principle and practice of
co-operation as the most certain indication of progress in society. He
wrote: 'As wealth increases and business capacity improves, we may
look forward to a great extension of establishments both for industrial
and other purposes, formed by the collective contributions of large
numbers, establishments like those called by the technical name of
joint-stock companies, or . . . those associations of workpeople either
for production, or to buy goods for their common consumption, which
are now specifically known by the name of Co-Operative Societies.'[6]
Mill even argued that co-operation would become the dominant form
of economic relationship in Britain. Speculating on 'the probable
future of the labouring classes', he wrote, 'I cannot think that they will
be permanently contented with the condition of labouring for wages
as their ultimate state. . . . The relation of masters and workpeople
will be gradually superseded by partnership, in one of two forms; in
some cases, association of the labourers with the capitalist; in others,
and perhaps finally in all, association of labourers among themselves.'[7]

Several Liberals went along with Mill in advocating the replacement
of the wage relationship by one of co-partnership between employer
and workman. Thomas Hughes, George Holyoake and Henry Fawcett
were leading advocates of the idea of profit-sharing and strongly supported those Liberal employers like Francis Crossley who allowed their
workers to obtain shares at preferential rates. There was considerable
interest in the first serious profit-sharing schemes which were set up in
the mid-1860s by Henry Briggs at Whitwood Colliery in West
Yorkshire and by Edward Greening at the Cobden Memorial Mills in
Lancashire. Both these and other experiments in industrial co-partnership failed, however, in the depression which began in the mid-1870s.
Briggs's scheme foundered in 1874 when trade declined and his workers
struck against threatened wage reductions.

While in the short term profit-sharing failed in Britain because of
industrial depression, in the long term it was killed by the opposition
of trade unionists who regarded it as a device for perpetuating capitalist
ownership. Between 1865 and 1929 there were 635 profit-sharing
schemes, including the large-scale ventures of famous early twentieth-
century Liberal employers like Seebohm Rowntree and William

Hesketh Lever, but nearly all of them foundered on trade union opposition.

If the suspicions of trade unionists killed profit-sharing, then the fears of employers helped to prevent the development of workers' co-operatives. Few Liberals shared Mill's enthusiasm for this ultimate extension of the co-operative principle or the eagerness with which he looked forward in his *Autobiography* to the time 'when it will no longer either be, or thought to be, impossible for human beings to exert themselves strenuously in procuring benefits which are not to be exclusively their own, but to be shared with the society they belong to'. To most of them there was something dangerously socialistic in his statement that the great social problem for the future was 'how to unite the greatest individual liberty of action with a common ownership of the raw materials of the globe, and an equal participation of all in the benefits of common labour'.[8] E. V. Neale, the Christian Socialist pioneer of the co-operative movement, rightly saw that Liberals sought merely to improve 'the institutions belonging to competitive society' and were not interested in constructing 'the better order of Co-Operative society'.[9] Philosophically, Liberals could never accept the idea of an economy organized wholly on the basis of co-operation and without competition. Even Mill insisted: 'I agree with the Socialist writers in their conception of the form which industrial operations tend to assume in the advance of improvement . . . but I utterly dissent from the most conspicuous and vehement part of their teaching, their declamations against competition.'[10]

Although they balked at the idea of workers' control of industry, many Liberals had a vision of a society where everyone had become a small capitalist and where there was no conflict between masters and men. The concept of inevitable class antagonism was wholly alien to them and they sought to prevent working people from regarding themselves as a separate class with interests distinct from and opposed to those of the rest of society. It was in this spirit that William Rathbone wrote a pamphlet in 1877 on *The Increased Earnings of the Working Classes* to show that the people were well on the way to becoming small capitalists, and that John Bright campaigned throughout the 1860s for the vote to be extended to at least the more respectable element of the working population.

Bright characteristically saw the problem of the development of a separate working-class consciousness as essentially a political one. In a revealing letter in 1860 he wrote: 'Our present system of political exclusion makes of the working classes a nation separated by a gulf from that other nation. . . . The class receiving wages is shut out from the questions and interests which occupy the minds and engage the energies of the employing class. Its members are limited to the consideration of their own individual, and local and class interest, and their mental activity is devoted to something like a servile war. . . . If the capitalists practically assert that the workman is born only to labour . . . and if, unhappily, the workman should practically acquiesce in this view and should abstain from efforts to invest himself with the rights of citizenship, let us be assured that his activity will not cease. . . . He will conclude that the only mode of bettering his condition is in the advance of wages forced from capital, it may be, at the risk of its destruction, and gained and secured only by combinations.'[11]

With the vote, however, Bright maintained that working men ceased to be mere passive objects motivated by class feelings and were transformed into active participants in society who helped to determine their own destiny. 'The workman of England is no longer a human machine,' he told the Rochdale Working Men's Club in 1877, 'he is a man into whom has been infused a new life, and to whom is given a new and wholesome responsibility. Every voting working man in England is now a ruler of men, and a joint ruler of many nations.'[12]

The Lib–Lab alliance which Bright had forged, very much on his terms, by rallying former Chartists behind the middle-class Liberal banner of reform in the 1860s, was not slow to produce results. Its most immediate and practical effect was the pact made between the Liberal party and the Reform League in 1868 whereby Samuel Morley, James Stansfeld and C. G. Glynn, the Liberal chief whip, gave George Howell £1,900 for the League in return for his promise that it would help the Liberals in the forthcoming General Election and not put up its own labour candidates. Significantly, one of the purposes of the money was to provide the League with a London club, the Adelphi, where its working-class members could mix with middle-class metropolitan Liberals. Two years later Morley and a group of Liberal industrialists which included Titus Salt gave substantial financial aid to the *Beehive*, a trade union paper, which was able as a result to reduce its price to one penny. In return, they secured a promise from the editor, George Potter, that the paper would support the Liberal cause.

It is not difficult to see why Karl Marx later bitterly criticized Howell and Potter for selling their working-class consciousness for a mess of pottage and allowing Bright and other Liberal capitalists to make them their henchmen. There was undoubtedly an element of pure self-interest in the courting of labour leaders by Liberal employers. It is evident in Bright's argument that the enfranchisement of working men made strikes and industrial action less likely, and in John Morley's conviction that the more violent features of trade unionism were best eliminated by 'active fraternisation . . . with the leaders of the workmen by members of the middle class, who represented the best moral and social elements in the public opinion of their time'.[13]

It would, however, be wrong to suggest that Lib–Labism was promoted by Liberal capitalists simply to give them a more compliant workforce and an easier life. Employers like Morley, Salt and Bass were genuinely interested in helping working men improve themselves. They were model employers in that they paid high wages and showed a genuine concern for their labour force which was more than just paternalistic. Bass was instrumental in setting up the Amalgamated Society of Railway Servants in 1871 even though its existence seemed to threaten his own interests. Salt took as much trouble to provide facilities for his workers' self-education and political development in Saltaire as he did to provide for their material comfort. Samuel Morley happily presided at meetings where Ernest Jones, a former Chartist leader, and others delivered speeches with markedly revolutionary tendencies. When chided for this by other employers, he said: 'It is better that large employers of labour should be willing to hear all that can be said by the advocates of the working class, rather than, from over sensitiveness as to their reputation, or indifference as to the condition of the people, or even fear of "unconscious irony", shut themselves within their own circle.'[14]

The enlightened interest of the model Liberal employers in labour questions helped to produce a number of important advances in the field of industrial relations in the second half of the nineteenth century. Perhaps the most important was the principle of putting disputes to arbitration. Although the concept of arbitration was widely accepted by Liberals in the field of foreign affairs, it was not at first so popular at home. Joseph Hume noted while attempting to arbitrate in a strike at Preston in 1853: 'I see on the list of advocates for arbitration to settle the disputes of nations instead of having recourse to war, many master manufacturers who are at this moment in dispute against their men.'[15] The widespread application of the principle of arbitration to industrial disputes was effectively the result of the work of one man, Mundella, who showed it to be in the interests of both employer and employee.

Mundella first employed the device of arbitration in 1860 after four consecutive strikes by Nottingham framework knitters had led employers to call for a lockout. At his instigation the dispute was settled by a conference of both sides and a Board of Arbitration was set up with six manufacturers and six operatives to resolve all future disputes within the Nottingham hosiery industry. The Board, which was the first of its kind in the country, was so successful that Mundella found himself in demand to settle other disputes. In 1867, after putting to arbitration a dispute involving South Yorkshire miners, he was asked by the Sheffield Organized Trades and Reform League to stand for election to Parliament. He became Liberal M.P. for the city the following year. In 1871, after he had been called in to arbitrate over a claim by Newcastle engineers for a nine-hour day, he was approached by George Howell with the suggestion that he should introduce a Bill establishing arbitration boards in all industries throughout the country. Although he was unhappy about the idea of compulsory arbitration and preferred the initiative to come from employees and employers themselves, he introduced and successfully carried in 1872 the Arbitration (Masters and Workers) Act which provided for the establishment of Courts of Conciliation to resolve industrial disputes. In 1894 Mundella secured a more effective Act authorizing the Board of Trade to take the initiative in establishing voluntary boards of conciliation and arbitration in any district or trade and to nominate such boards to act in actual disputes. This established the rudiments of the government machinery of arbitration which exists today.

Mundella stressed that as well as arbitration over actual disputes, there should be continuous discussion between representatives of management and labour. 'One of the results of this interchange of thoughts and opinion', he told the Royal Commission on the Trade Unions in 1867, 'is that the workman becomes better acquainted with the laws which govern trade and commerce and with the influence of foreign competition, and the master learns how to appreciate the difficulties of the workman and to sympathise more with his trials and struggles to maintain and improve his position.'[16] Many Liberal employers shared his views and maintained a regular dialogue with representatives of their workforce, and several were also active enthusiasts for arbitration. Morley devoted himself to increasing the number of Boards of Conciliation and Arbitration in the textile industry and R. Spence Watson, a Newcastle solicitor, served as arbitrator in more than a hundred trade disputes in the north-east.

One of the main points which Mundella sought to put across to his fellow employers in his advocacy of arbitration and discussion between workers and managers was that trade unions were a help rather than a hindrance to good business. The Manchester Party had been hostile to trade unions, which were regarded as dangerously class-based combinations in fundamental breach of Adam Smith's golden rule that contracts between labour and capital should be entered into freely and without coercion. Cobden regarded trade unions as 'founded upon principles of brutal tyranny and monopoly', and declared, 'I would rather live under a Bey of Algiers than a trades committee.'[17] Bright had no time for trade union pressure and in 1861 his firm prosecuted four of its workers for picketing. More conservative Liberals continued to be unhappy about the growth of trade unionism in the middle of the nineteenth century. Robert Lowe complained in 1867 that trade unions 'are all founded on the right of the majority to coerce the minority, on the absolute subjugation of the one to the many, and the employment of such means as may be necessary in order to give effect to these false and dangerous principles.'[18]

Several Liberals, however, came to welcome the growth of responsible trade unionism in the 1860s as a spontaneous expression of working-class self-help and political maturity. They were not a little influenced by the development of the new model unions like the Amalgamated Society of Engineers, founded in 1851, Robert Applegarth's Amalgamated Society of Carpenters and Joiners, and Joseph Arch's National Agricultural Labourer's Union. These were groupings of skilled workers who were more interested in campaigning for the vote, encouraging self-improvement and education and establishing mutual benefit schemes than in striking or combining to exert their industrial muscle. Enlightened Liberals saw that trade unions did not threaten the voluntary nature of the contract between master and man, but rather put their relationship on to more equal terms. In Mundella's view the growth of trade unionism actually facilitated free trade in labour: 'A master is a corporation and can deal singly with his men if they go to him singly. But if they go to him as a trade union, they are a body equal to himself and a bargain can be made on equal terms.'[19]

Samuel Morley, Mundella and Thomas Hughes laboured particularly hard to secure general Liberal support for the fledgling trade union movement. In 1869 Hughes introduced a Bill drafted by Frederic Harrison which would have allowed trade unions to hold funds under the security of the law, given them freedom of contract and abolished special offences arising out of industrial disputes. Morley and Mundella called on their fellow employers to meet and co-operate with the members of the new Trades Union Congress which had been set up in 1868. They themselves gave a well-publicized breakfast party to the delegates when the Congress met in Nottingham in 1872. 'I think it is highly desirable', Mundella wrote afterwards, 'that the members of the Trades Union Congress should not be left in a state of isolation. At recent meetings . . . a considerable number of employers attended and gave a moderate tone to their meetings, and deprived them of that exclusive class character which they are too prone to take if left to themselves. I think, moreover, that Liberal and sensible employers should manifest their sympathy with this labour Parliament in all efforts of a reasonable and laudable character tending to improve their class.'[20]

Gladstone's first Government failed to give trade unionism the support that its Liberal champions had hoped for. Although the 1871 Trade Unions Act established that unions could not be prosecuted as conspiracies in restraint of trade and could be registered as friendly societies, the Criminal Law Amendment Act of the same year made picketing illegal. Efforts by Mundella, Morley and Hughes to repeal it were unsuccessful and it was Disraeli's Conservative government that accorded trade unions the full recognition they had been denied by the Liberals when it legalized peaceful picketing in 1875. The Conservatives also passed an Employers and Workmen Act which made employers and employees equal partners to a civil contract and abolished imprisonment for breach of such a contract. A year earlier Gladstone had shown his own feelings about trade unions when he had threatened to evict from their homes a group of miners on his land near Hawarden who were striking in protest at a ten per cent reduction in wages. Although his attitude to trade unions became more favourable as he got older, and in 1887 he even told an audience in Swansea that they had 'upon the whole been productive of an enormous balance of good', trade unionists did not forget that his government had failed to give them what they regarded as a fundamental right.[21]

Recognition and protection of trade unions was, of course, only one way in which politicians could help the labour movement. They could also promote legislation to protect workers and improve their conditions. This was not a popular venture among Liberals since it ran directly counter to cherished notions of self-reliance and voluntaryism. The hostility to factory legislation which had first been expressed by

Cobden and Bright lingered long in the party and Gladstone's first
Government did little directly to promote the interests of working
people. Bass found only meagre Liberal support for his efforts to
secure a ten-hour working day for railway workers. A Bill introduced
by Mundella in 1872 to reduce the working week for women and
children employed in textile factories was defeated after it had been
opposed by such 'enlightened' Liberal employers as Titus Salt and
Henry Ashworth. It was not until the Conservatives were in office that
a measure similar to Mundella's was carried. Admittedly in 1871 Sir
John Lubbock, Liberal M.P. for Maidstone, had managed to carry his
Bank Holiday Act, which established fixed public holidays on Boxing
Day, Easter Monday, Whit Monday and the first Monday in August,
but it applied only to office workers until Disraeli's Government
extended its provisions to cover all workers in 1875.

It was not surprising that Alexander MacDonald, who with Burt
was the only representative of labour in the 1874 Parliament, told his
constituents in 1880 that the Conservatives had done more for the
working man in the last five years than the Liberals had done in the last
fifty years. The social and labour legislation of Disraeli's 1874–80
Government was certainly impressive. It included the 1875 Public
Health Act which gave new local sanitary authorities power to provide
hospitals financed out of the rates, and the Artisans' Dwelling Act which
allowed local authorities compulsorily to purchase land for house
building, as well as the Trade Unions Act and the Factory Act which
the Liberals had failed to pass. With their tendency towards paternalism
the Tories found it much easier to promote interventionist and regulatory legislation on behalf of the working classes. They also realized
that they needed, more than the Liberals, positively to go out and win
working-class votes by substantial concessions to labour. George
Howell told Goldwin Smith in 1877: 'I regret to say that the Liberals
not only did not help us in our great labour battles but they positively
threw everything in our way. . . . The Tories are doing their best to
conciliate the artisan classes, and they will be repaid with the gratitude
of those whom they help.'[22]

The Conservatives had also early realized what the Liberals would
only reluctantly and gradually accept, that the ordinary working men
enfranchised in 1867 were more susceptible to promises of immediate
material rewards and better conditions at home and at work than they
were to the remote ideals of political reform with which the Liberals
wooed them at the polls and which had appealed to some of their

leaders and more 'respectable' colleagues. In his Crystal Palace speech of 1872 Disraeli remarked that, 'from personal conversation with the labouring class . . . the policy of the Tory party, that would improve the condition of the people, is more appreciated by the people than the ineffable mysteries and all the pains and penalties of the Ballot Bill.'[23] The terrible truth only gradually dawned on the Liberals that enfranchisement had not suddenly made the workers into perfect citizens, interested in Parliamentary reform and foreign affairs, having forsaken their class interest. It came home with the Liberals' defeat in the 1874 election, when the working-class electorate apparently spurned Gladstone's great crusade for economy in favour of Disraeli's 'bribes' of social reform. It was the first sign that the masses, far from sharing Gladstone's interest in saving public money, were coming to see the public purse as the great provider.

Liberals began to start doubting their faith in labour. Looking back some years later on 'the ridiculous political action' of the working class in 1874, T. H. Green told C. A. Fyffe, 'We held our heads too high during Gladstone's ministry. We thought the working classes had made much more progress than they really had.' Fyffe noted that 'explaining this, he dwelt with great disappointment on the use made by the workmen of their half holiday and their shorter hours. He even said that he thought it was better they should not have a half holiday, but should be kept constantly at their work so that they should not have time to drink.'[24] Goldwin Smith sadly confirmed from his experience of the mechanic 'that it was rightly said that he is a Socialist at home and a Jingo abroad'.[25]

Lib–Labism was also under attack from the labour side. The mid-1870s saw the beginning of a series of economic slumps that continued for the next thirty years and reversed the prosperous conditions of the mid-Victorian decades. Industrial and agricultural depression hit particularly hard the skilled artisans who had been the strongest supporters of the Lib–Lab alliance. It weakened their self-reliance and thrift. By 1880 Liberalism was failing to fulfil its earlier promise of automatically producing rising levels of prosperity. The growing masses of unskilled factory hands and labourers were demanding positive measures of social welfare and protective legislation and were developing a new form of trade unionism based on very different principles from those of Howell and Arch.

The alliance between Liberals and labour was also being threatened by the rise of a new political and economic ideology wholly opposed to the principle of competitive individualism. The growing power of the unskilled working classes was contributing to the development of a collectivist outlook. In his contribution to the 1867 *Essays on Reform*, Richard Hutton had predicted that 'the most important of all the characteristic influences which may be anticipated from the representation of the artisan class, is the introduction into our national politics of those large, and still radically true and noble ideas of the claims of the organised whole over individuals that constitute it, which the artisan class have worked out at the expense of so much sacrifice, and too often, no doubt, at the expense of true freedom, in their trade societies. . . . It is probable that, as the working classes gain greater influence in the State, they will be able to show us that, in our undue confidence in unlimited competition, we have frittered away many national advantages.'[26] Although Britain's first Socialist political organization, the Democratic Federation, was an almost exclusively middle-class enterprise when it was set up by Henry Hyndman in 1881, working men had an obvious interest in its main demand for an end to the payment of wages by one class to another.

The working classes were also showing increasing signs of wanting their own independent representation in Parliament. In 1868 Holyoake stood as an independent Labour candidate in Birmingham and told the electors that as representatives of the 'master class', the Liberals could never legislate from the workers' point of view.[27] In the next twenty years, more and more working men felt that they were not being adequately represented in Parliament by Liberals who were more often than not their employers, and pressure grew for the creation of a separate Labour party. The dominance of class in politics, which Bright had so much dreaded, was coming about.

Lib–Labism was not necessarily dead, however. Admittedly, in the form in which it had been developed by Bright and the model Liberal employers it had no future. The old relationship between Liberal reformers and respectable artisans based on a shared faith in self-help and political emancipation was over. Howell and Samuel Morley made a vain bid to resurrect it in 1878 with a National Political Union, on the model of the Reform League, which was a spectacular failure. Two years later, however, Chamberlain won the cheers of working men when he persuaded Gladstone's second Government to put on to the statute book an interventionist measure which flew in the face of traditional Liberal principles. The Employers' Liability Act answered a major demand of labour by providing that workers should be paid compensation by their employers for accidents arising during the course of their work. The Act was limited in scope and only provided for modest amounts of compensation. None the less it marked a major departure in legislating for all working people rather than for the protection of a particularly vulnerable group and in interfering with the free contract between master and man.

The failure of Morley and Howell and the success of Chamberlain showed the need for Lib–Labism to be put on to a new foundation if it was to survive in the changed economic and social climate of the 1880s. The basis of the alliance needed to be restated on labour's terms, and not maintained, as hitherto, on the Liberals' terms. To keep the support of working men, the Liberals would have to accept labour candidates and legislate for social reform. They would need to become, in effect, the labour party. They would also have to modify one of their most cherished ideals, the principle of voluntaryism.

Chapter 8

The Voluntary Principle

In 1873 an appeal was made to Gladstone to introduce into Hawarden Board Schools as provided for in his 1870 Education Act. He refused on the grounds that there were perfectly adequate voluntarily run schools in the village. In a letter to Bright about the matter he explained: 'for myself, not in education only, but in all things, I prefer voluntary to legal machinery, when the thing can be well done either way.'[1] The conviction that voluntary spontaneous effort by individuals and groups was preferable to compulsory action by the state was a fundamental tenet of Victorian Liberalism. It appealed equally to up-and-coming manufacturers, to lovers of liberty and to the Nonconformist Conscience. The ideal of voluntaryism informed the Liberal attitude to the provision of education, health and social welfare, the intervention of government in industry and the desirability of legislative interference with the moral choice and responsibility of the individual. Yet paradoxically, it also inspired forms of collective social action which prompted many Liberals to call for greater state intervention.

Voluntaryism had an obvious appeal to manufacturers and merchants. Applied to industry, it stood for free trade, unrestricted competition, and the absence of protectionist or regulatory legislation which interfered with the free contract made between employer and worker. For Cobden and Bright voluntaryism meant the non-interference of the government in the workings of the economy. For lovers of liberty, it was a fundamental political principle which allowed maximum individual freedom and restricted to a minimum the activities of the state.

In essence, however, voluntaryism was a moral rather than an economic or political principle. It derived from the Liberal ideal of the responsible self-governing citizen and the Protestant ideal of obedience to the individual conscience, disciplined by Bible teaching and the values of the gathered church. Under a voluntary system of society individuals had to make moral choices and shoulder their own responsibilities. They could not shuffle them off on to others or on to the state. T. H. Green noted that morality lay in 'the disinterested performance of self-imposed duties'. Compulsory and interventionist action by the state negated morality 'by narrowing the room for the self-imposition of duties and for the play of disinterested motives'.[2] For Edward Miall, one of the leading proponents of voluntaryism, 'perhaps the greatest peril to which our social organization exposes us is the temptation it offers to shift from ourselves to our rulers all active care for the myriads around us, and to condense our whole duty into the payment of the Queen's taxes.'[3]

The best exposition of the principle of voluntaryism, which showed its stress both on individual moral responsibility and on collective social action, was made by Mill in his *Principles of Political Economy*. He wrote: 'The business of life is an essential part of the practical education of a people. . . . Instruction is only one of the desiderata of mental improvement; another, almost as indispensable, is a vigorous exercise of active agencies; labour, contrivance, judgement, self-control: and the natural stimulus to these is the difficulties of life. . . . A people among whom there is no habit of spontaneous action for a collective interest—who look habitually to their government to command or prompt them in all matters of joint concern—who expect to have everything done for them, except what can be made an affair of mere habit and routine—have their faculties only half developed. . . . It is therefore of supreme importance that all classes of the community, down to the lowest, should have much to do for themselves; that as great a demand should be made upon their intelligence and virtue as it is in any respect equal to; that the government should not only leave as much as possible to their own faculties the conduct of what concerns themselves alone, but should suffer them, or rather encourage them, to manage as many as possible of their joint concerns by voluntary operation.'[4]

The promotion of self-help and individual responsibility was an important part of the voluntaryist creed. Miall feared that government provision of welfare would sap the self-reliance of the people. He commented that those in favour of legislation for compulsory education of factory children 'would seem enamoured of Spartan government and to be willing to impose upon the legislature the duty of suckling, training and then taxing the whole population'.[5] Mill carried to extreme lengths his insistence that the government should not interfere with the individual's freedom of moral choice or protect him from his own irresponsibility. He opposed state action to control and regulate prostitution on the grounds that 'it was not part of the business of Government to provide securities beforehand against the consequences of immoralities of any kind.'[6] He similarly objected to Nonconformist proposals for legislation to promote temperance on the grounds that the use of alcohol was 'a subject on which every sane and grown-up person ought to judge for himself'. Harcourt initially took the same view and deplored 'grand-maternal Government which ties nightcaps on a grown-up nation by act of Parliament'.[7] In the same spirit the institution of a secret ballot for elections was opposed by Mill and also by Trollope, who argued that it was 'unworthy of a great people to free itself from the evil results of vicious conduct by unmanly restraints'.[8] Peter Taylor, who was an arch-voluntaryist, waged a vigorous campaign against compulsory vaccination which he felt to be an unwarrantable interference with the free moral choice of the individual.

Voluntaryism was championed above all, however, not so much because it encouraged individuals to be responsible for their own lives as for its effect on general social responsibility and active concern for the plight of others. Self-help was only a part of the voluntaryist principle, which as defined by Edward Baines, another of its leading exponents, encompassed 'all that is not Governmental or compulsory, all that men do for themselves, their neighbours or their posterity of their own free will'.[9] The voluntaryists were not opposing compulsory activity by the state so that the individual could sit back and ignore the needs of his fellow men. 'The contented man, or the contented family,' wrote Mill, 'who have no ambition to make anyone else happier, to promote the good of their country or their neighbourhood, or to improve themselves in moral excellence, excite in us neither admiration or approval.'[10]

At the heart of Gladstonian Liberalism was a belief in the importance and the effectiveness of spontaneous activity by individuals and communities as the main agency for providing education, health and welfare to those who could not provide it for themselves. Voluntaryism was based on the confident expectation that private charity, together with the activity of friendly societies, co-operative associations and the countless other agencies of voluntary community action would be adequate to combat the evils of illiteracy, disease and poverty. It rested on a supremely optimistic view of human nature. As Mill put it: 'This firm foundation is that of the social feelings of mankind; the desire to be in unity with our fellow creatures, which is already a powerful principle in human nature, and happily one of those which tend to become stronger, from the influences of civilisation. . . . The influences are constantly on the increase which tend to generate in each individual a feeling of unity with all the rest; which feeling, if perfect, would make him never think of, or desire, any beneficial condition for himself, in the benefits of which they are not included.'[11]

The voluntary principle was first seriously worked out and established in the Liberal consciousness in the 1840s and 1850s through the Nonconformist campaigns against the Established Church and government provision of education. It was not surprising that voluntaryism should initially have been a Nonconformist idea. The dissenting chapel, with its claim to be the 'gathered church' of believers and its numerous recreational, educational and social offshoots, was in many ways the perfect example of a voluntary society. Nonconformists also had every reason to be suspicious of extending the powers of a state which had only recently, and grudgingly, accepted them as full members and which was still dominated by churchmen, aristocrats and other such groups whom they despised. It was no coincidence that the young Herbert Spencer, who was later to become the most extreme advocate of voluntaryism in the late nineteenth century, first developed his views on the proper limits of state power in 1842 in the pages of Edward Miall's *Nonconformist*.

The attack on the Established Church, which was launched in 1836 with the establishment in Birmingham of a Voluntary Church Society, was based on the conviction that its dependence on compulsorily levied rates and legal privileges was at odds with the principles of Christianity. 'The state church cannot compel submission', Miall wrote, 'and yet leave conscience in a position of supremacy.'[12] Nonconformists argued that a free system of religion in which each church or sect competed for allegiance and support on the basis of conviction and voluntary donation rather than relying on legal establishment and compulsory levy or endowment would produce a more Christian country. 'An ounce of spontaneous action is worth more than a ton of compulsion,' Samuel Morley reflected; 'I am prepared to contend that to rely on the legislative enforcement of any Church system would be to wither up all that is fresh and vital in our religious communities.'[13]

The battle which Baines and Miall waged in the 1840s and 1850s against state provision of education was similarly inspired by a preference for voluntary over compulsory action and by dislike of a system which favoured one particular denomination. The voluntaryists took up their campaign when it was clear that no form of state education would be possible in Britain without a strong bias in favour of the role of the national Church. They were opposed by several Nonconformists and a good many Liberals, including those like Cobden who, while ideologically sympathetic to their position, saw that it was not a practical reality. They themselves were later to concede that the state must be involved in the provision of education. None the less, the ideas which they developed in their campaign had an important influence on Liberal thought.

The voluntaryists opposed increased governmental control over and support for education because they felt that it was both unhealthy and unnecessary. For Baines education was something to be provided 'by *individual* talent and energy and the *voluntary* combinations of a free people among themselves' rather than by the corporate action of the state and through compulsory taxes.[14] He saw a state school system as destroying the whole tradition of English education, the most notable characteristic of which was that 'it has been free. It has been left to the people themselves. The bequests of the enlightened dead, the benevolence and public spirit of the living, the zeal of Christian communities, the affection of parents, the skill and learning of schoolmasters competing with each other for patronage and fame, the force of a healthy public opinion, and perhaps above all, the genius of authors ever breathing the air of freedom, have combined to educate a people whom I fearlessly place foremost among the nations of the earth.'[15]

Behind these high-minded principles, a certain amount of self-interest underlay the voluntaryists' position. It was significant that as well as being Nonconformists, with a natural dislike of the Establishment's activities and a justified fear that government provision of education would naturally favour Anglicanism, they were also often manufacturers from the Midlands and the North, opposed to the doctrine of state paternalism which they saw being developed by southern landowners and bureaucrats. Edward Baines's *The Social, Educational and Religious State of the Manufacturing Districts* was written to counter the idea being expounded by Tory reformers like the Earl of Shaftesbury that factory children were left in a state of ignorance and neglect by their employers. Baines argued that their educational needs were in fact well provided for by voluntary schools run on the manufacturers' principles of competition and enlightened self-interest. The voluntaryists defended free trade in education against state paternalism just as they defended it in industry. Baines wrote: 'There is a great analogy between Government protection to industry and Government protection to Mind. They are attempted in great part from the same motives; they indicate the same distrust of individual exertion and prudence . . . if competition and interest stimulate manufacturers, merchants, artisans, farmers, professional men, and all this bustling world of industry, how is it that they should not equally stimulate schoolmasters and school committees? . . . Thousands of incompetent schoolmasters and bad schools have given way before the march of improvement, and all the rest must do the same, unless they advance with the demands of society . . . but if you want a receipt for perpetuating badness, I will give you one—put the thing under a Government, a Corporation, or a County Board that is to enforce uniformity.'[16]

Voluntaryists were seriously concerned about the consequences of the government providing the education that it was the duty of each man to provide for his own children. 'Relieve men of their duties,' wrote Baines, 'and you rob them of their virtues.'[17] Opposing a Bill providing for rate-supported schools in Lancashire in 1852, Miall wrote, 'We should like to ascertain . . . what amount is spent weekly in Manchester and Salford by the working and poorer classes at the various gin palaces and beer shops in these two boroughs. We should like to know what amount of money these classes could raise, without curtailment of a single domestic comfort, and merely by an exercise of self-denial in regard to what is positively pernicious in them.'[18] He pointed out that by sacrificing one pint of beer a week, any working man could afford to educate his child. That was the voluntaryists' answer to those who argued that the mass of the population could not or would not contribute to their children's education or send them to school unless it was compulsory to do so. 'This is an evil not to be cured by legislation,' wrote Baines, 'but by the gradual leavening of the working classes with more correct views and higher aspirations.'[19]

Voluntaryists conceded that a state system of education might provide better school buildings and facilities but they believed that it would be a body without a soul. 'Government interference to educate the poor would destroy voluntary efforts for that end, and, by destroying those efforts, would destroy the principles which sustain them,' Baines wrote: 'Would the nation be a gainer, even by the utmost conceivable perfection in the machinery of education, if you attained that end by suppressing the greatest school of national virtue—the spontaneous organisation of patriots and Christians for the enlightenment of their fellow-men?'[20] There was another serious objection to education provided by the state. In Miall's opinion, it constituted 'about the most fearful weapon with which a nation could entrust its rulers . . . to surrender to the "powers that be" the task of moulding the habits, shaping the character and fixing the elemental principles, political, social, moral and religious, of succeeding generations is just to let down the drawbridge and raise the portcullis which at present guard the citadel of national freedom'.[21] Baines believed that a system of state education 'would train the very children from their earliest entrance into the school to obsequious servility' and 'give to the people themselves habits of enervating dependence on the Government'.[22] A voluntary system, on the other hand, 'might give them habits of independent thought, of active benevolence, and of noble self-reliance'.[23]

The voluntaryists held that, as well as being thoroughly undesirable, state provision of education was also totally unnecessary. Baines wrote *The Social, Educational and Religious State of the Manufacturing Districts* to show 'the power of voluntary Christian zeal to provide the means of education and religious instruction, even for a rapidly increasing population'.[24] The same point was made by Henry Richard, the leading Welsh voluntaryist, in his *The Progress and Efficacy of Voluntary Education, as exemplified in Wales* (1847). Miall constantly pointed to the numerous mechanics' institutes and Sunday schools in existence, and held up as examples of voluntaryist achievement the people's colleges established at Nottingham and Sheffield and the teacher-training college set up by the Congregational Board of Education at Homerton. Mill, who as a young man was on the whole an enthusiastic supporter of voluntaryism in education as in other matters, was confident that 'as the people grow more enlightened, they will become more able to appreciate, and more willing to pay for, good instruction, so that the competition of the market will become more and more adequate to provide good education.'[25] Baines summed up the voluntaryists' confidence and optimism in 1847: 'the voluntary and independent action of the people in the cause of education, morals and religion is transcendentally more powerful than would be required to perfect the means of education in England. These points being established, there does not remain the shadow of a ground for demanding any further interference on the part of the Government, still less for any general scheme of state education.'[26]

In putting forward his own plan for a voluntary system of education in Lancashire, Baines wrote: 'Lancashire, of all counties, can most effectively organise itself, without asking the legislature to compel it.

Have we not seen its mighty League, its great Manchester Unity of Friendly Societies, its infant Union of Mechanics' Institutes, and many other associations for the reform of our laws and the improvement of the people? Whatever can be done by talent, public spirit, wealth, and the habit of co-operation, can be done by the men of Lancashire: and it is infinitely more safe and honourable to them to be the self-relying organisers of their own social improvement, than to call in legislative control and compulsion.'[27] The developing network of friendly societies and mutual benefit societies in the mid-nineteenth century encouraged Liberals to feel that voluntary activity would provide not only for the education but also for the welfare of the population. Where it failed to penetrate at the bottom level of society, they confidently looked to the application of that traditional voluntary instrument of relief, private charity.

A voluntary system of providing relief for the poor was as dear to Liberals' hearts as a voluntary system of education, although it was not pursued with the same fervour. Its main proponent was William Rathbone, the Liverpool merchant, who saw in his native city that the poverty arising from industrialization needed to be countered by a highly organized system of relief. In 1867 he wrote *Social Duties, Considered in Reference to the Organisation of Effort in Works of Benevolence and Public Utility* in which he argued for the organization of charity. Voluntaryism was at the heart of Rathbone's approach to dealing with poverty. He rejected the idea of state-provided welfare. 'Where good is to be done to the individual man,' he wrote, 'it should come from the free-will of fellow-men; the machinery should be in the background, and the voluntary benefactor should come into personal contact with his suffering brother.'[28]

In 1869 Rathbone's philosophy was put into practice with the foundation of the Charity Organisation Society to make arrangements for charitable relief throughout London. Liberal influences were strong in the Society. One of its founders was F. A. Maxse, the Liberal candidate at Southampton in 1868 on whom George Meredith had based his hero in *Beauchamp's Career*. Lord Lichfield, a former Liberal M.P., was its first chairman, Sir Charles Trevelyan sat on the Council, and Gladstone was a strong supporter. The Society's secretary from 1875 until 1913 was Charles Loch, a Balliol pupil of T. H. Green and a staunch Liberal and voluntaryist.

The Charity Organisation Society exemplified the principles of voluntaryism and individualism. It regarded personal character as the most important determinant of whether or not someone should be helped. Those who showed a sense of responsibility and could be returned to society, the deserving poor, were to be helped by voluntary effort. Those who did not, and were destitute, were consigned to the workhouse and the harsh treatment of the Poor Law. The Society's main objects included 'the promotion of habits of providence and self-reliance' and 'the repression of mendicity and imposture'.[29] Loch and the other leading members strongly resisted any move towards state intervention in welfare through the provision of old-age pensions and sickness or unemployment benefits. This was regarded as indiscriminate charity which would confirm the indolent in their ways and sap the moral fibre of those self-respecting families struggling to keep themselves from destitution.

Adherence to voluntaryism led most Liberals to see a distinctly limited role for government. Their ideal was a passive rather than a positive state which interfered as little as possible with the voluntary activity of individuals and communities. 'The duty of civil government', wrote Miall, 'is to provide "a clear stage and no favour", to remove impediments from the free agency of moral nature and religious zeal, and to see to it that nothing in the shape of its own fiscal exactions or of class injustices operates to prevent the fullest and freest play of those instincts and responsibilities by which the end is to be secured.'[30] The idea that the state might itself provide education and welfare or ameliorate human life was anathema to the voluntaryists: 'We would dispatch it on no mission of knight-errantry in search of social felicity; it is much better kept at home to perform a less exalted task. . . . Let it perform efficiently the duty of a police establishment and interfere with no man further than the demands of justice require . . . if happiness be not the result, the fault is not in government—for the production of happiness lies not within its sphere.'[31]

This minimal view of the function of the state commended itself to most Gladstonian Liberals. What they dreaded most was the assumption by the Government of duties and responsibilities which should properly be left to individuals or voluntary associations. C. S. Roundell, Postmaster General in Gladstone's second administration, held that 'Legislation which encourages the people rather to rest upon State-help than to rely upon themselves, however well-intentioned, will prove incalculably mischievous in the end, and to every measure which is brought forward with the object of improving the condition of the people, this simple test should be applied—will it tend to encourage them to rely upon self-help?'[32] T. H. Green, in his *Lectures On the Principles of Political Obligation*, attacked all laws and government prohibitions 'which interfere with the growth of self-reliance, with the formation of a manly conscience and sense of moral dignity', and 'legal institutions which take away the occasion for the exercise of certain moral virtues (e.g. the Poor Law which takes away the occasion for the exercise of parental forethought, filial reverence and neighbourly kindness)'.[33] Goldwin Smith demanded: 'let Government do only that which the citizen cannot do for himself with the aid of voluntary association.'[34]

The voluntaryists' view of the proper function of the state was worked out most fully by Mill. In his *Principles of Political Economy* he wrote: 'A good government will give its aid in such a shape, as to encourage and nurture any rudiments it may find of a spirit of individual exertion. It will be assiduous in removing obstacles and discouragements to voluntary enterprise and in giving whatever direction and guidance may be necessary: its pecuniary means will be applied, when practicable, in aid of private efforts rather than in supersession of them, and it will call into play its machinery of rewards and honours to elicit such efforts. Government aid, when given merely in default of private enterprise, should be so given as to be as far as possible a course of education for the people in the art of accomplishing great objects by individual energy and voluntary co-operation.'[35] If voluntary enterprise really was inadequate to meet some agreed need in society, then Mill suggested that while 'leaving individuals free to use their own means of pursuing any object of general interest, the government, not meddling with them, but not trusting the object solely to their care [should] establish, side by side with their arrangements, an agency of its own for a like purpose'.[36] It was possible, he argued, to have an Established Church without discriminating against other religions or sects, a state education system without prohibiting private schools and tutors, a state Post Office without penalizing private letter-conveyancing, and public hospitals alongside private medicine. In that way, the virtues of competition and voluntaryism were preserved.

Gladstone shared the voluntaryists' limited view of the functions of government and applied it both as Chancellor and Prime Minister. He believed that the greatest benefits which the state could confer on working people were the removal of obstacles to self-advancement and improvement and the provision of a fiscal system which kept prices and taxation low, so enabling individuals and communities to make the maximum use of their resources. This conviction underlay his early work in throwing careers open to talent and reducing duties and taxes. He was much less happy about involving the government in the business of social engineering and the positive provision of welfare, or what he disparagingly referred to as 'constructionism'. That meant constricting the resources of the taxpayer and lessening his capacity for moral choice and voluntary activity, and also sapping the self-reliance of the recipients of government handouts. 'If the Government takes into its hand that which the man ought to do for himself,' he told a gathering of working men in Saltney, Cheshire, 'it will inflict upon him greater mischiefs than all the benefits he will have received or all the advantages that would accrue from them. The essence of the whole thing is that the spirit of self-reliance, the spirit of true and genuine manly independence, should be preserved in the minds of every member of that class.'[37]

In so far as he engaged in 'constructionist' government activity, Gladstone very much followed Mill's demands that its purpose should be to strengthen self-reliance and that any public institutions established should co-exist with and supplement voluntary bodies. His first, and in many ways most successful, use of positive state power to stimulate self-help was the establishment in 1861 of the Post Office Savings Bank. Although voluntary trustee savings banks existed to encourage thrift among working men, they offered no guarantee for the security of funds deposited and were not used by many working people. Gladstone, who as Chancellor had tried to improve the constitution of private savings banks to make them more useful to the poorer classes, was persuaded that a national savings bank attached to the Post Office and backed by government guarantee would provide a simple, safe and readily accessible repository for the savings of working people and would positively encourage thrift.

The Post Office Savings Bank was immensely successful in gaining deposits from working people. Its potential for encouraging thrift was seized on and exploited particularly by Henry Fawcett who, as Postmaster General in Gladstone's second administration, greatly increased the number of post offices in small villages and poor urban areas which handled Savings Bank business. He also made special arrangements for navvies and labourers to deposit sums at their place of employment, and instituted an arrangement for making very small deposits by slips on which postage stamps could be stuck. In 1880 Fawcett issued a free pamphlet *Aids to Thrift* to explain in simple terms the benefits of saving with the Post Office. By 1895 nearly six million people had deposits totalling over £80,000,000 in the Post Office Savings Bank.

In 1864 Gladstone extended the scope of the Post Office Savings Bank by empowering it to conduct life assurance business. His aim was not to institute a compulsory state insurance scheme but simply to provide an alternative voluntary system to that operated by friendly and burial societies. He was concerned at the swindling character of many societies and pointed out that if a man defaulted on a single premium he lost everything that he had paid in. His scheme was strongly opposed, however, by those who saw it as crippling the friendly societies and giving the state a monopoly of life insurance and was substantially modified in Committee. The minimum sum for which a life could be insured was set at £20, too much for many working people, and the scheme was only operated in a small minority of post offices. As a result, very few people used it. In 1882 the scheme was widened to enable people to insure their lives for sums under £25 and to include children.

These activities showed that Gladstone was prepared to use the state positively to encourage thrift and providence. His preference remained for voluntary agencies in this sphere, but he was concerned that neither friendly societies nor savings banks offered sufficient protection to the small saver. He attempted to tighten up their management and Lord Lichfield introduced a Bill with that object in 1868, but it met with opposition from extreme voluntaryists, and legislation regulating the friendly societies was not finally passed until 1875 when it was carried by Disraeli's Conservative Government. Gladstone's interference with the friendly societies was construed as thoroughly interventionist and anti-voluntaryist, as in a sense it was. But its aim was to strengthen rather than weaken the societies. Ideally, he saw government and voluntary societies working together in partnership, with the former only supplementing or regulating the latter if there were evident inadequacies in their approach.

This philosophy underlay two important measures of Gladstone's first administration. The first was the Minute on Relief of the Poor in the Metropolis issued in 1869 by Goschen as President of the Poor Law Board. The 'Goschen Minute', as it came to be known, proposed that Poor Law relief should be given only to the destitute, and that the poor should be helped by charitable activity. The minute, which was drawn up in collaboration with the Charity Organisation Society and backed

G

by a strict application of the Poor Law by the Local Government Board under Stansfeld, embodied the voluntaryist Liberal hope that co-operation between the state and private charity would be sufficient to ensure that the government would not need to assume new duties in the prevention and relief of poverty. It rested on the belief that most poverty was the individual responsibility of the working man, and that he had the wherewithal to climb out of it with a little help from voluntary aid. Only in cases of extreme destitution should the state provide welfare, and then only after applying the workhouse test to all able-bodied applicants for relief.

The other major measure which combined governmental and voluntary activity to promote general welfare was, of course, Forster's Education Act of 1870. In many ways, the Act, in providing for Board Schools only where existing voluntary schools were inadequate, was a highly voluntaryist measure and was opposed as such by most enthusiasts for state education. At the same time, however, as the first statutory recognition that the state had direct responsibility for education, it represented an abandonment of the pure voluntaryist principle. As such, it could have been expected to meet with the whole-hearted opposition of Baines, Miall and Morley. In fact, they greeted it with mild enthusiasm and if they had an objection it was that the measure was too voluntaryist in that it allowed Church schools free sway. The three leaders of the voluntaryist movement in education had come to realize by the late 1860s that a wholly voluntary school system was inadequate to educate the rapidly rising urban population. By 1867 they accepted that the state had a positive role to play in the provision of education. It was the first significant Liberal retreat from the voluntaryist position. Morley and Miall joined the National Education League's campaign for state education financed out of the rates, while Baines supported the National Education Union's more limited call on the government to fill in the gaps in the voluntary system. 'I confess to a strong distrust of government action, and a passionate love for voluntary action and self-reliance,' Baines wrote in 1867, 'but though the passion still rules, I now acknowledge that it was allowed too absolute sway, and as a practical man I am compelled to abandon the purely voluntary system, as untenable in competition with that which combines voluntary action and state aid.'[38]

Matthew Arnold denounced the Liberals in the 1860s for their advocacy of a 'do nothing state'. Carlyle, in similar vein, equated Liberalism with *laissez-faire*, the notion of leaving everything to the competitive forces of the market which he saw as responsible for many of the social evils of the time. In fact, nothing could be further from the truth than to equate Victorian Liberalism with 'do nothingness' and *laissez-faire*, as so many historians, following A. V. Dicey, have mistakenly done. Voluntaryism was not a doctrine which implied inaction over social evils and which encouraged its adherents to let things be. On the contrary, it demanded considerable effort, albeit of an individual and spontaneous nature, to relieve poverty and suffering. Gladstone constantly upbraided those manufacturers who did not actively promote the welfare of their workers and who were 'so deluded as to make money the object of their worship, instead of using it as an instrument of good'. As a result, he was fiercely attacked for going against the sacred principle of the *Wealth of Nations* that 'employers of labour must be allowed at all times freely to carry out their business with a view to their own pecuniary profit.'[39] Voluntaryists were not implacably opposed to state action. They merely had a strong preference for men doing things both for themselves and for others because they wanted to, rather than because they were compelled to by the state.

The term *laissez-faire* was, indeed, remarkably little used by Victorian Liberals. It never figured at all, for example, during the agitation against the corn laws. The only Liberal thinker to declare his faith in the doctrine was Mill, who wrote in *The Principles of Political Economy* that '*Laisser-faire*, in short, should be the general practice: every departure from it, unless required by some great good, is a certain evil.'[40] He laid down as a general rule that in all areas of life the principles of the free market should operate since the individual, as a consumer, was the best judge of his own wants. He went on, however, to make so many exceptions to this rule as to emerge as strongly interventionist, if not positively paternalistic.

Mill's first area of exception to the general rule of *laissez-faire* was where the want was not felt by the consumers and yet their need was great. He instanced in particular education: 'Those who most need to be made wiser or better usually desire it least, and if they desired it, would be incapable of finding the way to it by their own lights. It will continually happen on the voluntary system that, the end not being desired, the means will not be provided at all, or that, the persons requiring improvement having an imperfect or altogether erroneous conception of what they want, the supply called forth by the demand of the market will be anything but what is really required . . . .

Education therefore is one of those things which it is admissible in principle that a government should provide for the people.'⁴¹ Mill further departed from strict *laissez-faire* principles in arguing that it was a legitimate function of government to impose on parents the legal obligation of giving elementary education to their children and to give financial support to elementary schools so as to make them accessible to all children. He was careful to insist, however, that the state should not have a monopoly in the provision of education.

Mill next went on to exclude from the operation of the general *laissez-faire* principle all areas of life where the individual could not judge his own good for himself. This exception covered lunatics and children and justified, for example, government intervention in industry to protect children from being overworked, since 'freedom of contract, in the case of children, is but another name for freedom of coercion.'⁴² Women, however, should not be so protected since they were able to judge their own good and negotiate with employers accordingly. He also excepted from his general rule those things delegated by individuals to other agencies, such as joint stock companies, and all monopoly organizations, which he argued should be subject to government control. He made a further exception where the law was required not to overrule the judgement of individuals but to give effect to it. As an example he cited the case of a group of operatives agreeing to work shorter hours. Such an agreement should be sanctioned by law so that it was no longer in the interest of one of the operatives to break it.

Mill also exempted from the 'do nothing' principle the whole area of welfare provision in society where, as he put it, individuals were not acting for their own interest but for that of others. He argued that the destitute should not have to rely on charity for their subsistence. The state, through the mechanism of the Poor Law, should provide the bare means of subsistence, but no more, to all those unable to make their own livelihood, while private charity should give additional support to the deserving poor. He also argued that the government should provide those services which no individual was likely to be particularly interested in providing, such as the building and upkeep of lighthouses, buoys and other navigational aids, the equipping of scientific expeditions and, characteristically, the maintenance of a learned class. 'It may be said generally', he concluded, 'that anything which it is desirable should be done for the general interests of those members of the community who require external aid, but which it is not of a nature to remunerate individuals or associations for undertaking it, is in itself a suitable thing to be undertaken by government: though, before making the work their own, governments ought always to consider if there be any rational probability of its being done on what is called the voluntary principle, and if so, whether it is likely to be done in a better or more effectual manner by government agency, than by the zeal and liberality of individuals.'[43]

Altogether, Mill had preserved few areas of life where state interference was forbidden and where the *laissez-faire* principle should at all times hold sway. 'In the particular circumstances of a given age or nation,' he wrote, 'there is scarcely anything really important to the general interest, which it may not be desirable, or even necessary, that the government should take upon itself.'[44] In the 1840s, when he wrote the *Principles of Political Economy*, he was still confident that individual effort would perform most of what was required for the well-being of society and that the need for government action would be minimal. As the century progressed, however, he saw a wider role for the state. He did not, as some commentators have said, increase the list of exceptions to the *laissez-faire* principle in subsequent editions of the *Principles*. He could hardly have widened them any further. But in his other writings, particularly his *Autobiography*, he revealed a reluctant but steady progress towards a more interventionist viewpoint as he saw the failure of voluntaryism to live up to its promise.

Voluntaryism rested on the principle that the individual was master of his own fate and that in those few cases where for some reason certain individuals were not able to help themselves, others, either singly or in groups, would always step in to provide assistance. This principle worked well enough during the years of the mid-Victorian economic boom and, indeed, helped to preserve Britain from 'Prussianism', the over-government and crushing of individual spirit that so struck visitors to Germany in the 1860s and 1870s. Most able-bodied men were in employment and with rising real wages were able to put something aside in a friendly society or savings bank to provide for sickness and old age. Employers were also able to be generous. During the brief trade recessions in the 1850s and 1860s, and particularly during the Lancashire cotton famine, factory and mill owners raised and distributed considerable sums of money to ease their workers' temporary distress. It has been calculated that during the 1860s private philanthropy may have been providing the poor with as much as £60 million annually as compared with only £6 million from the official Poor Law.[45]

With the ending of the economic boom in the 1870s, however, the failure of purely voluntary agencies to cope with the needs of the rapidly growing urban population, which Baines, Miall and Morley had come to realize in the field of education, was becoming obvious in other areas as well. At a time of falling prosperity and long-term unemployment, more and more individuals were becoming victims rather than masters of their circumstances. Friendly societies were no longer adequate to the demands being made on them. Employers, too, were facing harder times and were more inclined to cut the wages of their workers than offer them assistance.

Voluntaryism still had many Liberal champions in the early 1880s. The Charity Organisation Society continued to look to individual responsibility as the remedy for poverty and distress and to oppose state action. Loch and others argued that friendly societies, which by the mid-1880s had a membership of 6 million out of a population of $7\frac{1}{2}$ million males over 20, were more than adequate agencies to provide insurance against sickness, unemployment and old age. Characteristically, the Society reacted to the exceptional distress of the mid-1880s by producing a report which recommended the division of the poor into three categories: the thrifty and careful who should be helped by private charity, those who were not provident but who had decent housing, who should be given a modified workhouse test, and 'the idle, loafing, drinking class' who should be given the bare minimum of the Poor Law.[46] Bright continued to uphold the principle of free contracting between employer and worker and opposed all legislation which sought to protect workers. Gladstone's second administration was run on largely voluntaryist principles and refrained from interventionist legislation in the spheres of industry and welfare. Even the proposed temperance legislation, which was opposed by extreme voluntaryists because of its coercive nature, was highly voluntaryist in tone being in the form of a Permissive Bill requiring the spontaneous action of local ratepayers to secure a veto on the sale of liquor. Gladstone himself delighted Peter Taylor by announcing in 1883: 'I regard compulsory and penal provisions, such as those of the Vaccination Acts, with mistrust and misgiving, and were I engaged in an inquiry, I should require very clear proof of their necessity before giving them my approval.'[47]

Increasingly, however, the voluntary principle was coming under attack not just from the disciples of Arnold and Carlyle but from many Liberals themselves. During the 1880s many people were beginning to question whether self-help and philanthropic activity were sufficient to cope with the miseries of the age and whether the free contract of master and labourer and the enlightened self-interest of manufacturers were sufficient safeguards against the exploitation of labour. Ironically, it was often those most strongly influenced by voluntaryism who came to see its shortcomings most clearly. As they gained in self-confidence and moved further into the political society from which they had formerly been excluded, many Nonconformists lost their hostility to government and came to see that their concern for humanity and fraternity might best be expressed in the municipal or even the national community. Involvement in such voluntaryist campaigns as that against the Contagious Diseases Acts had led many Liberals to demand a positive role for the state in controlling the traffic in prostitutes. In a similar way, those involved in church and university settlements among the poor, which were often inspired by the ideology of the Charity Organisation Society, had come to see vast, impersonal forces rather than personal irresponsibility as the root causes of poverty. At least one of them, F. H. Stead, brother of W. H. Stead and himself warden of a Congregational settlement in Walworth, east London, had by the early 1880s espoused views directly contrary to those of Loch and was a leading advocate of old-age pensions and state insurance schemes against unemployment. The terrible reality of the drink problem had impressed both Harcourt and Green with the need for legislation interfering with the freedom of the individual for the good of society as a whole.

The fact was that ultra-voluntaryism, in the form of total *laissez-faire* and libertarianism, had never been a feature of the Liberal outlook. The only significant group who held to that position were the extreme individualists who followed Herbert Spencer into anarchic conservatism in the last decade of the nineteenth century. For most Victorian Liberals voluntaryism was always harnessed to a passion for social improvement. As such, it proved to be surprisingly compatible with the idea of state intervention.

Chapter 9

The Passion for Improvement

John Stuart Mill once described Gladstone as the statesman 'in whom the spirit of improvement is incarnate, and in whose career as minister the characteristic feature has been to seek out things that require or admit of improvement'.[1] Zeal for improving mankind was a characteristic feature of the Victorian Liberal mind. It manifested itself in an obsession with the efficiency and reform of institutions, in a desire to clear away anomalies and obstacles to social progress and advancement, and in the passionate involvement of so many Liberals in crusades to right some wrong and make the world a better place. The dedicated, almost professional social improver or 'faddist' who devoted himself to some specific cause, as Lawson and Caine did to temperance, Rathbone to the reform of the bankruptcy laws, Lubbock to securing holidays for working people and Stansfeld to the repeal of the Contagious Diseases Act, was as much a characteristic Liberal type as the up-and-coming manufacturer or the dissident Nonconformist.

There was, of course, a strong Whig tradition of concern with social reform and improvement which went back at least to the beginning of the nineteenth century when it was represented by such figures as Henry Brougham, Sir Samuel Romilly and Francis Place. In many ways, indeed, the Benthamite reformers of the 1820s and 1830s were more interventionist and 'advanced' in their approach to social questions than their Liberal heirs a generation later. The Constitutional Code which Bentham himself drew up with Southwood Smith and Edwin Chadwick envisaged the establishment of a series of government departments to superintend such social services as the relief of poverty, health and education. Most Gladstonians in the 1880s still shrank in horror from the prospect of such wholesale 'constructionism'.

At first, Liberals looked for social improvement through individual advancement aided by the removal of obstacles and restrictions and the opening of careers and opportunities to all. The Manchester School's view that the way to the general improvement of society lay through the free play of individual enterprise and voluntary effort and the onward march of prosperity and scientific progress continued to commend itself to most Gladstonians. It was challenged, however, by those younger Liberals who felt that improvement must come through social reorganization involving the use of the constructive power of the state. In 1874 Joseph Chamberlain, who became the leading exponent of this latter approach, although more perhaps through opportunism than conviction, shattered the confident optimism of Gladstonian Liberalism by pointing out that 'despite the perpetual adulation of ourselves and the constant recitals of our prosperity and of the progress we are making in science and general culture . . . we have in our midst a vast population more ignorant than the barbarians, more brutal than the savages whom we profess to convert, more miserable than the most wretched in other countries to whom we attempt from time to time to carry succour and relief.'[2] The constructionist policies which younger Liberals advocated, involving the use of the state as an agent of social improvement, initially filled Gladstonians with horror. However, as the voluntary and individualist approach increasingly showed its inability to combat the ignorance, poverty and squalor of a mass urban population, the idea of the positive state gradually gained ascendancy in the Liberal mind.

Probably the most important and united campaign for improvement in which Liberals engaged was the movement for land reform. Initiated by Cobden and Bright, it attracted Gladstone, Mill and the intellectuals, and Chamberlain and the constructionists. The survival of medieval laws restricting the transfer of property, chief of which were those relating to primogeniture and entail, was seen by all Liberals as conferring an unjustifiable privilege. It led to a pattern of land ownership in which, as the *New Domesday Book* of 1875 revealed, one half of the enclosed land of England was owned by a mere 2,250 families. Much of it was either uncultivated or farmed by tenants who stood to gain no benefits if they improved it.

The restrictive land laws offended a number of Liberal principles. They were a blatant form of protectionism which distorted the free working of the economy and prevented resources being put to their most productive use. A demand for free trade in land followed naturally from the call for free trade in corn. It also enabled Liberals to attack their favourite enemy, the landed aristocracy, and to champion the rights of tenants whose welfare was always closer to Liberal hearts than was that of factory workers. Reform of the land laws seemed to offer a way to improve both the self-reliance and the material condition of the lower classes which conveniently avoided the need for any interference with manufacturing industry or commerce. 'The whole history of the ownership of land in Europe', wrote T. H. Green, 'has been of a kind to lead to the agglomeration of a proletariat neither holding nor seeking property. . . . When we consider all this, we shall see the unfairness of laying on capitalism or the free development of individual wealth the blame which is really due to the arbitrary and violent manner in which rights over land have been acquired and exercised.'[3]

At the root of the Liberal campaign for land reform was a vision of a new rural lower-middle class of peasant proprietors on a par with the independent artisans and craftsmen in the towns. George Howell summed up the campaign's demands as 'security of tenure, at fair and fixed rents, with the right of free sale to British agriculturalists, and help to create a peasant propriety'.[4] There were considerable attractions in creating such a new class of property owners. The value of the acquisition by a labourer of a small landed property, wrote Fawcett in 1865, 'is not to be estimated by the amount of wealth with which it enriches him. It makes him a different man; it raises him from the position of a labourer, and calls forth all those active qualities of mind, which are sure to be exerted when a man has the consciousness that he is working on his own account.'[5]

The campaign for wider ownership of land was initially carried out through extra-Parliamentary pressure groups. The first of these was the National Freehold Land Society, set up in 1849. The object of the Society, in which Cobden was a leading member, was to encourage people to buy freehold plots, either outright or by subscription, and so become both property owners and voters, under the forty shilling qualification of the 1832 Reform Act. Although by 1852 20,000 allotments of sites worth at least forty shillings a year had been made by the Society, it became clear that a more radical approach was needed; and in 1869 Mill, with the support of Fawcett, John Morley and Thorold Rogers, set up the Land Tenure Reform Association. The objects of the Association, as set out in its programme for 1871, included the removal of all legal and fiscal impediments to the free transfer of land, the abolition of primogeniture, the encouragement of co-operative agriculture through the purchase of land by the state and its subsequent lease to co-operative associations, and the gradual takeover by the state of land belonging to the Crown, public bodies and charitable endowments so that it could be let to tenants.

These proposals of the Land Tenure Reform Association were

significant in their envisaging a positive role for the state in the field of social improvement. They stopped short of land nationalization, but not far short. In his *Principles of Political Economy*, Mill had argued that absolute ownership of land was inadmissible since it was a vital commodity, limited in quantity, which rightly belonged to the whole community. In this vein, both Mill and his Association called for the taxation of all increases in the value of land which occurred without any effort by the proprietors. The idea of taxing land in this way, which was powerfully canvassed by Henry George in his influential book *Progress and Poverty* (1879) and supported by many Nonconformists, was to become a feature of the Liberal programme of social improvement and found its way into Lloyd George's People's Budget of 1909.

The pattern of land ownership in Ireland aroused particularly strong feelings among Liberal reformers. Bright described it as displaying 'in perfection the fruits of aristocratic and territorial occupation and privilege'.[6] Over ninety per cent of the land was owned by British Protestant proprietors, most of them absentee landlords, whose largely Catholic tenants had no security of tenure. Liberals saw land as lying at the root of Ireland's political troubles. 'The great evil of Ireland is this,' wrote Bright, 'that the Irish people, the Irish nation, are dispossessed of the soil.'[7] There was a strong call from many Liberals in the 1860s for government action to secure tenant rights and create a native proprietary of the land. Bright himself suggested the establishment of a Parliamentary Commission empowered to use public money to buy land from absentee landlords and resell it to tenants over a long period. Mill called for existing tenants to be given a permanent tenure at a fixed rent to be assessed by the government.

Gladstone's governments proved unenthusiastic about legislating for land reform in England and largely confined themselves to trying to rectify the clear injustices of the Irish system of land tenure. The Irish Landlord and Tenant Act of 1870 gave tenants the right to claim compensation for improvements made to land during their occupancy and also for eviction for any reason other than non-payment of rent. It did not, however, satisfy Irish tenants who wanted security of tenure and fair rents enforced by law. Gladstone's 1881 Irish Land Act went a long way towards meeting their demands by establishing a tribunal to fix fair rents, guaranteeing fixity of tenure to all who paid rents, and establishing freedom of sale and the right of a tenant to part with his interest in a property. When it was clear that not even these measures would reconcile Irish tenants to their English landlords, Gladstone worked out his land purchase scheme of 1886 which gave the owners of land in Ireland an option to be bought out by the government at a sum of twenty times their annual net rental.

Gladstone's Irish land legislation marked a significant departure from the principles of absolute property rights and freedom of contract. By controlling rents, compensation and security of tenure, the laws asserted the state's right to determine the conditions on which private property could be enjoyed. The 1881 Act in particular alarmed many more conservative Liberals by its apparent disregard for the rights of landlords. It led to the resignation from the Cabinet of the Duke of Argyll, who himself owned 170,000 acres in Scotland. Gladstone admitted that the Act marked 'a great departure from the principles of free contract . . . but . . . it is required by the circumstances of the country'.[8] He made clear, however, that he had no intention of applying such drastic legislation to England.

The general efforts at land reform made by Liberal governments were insignificant compared with the particular measures applied to Ireland. The most important of the measures passed during Gladstone's second administration, the Settled Land Act of 1882, which broke down barriers to land transfer by allowing settled land to be freely sold or let, was carried through Parliament on the initiative of a Conservative peer, Lord Cairns. The only major piece of land legislation promoted by the government was the 1883 Agricultural Holdings Act which gave tenants a statutory right to compensation for improvements to land which they made during their occupancy.

Gladstone and many other Liberals continued to believe into the 1880s that the wider ownership of land which they wanted to see could be achieved through permissive and voluntary means and without compulsory purchase of land by the state. In 1880 Bradlaugh was instrumental in setting up the Land Reform League to campaign for interference by the state with the monopoly of landlords but to resist land nationalization. Five years later a group of Liberals and moderate Conservatives led by Auberon Herbert established the Small Farms and Labourer's Holding Company to buy large tracts of land, subdivide them, and sell them off as small-holdings. The Company was actively supported by the Duke of Argyll and Thorold Rogers but it aroused little response from landowners and little interest among agricultural labourers.

More radical Liberals were meanwhile coming to the view that compulsory state intervention and purchase were the only effective means of achieving reform in the system of land ownership. Chamberlain's famous Radical or 'Unauthorized' Programme of 1886 included a demand that local authorities should be empowered to purchase land compulsorily and then let it out for labourers' allotments and small-holdings and artisans' dwellings. Henry Labouchere called for 'the confiscation to the state of all lands owned by private individuals which might be cultivated, but which are not, and which are not part of the amenities of residence'.[9]

The ultimate objective of Chamberlain and Labouchere was the same as that of Gladstone and Bradlaugh—the creation of a new class of peasant proprietors. They differed from the older and more conservative Liberal land reformers, however, in believing that this end could not be achieved by voluntary means. Chamberlain and Jesse Collings had initially tried to promote their ideal of labourers' small-holdings with 'three acres and a cow' through permissive legislation like the 1882 Allotments Extension Act which encouraged the offering of small parcels of land on the market. They soon came to the view, however, that only the penal taxation of land, or even its nationalization, would induce owners to part with it and effect a fundamental change of ownership in favour of small proprietors. The Liberal campaign for land reform had begun as a demand for free trade and the abolition of privileges in the best tradition of the Manchester School. By the mid-1880s it was becoming a call for state intervention and even for state ownership.

A similar growing realization of the positive role that the state could play in improving society occurred in the field of education. The spread of education came second only to land reform in the Liberal catalogue of good causes. With their belief in progress and their trust in the people, Liberals had none of the dread of 'the all-conquering march of intellectual power' which was felt by some Tories.[10] From an early stage, they committed themselves to extending the provision of education in society. Cobden and Bright first met at a meeting of the British and Foreign School Society in Rochdale in 1837. Ten years later they were both actively involved in setting up the Lancashire Public Schools Association (leading later to the National Public Schools Association) to campaign for a system of elementary schools paid for out of the rates.

The Liberal campaign to establish a proper system of elementary education gathered momentum in the late 1860s. The voluntaryists conceded that a state scheme was necessary, after surveys had shown that voluntary schools were reaching less than twenty per cent of those between three and twelve, and that forty per cent of children had no schooling at all. The Taunton Commission reported in favour of much greater public control over the endowed schools through a central administrative board and local district commissioners. The 1867 Reform Act underlined the urgent need for a proper system of education, as Lowe put it, to enable 'our future masters to learn their letters'.[11] In both 1867 and 1868 Henry Bruce introduced Bills to set up local boards to provide schools funded out of the rates. In 1869 Chamberlain was instrumental in setting up the National Education League to campaign for free compulsory elementary education on the rates.

Forster's Education Act of 1870 was a significant milestone in recognizing for the first time that the state had direct responsibility for education. It brought elementary schools within reach of all children, although it stopped short of making their education either compulsory or free. The call to remedy these two deficiencies was taken up by Chamberlain and the National Education League and by younger Liberal politicians like Mundella who did not share their elders' aversion to compulsion and provision by the state. Of all Gladstonian Liberals, Mundella was perhaps the most committed to educational improvement. He was an ardent advocate of university extension and helped to establish Firth College in Sheffield (now Sheffield University) as the prototype of the technical colleges which he felt Britain must have to maintain its industrial competitiveness in the world. He battled against voluntaryist objections to promote state secondary schools. It was in the elementary sector that he achieved most, however. In 1880, as Vice-President of the Committee of the Privy Council with special responsibility for education, he secured legislation enforcing compulsory school attendance on all children from five to ten and making employers of children over ten liable to prosecution if they did not have certificates of education. By 1885 Gladstone himself, prompted by pressure from Mundella and the National Liberal Federation, had come near to accepting a system of free elementary schools paid for out of the rates, which would have horrified the voluntaryists thirty years earlier, although it was Lord Salisbury's Conservative Government which finally created free education by abolishing elementary school fees in 1891.

Just as in the 1860s Liberal enthusiasts for land reform and education had come to see a positive role for the state in improving society, so those involved in the temperance movement came to the same view in the 1870s. Initially, temperance had seemed a goal that could and should only be pursued by individual moral action and not by the use of the coercive power of the state. Gradually, however, it became clear that moral suasion would not be enough. T. H. Green came to the realization in 1873 that 'the drink curse is altogether too big a thing to be dealt with by individual effort only.'[12] Samuel Morley noted in 1878: 'I have come reluctantly to the opinion that we must have legislation. I do not see a chance of getting any substantial relief without legislative action.'[13] Harcourt experienced a similar conversion from his earlier opposition to legislation on temperance during his time as Home Secretary in the early 1880s. Predictably Chamberlain advocated a solution to the drink problem which involved state action. In 1877 he argued that the liquor trade should be taken out of private hands and put under municipal control where it could be properly regulated. His proposals proved too socialistic for most Liberals, and it was eventually the idea of a local veto of the drink trade by a majority of ratepayers, which happily combined spontaneous local action with legislative prohibition and regulation, that the party seized on as the way to create a sober society.

Land reform, education and temperance appealed to Gladstonian Liberals as improvements which, even if they could only be brought about by some compulsory government action, had the effect of encouraging self-help and promoting the moral and intellectual quality of the populace. More advanced Liberals, however, argued that there were even more basic improvements to be made before a sober and educated society could be created. The majority of the population were not rural peasants but urban labourers whose physical conditions of life made any kind of advancement difficult. Characteristically, it was once again Chamberlain who made the point most forcibly when he exclaimed in 1874: 'What folly it is to talk about the moral and intellectual elevation of the masses when the conditions of life are such as to render elevation impossible! What can the schoolmaster or the minister of religion do, when the influences of home undo all he does? We find bad air, polluted water, crowded and filthy homes, and ill-ventilated courts everywhere prevailing in the midst of our boasted wealth, luxury and civilisation.'[14]

The improvement of the urban environment was not a matter of indifference to traditional Liberals as their critics implied, but it was something that they felt was better done by individual voluntary effort than by compulsory state action. Titus Salt, for instance, gave the inhabitants of Saltaire clean air, sewage disposal and good ventilation as well as Nonconformist chapels. Such action by manufacturers on behalf of their workers was lauded by Liberals while compulsory regulations were deplored. Edwin Chadwick's great Public Health Act of 1848 had been strongly opposed by Cobden and Bright. In Parliament Liberals continued to be noticeably less enthusiastic than Tories about measures to promote Disraeli's dictum *'Sanitas sanitatum, omnia sanitas'*, although voluntaryist objections were overcome sufficiently for regulations on compulsory vaccination against smallpox to be tightened up in 1871 and for the enactment the following year of a Public Health Act which incorporated many of the recommendations of Disraeli's Royal Commission on Sanitation, including the compulsory appointment of medical officers of health by all local authorities. When the Tory leader suggested in his 1872 Manchester speech that the health of the people should be the most important question for politicians, he was derided in the Liberal press for advocating the 'policy of sewage'. 'It may be the "policy of sewage" to a Liberal member of Parliament,' Disraeli observed in his subsequent Crystal Palace speech, 'but to one of the labouring multitude of England . . . it is a question of life and death.'[15]

Liberals at Westminster may not have been much interested in sewage, but many of those who lived and worked in the overcrowded cities of the Midlands and the North did not deserve Disraeli's sarcastic jibe. In Birmingham, for example, a group of Liberals under the influence of George Dawson and R. W. Dale developed a positive approach to urban environmental improvement which had a considerable impact on Liberal policy. From their work, and as a result of the activities of many other local politicians and reformers, there developed the idea of municipal provision of public amenities and of local government as the main agency for promoting the physical health and welfare of the people.

Dawson was in many ways an archetypal Gladstonian. He was an ardent Nonconformist and a lover of liberty who organized the first public meeting in England on behalf of the Hungarian nationalists. His Nonconformist conscience and his idealistic nationalism led him away from the traditional individualism of most Liberals, however, and towards a doctrine of fraternity and corporate responsibility. He found an expression of that doctrine in the new municipal communities which were developing in the industrial North and Midlands. 'A great town', he wrote, 'exists to discharge towards the people of that town the duties that a great nation exists to discharge towards the people of that nation.'[16] In a speech in 1861 at the opening of the first free public library in the country which he had been instrumental in securing for Birmingham, he developed his municipal gospel. The town council, he argued, was a new church 'where men might forget sectarianism and political economy ... and find a brotherhood'.[17]

Dale took up the municipal gospel which Dawson was spreading and preached to the members of his own congregation that 'they ought to be Aldermen and Town Councillors. They ought to give their time as well as their money to whatever improvements are intended to develop the intelligence of the community. They ought to be reformers of local abuses. They ought to see to it that the towns and parishes in which they live are well drained, well lighted, and well paved; that there are good schools for every class of the population; that there are harmless public amusements; that all parochial and municipal affairs are conducted honourably and equitably.'[18]

Dale's followers responded to his appeal. 'Towards the end of the sixties,' he noted later, 'a few Birmingham men made the discovery that perhaps a strong and able Town Council might do almost as much to improve the conditions of life in the town as Parliament itself ... instead of discussing small questions of administration and of economy, [they] dwelt with glowing enthusiasm on what a great and prosperous town like Birmingham might do for its people. They spoke of sweeping away streets in which it was not possible to live a healthy and decent life; of making the town cleaner, sweeter and brighter; of providing gardens and parks and music; of erecting baths and free libraries, an art gallery and a museum. They insisted that the great monopolies like the gas and water supply should be in the hands of the Corporation; that good water should be supplied without stint at the lowest possible prices; that the profits of the gas supply should relieve the pressure of the rates.'[19]

No one was more enthusiastic about this new idea of municipal improvement than Chamberlain, who joined the Birmingham Town Council in 1869 and became mayor in 1873. He initiated a massive programme of slum clearance and urban improvement, partially funded out of the profits of the town's gas and water companies which he brought under municipal ownership. The results were spectacular. In 1883, when he had left local for national politics, he told John Morley that since his mayoralty there had been 'a saving of seven per thousand in the death rate—2,800 lives per annum in the town. And as five people are ill for everyone who dies, there must be a diminution of 14,000 cases of sickness. . . . Unless I can secure for the nation results similar to these which have followed the adoption of my policy in Birmingham, it will have been a sorry exchange to give up the Town Council for the Cabinet.'[20]

Chamberlain's activities in Birmingham had extended considerably the demesne of public ownership and the principle of interventionist and compulsory legislation. By the end of the 1880s it was not just the city's gas and water companies that were under municipal ownership, but also its parks and gardens, museums, art galleries and libraries, baths and wash houses, technical schools, cattle markets, street railways, concert halls, piers and harbours, dispensaries and hospitals and artisans' dwellings. Chamberlain seemed to have scant regard for the traditional Liberal values of voluntaryism and free enterprise. On the occasion of his third election as mayor he told the Town Council: 'All private effort, all individual philanthropy sinks into insignificance compared with the organised power of a great representative assembly like this.'[21]

In Parliament, Chamberlain worked to extend to other parts of the country the system which he had established in Birmingham. The way had already been paved by Mundella who with George Leeman, M.P. for York, had been largely responsible for the 1872 Municipal Corporations (Borough Funds) Act which allowed local authorities to use public money to take over and run public utilities. In 1879 Chamberlain opposed a Bill to limit the amount that could be loaned to local authorities with words which must have worried Gladstone: 'The expenditure by local authorities is increasing and ought to increase.'[22] The following year he strongly backed the Metropolitan Water Works Purchase Act which enabled London to follow Birmingham's example. In 1882 he succeeded in carrying through Parliament an Electric Lighting Bill which enabled municipalities to adopt electric lighting and limited its supply by private enterprise to a period of twenty-one years. By 1884, twenty-four local authorities had obtained authorization to issue stock to pay for housing, sanitation, educational and welfare schemes.

The fact that this great increase in public ownership and intervention had come at local rather than national level made it less of a shock than it would otherwise have been. The responsibility for housing, health and recreation assumed by many town councils by the mid-1880s would never have been accepted if it had been undertaken by government departments. There was considerably less suspicion in Liberal minds about the growth of local government power, which was at least near the people and reasonably representative, than there was about the spread of central government. Chamberlain himself wrote in 1885: 'While I am myself afraid of anything in the nature of centralisation or state interference, I have no jealousy at all of the growth and spread of these municipal institutions, which are the great honour and glory of this country.'[23] There was no doubt, however, that he was a man who saw a strong positive role for government of all kinds and that his presence in Gladstone's second administration would help the already growing trend towards interventionist legislation, increased spending of public money for the public good, and shifting responsibilities from the individual to the state.

In fact, that trend was already well under way by the time that Chamberlain came into the Liberal Government. In 1878 Dale noted 'even within the last thirty years a very great and remarkable change has passed upon the theoretical views of the advanced Liberal party. In my early years . . . one chief article of the creed of extreme Radicalism was this—that the powers of government, municipal and national, should be restrained within the narrowest possible limits; that governments should do nothing for us except protect us against force and against fraud . . . but Radicalism has gradually come to discover that with political power in the hands of the people, municipal and national government may contribute very much to the positive development of national life. We still hold fast to the great principle, that so far as the industry of the country is concerned, it will prosper most if it is left unfettered, but we say that in many directions the interference of Government, national and local, may very greatly contribute to national advance.'[24] He cited specifically the growing interference with landowning, the assumption of government responsibility for education, and the development of local government control over public health and the urban environment.

During Gladstone's second administration of 1880 to 1885 the positive role of the state in improving society was confirmed. Beatrice Webb saw it as a no-man's-land between the old Radicalism and the new Socialism and wrote: 'this ministry of all the talents wandered in and out of the trenches of the old individualists and the scouting parties of the new Socialists.'[25] Dicey's over-simplified picture of a period of Benthamite *laissez-faire* giving way to a period of collectivism, 'favouring the intervention of the state, even at some sacrifice of individual freedom, for the purpose of conferring benefit upon the mass of people', has some truth if applied to these years.[26] The interventionist actions of Gladstone's first Government in the fields of education, land law and personal savings, could be construed as actions to stimulate self-help and create an educated, independent population which could stand on its own feet. They did not involve continuing commitments by the state to the public welfare and, indeed, envisaged the state being able to pull back from this area. The legislation of the second administration was, however, of a very different order. It involved central and local government in continuing commitments such as ensuring compulsory attendance at school and safeguarding public health. Not only were the sacred canons of voluntaryism breached by such measures as the Irish Land Act, but in measures like the Allotments Extension Act and the Irish land purchase scheme, the government had shouldered new responsibilities which were capable of infinite expansion. Improvement was no longer being sought by removing obstacles, but rather by creating new institutions. 'Constructionism' was the order of the day.

This change from a largely negative to a positive view of the role of the state was partly the result of a growing realization in the 1880s of the extent of poverty and disease in Britain. The serious depression which broke the prosperity of the mid-Victorian economy in the late 1870s greatly increased the number of poor and unemployed. It also cast grave doubts on the central assumption of economic liberalism that, provided attention was paid to the production of wealth, the distribution would look after itself. Social scientists, using the new tools of statistical investigation and quantitative analysis, showed that poverty had remained persistent and widespread despite the long years of prosperity arising from free trade and low taxation. They also suggested that it was not so much a matter of individual moral responsibility, as a product of vast impersonal forces which could only be tackled by collective action.

Similar sentiments were also being voiced increasingly by Nonconformists. With the achievement of their political goals, Nonconformist ministers and publicists turned their attention to social matters. It was significant that many of the Liberals' first steps in the direction of positive state intervention were taken because of the promptings of this newly directed Nonconformist Conscience. The United Kingdom Alliance's insistence that the state could not remain morally neutral on a subject like drink had helped to establish the case for temperance legislation. Dawson's gospel of municipal reform had sanctioned the

interventionist activities of local government. Tracts like Andrew
Mearns's *Bitter Cry of Outcast London* showed the squalor and disease
that voluntary charitable effort was hardly touching. A new breed of
Nonconformist Liberal politicians was emerging, like John Benn, a
leading Congregationalist and grandfather of Anthony Wedgwood
Benn, who joined the London County Council in 1889 determined to
apply constructionist and interventionist policies in the spheres of social
services, health, education and housing.

Hardly less important in changing Liberal attitudes to the role of the
state than the effects of the depression, the revelations of social scientists,
and the promptings of the Nonconformist Conscience was the growing
power of the unskilled working classes. These men, who formed the
bulk of the two million people enfranchised in 1884, were very different
in their attitudes and demands from the skilled artisans who had formed
the backbone of the Liberal party from 1867. Self-help and low taxation
had little appeal to labourers who were accustomed to collective action
and who looked to the state to provide them with welfare. Chamberlain
caught the new spirit of the times perfectly when he wrote to a friend
in 1883: 'The politics of the future are social politics, and the problem
is still how to secure the greatest happiness of the greatest number and
especially of those whom all previous legislation and reform seem to
have left very much where they were before.'[27]

Gladstone did not relish the intrusion of social issues into politics.
They were entirely alien to his conception of the proper concerns of
statesmen and governments and smacked dangerously of materialism
and crude populism. J. A. Hobson, one of the moving spirits behind
the 'New Liberalism' of the early twentieth century, recalled that as a
boy brought up in the high noon of Gladstonianism in the late 1860s
and early 1870s, 'I had no idea that politics had anything to do with
industry or standards of living.' Rather, it seemed to consist of 'those
stage monsters of foreign or imperial policy, the menace or the mis-
deeds of France, Russia, Turkey or Germany'.[28] For Gladstone, social
improvement was something to be achieved by individual moral
effort and not by the collective and compulsory activity of the state.
He was not in the least enamoured of the great municipal improvements wrought by Chamberlain in Birmingham. When he commended
that city in a speech in 1877, it was not for its sanitation and slum
clearance programme, but for 'the extraordinary energy that pervades
the whole place. Men have their own opinions and entertain them
freely; but with regard to one another they do not attempt to coerce

one another.'[29] Characteristically, he set more store by the free play of minds than by the free passage of sewage.

While Gladstone was no friend to 'constructionist' legislation and retained an essentially negative view of the state, he was never prevented by any doctrinaire attachment to the principle of *laissez-faire* from invoking the positive power of government when he felt it was genuinely needed to promote the public good. As President of the Board of Trade in the 1840s he had sought, to the consternation of Bright, to regulate the activities of the railway companies in the interests of passengers, a subject to which he returned in the 1880s. Introducing his proposal for a Post Office Life Insurance Scheme in 1864, he had commended such interventionist measures as the Factory Acts and sanitary regulations. 'There is here,' he said, 'undoubtedly, a very great interference with the liberty of private action. . . . On the whole it has been adopted by Parliament, not from any foregone conclusion in favour of that mode of meddling with private concerns, but under a sense of the exceedingly grave evils to be remedied. . . . I am bound to add that I believe it has been, in general, beneficial.'[30]

Gladstone responded to the growing cry for social improvement in the early 1880s by setting up Royal Commissions on rural depression (1882), contagious diseases (1883) and working-class housing (1884). The three commissions recommended interventionist legislation to deal with the problems that they studied. The most radical proposals came from the Royal Commission on housing which recommended the compulsory purchase of land by local authorities and the provision of government money for municipal housing schemes. George Goschen and Samuel Morley signed a dissenting memorandum expressing their reluctance 'to create an expectation, either of state subsidies, or of the building of working class dwellings at the public expense. . . . We are opposed to measures which . . . are calculated to weaken the motives which prompt the steady development of private enterprise.'[31] In the event, the commission's recommendations were not implemented until 1890 when the Tories introduced a Housing Act empowering local authorities to buy up and demolish substandard buildings and erect new houses in their place.

Traditional Gladstonian Liberals continued to look to individual moral effort rather than collective action as the main agency for improving society. Samuel Morley remained convinced that in seeking the reason and therefore the remedy for social ills 'many people begin at the wrong end. They say people drink because they live in bad dwellings; I say they live in bad dwellings because they drink. It makes all the difference which way you put it. The first essential is not to deal with the habitation, but the habit.'[32] Zeal for economy and dislike of increasing the power of the state made Gladstone's generation wary about turning the government into a provider of welfare for the people. Younger Liberals, however, took a very much more positive view of the state. By 1886 Hugh Price Hughes could talk of a 'New Liberalism' which 'rejects the heartless conclusions of doctrinaire political economy. . . . The old dread of state action has passed away now that there is some guarantee that the resources of the government will be used not to create or buttress the privilege of the few but to promote the well-being of the entire community.'[33] Initially this 'New Liberalism' had two major exponents, Joseph Chamberlain and T. H. Green, both of whom saw the state as a positive instrument for social improvement, although they differed in their emphasis.

It was inevitable that Chamberlain should formulate the most advanced and unqualified view of the positive role of the state as social improver. As the architect of municipal improvement in Birmingham and as chief exponent of the programme of 'Free Land' and 'Free Schools' in the 1870s, he had been at the forefront of the movement to use local and central government as agents of social improvement. He developed his ideas in the *Radical Programme* which he and other like-minded social improvers drew up in 1885. In the preface, he linked his demand for a new style of Liberal policy to the changed political situation brought about by the 1884 Reform Act: 'At last the majority of the nation will be represented by a majority of the House of Commons, and ideas and wants and claims which have been hitherto ignored in legislation will find a voice in Parliament, and will compel the attention of statesmen. New conceptions of public duty, new developments of social enterprise, new estimates of the natural obligations of the members of the community to one another, have come into view and demand consideration.'[34] The editor of the *Programme*, T. H. Escott, announced that it was time to 'sound the death-knell of the *laissez-faire* system. . . . The goal towards which the advance will probably be made at an accelerated pace is that in the direction of which the legislation of the last quarter of a century has been tending—the intervention, in other words, of the State on behalf of the weak against the strong, in the interests of labour against capital, of want and suffering against luxury and ease.'[35]

The proposals in the *Radical Programme* were not, in fact, very different from those being canvassed by Gladstone. Chamberlain himself had tempered many of the ideas of his Radical colleagues. In essence, the *Programme* called for free education, local government for rural areas and the right of local authorities compulsorily to purchase land to create houses and small-holdings for working people. It also proposed a redistributive system of taxation, with a graduated system of income tax, a tax on ground rents, higher death duties and a contribution by personal property to local rates.

Although Gladstone agreed with its proposals on taxation and local government, other Liberals were deeply unhappy about the *Radical Programme*. In the field of taxation at least it seemed to advocate socialism. Chamberlain himself stated in Hull during the great country-wide tour when he publicized the *Programme*: 'I believe the great difficulty with which we have to deal is the excessive inequality in the distribution of riches.'[36] He admittedly went on to say in Bradford: 'I do not believe that there can ever be an absolute equality of conditions and I think that nothing would be more undesirable than that we should remove the stimulus to industry and thrift and exertion which is afforded by the security given to every man in the enjoyment of the fruits of his own individual exertions. I am opposed to confiscation in every shape or form, because I believe that it would destroy that security and lessen that stimulus.'[37] But there was no doubt as to the general drift of his policy. As he said in Warrington: 'Of course it is Socialism. The Poor Law is Socialism; The Education Act is Socialism; the greater part of municipal work is Socialism; and every kindly act of legislation by which the community has sought to discharge its responsibilities and obligations to the poor is Socialism, but it is none the worse for that.'[38]

Gladstonian Liberals were also worried by the strongly positive role which the *Radical Programme* accorded the state. John Morley had diverged from his previous close association with Chamberlain in the early 1880s because of the latter's increasingly 'constructionist' stand. Chamberlain maintained that with the passing of the 1884 Reform Act it was no longer true that government power could be exercised only in the interests of a particular class. 'Now Government is the organised expression of the wishes and the wants of the people, and under these circumstances let us cease to regard it with suspicion.'[39] For many Liberals, however, it was impossible to regard government with anything other than suspicion and to them Chamberlain seemed to strike a distinctly un-Liberal note when he insisted that: 'My Radicalism, at all events, desires to see established a strong Government.'[40]

T. H. Green was very much closer than Chamberlain to the Victorian Liberal tradition. He was a firm believer in the value of spontaneous voluntary action by individuals and communities and was intensely optimistic about human nature, being convinced that man possessed a unique capacity for doing good. He felt that only by seeking to realize this moral capacity could man attain his full humanity, and therefore his freedom. Freedom for him had a positive meaning that went far beyond the negative doctrine of Mill and the Manchester School. 'When we speak of freedom,' he said, 'we do not mean merely freedom to do as we like irrespective of what it is we like. We mean the greatest power on the part of the citizens as a body to make the most and best of themselves.'[41] In his efforts to promote this ideal of freedom through his participation in the temperance movement and the Taunton Commission on Endowed Schools, Green had come to see that compulsory legislation, far from shackling men, was often needed to liberate them.

Green worked out his doctrine of the positive state in a lecture which he delivered in 1880 on *Liberal Legislation and Freedom of Contract*. The purpose of the lecture, he said, was to support recent and potential actions by the Liberal party which appeared to conflict with the cherished Liberal principle of liberty and freedom of contract. He distinguished three distinct periods of reform since the Liberal awakening in Britain. The first, from 1832 to 1846, had seen the struggle for a free society against privileged closed Corporations and the Church. It had involved no interference with the rights of the individual. The second period, from 1846 to 1868, had seen the liberation of trade and the realization of complete freedom of contract. The movement of reform since 1868, however, had been less readily identifiable as a work of liberation. It had involved land laws restricting the freedom of contract between landlord and tenant in England and Ireland, factory laws interfering with the free contract between master and labourer, and legislation on public health, temperance and education which introduced an element of compulsion and regulation into the behaviour of individuals and curbed their absolute liberties.

At first sight, Green admitted, these measures were all contrary to Liberal ideals of freedom of contract and individual liberty. But these ideals were not, he insisted, ends in themselves, but merely means to an end: 'That end is what I call freedom in the positive sense: in other words, the liberation of the powers of all men equally for contributions to a common good.' It followed, in this social definition of freedom, that 'the mere removal of compulsion, the mere enabling a man to do as he likes, is in itself no contribution to true freedom.' A drunkard or a man imprisoned in slum conditions was in no sense free. He had to be liberated by the state, the only agency capable of creating the conditions in which true freedom could be exercised. 'Our modern legislation then,' he continued, 'with reference to labour, and education, and health, involving as it does manifold interference with freedom of contract, is justified on the ground that it is the business of the state, not indeed directly to promote moral goodness, for that, from the very nature of moral goodness, it cannot do, but to maintain the conditions without which a free exercise of the human faculties is impossible.'[42]

Green retained his deep commitment to voluntaryism. It was tempered, however, by a realization that not all men would voluntarily educate their children or refrain from excessive drinking. 'We shall probably all agree', he wrote, 'that a society in which the public health was duly protected, and necessary education duly provided for, by the spontaneous action of individuals, was in a higher condition than one in which the compulsion of law was needed to secure these ends. But we must take men as we find them. Until such a condition of society is reached, it is the business of the state to take the best security it can for the young citizens' growing up in such health and with so much knowledge as is necessary for their real freedom. In so doing, it need not at all interfere with the individualism and self-reliance of those whom it requires to do what they would otherwise do for themselves. The man who, of his own right feeling, saves his wife from overwork and sends his children to school, suffers no moral degradation from a law which, if he did not do this for himself, would seek to make him do it.'[43]

There was no doubt, however, that in *Liberal Legislation and Freedom of Contract* Green appeared to adopt a position that was fundamentally at odds with the Liberalism of Cobden and Gladstone. He had written the lecture specifically to defend two Liberal measures of the previous Parliamentary session; the Ground Game Act, which withdrew the sanction of the law from agreements by which the occupier of land transferred to the owner the exclusive right of killing game, and the Employers' Liability Act which encouraged workmen to look for protection from the law rather than from their contract of employment. The principle of free contract was similarly threatened by other Liberal proposals to give Irish tenants security of tenure, just rents and compensation for improvements and to regulate the system of settling and bequeathing land. In defending state interference in those areas, Green laid it down that there was no absolute right of property in respect of either land or labour. The institution of property was only justifiable as a means towards an end: the free exercise of the social capabilities of all. Where it interfered with that end, as in the case of land occupied by tenants without the freedom to improve it or secure rights of tenure, or labour treated purely as a commodity, private property was being abused and it was right that the state should step in to regulate its ownership in the interests of the weaker party to the contract.

Green also departed from traditional Liberalism in rejecting the atomistic individualism of the Manchester School and developing instead a social conception of freedom. He rejected the old Millite notion that society had no right to interfere with the behaviour of the individual because it concerned only himself. 'It used to be the fashion', he wrote, 'to look on drunkenness as a vice which was the concern only of the person who fell into it, so long as it did not lead him to commit an assault on his neighbours. No thoughtful man any longer looks at it in this way. We know that, however decently carried on, the excessive drinking of one man means an injury to others in health, purse and capability, to which no limits can be placed.'[44] Green saw society as an interdependent organic community rather than as an artificial unit made up of competing, self-dependent individuals. With this view of freedom as a social rather than an individual phenomenon, he saw a clearly positive role for the state in helping men to attain it.

Green was not the only Liberal intellectual in the early 1880s to argue a positive role for the state. D. G. Ritchie, a fellow of Jesus College, Oxford, argued in much the same vein that in an age of popular democracy and sovereignty there could no longer be the antithesis between the state and the individual that there had been in the days of Cobden and Mill. The state was now 'us' rather than 'them' and, if its actions interfered in strict terms with the rights of the individual, they nevertheless promoted the interests of the individual as a collective member of the community. Arnold Toynbee, an economics tutor at Balliol College, Oxford, developed a similar argument in 1882 in a lecture to working men entitled *Are Radicals Socialists?* 'We have not abandoned our old belief in liberty, justice and self-help,' he said, 'but we say that under certain conditions the people cannot help themselves, and that then they should be helped by the state representing directly the whole people. In giving this State help, we make three conditions: first, the matter must be one of primary social importance; next, it must be proved to be practicable; thirdly, the State interference must not diminish self-reliance. Even if the chance should arise of removing a great social evil, nothing must be done to weaken those habits of individual self-reliance and voluntary association which have built up the greatness of the English people.'[45]

In fact, Green and his Oxford colleagues remained essentially Gladstonian in their approach to social improvement. Their bias was still towards voluntaryism and towards the traditional Liberal idea of removing hindrances to the exercise of man's freedom and responsibility. If they seemed to go further than the Liberals of the 1860s in suggesting positive rather than purely negative ways of increasing freedom, then, Green insisted, it was only the appearance and not the reality that had changed: 'The nature of the political reformer is always the same. The passion for improving mankind, in its ultimate object, does not vary.'[46] Green had invoked the idea of the common good of society not as a rationale for collectivism, but as a spur to a more strenuous individualism. It is difficult to see him as the architect of the collectivist Welfare State. Admittedly, there was a certain ambiguity in his arguments, as shown by the fact that they were taken up in the 1890s with equal alacrity by arch-voluntaryists like Bernard Bosanquet of the Charity Organisation Society and ardent interventionists like L. T. Hobhouse, the young Liberal journalist, to support directly contradictory points of view about the desirability of social reform by the state. In *Liberal Legislation and Freedom of Contract*, at least, however, Green's position had been fairly clear and strongly traditional. He had said nothing about government intervention in the fields of industry or social welfare, and instead had limited himself to temperance legislation and the 'liberation of the soil' through reform of the land laws, both causes over which even Cobden and Bright had supported the principle of interventionist legislation, as 'the next great conquests which our democracy, on behalf of its own true freedom, has to make'.[47]

A rising new generation of Liberals, most of whom were recent Oxford graduates, were not, however, as sensitive as their tutors had been about rejecting traditional Liberal tenets. J. A. Hobson, L. T. Hobhouse, H. H. Asquith, Herbert Samuel, H. W. Massingham and their circle of New Liberals were developing a doctrine that envisaged considerable 'constructionist' legislation to promote social welfare and linked the idea of positive state action at home with imperialism abroad. Other Liberals were coming to the same view. Hugh Price Hughes called on Nonconformists to discard their old individualism and espouse collectivism. W. T. Stead laid down as one of the main aims of the new school of advanced Liberalism which would be supported by the *Pall Mall* under his editorship: 'to vivify the stagnant squalor of the life of great masses of the population by associated effort, voluntary, municipal and imperial'.[48]

By 1885 a significant number of Liberals were calling on their party to embrace as its central object social improvement through legislative action. Chamberlain and his advanced Radicals, the New Liberals like Hobson and Asquith, and Nonconformists like Stead and Hughes all wanted to see the adoption of a programme of domestic social reform. It was not to be, however. Gladstone remained firmly committed to the traditional Liberal aims of political emancipation and individual moral improvement. He took the party into the 1885 election on the single issue of Home Rule for Ireland, at the head of a moral crusade of the kind so many now wanted to get away from. Chamberlain fought the election on what became the Unauthorized Programme. It was an ominous portent of a division that in less than a year was to split the Liberal ranks asunder.

Chapter 10

The Waning of Optimism

By the middle of the 1880s it was clear to its friends and foes alike that not all was well with Liberalism. Liberals no longer seemed to have a clear agreed understanding of what their beliefs were and what they should be doing. When in 1885 Andrew Reid asked 'the best minds of the Liberal Party' for their 'definitions and personal confessions of faith' for his book, *Why I am a Liberal*, the result was a myriad of widely different replies which reflected a lack of any consistency or consensus about the basis of their beliefs.

There was, of course, nothing new about diversity in the Liberal ranks. The party had always been a coalition of widely diverse interest groups and 'faddists' pursuing their own ideals and its heterogeneity had long been a worry to its leaders and whips. Following Gladstone's resignation in 1875, Lord Hartington had suggested that the Liberals should have three leaders, one for the Whigs, one for the Radicals and one for the Irish. The split within the party over the issue of Irish Home Rule, which came to a head in 1886 was, however, of a scale and importance quite unlike any previous internal disagreements. Ninety-three Liberal M.P.s joined the Tories in voting against the second reading of the Home Rule Bill in July 1886. Among those who broke decisively with Gladstone over the issue were Bright, Chamberlain, Forster and Dale. Home Rule alienated Whigs, Radicals, Nonconformists and intellectuals. It severed men from the allegiance of a lifetime and put old friends in opposing camps. 'The split of the Liberal party has made an immense difference to my private life,' Dale wrote. 'There are two clubs, and I belong to neither.'[1]

Irish Home Rule was recognized by both its supporters and its opponents as the supreme expression of Gladstonian Liberalism. For Gladstone and John Morley it was the issue which would restore a sense of unity and purpose to the Liberal party by reviving its energies and emotions in another great moral crusade. They saw it, together with the accompanying land purchase scheme, as embodying the central principles of Liberalism: self-determination for a small nation eager and ready for freedom, and the creation of a sturdy independent class of peasant proprietors. To the Whigs, however, it marked the culmination of Gladstone's dangerous desire to interfere with free contracts between landlord and tenant and to capitulate to wild men with guns. For Chamberlain and for the growing band of younger Liberals with imperialist sympathies, Irish Home Rule was a separatist and nationalist gesture which went wholly against their notion of an imperial federation in which the countries of the Empire would be united under one Parliament. To Radicals and social reformers, the preoccupation with the constitutional position of Ireland was an utter irrelevance which diverted attention from the urgent need for economic and social reform at home. As Andrew Reid put it, Home Rule might have 'a picturesqueness and grandeur,' but 'the English Labourer is a Hungry man and Irish liberty may not fill his belly.'[a]

The split over Home Rule in 1886 brought to a head serious differences which had been fermenting in the Liberal camp since the beginning of Gladstone's second administration. To those on the right of the party, the Government's actions seemed to conflict with the sacred principles of *laissez-faire* and freedom of contract and its philosophy seemed to be dangerously democratic and socialist. To those on the left, the administration seemed obsessed with old-fashioned constitutional and political reform and oblivious to the desperate social and economic conditions of much of the population. From both sides came a growing questioning of the continuing relevance and value of Gladstonian Liberalism, and a realization that its earlier critics might have been right after all. Even before the defections of 1886, a significant number of Liberals had already left the party and abandoned Liberalism in favour of either extreme individualism or socialism.

There had always been Liberals who worried about the populist and collectivist tendencies of their philosophy. As far back as 1859, in his introduction to *On Liberty*, Mill had pointed to a new threat to human freedom which might paradoxically emerge from democracy itself. Liberalism flourished in an atmosphere where most men thought of government as alien and hostile, but what would happen if they came to think of it as representing themselves and being on their side? Would they still be vigilant about restricting its powers? Subsequently other Liberals had taken up the same theme. Lowe and Bagehot had expressed grave reservations about the Liberal drive to extend the franchise because they saw it leading to the rule of the ignorant and to shameless populism in politics. 'Both our political parties will bid for

the support of the working man,' Bagehot wrote in 1867, 'both of them
will promise to do as he likes.'[3] Six years later James Fitzjames Stephen
launched his great attack on Liberal optimism about the effects of
democracy in *Liberty, Equality, Fraternity*, and in 1877 George Goschen
lamented that, as a result of granting the franchise to working men,
political economy was no longer the ruling principle in Parliament, and
indiscriminate philanthropy had taken its place.

During the early 1880s these fears ceased to be confined to a few
isolated intellectuals and came to be held much more widely by
manufacturers, professional people and even politicians, who had
hitherto been staunch Liberals, but who now deserted the Gladstonian
fold. The new mood was well caught by Trollope in the last of his
Palliser novels, *The Duke's Children*, published in 1880, where he had
the young Viscount Silverbridge desert his father's Liberalism and
become a Conservative because he felt, under the influence of his friend
Tregear, that the Liberals were now playing the game of Socialists and
Communists.

The immediate cause of many of these defections was the collectivist
and populist character of much of the legislation of Gladstone's 1880–85
administration. Acton spoke for many when he noted with some
concern in 1885 that 'there is latent socialism in the Gladstone philosophy', while Queen Victoria felt compelled to write to her Prime
Minister in the same year: 'There are very many persons who are
greatly alarmed by the *destructive* doctrines which are taught, who
would welcome warmly any words of Mr. Gladstone's which affirmed
that *liberalism* is *not socialism*, and that *progress* does not mean Revolution.'[4] Two measures in particular, the Employers' Liability Act of
1880 and the Irish Land Act of 1881, disquieted right-wing Liberals in
their departure from the principles of free contract and their apparent
capitulation to the demands of the mob. The first provoked the defection from the Liberal party of a number of manufacturers, including
H. D. Pochin, a well-known soap tycoon who had three times stood as
a Liberal Parliamentary candidate, and the second, which was described
by George Goschen as 'probably the most gigantic invasion of the
principle of *"Laissez-faire"* in recent times', led to the resignation from
the Government of the Duke of Argyll.[5] As a direct response to these
two Acts, and to the calls for further collectivist measures by
Chamberlain and others in the Government, a group of discontented
Liberal businessmen and individualists joined forces with Conservatives
to set up the State Resistance Union, later called the Liberty and Property

Defence League, 'for resisting over-legislation, for maintaining Freedom of Contract, and for advocating individualism as opposed to Socialism'.[6]

The members of the Liberty and Property Defence League, who included Pochin and at least two Liberal M.P.s, attacked Gladstone for drifting towards collectivism and argued for strict adherence to the principle of *laissez-faire* and for a free market economy. They deplored the increasing tendency towards public provision of health, welfare, education and housing, which Goschen contemptuously predicted would lead to 'Punch and Judy on the rates', and maintained that all these matters were much better left to private enterprise.[7] They attacked what they saw as the growing tide of collectivism, especially in the trade union movement, and upheld the values of competition and individual moral responsibility. In its most extreme form, their ideal was that of the survival of the fittest in accordance with the doctrine of Social Darwinism to which many of them adhered.

These principles went beyond the traditional Liberal preference for voluntary action and suspicion of state interference. If they had a pedigree it lay in the tradition of extreme individualism in Victorian thought exemplified by such figures as Baron Bramwell, a leading High Court judge in the 1870s who opposed all collectivist and protectionist legislation. Those who argued the case for *laissez-faire* and the free operation of the market in the 1880s did not accept, however, that they were departing from the true Liberal faith. Rather they held that it was Gladstone and those who still called themselves Liberals who had betrayed it. Thomas Mackay, one of the leading members of the new anti-collectivist movement, looked back to a time when 'liberal principles wielded an undoubted authority' and when 'the liberal was guided by a belief in the salutary principle of liberty and working class independence.'[8] Herbert Spencer, who became the leading philosopher of the movement, and at whose suggestion the Liberty and Property Defence League had been formed, began his *Man Versus the State* (1884) by pointing out that 'most of those who now pass as Liberals are Tories of a new type.' In the past, he argued, 'all truly Liberal changes diminished compulsory co-operation throughout social life and increased voluntary co-operation. . . . Liberalism habitually stood for individual freedom versus state coercion.' Now, however, in extending regulations, promoting coercive legislation and creating monopolies of public services, all in the name of the popular good, Liberals had taken over the Tories' paternalistic style of government.[9]

H

Spencer was not the only former believer to turn away from the Liberal creed on the grounds that it had changed from the pure gospel of his youth. In 1885 A. V. Dicey argued substantially the same case in his *Plea Of A Malcontent Liberal*. 'We olden-time English Liberals', he wrote, 'did not rest our case on any abstract theory, such as Rousseau's *Contrat Social*, nor did we attach much value to written expositions of theoretical principles, such as the American Declaration of Independence. We based our plea on the broad ground that in the long run the world fared better if people were left to manage their own affairs, to do the best they could for themselves, and to fight their own way without legal or social interference. . . . The whole theory of modern Liberals is that the State is to take in hand the control of the masses, and override the rights of individuals. . . . Common sense tells me that there is less practical risk of individual liberty being seriously endangered under a Conservative than under a Liberal administration. . . . Once you desert the solid ground of individual freedom, you can find no resting place till you reach the abyss of Socialism.'[10]

This feeling by intellectuals in the early 1880s that the Liberal party was no longer the party of individualism and that the Liberal faith in freedom was no longer well founded is remarkably similar in many ways to the disillusionment with the Labour party and the philosophy of social democracy on the part of a number of intellectuals in the late 1970s. The arguments used by Dicey and Spencer to justify their defection from the Victorian Liberal party are substantially the same as those that have recently been advanced by Paul Johnson, the former editor of the *New Statesman*, and Hugh Thomas, the historian, to explain their decision to leave the Labour party after many years of active membership. All four argued that the political faith in which they had been brought up had changed out of all recognition and from being lively and crusading had become bureaucratic and authoritarian. There was too a similar concern that freedom had been eroded. The intellectuals of the 1880s were particularly concerned with the effects of the mass democracy established by the 1884 Reform Act which so many of them had opposed. James Fitzjames Stephen complained: 'The old Liberalism . . . has been and is being utterly given up, and in its place is being erected a tyrannical democracy.'[11] Spencer deplored the advent of populism, and noted that 'popular good has come to be sought by the Liberals, not as an end to be indirectly gained by relaxations and restraints, but as the end to be directly gained.'[12] In his influential book on *Popular Government* (1885), Sir Henry Maine, a distinguished lawyer who, like Stephen, had deserted the Liberalism of his youth as a result of his experiences as an administrator in India, scathingly attacked Gladstonian optimism and faith in the people and predicted that the advance of the common man through democracy would be at the expense of ability and intelligence and would lead inexorably to less freedom, more bureaucracy and eventually to socialism.

It was not only Gladstone's democratic and collectivist tendencies which frightened Liberal intellectuals into the Conservative fold. There was also considerable unease about his foreign policy which seemed to be inspired by the interests of almost every nation save his own and which apparently involved appeasing enemies of the Empire like the Afrikaners in the Transvaal, the Parnellites in Ireland and the nationalists in India. Stephen complained in 1885 that 'England seems to have become a huge Gladstone with a conscience like the liver of a Strasbourg goose.'[13] Montagu Butler, the celebrated Master of Trinity College, Cambridge, who had earlier been an ardent Gladstonian, commented in 1887 that the Liberals' policy would lead to 'the relinquishment of Gibraltar, the abandonment of India, the repudiation of the colonies, and the resignation of our duties as a great fighting power in Europe'.[14] Gladstone's determination to spend as little as possible on defence caused particular concern. Dicey wrote that 'of all the delusions cherished by our home-bred Liberals, the greatest, perhaps, is the belief that England has only to cease giving offence abroad to be secure against attack.'[15] Tennyson was moved by Gladstone's efforts to reduce spending on the Navy in 1885 to pen a blistering attack on his old hero:

> *You, you if you fail to understand*
> *What England is, and what her all-in-all,*
> *On you will come the curse of all the land,*
> *Should this old England fall which Nelson left so great.*[16]

The policy of Home Rule for Ireland embodied all three strands of Gladstonianism that its conservative critics so much deplored. It was socialistic in compulsorily taking property away from landlords and giving it to tenants. It was populist and democratic in giving way to the demands of the nationalists. It was anti-imperialist and smacked of 'Little Englandism' in granting separation to an integral part of the United Kingdom. The elevation of Home Rule to be the central plank of Liberal policy in 1886 led to the final defection of the Liberal intellectuals who had become increasingly uneasy about the direction in which the party was going. Along with Hartington and the Whigs, Goschen, Stephen, Dicey, Butler and Maine forsook the party.

One of the most distinguished defectors from the Liberal party in 1886 was the historian William Lecky, who had previously been a devoted, if inactive, Gladstonian. In his book, *Democracy and Liberty* (1896), he depicted the disastrous policy of Home Rule as the inevitable culmination of the democratic and populist trends which had become increasingly evident in Liberalism in the past thirty years. Such a policy, he argued, would have been impossible before the Reform Act of 1867. 'In the days of middle-class ascendancy every politician found it necessary to place himself in general harmony with average educated opinion. . . . Mere rhetoric and claptrap; brilliant talent, unallied with judgement; coalitions to carry some measure which the country condemned by uniting it with a number of bribes offered to many different classes; policies in which great national interests were sacrificed to personal ambition or to party tricks; the dexterity which multiplies, evades or confuses issues, had seldom even a temporary success . . . but the changes that introduced into the constituencies a much larger proportion of ignorance, indifference, or credulity soon altered the conditions of politics.'[17]

Democracy and Liberty summed up the argument of those intellectuals who deserted the Liberal party in the 1880s because they felt it had become populist and collectivist. For Lecky the rot had set in with the granting of the vote to the uneducated and dependent masses in 1867. Their admission into the electorate had reduced politics to the practice of bribery and had led to such sordid attempts to buy votes as Gladstone's promise to abolish income tax in 1874 and the Irish land legislation of 1881. Almost worse, it had seriously weakened liberty, since the working classes, unlike their social superiors, favoured regulation and restraint. Popular government, Lecky predicted, would lead to 'a weakening of private enterprise and philanthropy; a lowered sense of individual responsibility; diminished love of freedom; the creation of an array of officials, regulating in all departments the affairs of life; the formation of a state of society in which vast multitudes depend for their subsistence on the bounty of the state'.[18] His message was clear: the realization of universal suffrage on which the Liberals were bent would turn Britain into a Socialist state.

There was another group of malcontent Liberal intellectuals who agreed with Lecky that the natural corollary of Gladstonian Liberalism was Socialism. But while he deplored it, they welcomed it. Their complaint was that the Liberals were not moving towards collectivism fast enough. For these left-wing critics, as for those on the right, the Liberal administration of 1880 to 1885 was a bitter disappointment and played an important role in their later defection. Younger advanced Liberals had high hopes that the party in government would take up serious social reform. Instead it concentrated largely on the traditional Liberal obsessions of administrative reform and civil liberty, passing such measures as the Corrupt Practices Act, the Nonconformists' Burial Act, and the abolition of flogging in the armed forces, and shied away from legislating on such important social questions as an eight-hour day for workers or state old-age pensions. To the Radicals, the Home Rule policy summed up Gladstone's out-of-date attachment to constitutional reform and political emancipation to the neglect of more pressing social and economic questions.

The criticism that Liberalism paid too much heed to political and religious emancipation and not enough to social reform was not, of course, a new one. Arnold had stated it forcefully in *Culture and Anarchy* when he argued: 'It is not fatal to our Liberal friends to labour for free trade, extension of the suffrage and abolition of church rates, instead of graver social ends; but it is fatal to them to . . . believe, with our pauperism increasing more rapidly than our population, that they have performed a great, an heroic work, by occupying themselves exclusively, for the last thirty years, with these Liberal nostrums, and that the right and good course for them now is to go on occupying themselves with the like for the future.'[19] In an important article in the *Fortnightly Review* of September 1873 Chamberlain argued that Gladstone was ruining the Liberal party by his refusal to see that social questions would henceforth dominate politics. The only hope for the party lay in the adoption of a programme 'which shall satisfy the just expectations of the representatives of labour as well as conciliate the Nonconformists'.[20]

The disillusionment with Gladstone among intellectuals on the left of the Liberal party grew in the early 1880s. After campaigning hard for them in the 1880 election, William Morris left the Liberals in 1881, largely in protest against the Irish Coercion Act and the lack of interest in social questions. In 1883 a group of advanced Liberals, disenchanted with the party's traditional individualism and antipathy to social reform, came together under the leadership of Sidney and Beatrice Webb to form the Fabian Society. At a local level, groups like the London Liberal and Radical Union proposed socialistic measures such as the rebuilding of slums at the sole expense of the ground landlord, which radically departed from the voluntaryism and political economy of the Liberal leadership. In 1885, in a book entitled *The Limits of Individual Liberty*, Francis Montague, a young Oxford academic, questioned whether the traditional Liberal goal of individual freedom had produced a happier and better society. He attacked the Millite notion that man was not primarily a social being and that human development was best promoted through 'unlimited competition and unrestrained discussion'. Montague argued that Liberal individualism and competition had led to exploitation and class conflict and concluded: 'Modern socialism expresses the practical revolt against the doctrine of negative freedom.'[21]

The unease among advanced Liberals about their party's refusal to shake off its traditional obsessions and commit itself to new doctrines of social reform reached its peak in the latter part of 1885. Gladstone's single-minded pursuit of Irish Home Rule to the exclusion of all other policies brought his more advanced followers into near open rebellion. The dissidents looked naturally for leadership to Chamberlain, who had consistently campaigned for the Liberals to become a party of social rather than constitutional reform, and whom Gladstone himself described as 'the most active and efficient representative of what may be termed the left wing of the Liberal Party'.[22] In the long run, he was a bad choice. Chamberlain was too much of an opportunist and his subsequent career with the Conservatives showed how little he really cared for social radicalism. Dilke would perhaps have been a better choice as a leader for the Radicals. In the short term, however, Chamberlain did not disappoint them. After very seriously considering forming his own separate Radical party, he launched in the autumn of 1885 his famous Radical or Unauthorized Programme of wide-ranging social and economic reforms as a direct challenge to the single-issue moral and political crusades on which the Liberals had traditionally fought elections and of which Home Rule was the supreme example. In the General Election of November 1885, at least 180 Liberal candidates stood on the Unauthorized Programme.

Surprisingly, the great split over Home Rule in 1886 produced remarkably few Radical defectors from the Liberal ranks. Chamberlain finally severed his connection with Gladstonianism over a measure which he regarded as the abnegation of his guiding political principle, the constructive use of the power of the state to improve the condition of the people. He took with him into the Liberal Unionist camp close

Birmingham colleagues like Jesse Collings and a number, although a distinct minority, of the local Liberal associations which made up the National Liberal Federation. Most advanced and radically inclined Liberals chose to stay with Gladstone or, like Sir George Trevelyan, to return to the fold after a brief period of self-imposed exile in protest against Home Rule. At the end of 1886 the Fabians, the London Liberal and Radical Union, and the growing band of young Liberals attracted to the 'New Liberalism' of social reform and collectivism were all still more or less loyal to Gladstonianism. But that loyalty was already sorely strained, and it would not be many years before some of the more advanced and progressive elements in Liberalism would move their allegiance to a new party dedicated to Socialism and the furtherance of the interests of labour.

The frustration of these two opposed groups of dissentient intellectuals helps to explain the subsequent sundering of Victorian Liberalism. Both for those who retreated into extreme individualism and for those who progressed into Socialism, Liberalism was a creed that had failed. In the eyes of the conservatives, it had lost its high ideals of freedom and created a mass democracy run on the principles of demagogy, bribery and collectivism. The Radicals felt that it had failed to liberate all men from poverty and oppression and had become fossilized in an outmoded set of economic ideas. In the early twentieth century many close friends who had been united in their Liberalism followed either its individualist or its collectivist strains to their logical conclusion and forsook their old creed for diametrically opposed new philosophies. The tendency is dramatically illustrated by the divergent paths taken in the 1920s by two brothers, William Wedgwood Benn, a strong Congregationalist and Radical politician, and Ernest Benn, the publisher. William, in the words of his son, Anthony Wedgwood Benn, the modern Labour politician, 'followed radicalism through to the shift from a Liberal Party that he felt had outlived its historical purpose into the Labour Party. My Uncle Ernest, who was a founder of the Society of Individualism, followed it through into the monetarist school. These two men shared a great belief in the rights of the individual, leading them in opposite directions in a way you find in the ex-Liberals in British politics today.'[23]

It was not only intellectuals who were beginning to desert Liberalism at this time. So also were the middle-class professionals and manufacturers who had for so long been among its staunchest supporters. As with the intellectuals, Home Rule provided the occasion for a final

severance with Gladstonianism by those who were already deeply discontented. In an article on the defection of the middle classes from
Liberalism in 1889, L. A. Atherley-Jones, son of Ernest Jones the
Chartist leader, noted that 'the Home Rule policy precipitated and
almost completed an exodus which hitherto had been gradual and
therefore less perceptible.'[24] Gladstone discerned the same trend. 'For a
long time before 1886,' he told a meeting of the National Liberal
Federation in 1889, 'the wealthy and powerful had been gradually
detaching themselves from the body of the Liberal Party and finding
their most natural associations in Toryism, in stagnation and
resistance.'[25]

Several explanations were given for this trend. Rosebery put it down
to reaction against the anti-imperialistic character of Liberal foreign
policy. Harcourt saw it as the response of the wealthy and privileged
to the party's growing collectivism and the advent of equal justice for
the poor. Atherley-Jones was probably nearest the mark when he
wrote: 'the battle of the middle class has been fought and won. Free
trade, the removal of religious disabilities, the participation and perhaps
preponderance of the commercial interest in the work of government
have transferred the bourgeoisie from the party of progress to the party
of rest. The reforms of the future menace, or appear to menace, the
interests of the middle class. Nationalisation of the land, a graduated
scale of taxation, free education, in a word, legislative enforcement of
the Benthamist doctrine of "the greatest happiness of the greatest
number" are regarded by that class with apprehension and dismay.'[26]

The desertion of the middle classes was a serious blow to the Liberals.
Lord Randolph Churchill wrote: 'it is the end of an epoch. The long
dominion of the middle classes, which had begun in 1832, had come
to its close, and with it the almost equal reign of Liberalism.'[27] But was
it necessary to be so pessimistic? The middle classes might feel that they
had obtained all they wanted and were now threatened by new reforms,
but that was no reason for the working classes to follow suit. On the
contrary, there were good grounds for arguing, as Atherley-Jones did,
that 'now, indeed, for the first time in the history of politics, we find
Liberalism almost exclusively identified with the particular interests of
the working class.'[28] This point of view overlooked the fact, however,
that there was a marked difference between the way the working class
themselves saw their interests and the way they were perceived by most
Liberals. As Lord Randolph Churchill put it: 'Slaves were free, Conscience was free, Trade was free. But hunger and squalor and cold

were also free and the people demanded something more than liberty. . . . How to fill the void was the riddle that split the Liberal Party.'[29]

Gladstonian Liberalism had courted working men on the basis of an appeal to the ideals of liberty and self-help, independence and altruism. For more than twenty years, in conditions of economic boom and with a restricted electorate, that appeal had succeeded. It continued to work even when the economy began to decline and when social questions might seem more pressing to the average voter than the fate of some obscure eastern European state. One of the most conspicuous social and political features of Britain in the 1880s and early 1890s was the continuing popular appeal of Gladstone and the style of politics that he represented. In the 1885 General Election, G. W. E. Russell, campaigning as a 'New Liberal' on a platform of social reform, in a constituency composed primarily of working men, was surprised to find that his promises of free education, public recreation, better housing for the poor and a purer water supply 'fell on deaf ears. My hearers are very keen about the blasphemy laws and the grant to Princess Beatrice, but for the physical and moral welfare of themselves and their neighbours they did not seem to care a straw.'[30]

The appeal of Liberalism to working men, and indeed to manufacturers, could not but be affected, however, by the depression in agriculture and industry which followed the collapse of the mid-Victorian economic boom in the mid-1870s. Under the impact of foreign competition, Britain lost the primacy which it had so long held as the world's first industrialized economy and leading trading nation. For the first time the country became dependent on imports for its staple food as technological advances brought in cheap American prairie wheat and refrigerated meat from Australasia to feed the rapidly growing population. As a result, agriculture collapsed and the capital value of agricultural land was halved in twenty years. Manufacturing industry fared no better. European and American competition captured many traditional British markets. The value of British exports fell steadily from the mid-1870s. The decline was particularly dramatic in the iron and steel industry, where Britain had been traditionally pre-eminent, and where exports were halved in one seven-year period.

The most immediate effect of this serious economic decline was to undermine faith in the kernel of Liberal economic policy, the gospel of free trade, which had gone almost unchallenged since it was preached by Cobden and Bright. Britain's competitors were now resorting to protectionism, erecting high tariff barriers to keep up prices at home and keep out foreign goods and subsidizing cheap exports which could undercut those from Britain. Germany had done so in 1879, Russia in 1881, France and Austria–Hungary in 1882, the United States was to do so in 1890. It was not surprising that the cry for protectionism went up from both workers and manufacturers in Britain as the trade figures got steadily worse. In 1887 the Conference of the National Union of Conservative Associations passed a resolution in favour of tariffs on imports. It was the first serious political challenge to the policy of free trade to which the Liberals remained wedded, and a sign of important battles to come in the early twentieth century.

The agricultural and industrial depression of the late 1870s and 1880s hit particularly hard the independent artisans and craftsmen who made up the 'aristocracy' of the labour movement and the most devoted adherents of Gladstonian Liberalism. It killed many of their co-operative schemes and weakened their independence. At the same time, however, it actually improved the condition of many factory and agricultural labourers by reducing prices and producing perhaps the first rise in real wages and in the standard of living for ordinary workers for more than forty years. These beneficiaries of the new economic situation, many of whom were also the recipients of the vote in 1884, might well have been expected to become the new backbone of the Liberal party. Some of them, indeed, did so, but many others found that Liberalism had little appeal and felt compelled to set up their own Labour party.

The single most important factor which prevented many of the ordinary workmen, recently enfranchised and made prosperous in the mid-1880s, from committing themselves to Liberalism was their new-found consciousness of class. This arose partly from the development of the so-called 'new unions' of unskilled workers like railwaymen, dockers, factory hands and labourers. These new unions, led by men like Ben Tillett, Tom Mann and John Burns, were very different from the old craft unions of Henry Broadhurst, Thomas Burt and George Howell. The old unions, made up of skilled men, had seen their role as essentially benevolent rather than political. Their main concern had been to maintain benefit funds for sickness and unemployment. Operating in an expanding economy, and with full employment, they had seen their own interest as one with that of their employers and happily subscribed to the values of self-help and individual responsibility. Broadhurst and Burt actually opposed legislation to give workers an eight-hour day on the grounds that it was demeaning and diminished their self-reliance. The new unions, born in an age of depression and unemployment, saw no common interest between workers and employers. Unskilled workers were not attracted to the self-help ethic as artisans were. Their method of work in factories or labouring gangs and their conditions of employment made them look more naturally to collective agencies, including the state, for help. The leaders of the new unions saw their role as political and organized mass industrial action like the gas workers' and dockers' strikes of 1889.

With this heightened class consciousness many ordinary workers saw the Liberals as enemies rather than allies. Where the older generation of artisans and craftsmen had revered Liberal M.P.s like Samuel Morley and John Bright as exemplars of the principles of self-help and crusading Nonconformity, younger unskilled workers despised them as employers of labour who refused just demands for higher wages and shorter hours. It had not mattered to Howell and Burt that many of the Liberal politicians they actively supported were middle-class manufacturers and industrialists. It mattered passionately to Mann and Tillett, however. In the General Election of 1892 Tillett stood against the veteran Gladstonian and Liberal M.P. for Bradford, Alfred Illingworth, and vigorously denounced him as an employer and capitalist. Four years later a Labour paper in Reading described the local Liberal candidate, George Palmer, the biscuit manufacturer, as 'the man who discharges and tries to starve workmen, the man who has built up a fortune by sweating the workers of Reading, the man who of all others the industrial workers of Reading ought to reject with contempt'.[31]

The increasing identification by working men of Liberals as employers and therefore as class enemies, which played such an important part in creating an independent Labour party in Britain, was perhaps as much a result of changes on the Liberal side as of the new class consciousness of the workers. The Liberals had always been to a large extent an employers' party. That in itself had caused little friction with working men during the years of economic boom when so many Liberals were model employers. Inevitably, however, Liberal manufacturers and entrepreneurs were forced to react to the depression of the late 1870s and 1880s by laying off workers and seeking to reduce costs. In the face of economic decline and the challenge of the new unions, some Liberal employers became as class conscious as their workers and organized themselves accordingly. Joseph Cowen was not alone in seeing the National Liberal Federation as a device to enable local caucuses of Liberal capitalists to keep working men out of politics. Certainly Chamberlain was always viewed with extreme suspicion by most trade union and labour leaders because of his activities as a manufacturer and employer. As a result, he was in many ways less attractive to them than Gladstone.

The new working-class consciousness also weakened the hold of Liberalism on ordinary men and women by its stress on the power of collective rather than individual action. It produced its own ideology, just as forty years earlier, the great rise in middle-class confidence and power had helped to produce the ideology of Gladstonian Liberalism. As Sidney Webb wrote in 1901: 'The historian of the future will recognise, in the last quarter of the nineteenth century, the birth of another new England. . . . This time it is not a new continent that the ordinary man has discovered, but a new category. We have become aware, almost in a flash, that we are not merely individuals, but members of a community. The labourer in the slum tenement, competing for employment at the factory gate, has become conscious that his comfort and his progress depend, not wholly or mainly on himself, or on any other individual, but upon the proper organisation of his trade union and the activity of the factory inspector. . . . The opening of the twentieth century finds us all, to the dismay of the old fashioned individualist, "thinking in communities". Now the trouble with Gladstonian Liberalism is that, by instinct, by tradition, and by the positive precepts of its past exponents, it "thinks in individuals". It visualises the world as a world of independent Roundheads, with separate ends, and abstract rights to pursue those ends. Their conception of freedom means only breaking somebody's bonds asunder. When the "higher freedom" of corporate life is in question, they become angrily reactionary and denounce and obstruct every new development of common action.'[32]

It was significant that it was a middle-class intellectual like Webb who spoke most confidently about the growth of collectivism among the working classes. Throughout the nineteenth century Socialism was a predominantly middle-class ideology. Even when it gradually began to reach working people in the late 1880s and 1890s it was only through the old 'aristocratic' craft unions, hit by structural changes in the economy. The pressure from ordinary workers was for the creation of a Labour party, not a Socialist party, distinguished from the Liberals by class and not doctrine. In some ways, indeed, Socialism was an inevitable, if not exactly a natural development from Liberalism. George

Howell remarked of the programme of the First Socialist International in 1864 that 'a Gladstone or a Bright could have accepted it with a good conscience.'[33] As early as 1857 Harcourt, who was to achieve fame in 1888 with his declaration 'we are all Socialists now', had written that 'Socialism is the legitimate and inevitable corollary of Mr. Bright's doctrine.'[34]

It was true that there was a socialistic element in Bright's assault on landed privilege and Gladstone's fulminations against the upper ten thousand. Yet in essence Socialism and Liberalism were fundamentally incompatible doctrines and the spread of the one could not but lead to the decline of the other. Webb in his remarks quoted above identified what was perhaps the most important difference. The Liberal sought social improvement through individual self-help, the Socialist through the collective action of a trade union or the state. Liberals would never have accepted the primacy of materialism implicit in the statement in William Morris's and Henry Hyndman's *Summary of the Principles of Socialism* (1884) that 'the first object of every animal, man included, is to feed itself and its offspring.'[35] It was an altogether loftier object with which they credited the human race. There were other important differences. Liberals believed in competition, Socialists deplored it. Liberals put more stress on the production of wealth, Socialists on its distribution. Socialists worshipped equality and felt that the power of the state should be used to bring it about. Liberals certainly wanted to narrow the divisions in society. Indeed, Plantagenet Palliser had told Phineas Finn in *The Prime Minister* that it was 'the idea of lessening distances—of bringing the coachman and the Duke nearer together' which most clearly distinguished Liberals from Conservatives.[36] But there was a dread in Liberalism of the dull uniformity and mediocrity which would result from the application of a policy of absolute equality enforced by the state, and a strong conviction that the talented should be allowed to rise above the common herd. Gladstone believed that 'there is no political idea which has entered less into the formation of the political system of this country than the love of equality,' and he dismayed Ruskin by declaring himself to be 'a firm believer in the aristocratic principle—the rule of the best. I am an out-and-out inegalitarian.'[37]

Socialism was not the only new doctrine to come out of the heightened class feeling of the 1880s. On the employers' side there was a new aggressive capitalism developed as a response both to the general economic depression and also to the new militancy of the unions.

Already, even before the economic slump, the trend had begun towards the amalgamation of small businesses into large corporations each with several factories. Firms like Huntley & Palmers were turning from family concerns run on paternalistic and co-operative lines into amorphous units geared to mass production. Businessmen who before had been owner-managers of their own factory or mill, closely interested in the lives of their workers, were now members of corporate boards with a wholly different outlook. When the economic slump came they responded like their workers, by acting collectively, establishing price rings and employers' associations and presenting a united front against strikes and trade union activity. Labour costs suddenly became too high and employers sought to reduce them. If unions protested, they used the courts to outlaw picketing and banded together to employ only 'free' non-trade-union labour. Collectivism and corporatism, those two great ideologies of the twentieth century, were developing hand in hand. As a pamphlet of 1893 put it: 'the battle cry of the future must not be Liberalism against Toryism, but Labourism against Capitalism.'[38]

Not surprisingly, Liberals deplored this increasing polarization between capital and labour. As one of the old 'model' employers, Samuel Morley complained that the new trade unionism, by putting negotiations on wages and conditions of work into the hands of professional middleman, had 'altered materially the character of the relationship between the two classes—there is, I fear, ceasing to be the intimacy between masters and men which existed some years ago'.[39] He felt that 'a mischievous attempt was being made nowadays in some quarters to set class against class—to produce estrangement between different sections of the community.'[40] On the other side, R. T. Reid, a Liberal M.P. who was to become Lord Chancellor in the 1905 Government, complained that he heard from many Liberal employers 'sentiments upon the relation of capital and labour analogous to the sentiments of Tory squires on the relation of squire and labourer'.[41] John Morley reflected sadly: 'the division of parties now had become to a very considerable extent also a division of classes . . . the wealthy and the great were on one side and the numbers were on the other side.'[42]

The emergence of class as the main determinant of political behaviour was the most important result of this polarization between capital and labour. It was confirmed by the redistribution clauses of the 1884 Reform Act which established as the basic electoral unit in Britain the single member constituency, with its boundary more often than not drawn along rather than across class lines. Liberalism could only suffer as a consequence of this development. Gladstone had successfully run a democratic party by keeping class issues out of politics. Once they came in, and became central, working men wanted their own Labour party, and businessmen turned to the Conservatives who became the capitalist party. Significantly, it was those businessmen with corporate and commercial interests, like finance, the railways, shipping and transport, who first defected to the Tories in the 1880s and those in more typically entrepreneurial manufacturing industries, like cotton, coal, metals and engineering, who tended to remain loyal to the Liberals. By the end of the century Liberalism was, in the graphic words of L. T. Hobhouse, 'occupying an awkward position between two energetically moving grindstones—the upper grindstone of plutocratic imperialism, and the nether grindstone of social democracy'.[43]

The sharp class polarization and the clash of capital and labour were not the only features of British society in the 1880s to weaken the hold and appeal of Liberalism. Perhaps even more damaging was the beginning of a retreat from the religious zeal, political activism and voluntary charitable work of the high Victorian period into the secularity, smugness and suburbanism which have been among the dominant characteristics of twentieth-century British life. In religion, in politics and in social life, people were ceasing to look outwards and were turning in on themselves. New forms of popular entertainment were emptying the chapels and debating societies. Even the secularist movement was affected by the general move away from commitment and activism. George Standring, a secularist journalist, lamented the failure of lemonade and abstract politics in working-men's clubs. When the *National Reformer* ceased publication in 1893, J. M. Robertson, its last editor, who later became a prominent Liberal politician, attributed its collapse to 'music hall-ism'.[44]

One aspect of this general social trend was the withdrawal of many Nonconformists from active Liberal politics. In 1883 Mundella noted with alarm that several prominent Sheffield Dissenters were deserting to the Conservatives. Home Rule took Dale and many others away from their traditional Liberal allegiance and into the Tory–Unionist camp. Several of those who stayed loyal to Gladstone in 1886, like Hugh Price Hughes and John Clifford, were increasingly attracted to imperialism and socialism. The old identification of Nonconformity with Liberalism was breaking up, and with it was disappearing that peculiar brand of moral fervour and righteous indignation which had sustained Gladstonianism. There could be no clearer evidence of that disappearance than the declaration of Dale, for so long the great apostle of Nonconformist political activism, when opposing the creation of a political Free Church Council in 1892, that 'we have come to the conclusion that the interference of organised churches with organised political societies has proved after all a false method of effecting the great objects of the Christian Gospel.'[45]

Nonconformists were also retreating from participation in local life, from voluntary charitable work and from a lively interest in the affairs of the day. Beatrice Webb lamented on a visit to Liverpool in the 1890s that the great Unitarian families who had dominated the city's local government and philanthropic ventures for so long 'are petering out, and the sons are not worthy of the fathers. . . . The present generation of rich folk want to enjoy themselves, find nothing to resist, no class or creed interest to fight for, so that they have ceased to consider anything but their pleasures.'[46] The trend was not confined to Nonconformists, of course. It was a general feature of society which showed itself in numerous different ways, in the decline of almsgiving which Beatrice Webb noted as the most striking change of her lifetime, in the collapse of voluntary societies and religious activities in the face of the rise of a mass leisure industry, and in the growth of a new popular press which gave bigger headlines to the names of footballers than politicians.

Perhaps the most striking feature of the new society was its smugness. As the *Manchester Guardian* pointed out, this was in some sense a result of the very successes of Liberalism, but augured ill for its future: 'The work of enfranchisement, though not complete, has been carried so far that whole classes have become satisfied with the existing order— that is to say, have become, by natural inclination and in the strict meaning of the term, Conservative. The forces on which the Liberalism of the sixties could rely are no longer at its disposal.'[47] The respectable lower-middle classes, the small traders and clerks, had attained the complacency and overriding sense of self-interest that was to make them the bedrock of the Conservative party for the next century. As early as 1874 Frederic Harrison had identified them as 'the sleek citizens, who pour forth daily from thousands and thousands of smart villas around London, Manchester and Liverpool, read their *Standard*, and believe that the country will do very well as it is'.[48]

The smart suburban villas from which Harrison's sleek citizens came nicely symbolized the new society which was growing up in Britain at the end of the nineteenth century. It was a society which was retreating physically as well as spiritually. John Carvell Williams, a leading Congregationalist who was chairman of the Liberation Society, and later became a Liberal M.P., warned his fellow Nonconformists in 1879 of 'that modern political evil which I may designate as suburbanism. That means in a large number of cases respectability, which is incompatible with enthusiasm, great apathy, and sometimes downright snobbishness, and a recantation of principles firmly held in days gone by.'[49]

Suburbanism and the attitudes which went with it were both a cause and an effect of the retreating society. After moving into their villas, Nonconformists became Anglicans and Liberals became Tories. The middle classes stopped taking part in local political and voluntary work and instead took to tending their gardens and reading the *Daily Mail*. Small businessmen no longer lived 'over the shop', manufacturers moved far away from their works and were no longer available for handing out wages, distributing prizes and delivering lectures on self-help and improvement. They left the care of their workers to hired managers and impersonal welfare departments, and in doing so stored up trouble ahead. Reflecting on the life of Thomas Thomasson, a Bolton cotton manufacturer and a leading figure in the Anti-Corn Law League, who died in 1876, Goldwin Smith wrote: 'I should think he was about the last of those who lived close to his works and among his men. Now the master, if he is a man and not a company, lives in a suburban villa, on which the working-man, going out for his Sunday walk, looks perhaps with a sinister eye, thinking, as his Socialist prophet tells him, it is all the product of his labour.'[50]

The retreat of the British into smugness and suburbanism inevitably hit Liberalism hard. It led most directly to a serious loss of party members and of party funds. So small had the membership become in one inner London Liberal association in the 1890s that Bernard Shaw was able to walk in off the street and demand to be elected to its executive committee, 'which was done on the spot by the astonished Association, ten strong or thereabouts'.[51] Liberal finances were gravely weakened by the defection of so many wealthy supporters over Home Rule. While the Midlothian Association had found no difficulty in reimbursing Gladstone for the £1,000 he spent in the 1885 election, only one subscriber could be found to contribute to the paltry £191 that he spent in the following year. Liberalism also suffered in other less tangible ways from the changes in society. It is impossible, for example, to measure the effect of the decline of provincialism as a force in English life, which showed itself in the eclipse of the provincial papers by the new popular national press and in the removal from Birmingham to London of the headquarters of the National Liberal Federation in 1886.

It was not just in Britain that society was in retreat and Liberalism on the wane. In the Habsburg Empire the Liberal party suffered a major defeat in 1879, having alienated the workers by its attachment to *laissez-faire*. It never again achieved a majority in Parliament and was subsequently destroyed by the Emperor Franz Josef. In France, after achieving victory in 1876 in alliance with the Radicals under Thiers and Gambetta, the Liberals ceased to be a major political force within the next twenty years because of their failure to implement social reform. The Italian masses also preferred immediate material benefits to the ideals of Liberalism. The Belgian Liberal party began losing the initiative to the Socialist party founded by Émile Vandervelde in 1885. In the German Reich Bismarck destroyed the Liberals in 1879 once they had put him into power and instead fashioned a Conservative and Catholic alliance which pursued imperialism and secret diplomacy abroad, centralized social welfare and military efficiency at home, and extreme protectionism in the economic sphere.

The Europe which Bismarck dominated in the 1880s was very different from the Europe of the 1860s. Hegelian ideas of the state had produced a new aggressive nationalism which was finding its expression in the scramble for more imperial possessions in Africa and the rush to re-arm. Secret alliances had put an end to the old Concert of Europe. Both Socialists and nationalists sought national efficiency through the creation of a powerful state and the encouragement of discipline and organization. L. T. Hobhouse gloomily observed at the turn of the century that Europe's 'efforts at internationalism have yielded to a revival of national exclusiveness, seen in the growth of armaments, the revival of aggravation and protectionism, the growth of anti-alien legislation. The doctrine of democratic rights has been replaced by the demand for efficiency, or by the unadorned gospel of blood and iron.'[52]

Bismarckian illiberalism found its echo in Britain. Social Darwinism encouraged the belief that might was right and led to an increased interest in eugenics and the possibilities of biological engineering. Economic decline prompted a renewed call for imperialism. Sir John Seeley's influential *The Expansion of England* (1883) inspired a campaign for a new British Empire which was powerfully encouraged by those reacting against Home Rule. The desire for national efficiency and for a new imperial role for Britain linked Chamberlain, the Fabians, and the young Liberal Imperialists like Asquith, Grey, Rosebery and R. B. Haldane against Gladstonianism. Traditional Liberal concerns with the rights of the individual, the freedom of trade and the limits on the power of the state were giving way to pragmatism, corporatism and a belief in the positive state as an agent of social reform and imperial expansion.

Behind these new ideas lay a deep sense of pessimism and despair. It is to be found in the art and literature of Britain and Europe in the 1880s, just as surely as optimism is found in that of the 1860s. Friedrich Nietzsche was announcing the death of God, Thomas Hardy was writing his novels of doom and hopelessness. Art reflected the *fin de siècle* mood of decadence and effeteness. The idea of progress was losing its central place in European thought. Men were beginning to wonder whether the world really did inevitably become a better and better place, or whether it was not destroying itself. Sir Henry Maine announced in 1885 that the assumption of progress, which had been integral to the development of liberalism and democratic idealism, is 'not in harmony with the normal forces ruling human nature, and is therefore apt to lead to cruel disappointment and serious disaster'.[53] Less clinically, but far more tellingly, Tennyson pinpointed the change of mood which had overcome the world when in 1886 he had the hero of *Locksley Hall* reflect on the failure of his youthful hopes of fifty years earlier:

> *Gone the cry of 'Forward, Forward', lost within a growing gloom;*
> *Lost, or only heard in silence from the silence of a tomb.*
> *Half the marvels of my morning, triumphs over time and space,*
> *Staled by frequence, shrunk by usage into commonest common place.*
> *'Forward' rang the voices then, and of the many mine was one.*
> *Let us hush the cry of 'Forward' till ten thousand years have gone.*[54]

By the mid-1880s even those who still remained in the Liberal fold were becoming affected by this universal pessimism. Many were disillusioned by the results of their efforts at emancipation and by the way that the masses whom they had entrusted with political power seemed to prefer socialism and jingoism to self-help and liberty. They were disturbed by the revelations of social scientists that for all the economic progress of the past forty years there were still large pockets of appalling poverty. They were bewildered by Europe's resort to protectionism and rearmament. Many of the old optimists were no more. Miall had died in 1881, T. H. Green in 1883, Samuel Morley in 1886. Bright died three years after he broke with the Liberals over Home Rule. Several Nonconformists followed Dale out of Liberalism and active political involvement. Stead became increasingly immersed in imperialism and spiritualism. Mundella joined other younger Liberals like G. W. E. Russell in pressing for social reform.

There were still some, however, who after 1886, remained true to the principles of Gladstonianism. The most faithful, apart from Gladstone himself, was John Morley who had described himself and his leader in 1885 as 'the last of the Cobdenites'.[55] His essay *On Compromise*, first published in 1874 and constantly reprinted throughout the 1880s, expressed the anguish of the Liberal optimist who saw his ideals threatened by a rising tide of complacency and class bitterness and who yet refused to give them up. 'Ours is a country', he wrote, 'where love of constant improvement ought to be greater than anywhere else, because fear of revolution is less. Yet the art of politics is growing to be as meanly conceived as all the rest. At elections, the man of principle has not often a chance against the man of a class.' He saw the cause of this malaise as a failure of moral nerve: 'Conscience has lost its strong and on-pressing energy, and the sense of personal responsibility lacks sharpness of edge. The native hue of spiritual resolution is sicklied o'er with the pale cast of distracted, wavering, confused thought. The souls of men have become void. Our modern way is . . . Beware of the high and hold fast to the safe. Dismiss conviction and study general consensus. No zeal, no faith, no intellectual trenchancy.'[56]

Morley proposed a simple remedy to cure this malaise in contemporary British politics: 'Those who use the watchwords of Liberalism [should] return upon its principles.'[57] He campaigned vigorously on the traditional themes of voluntaryism, individual responsibility, anti-imperialism, self-determination, and collaboration between middle-class and working-class reformers. He attacked efforts to increase the power and responsibility of the state, to further national pride and position overseas and to set one class against another. Significantly, he appealed increasingly in speeches to what he called the 'solid, serious, and reflective' Liberalism of the North and the Celtic fringe which he contrasted with the Socialist collectivism and the suburban complacency of London Liberalism. 'I am bound to say that it is when I come northward,' he told a delighted audience in his own Newcastle constituency in 1888, 'that I am in the presence of that kind of Liberalism which I, for one, most sympathize with, most rejoice in, and to which I look forward most confidently for the safe progress of the fortunes of our country.'[58]

Gladstone also turned to the heartlands of traditional Nonconformist Liberalism to escape from those metropolitan trends that seemed to threaten it. He had chosen the Scottish constituency of Midlothian for his great appeal to the electorate in 1879–80. In 1885 he chose a Celtic issue, Irish Home Rule, as the dominant item of Liberal policy for the next nine years. Second to Home Rule in his list of priorities for much of the period came the disestablishment of the Welsh Church, with Scottish disestablishment not far behind. He spoke less and less to metropolitan and English audiences and more and more to gatherings in Scotland and Wales where, like Morley, he stuck to the old policies of anti-imperialism and constitutional reform, as well as promising self government to the four component states of the United Kingdom.

Like Morley also, Gladstone retained his optimism and his belief in progress in the face of the growing pessimism of his contemporaries. In 1886 he produced a long catalogue of the triumphs and achievements of the past sixty years to refute the argument of Tennyson's *Locksley Hall Sixty Years On*. 'Men have no business to talk of disenchantment,' he told Morley, 'ideals are never realised.'[59] He was admittedly profoundly unhappy about current political trends, commenting to the Duke of Argyll: 'I deeply deplore the oblivion into which public economy has fallen, the prevailing disposition to make a luxury of panics, which multitudes enjoy as they would a sensational novel or a highly seasoned cookery; and the leaning of both parties to socialism.'[60] He wrote to Acton in similar vein, complaining that 'the Liberalism of today . . . its pet idea is what they call construction, that is to say, taking into the hands of the State the business of the individual man'. He went on, however: 'I have even the hope that while the coming change may give undue encouragement to "construction", it will be favourable to the economic, pacific, law-regarding elements; and the sense of justice which abides tenaciously in the masses will never knowingly join hands with the Fiend of Jingoism.'[61]

When, following the defeat of his third brief Government in 1886, Gladstone was asked to contribute to a symposium on 'the new Liberal programme', he replied that he had nothing to offer: 'I hold on to politics in the hope of possibly helping to settle the Irish question, but the general operations both of party and of particular subjects I am obliged, and intend, to leave in the hands of others.'[62] For the next six years while he led the party in opposition he refused seriously to consider the formulation of policy on any subject other than Home Rule. His colleagues were exasperated by his blindness to the demands of the times. It was clear to them, as Lord Ripon put it, that 'a whole series of labour questions would come to the front' on which the Liberals must have a policy.[63] The younger element in the party were working out their own 'New Liberalism' of social reform through the state. Other Radicals and labour representatives were trying to press for new initiatives through the National Liberal Federation. It was left largely to John Morley to devise some Gladstonian response to the labour questions which were coming to dominate domestic politics.

Morley was not as hostile to the idea of constructionism as Gladstone. He did not share his leader's consternation that 'interest has moved away from politics and theology towards the vague something which they call social reform.'[64] He even tried to pick up the pieces of the Unauthorized Programme which his erstwhile friend Chamberlain had abandoned in 1886. He was prepared to advocate considerable intervention by central and local government to promote social welfare. After a speech in 1889 in which he called for local authorities to be given powers compulsorily to purchase land for public purposes, to control the drink trade and to provide free school meals, paid for out of the rates, for hungry children at Board Schools, *The Times* accused him of forsaking true Liberal principles and asked: 'If we are to rear and educate other people's children for nothing, why not clothe them too and start them up in business? Where is the eleemosynary business to stop?'[65] Yet he was no dangerous collectivist. His natural sympathies were for voluntaryism and against interventionism. At the beginning of the same speech he had made clear his own position: 'My view is that we ought, in looking forward to social reform, to rely as much as we possibly can on organised co-operation outside of the law, and by that I mean without statutory interference.'[66]

It was as a voluntaryist that Morley approached the two great labour questions of the late 1880s, the desirability of a national state scheme of insurance for old age, sickness and unemployment, and the limitation by law of the hours to be worked each day. The idea of a national insurance scheme administered by the state, and paid for out of contributions by both workers and employers, had been put forward by several social reformers and found favour with Chamberlain. Morley dismissed it on the grounds that it would encourage malingering and irresponsibility, that the state was an inefficient agency for organizing relief, and that it was better to rely on the existing voluntary friendly and benefit societies and the Poor Law. He told an audience of working men in Newcastle in 1889: 'I am in favour of sticking to the old system by which you yourselves shall use your own judgment and your own energy in order to cultivate the virtue of thrift, and in order to see that thrift is rewarded.'[67]

The legal enforcement of an eight-hour working day in factories and workshops was perhaps the most insistent demand of the emerging Labour movement. It was taken up by many younger Liberals and Radicals. To the older Gladstonians, however, it was anathema. They felt it was for employers to limit the hours of work of their workers voluntarily out of humanitarian considerations and not because of legal compulsion. In 1884 Bright had declared: 'I still hold the opinion that to limit by law the time during which adults may work is unwise, and in many cases oppressive.'[68] In 1888 Bradlaugh fiercely attacked a Bill introduced by Sir John Lubbock to limit the hours of shop workers as 'a blow at the self-reliance of the individual'.[69] Morley was not quite so hostile to the idea of controlling working hours where this had been voluntarily agreed by both workers and employers, but he remained implacably opposed to compulsory action by the state. 'I am all for reducing the hours of labour to such limits as may be practicable,' he said in his speech at Newcastle in 1889, 'but I, for one, am firm on this: that the limitation must be effected, as some of the greatest reforms have been, by your own firm individual effort, and not by giving to Parliament to do that which Parliament is not very well fitted to do. What business has Parliament to prescribe to the people of Manchester and Birmingham and Newcastle the terms upon which they shall employ their men?'[70]

Gladstone shared Morley's voluntaryist objections to proposals for state intervention to provide welfare and protection for workers. He studiously ignored the demand for a national insurance scheme and rejected the Eight Hour Day as a Liberal slogan for the 1892 election. The strong pressure for its adoption was, in his view, a sign of 'the labouring class beginning to be corrupted by the semblance of power as the other classes have been tainted and warped by its reality'.[71] He made his own preferences clear in a speech at the opening of a recreation room in a Cheshire village in 1889: 'We live at a time when there is a disposition to think that the Government ought to do this and that, and that the Government ought to do everything. . . . The spirit of self-reliance, the spirit of true and genuine manly independence, should be preserved in the minds of the people.'[72] Significantly, when he recorded a message on Edison's new phonograph in 1890 it was on the theme of self-help and thrift.

In 1890 Gladstone contributed an article to the *Nineteenth Century* on 'Mr. Carnegie's Gospel of Wealth'. In it, he commended the doctrine of the Scottish-born industrialist and philanthropist, Andrew Carnegie, that the antidote to the present unequal distribution of wealth and the appalling pockets of disease and suffering in society lay in the charitable activity of the rich. Taking as his starting point Carnegie's notion that the surplus property of the wealthy should be given for the common good, Gladstone proposed a Universal Beneficent Society, which he himself offered to set up, in which the rich would bind themselves to devote a fixed proportion of their income for the benefit of their countrymen. His scheme, which was little noticed at the time, could be said to be the swan-song of voluntaryism. It was a final attempt to solve the problems of disease and poverty in society by an appeal to man's better nature rather than by setting up a compulsory welfare state. It came too late, however. Gladstone's scheme could only have succeeded, if at all, in an earlier age when wealth was still in the hands of individuals rather than corporations and before the poor had begun to look to the state for succour and support.

Gladstone and Morley's continued attachment to voluntaryism played a decisive part in the final severance of the Labour movement from Liberalism. In 1889 working men in Newcastle set up their own Labour Electoral Organisation with the specific object of ousting Morley because of his opposition to legislation on an eight-hour working day. He was defeated at the polls in both the 1892 and 1895 elections as a result of the defection of working-class voters in his Newcastle constituency. Several leading Socialists left the Liberal party because of its refusal to contemplate legislation on the subject. George Lansbury tried to move for an Eight Hours Bill at the 1889 congress of the National Liberal Federation. He wrote later: 'After a few minutes I was gently but firmly pushed down the steps, and thus ended my connection with Liberalism.'[73] After trying equally unsuccessfully to propose the measure at the 1890 and 1891 congresses, Sidney Webb wrote: 'the Liberal Party is shrinking up into a middle class group.'[74]

In addition to their disappointment over the Eight Hours Bill, the Labour movement was becoming increasingly frustrated over the Liberal party's continued reluctance to adopt working-class candidates. This single factor, which resulted at least as much from the poverty of most constituency associations as from any prejudice among the employers who dominated them, was probably more responsible than any other for the final severance of the Labour movement from the Liberals and its organization as an independent political party in the early 1890s. Three leading figures in the infant Labour party all left the Liberals because of their failure to be adopted as Parliamentary candidates. Keir Hardie unsuccessfully sought adoption at mid-Lanark in 1888, Ramsay MacDonald at Attercliffe in 1894 and Arthur Henderson at Newcastle in 1895. Hardie went on to contest the 1892 election independently and to become one of the first two Labour M.P.s, the other being John Burns. Although twenty-five working-class candidates contested the 1892 election as Liberals, most of the ten elected were miners who, under the leadership of Thomas Burt, opposed such measures as the Eight Hours Bill and were regarded as traitors by most members of the Labour movement. Gladstone himself was deeply worried about the lack of working-class M.P.s in the Liberal party but characteristically he refused to contemplate the remedy canvassed by the Labour movement, the payment of M.P.s, and instead called for voluntary financial sponsorship by wealthy Liberal industrialists.

On the eve of Gladstone's fourth administration, the leaders of the Labour movement had little doubt that after their lengthy prevarications, the Liberals would shortly be forced to reveal themselves in their true colours as individualists and capitalists opposed to social reform. A Fabian pamphlet of 1889 predicted: 'The dodgy Liberal will see his chance of the indefinite postponement of the socializing of politics. Manhood suffrage, female suffrage, the woes of deceased wife's sisters, the social ambition of dissenting ministers, the legal obstacles to the "free" acquirement of landed property, home rule for "dear old Scotland" and "neglected little Wales", extraordinary tithes, reform of the House of Lords: all these and any number of other obstacles may be successfully thrown in the way of the forward march of the Socialist Army.' Whatever delaying tactics he used, however, the day could not be far off when the Liberal would finally have to decide 'either to throw over private capital or to frankly acknowledge that it is a distinction without a difference which separates him from the Conservative against whom he has for years been fulminating'.[75]

In fact, Gladstone's last Government went a surprisingly long way down the Socialist road. Harcourt, the Chancellor of the Exchequer, introduced death duties on landed estates, much to the alarm of the Prime Minister. As President of the Board of Trade, Mundella set up a special Labour Department and collected statistics on unemployment for the first time. He also carried a Bill giving railwaymen an eight-hour day. Asquith, the Home Secretary, greatly increased the number of factory inspectors and instituted inquiries into working conditions which led to a more stringent code of sanitary and safety precautions for all places of work. He also introduced an Employers' Liability Bill to ensure workers were compensated for industrial injuries. Gladstone subsequently dropped the measure, however, after it had been fiercely opposed in the House of Lords. Henry Campbell-Bannerman, the Secretary of State for War, increased the wages of government employees in defence establishments to standard trade union rates and reduced their working week to forty-eight hours. Arthur Acland, Vice-President of the Council with responsibility for education, greatly increased government supervision of both teaching and school building standards and raised the compulsory school-leaving age from ten to eleven. He was also responsible for the appointment of a Royal Commission on secondary education under James Bryce which recommended the creation of a fully fledged Ministry of Education. H. H. Fowler, President of the Local Government Board, carried a Local Government Act in 1894 which set up nearly 7,000 parish councils and gave increased powers to urban and rural district councils.

Gladstone fully supported the interventionist activities of his younger ministers. He himself spoke in favour of such socialistic proposals as free elementary education, employers' liability and the taxation of land values. He strongly defended the legal rights of trade unions and deplored the efforts of employers to use the courts and the law of conspiracy against strikes and picketing. Much influenced by his friend Cardinal Manning's sympathy for the dockers, he had even praised the 1889 dock strike for strengthening 'the condition of labour in the face of capital'.[76] He cheerfully endorsed the contents of the National Liberal Federation's Newcastle Programme of 1891, which included demands for old-age pensions and an Eight Hours Bill, although he carefully selected items which he thought were important and neglected more constructionist proposals which he did not like. He came near to committing himself to state old-age pensions, commenting that 'until society is able to offer to the industrious labourer at the end of a long and blameless life something better than the workhouse, society will not have discharged its duties to its poorest members', and telling the House of Commons in 1892 that the Liberal party had 'come generally to the conclusion that . . . it is hard even for the industrious and sober man, under ordinary conditions, to secure a provision for his own old age'.[77] In 1893 he even voted in favour of a Bill to give miners an eight-hour day and declared that 'the present epoch is one a little too late . . . for us to say we will adhere rigidly to the principle of non-interference with adult labour.'[78]

It was little wonder that many older Liberals were horrified at what they took to be Gladstone's desertion of the principles of individualism and voluntaryism. George Howell bitterly attacked the proposed Eight Hours Bill in *A Plea for Liberty* (1891) as marking 'an epoch of dependence, the sure precursor of decay in men and nations'.[79] Sir William Mather, a leading Lancashire industrialist, quit his seat in Parliament in 1895 to devote himself to converting his fellow employers to the principle of securing an eight-hour working day by voluntary means so that legislation on the subject could still be averted, Parliament saved from degradation and the essentials of Liberalism preserved. Spence Watson commented wistfully on Gladstone's endorsement of the Newcastle Programme: 'some of us look back at the good old time when we took up one great burning question and fought it.'[80]

In fact, the critics need not have been so worried. Gladstone's basic convictions were still with them and not with the interventionists and collectivists. For him, the main aim of social policy was still to remove the obstacles to a full expression of the individual moral personality and not to establish a collective welfare state. The issues which interested him most remained Ireland, the temperance question, constitutional reform and foreign affairs. The granting of responsible government to Natal, the struggle to prevent Uganda being made a British protectorate, the Scottish and Welsh Church suspensory Bills, and the tightening up of electoral registration; these were the achievements of his last administration which gave him greatest pleasure, not the various pieces of 'constructionism' over which he had presided. He remained passionately opposed to any new activity which increased public expenditure. As Harcourt put it in 1893: 'I believe the Prime Minister and myself are the last representatives of the vanished creed [economy].'[81]

Certainly the Labour movement had no doubt as to where Gladstone's priorities lay. In 1893 a Fabian pamphlet, *To Your Tents, O Israel*, argued that his complete absorption in Home Rule, together with John Morley's doctrinaire adherence to the principles of the Manchester School, had finally and effectively killed any chance that there might have been of the emergence of a new Liberalism as advocated in the Government by Asquith, Acland, Mundella, Rosebery, Bryce and

Ripon. It called for the creation of a separate Labour party firmly anchored to the trade union movement. On 13 January 1893, as Gladstone introduced yet another Home Rule Bill into Parliament, a conference in Bradford resolved to establish an Independent Labour party in Britain.

As long as Gladstone remained at the helm, so long at least would Liberalism survive. Contemporaries could not help speculating, however, as he entered his eighties, what would happen after he went. William Morris put the question in *The Commonweal* in 1888: 'What will be left of Liberalism when this old man has gone?'[82] Three years later Acton asked: 'How is Liberalism to govern the Empire when its halo is gone . . . and there is nobody to play Hamlet?' and John Morley observed: 'Talk of the Liberal Party? Why it consists of Mr. G. After him it will disappear and all will be chaos.'[83]

In fact, they did not have to wait long for their answer. Gladstone resigned the leadership of the Liberal party in 1894 in defence of the principles of peace, retrenchment and reform which had sustained him throughout the nearly thirty years he had been at its head. In the face of Europe's race to rearm, the Admiralty wanted to build seven new British battleships at a cost of over £3 millions. Gladstone warned the Cabinet that if it approved the naval estimates, he would resign, since they 'would end in a race towards bankruptcy by all the powers of Europe'.[84] Both his sense of economy and his dislike of militarism were outraged by the thought that a government over which he had presided might approve the estimates. 'Liberalism cannot put on the garb of Jingoism,' he wrote to Mundella in a letter which went on to describe his lifetime in politics as 'for sixty years a constant effort to do all I could for economy and peace'.[85]

The Cabinet approved the estimates, however, and Gladstone resigned. 'The world of today is not the world in which I was bred and trained and principally lived,' he wrote to Acton at the time. 'I take the worst at the worst and say that if the whole generation is against me, even that is far better than that I should with my eyes open do anything to accelerate, exasperate, widen or prematurely take or verge towards taking a part in the controversies of blood which we all fear and seem to see hanging over Europe.'[86] A few days later, and sixty-one years after he had made his maiden speech in Parliament, he made his last speech there, a vigorous assault on the House of Lords.

As his friends and enemies alike had predicted, Gladstone's brand of Liberalism was all but finished with his own departure from politics.

His successor, Rosebery, was an imperialist, strongly sympathetic to 'constructionist' legislation, with a passion for national efficiency and horse-racing. Old-style Liberals were disturbed by his establishment of a protectorate over Uganda and his insistence on maintaining British control over Egypt. The London Nonconformist Council passed a resolution calling on all Nonconformists to refrain from supporting political leaders connected with the Turf. Gladstone himself realized that an era had ended with his departure from the Liberal leadership. The sixty years in which he had been politically active, he told friends shortly after his resignation, had been 'a period of emancipation, political, economical, social, moral, intellectual. . . . Another period has opened and is opening still, a period possibly of yet greater moral dangers. . . . To emancipate is comparatively easy. It is simple to remove restrictions, to allow natural forces free play. We have to face the problem of constructive legislation. . . . I am thankful I have borne a great part in the emancipating labours of the last sixty years, but entirely uncertain how, had I now to begin my life, I could face the very different problems of the next sixty years. Of one thing I am, and always have been, convinced—it is not by the state that man can be regenerated and the terrible woes of this darkened world effectually dealt with.'[87]

The General Election of July 1895 was the first in 63 years which Gladstone had not contested. He took no part in it, beyond delivering a farewell address to his Midlothian constituents reminding them that 'the century now expiring has exhibited a period of unexampled activity both in legislative and administrative changes, these changes have been in the direction of true and most beneficial progress . . . and the overwhelming proportion have been effected by direct action of the liberal party.'[88] Despite his own non-involvement, it was essentially Gladstonian Liberalism which was offered for a last time to the electors, and which was decisively and utterly rejected. Hopelessly split, Liberals appealed to the country with an amalgam of all the great rallying cries of the past—Church disestablishment, temperance reform, anti-imperialism and national self-determination—none of which any longer excited the electorate. Dale had reflected sadly in 1894 that the great Nonconformist goals of disestablishment and temperance reform seemed further off than ever now that 'the popular passion has all run into the channels of the various labour questions'.[89] Beatrice Webb noted in her diary on the eve of the election: 'The Liberal Party is pledged to three measures which offend all the conservative instincts of the people, Home Rule, local veto and Church Disestablishment, without exciting the slightest enthusiasm among the advanced section of the party.'[90] The result was catastrophic. The Conservatives increased their representation from 269 to 340 seats, and the Liberal Unionists from 46 to 71, while the Liberals dropped from 273 to 177 M.P.s, their smallest presence in Parliament since the early 1860s.

Friend and foe alike were agreed that the 1895 election defeat struck a mortal blow at Gladstonianism. 'Down goes the middle class Radicalism and the Nonconformist conscience,' wrote the Revd. Henry Scott-Holland, a pioneer Christian Socialist: 'How shall we do without them?'[91] William Clarke, a Fabian Socialist, commented that 'the Liberal Party is smashed into atoms. . . . An organised hypocrisy has come to an end.'[92] Lord Rosebery, who resigned the leadership following the defeat, wrote: 'it is always possible that that may happen here which has happened in Belgium—the elimination of Liberalism, leaving the two forces of Socialism and Reaction face to face.'[93]

Liberals advanced contradictory reasons for their diastrous electoral defeat. The young Herbert Samuel told the National Liberal Federation that it showed the consequences of failing to adopt collectivist policies of social reform, a view that was shared by many younger members of the party. Others, however, saw the defeat as a result of the Liberals' abandonment of their historical principles and their foolish attempt to compromise with modern trends. The most powerful expression of this latter view came in a volume of *Essays in Liberalism* published in 1897 and dedicated to John Morley. It was the work of six recent Oxford graduates, Hilaire Belloc, F. W. Hirst, J. A. Simon, J. S. Phillimore, J. L. Hammond and P. J. Macdonell. The book was similar in style to the *Essays on Reform* which had been written thirty years earlier by another group of young Liberals. The main difference was that while the *Essays on Reform* looked forward, the *Essays in Liberalism* looked back. Their theme was sounded by Belloc in his introductory essay: 'Is it possible to revert at this hour to the simple doctrines which formed the strength of our first leaders?'[94]

The young authors of the *Essays in Liberalism* were convinced that it was not only possible, but essential, for the Liberal party to return to its historic principles if it was to survive. The evils of the present, wrote Belloc, were Jingoism, 'a dream of mere conquest and a glory of mere empire', and Socialism, 'an attack upon personal production, personal accumulation and consequent personal possession'.[95] They could only be combated by a bold reassertion of the principles of free trade, self-determination, constitutional reform and voluntaryism. The essays were a lament for the lost values of Gladstonianism. Hirst in his essay on Liberalism and wealth lauded the virtues of free trade and individualism and called on the Liberals 'by amending the land laws to foster a race of yeomen, and by encouraging co-operation to smooth away the antithesis of capital and labour'.[96] Phillimore's contribution on foreign policy was pure Cobdenism. Simon stoutly defended competition in industry in his essay on Liberals and Labour. Belloc devoted eleven pages of his essay to the land question and less than one to the condition of industrial society. The whole volume breathed the spirit of a world that had disappeared, where workers and employers stood together rather than opposing one another and where men cared more about liberty than about the size of their next wage packet. All six essayists agreed that the Liberals' greatest mistake was their retreat from the politics of idealism into the politics of materialism. As P. J. Macdonell put it: 'The Liberal Party has been beaten because it has attempted to meet the collectivist on his own ground—because it has tried to compete with him in materialist programmes and promises of increased comfort. It must return to its earlier, better ideal. It must take its stand on the moral grounds of liberty and justice. It must teach the individual his duties as a citizen, and material prosperity will follow, stimulate his intelligence, his thrift, his patriotism, and he will take good care to improve his surroundings. . . . The remedy is simply this: Liberalism must once again base its claims on broad, abstract, moral lines. Its measures aim to fulfil great moral ideas, not merely to confer small material gains. In the days of Bright and Cobden Liberalism appealed to great abstract conceptions.'[97]

As the young authors of *Essays in Liberalism* called for a return to first principles, other Liberals ended the nineteenth century with equally idealistic appeals to the moral roots of their creed. Gladstone led a national campaign in 1896 over the Turks' massacre of the Armenians and made the last great public speech of his life in Liverpool, lasting an hour and twenty minutes, calling for British intervention to avenge the slaughter. The following year, in the last twelve months of his life, he turned his attention to the liberation of Crete. Joseph Arch continued to preach the traditional Gladstonian gospel to workers on the land. 'I do not believe in State-aid and land nationalisation,' he told young men in 1898, 'self-help and liberty, order and progress—these are what I advocate. Present day socialism will die a natural death sooner or later.'[98] W. T. Stead, strongly backed by John Morley and by many Nonconformists, toured Europe in 1898 to gain support for Tsar Nicholas II's proposal for a world peace conference to end the armaments race and establish a permanent international court of arbitration.

Had he lived a little longer Gladstone would have warmly approved of Stead's mission and of the results of the Peace Conference held in 1899 which secured international agreement on the outlawing of certain weapons and established a permanent court of arbitration in the Hague. One of his last recorded utterances before he died in May 1898 was a gloomy prediction that the European arms race would end in war and that 'materialism and militarism will be the Devil's agents during the twentieth century.'[99] Even as he lay dying, his prophecies seemed near fulfilment. At home, employers were engaged in lock-outs against their workers and the Trades Union Congress passed a resolution recommending trade unionists to support only 'working-class socialist parties'. Abroad, rumours of war filled the air. The United States opened hostilities with Spain over Cuba. Kitchener moved south down the valley of the Nile to annihilate the Khalifa's forces and collided with French troops advancing north. Russia menaced Britain's position in the Far East. The collapse of China threatened a new European scramble for imperial possessions. In South Africa the stage was being set for a bloody conflict between the British and the Boers. Meanwhile the naval dockyards and armaments factories of Germany teemed with activity. Gladstone's world, the world of peace, retrenchment and reform, seemed to have died with him. When at the turn of the century, a clergyman announced his intention of starting a new periodical called *The Optimist*, Sir Wilfrid Lawson wrote to him: 'Is there anything to sustain such a name in the present condition of the world? Here you have more people trained and armed for the slaughter of their fellow-men than have ever been seen before.'[100]

In fact, of course, Liberalism survived into the twentieth century and even flourished in an apparently unpropitious climate. But it was a very different Liberalism from that of Gladstone. Historians disagree as to the exact point when the Liberal party lost its individualism and voluntaryism and became the collectivist, social democratic organ that it is today. Some follow Maine and Spencer in seeing the change occurring as far back as the early 1880s with Green's lecture on *Liberal Legislation and Freedom of Contract* and the socialistic measures of Gladstone's second administration. Others have maintained that it was not until the 1930s, when Liberal thinking was dominated by J. M. Keynes and

William Beveridge, that the party finally broke with its Gladstonian past. There are good grounds, however, for dating the decisive change in the Liberal outlook to the turn of the century and the years immediately before and after Gladstone's death. Certainly it was in that period that contemporaries were conscious of the emergence of a 'New Liberalism'.[101]

During the early 1890s a group of young Liberals, most of whom were in their late twenties, had started meeting regularly together to discuss social and labour questions. They included J. A. Simon, one of the recent Oxford graduates who had contributed to the *Essays in Liberalism*, L. T. Hobhouse, another Oxford graduate who was shortly to join the *Manchester Guardian*, J. A. Hobson, a lecturer in economics for the Oxford University Extension movement, Charles Trevelyan, son of Sir George Trevelyan and himself a Liberal candidate in the 1895 election, R. B. Haldane, M.P. for East Lothian and a keen amateur philosopher, Herbert Samuel, who had just come down from Balliol College, Oxford, and J. M. Robertson, the secularist and journalist. The group had close contacts with trade union leaders like Tom Mann and Ben Tillett, Fabians like Sidney Webb and Sydney Olivier, and with the emerging Labour party through one of its founder members, Ramsay MacDonald. By 1894 the group had become known as the Rainbow Circle, taking its name from the tavern in Fleet Street where it regularly met to discuss such topics as 'Economic Deficiencies of the Manchester School' and 'Political defects of the old Radicalism'. In 1896 its members established the *Progressive Review*, which was dedicated to promoting a 'New Liberalism' based on 'a specific policy of reconstruction, the conscious organization of society and an enlarged and enlightened conception of the functions of the state'.[102]

These self-styled 'New Liberals', who with the Liberal Imperialists like Asquith and Grey rapidly came to dominate the policy and outlook of the party in the early twentieth century, had a very different conception of Liberalism from the old Gladstonians. They believed that most problems had social rather than personal causes and that the way to improvement lay through state action and not individual moral regeneration. They saw themselves fighting altogether different battles from their predecessors. 'Today it is not for individual freedom that we have to struggle against classes and privilege,' Haldane wrote in the first number of the *Progressive Review*. 'We have to win a yet harder fight, a fight for emancipation from conditions which deny fair play

I

to the collective energy for the good of society as a whole.'[103] Asquith told his electors in 1892: 'I am one of those who believe that the collective action of the community may and ought to be employed positively as well as negatively.'[104] David Lloyd George, the fiery Welsh Radical who had entered Parliament in 1890, summed up the difference between the old and the new Liberalism in a speech at Swansea in 1908: 'The old Liberals used the natural discontent of the people with the poverty and precariousness of the means of subsistence as a motive power to win for them a better, more influential, and more honourable status in the citizenship of their native land. The new Liberalism, while pursuing this great political ideal with unflinching energy, devotes a part of its endeavour also to the removing of the immediate causes of discontent. It is true that man cannot live by bread alone. It is equally true that a man cannot live without bread.'[105]

It was certainly the new rather than the old Liberalism which underlay the policies and achievements of the last Liberal Government in Britain, Asquith's administration of 1908 to 1915. The measures laying the foundation of the Welfare State, like the Old Age Pensions Act and the National Insurance Act, reflected the collectivism of the Rainbow Circle rather than Gladstonian voluntaryism. None the less, there were still traces of the persistence of Victorian Liberal principles. Asquith envisaged a partnership between voluntary and statutory agencies in promoting social reform and was reluctant to throw the whole task on to the state. As Foreign Secretary, Sir Edward Grey remained faithful to the ideal of the Concert of Europe and the principle of international arbitration. Old values continued to be held. There were still those who retained the essentially Victorian faith that the writer Kathleen Nott identified in her father's Liberalism on the eve of the First World War as: 'disapproval of war, disapproval of capitalism, disapproval of Labour: disapproval of God (and since he happened to be a first-class choir bass, mild contempt of vicars); and a Utopian chiliasm based on a belief in Original Virtue, that looked forward to lotus eating rather than general prosperity'.[106]

The last survivor from the age of optimism was, appropriately, Gladstone's greatest disciple and principal lieutenant, John Morley. Shortly before his mentor died, Morley had announced the ending of his official association with the Liberal party in terms that left no doubt of his own conviction that Gladstonianism would die with its creator: 'I will not go around the country saying fine things or listening to fine things about Mr. Gladstone, and at the same time sponging off the slate all the lessons that Mr. Gladstone taught us and all the lessons that he set.'[107] He threw himself into the task of writing his monumental biography of Gladstone and speaking around the country in defence of his policies. In the book and in his speeches Morley vigorously denounced imperialism, militarism and Socialism and championed self-determination, non-intervention and individual responsibility. He castigated his contemporaries for sinking further every year into cynical compromise and despair. 'They have ceased either to trust or distrust liberty', he had commented sadly to Gladstone in 1891, 'and have come to the mind that it matters little either way. Men are disenchanted. They have got what they wanted in the days of their youth, yet what of it, they ask.'[108]

In the event, Morley did not end his association with the Liberal party after Gladstone's death. From 1905 to 1914 he sat in Campbell-Bannerman's and Asquith's Cabinets as Secretary for India and Lord President of the Council, but he found himself increasingly out of sympathy with his colleagues. In 1907 he regretfully noted that Socialism had become 'the key to our politics' and 'the catchword of the hour'.[109] In August 1914 he finally resigned from Asquith's Government when it took Britain into war with Germany and so, in his view, overturned the sacred Liberal commitment to let reason rather than force be the arbiter in international disputes. The jingoism and resort to conscription which followed the declaration of war filled him with horror. Early in 1915 he told a friend: 'Liberalism, as we have known it, is dead beyond resurrection.'[110]

The horror of the First World War destroyed in Morley, as it did in many others, the last flickerings of the optimism and the belief in progress which had been at the heart of their Liberalism. Harold Laski reported on a visit to Morley in 1920: 'I was glad to find him free from the cant of progress. He has a little outlived his generation, in the sense that the pure milk of the Cobdenite word remains pure even in the midst of changes.'[111] In one of his last published works, *Notes on Politics and History*, Morley even questioned whether it was any more than an 'optimist superstition' to believe 'that civilised communities are universally bound somehow or another to be progressive'.[112] So far had the militarism and materialism of the twentieth century weakened the faith of one who had belonged to a group of men who had been fired by optimism about the potential of the human spirit. When Morley died in 1924, Francis Hirst commented, 'it is the end of a chapter', and H. W. Massingham wrote that 'he was the last of the great, the true Liberals.'[113] Asquith simply commented: 'This means the disappearance of the last survivor of the heroic age.'[114]

Although the great Liberal figures in the twentieth century have shown some of the same qualities which distinguished their Victorian predecessors, they seem rather diminished in comparison. It is not too difficult, for example, to see Hilaire Belloc and Gilbert Murray as the intellectual heirs of John Morley and John Stuart Mill; H. A. L. Fisher and G. M. Trevelyan as imbued with the same historical spirit as Acton; and George Cadbury, Seebohm Rowntree and William Hesketh Lever as benevolent Nonconformist industrialists in the mould of Samuel Morley and Titus Salt; although it does require a considerable leap of imagination to see Keynes and Beveridge as the lineal descendants of Cobden and Bright. Not even their most ardent admirers would claim, however, that this admittedly talented generation of Liberals had the same faith in the human spirit as the generation of Gladstone.

Chronology

THE LIBERAL AWAKENING 1832–1868

1832 Great Reform Act
1839 Mill's article on 'The Reorganisation of the Reform Party' in the *Westminster Review*
Anti-Corn Law League set up in Manchester
1840 Bright leads campaign against church rates in Rochdale
1841 Cobden elected M.P. for Stockport
Complete Suffrage Union started by Sturge
Nonconformist founded by Miall
1844 Anti-State Church Association founded (later Liberation Society)
1846 Peel repeals the corn laws
1847 Baines begins campaign against state education
1850 Cobden and Bright first oppose Palmerston's foreign policy over Don Pacifico incident
1855 Administrative Reform Association set up by Samuel Morley
Trevelyan–Northcote report on entry to Civil Service
Stamp duty on newspapers abolished by Gladstone
1859 Meeting in Willis's Rooms taken to mark formation of Liberal party
Gladstone joins Liberals on return from Italy
Mill's *On Liberty* published
1860 Anglo-French Commercial Treaty negotiated by Gladstone and Cobden
1861 Gladstone sets up Post Office Savings Bank
1864 Baines's Bill to reduce borough franchise qualification
Gladstone commits himself to Parliamentary reform
1865 Death of Palmerston. Russell takes over Whig leadership
Reform League formed
Fortnightly Review set up by Liberal intellectuals
Governor Eyre case and victory of North in American Civil War unite Liberals

1866   Gladstone introduces Reform Bill
1867   Gladstone carries abolition of church rates
       Second Reform Act gives vote to all householders in boroughs
       and enfranchises one million workers
1868   Compact between George Howell of the Reform League and
       Samuel Morley and others on behalf of the Liberal party
       cements Lib–Lab alliance

GLADSTONE'S FIRST GOVERNMENT 1868–1874

1869   Disestablishment of the Irish Church
       Foundation of Charity Organisation Society
       Chamberlain sets up National Education League in Birmingham
       to campaign for free, non-sectarian education
1870   Forster's Elementary Education Act provides Board Schools
       where voluntary schools inadequate
       Irish Landlord and Tenant Act
       Entry to Civil Service thrown open to competitive examination
1871   Cardwell's Army reforms include abolition of purchase of com-
       missions
       Trades Union Act gives unions legal status and protection
       Criminal Law Amendment Act outlaws picketing
       University Tests Act abolishes religious tests at Oxford and
       Cambridge
       Poor Law Board established
       Sunday observance laws eased
       Bank Holiday Act
1872   Bruce's Licensing Act
       Ballot Act establishes secret voting
       Mundella's Arbitration (Masters & Workers) Act sets up arbitra-
       tion machinery
       Municipal Corporations (Borough Funds) Act enables local
       authorities to take over public utilities
       Mundella unsuccessfully introduces Bill to reduce hours of work
       of women and children in textile factories
1873   Selborne's Judicature Act fuses common law and equity
       Chamberlain becomes Lord Mayor of Birmingham and begins
       municipal improvements

1875 Gladstone resigns Liberal leadership following electoral defeat in 1874. Hartington in the Commons and Granville in the Lords take over

1876 Gladstone takes up and leads national agitation against Bulgarian atrocities

1877 Chamberlain sets up National Liberal Federation

1879 Midlothian Campaign re-establishes Gladstone as Liberal leader

GLADSTONE'S SECOND GOVERNMENT 1880–1885

1880 Burials Act allows Nonconformists and others burial in church-yards
Ground Game Act transfers game rights from landlords to tenants
Employers' Liability Act protects industrial workers
Compulsory school attendance from five to ten established

1881 Pretoria Convention recognizes independence of Transvaal
Irish Land Act gives tenants fair rents, free sale and fixity of tenure
Irish Coercion Act
Flogging abolished in the Army
Welsh Sunday Closing Act

1882 Occupation of Egypt and shelling of Alexandria
Married Women's Property Act
Allotments Extension Act
Settled Land Act eases transfer of land

1883 Agricultural Holdings Act gives tenants right to compensation for improvements
Corrupt Practices Act stops abuses in elections

1884 Third Reform Act enfranchises two million people, gives vote to agricultural workers and establishes single-member constituencies

1885 Scottish Office established
Chamberlain fights election on Unauthorized or Radical Programme

GLADSTONE'S THIRD GOVERNMENT 1886

1886 Irish Home Rule Bill introduced but defeated
Repeal of Contagious Diseases Acts

1891 Newcastle Programme endorsed by Gladstone

GLADSTONE'S FOURTH GOVERNMENT 1892-1894

1892   Formation of labour department in Board of Trade by Mundella
Smallholdings Act

1893   Second Irish Home Rule Bill introduced and defeated
Acland raises school-leaving age from ten to eleven
Hours of Labour (Railway Servants) Act establishes eight-hour
day
Harcourt unsuccessfully introduces Permissive Bill allowing
local veto of drink trade

1894   Local Government Act sets up parish and urban district councils
Asquith's Employers' Liability Bill defeated by Lords
Gladstone resigns over naval estimates; Rosebery takes over as
Liberal leader

ROSEBERY'S GOVERNMENT 1894-1895

1894   Death duties introduced by Harcourt

1895   Asquith introduces Welsh Disestablishment Bill
British Protectorate established over Uganda

1898   Death of Gladstone

Biographical Notes

The main purpose of these notes is to give brief biographical information about those referred to in this book. They are not intended to provide an exhaustive list of leading Gladstonian Liberals, although most of the important figures in the Liberal movement between the mid-1850s and the mid-1880s are included. The biographical notes are confined to Gladstonian Liberals and certain Radicals; Whigs, Liberal Imperialists and New Liberals are excluded.

ACLAND, ARTHUR (1847–1926): Fellow of Keble College, Oxford, 1871–5. M.P. for Rotherham, 1885–99. Vice-President of the Council with responsibility for education, 1892–5.

ACTON, JOHN (1834–1902): M.P. for Carlow, 1859–65. Raised to peerage 1869. Professor of Modern History at Cambridge from 1895. Leading Liberal Roman Catholic in Britain.

ARCH, JOSEPH (1826–1919): Founder and leader of National Agricultural Labourers' Union. M.P. for N.W. Norfolk, 1885–6, 1892–1902. Leading Lib–Lab.

ARGYLL, 8TH DUKE OF (1823–1900): Peelite and free trader in 1840s. Succeeded to title 1847. Strong supporter of North in American Civil War. Secretary of State for India, 1868–74. Lord Privy Seal, 1880–1. Resigned over Irish Land Act and subsequently opposed Home Rule.

ASHWORTH, HENRY (1794–1880): Lancashire cotton mill owner. Candidate for Salford, 1859.

BAGEHOT, WALTER (1826–77): Editor of the *Economist*, 1860–77. Candidate for Bridgewater, 1866. Author of *The English Constitution* (1867). Moved away from Liberalism in 1870s.

BAINES, EDWARD (1800–90): M.P. for Leeds, 1859–74. Proprietor of *Leeds Mercury*. Led educational voluntaryists and introduced Parliamentary Reform Bill in 1864.

BASS, MICHAEL THOMAS (1799–1884): Head of Burton-on-Trent brewing business. M.P. for Derby, 1848–83. Strong advocate of Lib–Labism and supported railway workers in their call for shorter working hours.

BEALES, EDMUND (1803–81): Radical reformer and lawyer. Joint founder of the Reform League.

BRADLAUGH, CHARLES (1833–91): M.P. for Nottingham, 1880–91. Leading atheist. Founded National Secular Society, 1866. Refused to take oath on election as M.P. and led campaign for M.P.s to make secular affirmations. Republican sympathies and strong individualist.

BRIGHT, JACOB (1821–99): Partner in firm of John Bright and brothers, cotton spinners and manufacturers, Rochdale. M.P. for Manchester, 1867–74, 1876–85, S.W. Manchester, 1886–95. Introduced Bills to give votes to women.

BRIGHT, JOHN (1811–89): Brother of above. Led campaign against church rates in Rochdale in 1840s. M.P. for Durham, 1843–7, Manchester, 1847–57, Birmingham, 1857–89. President, Board of Trade, 1868–70. Chancellor of the Duchy of Lancaster, 1873, 1880–2. Leading advocate of Parliamentary reform. First English Nonconformist to sit in Cabinet. Resigned in protest against bombardment of Alexandria and subsequently opposed Home Rule.

BROADHURST, HENRY (1840–1911): Stonemason. Parliamentary Secretary, T.U.C., 1875–90. M.P. for Stoke-on-Trent, 1880–5, Bordesley, 1885–6, W. Nottingham, 1886–92, Leicester, 1894–1906. Under Secretary, Home Office, 1886. First working man in British government. Strong opponent of Eight Hours Bill.

BRODRICK, GEORGE CHARLES (1831–1903): Barrister. Involved in University Tests agitation. Leader writer on *The Times*, 1860–73. Candidate for Woodstock, 1868 and 1874, Monmouthshire, 1880. Warden of Merton College, Oxford, 1881–1903. Became disillusioned with Gladstonianism in 1880s.

BRUCE, HENRY (1815–95): South Wales mine owner and ironmaster. M.P. for Merthyr Tydfil, 1857–68, Renfrewshire, 1869–73. Home Secretary, 1868–73. Responsible for 1872 Licensing Act. Created 1st Baron Aberdare, 1873.

BRYCE, JAMES (1838–1922): On Taunton Commission on Endowed Schools, 1865–6. Regius Professor of Civil Law at Oxford, 1870–93. M.P., Tower Hamlets, 1880–5, S. Aberdeen, 1885–1906. Chancellor of the Duchy of Lancaster, 1892–4. President, Board of Trade, 1894–5. Subsequently British Ambassador to Washington.

BURT, THOMAS (1837–1922): Miners' leader in the north-east. M.P. for Morpeth, 1874–1918. Secretary, Board of Trade, 1892–5. One of first working men elected to Parliament.

CAINE, WILLIAM (1842–1903): Iron miner. M.P. for Scarborough, 1880–5, Barrow-in-Furness, 1886–90, E. Bradford, 1892–5. Civil Lord of Admiralty, 1884–5. Baptist and temperance reformer. Left Gladstonians over Home Rule in 1886 but rejoined them in 1890.

CAMPBELL, SIR GEORGE (1824–92): Judge. Lieutenant-Governor of Bengal. M.P. for Kirkcaldy, 1875–92. Advocate of Scottish and Irish Home Rule.

CAMPBELL-BANNERMAN, HENRY (1834–1908): M.P. for Stirling, 1868–1908. Financial Secretary for War, 1871–4, 1880–2. Secretary to Admiralty, 1882–4. Chief Secretary for Ireland, 1884–5. Secretary of State for War, 1892–5. Liberal leader, 1899. Prime Minister, 1905–8.

CARDWELL, EDWARD (1813–86): Peelite M.P. in 1840s and 1850s. M.P. for Oxford, 1857–74. Secretary of State for War, 1868–74. Author of Army reforms. Created 1st Viscount Cardwell, 1874.

CHAMBERLAIN, JOSEPH (1836–1914): Birmingham screw manufacturer. Unitarian. Founded National Education League, 1869. Mayor of Birmingham, 1873–6. M.P. for Birmingham, 1876–86. President, Board of Trade, 1880–5. President, Local Government Board, 1886. Never really a Gladstonian and split from the Liberals over Home Rule to lead Unionists. Subsequently a Conservative.

CHILDERS, HUGH (1827–96): Member of Government of Victoria, Australia, 1851–7. M.P. for Pontefract, 1860–85, Edinburgh South, 1886–92. First Lord of Admiralty, 1868–71. Chancellor of the Duchy of Lancaster, 1872–3. Secretary of State for War, 1880–2. Chancellor of Exchequer, 1882–5. Home Secretary, 1886.

CLIFFORD, JOHN (1836–1923): Minister, Praed Street Baptist Chapel, London, from 1858. Nonconformist leader. Remained loyal to Liberalism although moved towards Socialism.

COBDEN, RICHARD (1804–65): Sussex-born calico printer in Lancashire. Founder and leading member of Anti-Corn Law League. M.P. for W. Riding of Yorkshire, 1847–57, Rochdale, 1859–65. Arranged Anglo–French Commercial Treaty, 1860.

COLLINGS, JESSE (1831–1920): Birmingham merchant. Secretary of National Education League. Founder of Allotments and Smallholdings Association. Mayor of Birmingham, 1878–9. M.P. for Ipswich, 1880–6. Parliamentary Secretary to Local Government Board, 1886. Follower of Chamberlain and quit Liberals over Home Rule. Subsequently Unionist M.P.

COLMAN, JEREMIAH JAMES (1830–98): Norwich mustard and starch manufacturer. Baptist. M.P. for Norwich, 1871–95.

COWEN, JOSEPH (1831–99): Newcastle mine owner, manufacturer and journalist. Proprietor of *Newcastle Chronicle*. M.P. for Newcastle, 1873–86. Radical and Friend of Italy.

CROSSLEY, SIR FRANCIS (1817–72): Halifax carpet manufacturer and philanthropist. M.P. for Halifax, 1852–9, W. Riding of Yorkshire, 1859–72.

DALE, ROBERT WILLIAM (1829–95): Congregational minister at Carr's Lane Chapel, Birmingham, from 1859. Strong advocate of Nonconformist involvement in politics but opposed Home Rule and subsequently withdrew from politics.

DAWSON, GEORGE (1821–76): Minister at Mount Zion Baptist Chapel,

1844–7, and the independent Church of the Saviour, 1847–76 (both Birmingham). Leading proponent of municipal reform.

DICEY, ALBERT VENN (1835–1922): Constitutional lawyer and historian. Fellow of Trinity College, Oxford, 1860–72. Professor of English Law at Oxford, 1882–1909. Opposed Home Rule and after 1886 became most ardent defender of Unionist position outside Parliament.

DILKE, SIR CHARLES (1843–1911): Barrister. M.P. for Chelsea, 1868–86. Under Secretary at Foreign Office, 1880–2. President, Local Government Board, 1882–5. Radical Republican. Career ended by divorce scandal, 1885.

DOULTON, HENRY (1820–97): Pottery and ceramic manufacturer in Lambeth.

FAWCETT, HENRY (1833–84): Blind political economist. Professor of Political Economy at Cambridge, 1863–84. M.P. for Brighton, 1865–1874, Hackney, 1874–84. Postmaster General, 1880–4.

FORSTER, WILLIAM EDWARD (1819–86): Barrister but went to work in worsted factory near Bradford. M.P. for Bradford, 1861–86. Vice-President of Council with responsibility for education, 1868–74. Author of Elementary Education Act, 1870. Carried Ballot Act through Commons, 1872. Chief Secretary for Ireland, 1880–2. Broke with Gladstone in 1882 over Irish policy and opposed Home Rule.

FOX, WILLIAM JOHNSON (1786–1864): Unitarian and rationalist. Active in Anti-Corn Law League. M.P. for Oldham, 1847–62. Introduced Bill for compulsory secular education, 1850.

FREEMAN, EDWARD AUGUSTUS (1823–92): Fellow of Trinity College, Oxford, 1845–84. Regius Professor of Modern History, Oxford, 1884–92. Candidate for mid-Somerset, 1868. Took leading part in Bulgarian atrocities campaign.

GIBSON, THOMAS MILNER (1806–84): M.P. for Manchester, 1841–57, Ashton-under-Lyne, 1857–68. Instrumental in securing repeal of newspaper stamp duty, 1855. Founder member of the Manchester School.

GLADSTONE, WILLIAM EWART (1809–98): Peelite Conservative M.P., 1832–65. M.P. for S. Lancashire, 1865–8, Greenwich, 1868–80, Midlothian, 1880–95. Chancellor of Exchequer, 1852–5, 1859–66. Leader of Commons, 1865–6. Prime Minister, 1868–74. Retired from Liberal leadership in 1875 but resumed in 1880. Prime Minister, 1880–5, 1886, 1892–4.

GOSCHEN, GEORGE JOACHIM (1831–1907): City financier. M.P. for City of London, 1863–80, Ripon, 1880–5. President, Poor Law Board, 1868–71. First Lord of Admiralty, 1871–4. Opposed extension of franchise and Home Rule in 1880s and joined Conservative Cabinet in 1887.

GRANVILLE, 2ND EARL OF (1815–91): Staffordshire ironmaster. Succeeded to title, 1846. Foreign Secretary, 1851–2, 1870–4, 1880–5. Colonial Secretary, 1868–70, 1886.

GREEN, THOMAS HILL (1836–83): Philosopher. Fellow of Balliol College, Oxford, 1860–82. Professor of Moral Philosophy, Oxford, from 1877. Liberal member of Oxford City Council and Oxford School Board. Author of *Liberal Legislation and Freedom of Contract* (1880).

HARCOURT, SIR WILLIAM VERNON (1827–1904): Barrister. M.P. for Oxford, 1868–80, Derby, 1880–95, W. Monmouthshire, 1895–1904. Solicitor General, 1873–4. Home Secretary, 1880–5. Chancellor of the Exchequer, 1886, 1892–5. Liberal leader in the Commons, 1894–8. Convert to temperance legislation and reluctant supporter of Home Rule.

HARRISON, FREDERIC (1831–1923): Barrister. Professor of Jurisprudence, Council for Legal Education, 1877–89. Leading Positivist. Contested London University as Home Rule candidate in 1886. London County Council Alderman, 1889–92.

HERBERT, AUBERON (1838–1906): Political philosopher and author. M.P. for Nottingham, 1870–74. Free-thinker and Republican. Active in Bulgarian agitation. Later became ardent disciple of Herbert Spencer.

HOLYOAKE, GEORGE JACOB (1817–1906): Founder of secularism. Last person in Britain to be imprisoned on charge of atheism. Edited the

Reasoner. Leading advocate of Lib–Labism and co-operation. Offered himself as Liberal candidate in 1857, 1868 and 1884 but never went to the poll.

HOWELL, GEORGE (1833–1910): Bricklayer. Secretary of the Reform League, 1864–9. Parliamentary Secretary of Trades Union Congress, 1871–5. M.P. for Bethnal Green N.E., 1885–95. Leading Lib–Lab. Became extreme individualist.

HUGHES, HUGH PRICE (1847–1902): Wesleyan Methodist minister. Started *Methodist Times*, 1885. Promoted Free Church Congress, 1892. Began as Gladstonian but became Liberal Imperialist and strongly supported Boer War.

HUGHES, THOMAS (1822–96): Novelist and author of *Tom Brown's Schooldays.* M.P. for Lambeth, 1865–8, Frome, 1868–74. Enthusiast for co-operative movement and for legislation to help trade union movement. Opposed Home Rule and became Unionist.

HUTTON, RICHARD HOLT (1826–97): Unitarian minister and journalist. Editor and joint-proprietor of the *Spectator* from 1861.

ILLINGWORTH, ALFRED (1827–1907): Bradford worsted spinner. M.P. for Knaresborough, 1868–74, Bradford, 1880–5, Bradford W., 1885–95.

JAMES, SIR HENRY (1828–1911): Barrister. M.P. for Taunton, 1869–85, Bury, 1885–95. Attorney General, 1873–4, 1880–5. Drafted and carried Corrupt Practices Act, 1883. Opposed Home Rule and became prominent Liberal Unionist. Created 1st Baron James of Hereford, 1895.

LABOUCHERE, HENRY (1831–1912): Diplomat and journalist. Founder and proprietor of *Truth.* M.P. for Windsor, 1865–6, Middlesex, 1867–8, Northampton, 1880–1906. Advanced Radical.

LAWSON, SIR WILFRID (1829–1906): M.P. for Carlisle, 1859–65, 1868–85, Cockermouth, 1886–1906. Congregationalist. Parliamentary spokesman for U.K. Alliance and leading temperance reformer.

LICHFIELD, 2ND EARL OF (1825–92): As Thomas George Anson, M.P.

for Lichfield, 1847–54. First chairman of Charity Organisation Society.

LOCH, CHARLES (1849–1923): Balliol pupil of T. H. Green. Secretary of Charity Organisation Society, 1875–1913. Strong opponent of state intervention in social welfare.

LOWE, ROBERT (1811–92): Barrister and M.P. in Australia in 1840s. Leader writer on *The Times*. M.P. for Kidderminster, 1852–9, Calne, 1859–68, London University, 1868–80. Vice-President of Committee of Council with responsibility for education, 1859–64. Chancellor of the Exchequer, 1868–73. Home Secretary, 1873–4. Created 1st Viscount Sherbrooke, 1880. Conservative Liberal, opposing Parliamentary reform.

LUBBOCK, SIR JOHN (1834–1913): Banker and scientist. Vice-Chancellor, London University, 1874–80. M.P. for Maidstone, 1870–80, London University, 1880–1900. Introduced bank holidays (1871) and promoted legislation to preserve ancient monuments and reduce hours of work in shops. Created 1st Earl of Avebury, 1900.

MATHER, SIR WILLIAM (1838–1920): Chairman, Mather & Platt Ltd., Salford iron manufacturers. M.P. for Salford S., 1885–6, Gorton, 1889–95, Rossendale, 1900–4. Opponent of compulsory eight-hour working day.

MEREDITH, GEORGE (1828–1909): Novelist. Actively assisted F. A. Maxse, Liberal candidate for Southampton in 1868, and subsequently wrote *Beauchamp's Career*. One of founders of *Fortnightly Review*.

MIALL, EDWARD (1809–81): Congregational minister. Founder and editor of the *Nonconformist*. Leading campaigner for educational voluntaryism and disestablishment of the Church of England. M.P. for Bradford, 1869–74.

MILL, JOHN STUART (1806–73): Philosopher. Author of *Principles of Political Economy* (1848), *On Liberty* (1859), *Thoughts on Parliamentary Reform* (1859), *Considerations on Representative Government* (1861). M.P. for Westminster, 1865–8. Enthusiast for votes for women, Parliamentary reform and civil liberties.

MORLEY, JOHN (1838–1923): Journalist. Editor of *Fortnightly Review*,

1867–82, *Pall Mall Gazette*, 1880–3. M.P. for Newcastle-on-Tyne, 1883–95, Montrose, 1896–1908. Chief Secretary for Ireland, 1886, 1892–5. Secretary of State for India, 1905–10. Free-thinker. Biographer of Gladstone and Cobden. Created Viscount Morley in 1908.

MORLEY, SAMUEL (1809–86): East Midlands hosiery manufacturer. Congregationalist. Proprietor of the *Daily News*. Founded Administrative Reform Association, 1855. M.P. for Bristol, 1868–85. Leading Nonconformist representative in Parliament.

MUNDELLA, ANTHONY JOHN (1825–97): Son of Italian refugee. Nottingham hosiery manufacturer. M.P. for Sheffield, 1868–85, Sheffield Brightside, 1885–97. Leading advocate of Lib–Labism and principle of arbitration in industrial disputes. Vice-President of Committee of Council with responsibility for education, 1880–5. President of Board of Trade, 1886, 1892–4. Established labour department at Board of Trade.

PALMER, GEORGE (1818–97): Reading biscuit manufacturer. M.P. for Reading, 1878–85.

POCHIN, HENRY DAVIS (1824–95): Salford soap manufacturer. Mayor of Salford, 1866–8. M.P. for Stafford, 1868–9. Leading advocate of Parliamentary and educational reform and church disestablishment in 1860s and 1870s, but left Liberals in protest against Employers' Liability Act in 1880 and became founder member of Liberty and Property Defence League.

RATHBONE, WILLIAM (1819–1902): Liverpool merchant. Unitarian. M.P. for Liverpool, 1868–80, Caernarvonshire, 1880–5, N. Caernarvonshire, 1885–95. Advocate and promoter of voluntary charitable activity.

REID, SIR ROBERT THRESHIE (1846–1923): Barrister. M.P. for Hereford, 1880–5, Dumfries, 1886–1905. Solicitor General, 1894. Attorney General, 1894–5. Lord Chancellor, 1905–12. Created 1st Baron Loreburn, 1906.

REID, THOMAS WEMYSS (1842–1905): Journalist and novelist. Editor, *Leeds Mercury*, 1870–87, the *Speaker*, 1890–9.

K

RENDEL, STUART (1834–1913): M.P. for Montgomeryshire, 1880–94. Chairman of Parliamentary Association of Welsh Liberals from 1888. Created 1st Baron Rendel, 1894.

RICHARD, HENRY (1812–88): Congregational minister. Secretary of Peace Society, 1848–85. M.P. for Merthyr, 1868–88. Leading advocate of international arbitration.

RIPON, MARQUESS OF (1827–1909): Succeeded to title, 1859. Lord President of the Council, 1868–73. Governor-General of India, 1880–4. First Lord of Admiralty, 1886. Colonial Secretary, 1892–5.

ROGERS, JAMES EDWIN THOROLD (1823–90): Political economist. Professor of Statistics and Economics, King's College, London, 1859–90. Professor of Political Economy, Oxford, 1862–7. M.P. for Southwark, 1880–5, Bermondsey, 1885–6.

ROGERS, JAMES GUINNESS (1822–1911): Congregational minister in London, 1865–1900.

ROUNDELL, CHARLES SAVILE (1827–1906): Barrister. Secretary to Royal Commission on Governor Eyre affair, 1865. M.P. for Grantham, 1880–5, Skipton, 1892–5. Postmaster-General, 1880.

RYLANDS, PETER (1820–87): Iron and steel manufacturer in Warrington. Active in Anti-Corn Law League and Lancashire Public Schools Association. M.P. for Warrington, 1868–74, Burnley, 1876–87. Fought for reform of Diplomatic Service. Opposed Home Rule.

SALT, SIR TITUS (1803–76): Yorkshire worsted and mohair manufacturer. M.P. for Bradford, 1859–61. Created model town of Saltaire.

SELBORNE, 1ST EARL OF (1812–95): As Roundell Palmer, M.P. for Richmond, 1861–72. Solicitor General, 1861–3. Attorney General, 1863–6. Created 1st Baron Selborne, 1872 and Lord Chancellor, 1872–4, 1880–5. Responsible for 1873 Judicature Act. Opposed Home Rule.

SMITH, GOLDWIN (1823–1910): Regius Professor of Modern History, Oxford, 1858–66. Involved in Liberal agitations over Governor Eyre case, American Civil War and University tests. From 1868 was resident in United States and Canada.

SPENCER, HERBERT (1820–1903): Philosopher and extreme individualist. Sub-editor on the *Economist*, 1848–53. Moved away from Liberalism in 1870s towards social Darwinism and Conservatism.

STANSFELD, SIR JAMES (1820–98): Barrister. Strong supporter of Garibaldi and Mazzini in 1840s. M.P. for Halifax, 1859–95. Lord of Treasury, 1868–9. President, Poor Law Board, 1871. President, Local Government Board, 1871–4. Resigned to devote himself to securing repeal of Contagious Diseases Acts and resumed office again in 1886.

STEAD, WILLIAM THOMAS (1849–1912): Journalist. Editor, *Northern Echo*, 1871–80, *Pall Mall Gazette*, 1883–9. Congregationalist. Established 'New Journalism' and campaigned for ending of juvenile prostitution, for international arbitration and social reform. Later became Liberal Imperialist.

STEPHEN, SIR JAMES FITZJAMES (1829–94): Barrister. Liberal candidate for Harwich, 1865, Dundee, 1873. Legal member of Viceroy's Council in India, 1869–72. Deserted Liberalism in 1870s for Conservatism.

STEPHEN, SIR LESLIE (1832–1904): Brother of above. Man of letters and founder of *Dictionary of National Biography*. Leading agnostic. Strong supporter of North in American Civil War and helped Henry Fawcett contest Cambridge in 1863 and Brighton in 1864 for the Liberals. Later drifted away from Liberalism.

TAYLOR, PETER (1819–91): Partner in Courtauld & Co., silk mercers. Chairman of Friends of Italy and active in Anti-Corn Law League in 1840s. M.P. for Leicester, 1862–84. Led campaign against compulsory vaccination. Opposed Home Rule.

THACKERAY, WILLIAM MAKEPEACE (1811–63): Novelist. Active in Administrative Reform Association. Contested Oxford for Liberals in 1857.

THOMAS, ALFRED (1840–1927): Cardiff merchant. M.P. for

E. Glamorganshire, 1885–1910. Advocate of Home Rule for Wales. Created 1st Baron Pontypridd, 1912.

TREVELYAN, SIR CHARLES (1807–86): Administrator. With Sir Stafford Northcote, advocated entry to the Civil Service by competitive examination in 1855. Governor of Madras, 1859–60. On Council of Charity Organisation Society. Active in Northumberland Liberal politics.

TREVELYAN, SIR GEORGE OTTO (1838–1928): Son of above. M.P. for Tynemouth, 1865–8, Border Burghs, 1868–86, Bridgeton, 1887–97. Civil Lord of Admiralty, 1868–70. Parliamentary Secretary to Admiralty, 1881. Chief Secretary to Ireland, 1882–4. Chancellor of Duchy of Lancaster, 1884–5. Chief Secretary for Scotland, 1886, 1892–5. Advocate of temperance legislation and granting franchise to agricultural labourers. Opposed Home Rule in 1886 but rejoined Gladstonian Liberals in 1887.

TROLLOPE, ANTHONY (1815–82): Novelist. Contested Beverley for Liberals in 1868. Expressed Liberal views in his Palliser novels.

WATSON, ROBERT SPENCE (1837–1911): Newcastle solicitor. President of National Liberal Federation, 1890–1902. Pioneer in settlement of industrial disputes by arbitration.

WILLIAMS, JOHN CARVELL (1821–1907): Secretary, British Anti-State Church Association (later Liberation Society), 1844–77. Chairman of Liberation Society, 1877–98. M.P. for Nottingham S., 1885–6, Mansfield, 1892–1900. Promoted 1880 Burials Act. Enthusiast for temperance, disestablishment and international arbitration.

Notes

Except where otherwise indicated, the place of publication of all books mentioned is London. Full details of each publication are included at the first citation in each chapter.

Preface (*between pages 11 and 15*)

1. J. H. Newman, *Apologia Pro Vita Sua*, ed. M. J. Svaglic (Oxford, 1967); pp. 233–4.
2. M. Arnold, *Culture and Anarchy*, ed. J. Dover Wilson (Cambridge paperback edn., 1971), p. 62.
3. Quoted in J. Vincent, *The Formation of the British Liberal Party 1857–1868* (paperback edn., 1972), p. 252.
4. G. M. Trevelyan, *English Songs of Italian Freedom* (1911), p. xv; R. Kelley, *The Transatlantic Persuasion: The Liberal–Democratic Mind in the Age of Gladstone* (New York, 1969), p. 149.

Chapter 1: The Liberal Awakening (*between pages 17 and 48*)

1. *The Diaries of John Bright*, ed. R. A. J. Walling (1930), p. 13.
2. B. Mallet, *Thomas George, Earl of Northbrook, A Memoir* (1908), pp. 32–3.
3. Quoted in J. Hamburger, *Intellectuals in Politics: John Stuart Mill and the Philosophic Radicals* (New Haven, 1965), p. 32.
4. Mill's article is in the *Westminster Review*, XXXII (1839), pp. 475–508.
5. M. Arnold, *Culture and Anarchy*, ed. J. Dover Wilson (Cambridge paperback edn., 1971), p. 56.
6. G. Meredith, *Beauchamp's Career* (Memorial edn., 1910), I, p. 139.
7. J. Morley, *The Life of Richard Cobden* (1881), I, p. 392.
8. *Ibid.* II, p. 146.
9. L. Hunt, *Autobiography* (1850), II, p. 77.
10. *Hansard*, 3rd series, CLIV (1859), 233–4.
11. *Saturday Review*, 17 November 1885.
12. A. Trollope, *Autobiography* (Oxford, 1929), p. 215.
13. *Fortnightly Review*, old series, II (August 1865), p. 761.
14. J. Morley, *Studies in Literature* (1891), p. 54.
15. J. S. Mill, *Principles of Political Economy*, ed. W. J. Ashley (Oxford, 1920), p. 976.
16. J. Bryce, *Studies in Contemporary Biography* (1903), p. 120.
17. T. Carlyle, *Past and Present* (Centenary edn., 1897), p. 28.
18. *Fortnightly Review*, new series, VIII (October 1870), p. 479.

19. J. S. Mill, *Autobiography*, ed. J. Stillinger (Oxford paperback edn., 1971), p. 159.
20. Quoted in D. A. Hamer, *Liberal Politics in the Age of Gladstone and Rosebery* (Oxford, 1972), p. 165.
21. P. Magnus, *Gladstone* (paperback edn., 1963), p. 271.
22. Meredith, *Beauchamp's Career*, I, p. 294.
23. A. Trollope, *Phineas Redux* (1873), I, p. 16.
24. Quoted in G. W. E. Russell, *Social Silhouettes* (1906), p. 151.
25. Trollope, *Phineas Redux*, I, pp. 137–8.
26. Morley, *Life of Cobden*, I, p. 249.
27. Arnold, *Culture and Anarchy*, p. 63.
28. Quoted in W. E. Mosse, *Liberal Europe: The Age of Bourgeois Realism* (paperback edn., 1974), pp. 81–2.
29. *The Collected Works of William Morris*, ed. M. Morris (1915), XXIII, pp. 71–2.
30. Quoted in G. Watson, *The English Ideology* (1973), p. 16.
31. Quoted in J. Roach, 'Liberalism and the Victorian Intelligentsia', *Cambridge Historical Journal*, XIII (1957), p. 58.
32. A. Lunn, *Come What May* (1940), p. 11.
33. J. S. Mill, *Three Essays*, ed. R. Wollheim (Oxford paperback edn., 1975), p. 155.
34. J. S. Mill, *Earlier Letters 1812–1848*, ed. F. E. Mineka (Toronto, 1963), pp. 27–8.
35. Mill, *Principles of Political Economy*, p. 795.
36. *Fortnightly Review*, new series, I (April 1867), pp. 491–2.
37. A. Trollope, *The Prime Minister* (Oxford edn., 1952), II, p. 265.
38. Quoted in E. M. Everett, *The Party of Humanity* (Chapel Hill, N.C., 1939), p. 329.
39. E. Hodder, *The Life of Samuel Morley* (1887), p. 446.
40. C. Brinton, *English Political Thought in the Nineteenth Century* (1933), p. 203.
41. *Why I Am A Liberal*, ed. A. Reid (1885), p. 15.
42. Quoted in Mosse, *Liberal Europe*, p. 42.
43. Quoted in Watson, *The English Ideology*, p. 260.
44. Arnold, *Culture and Anarchy*, p. 59; Preface to 'Schools and Universities On the Continent', in *The Collected Works of Matthew Arnold* (1903), XII, p. 129.
45. J. Morley, *Recollections* (1918), I, p. 27.
46. J. S. Mill, *Utilitarianism* (10th edn., 1888), p. 21.
47. *The Public Addresses of John Bright*, ed. J. T. Rogers (1879), p. 137.
48. T. Hughes, *Tom Brown At Oxford* (1861), p. 487.
49. G. Eliot, *Felix Holt the Radical* (Illustrated copyright edn., n.d.), I, pp. 266–7.
50. *A Diary of the Gladstone Government* (Edinburgh, 1886), p. 3.
51. Quoted in A. Briggs, *Victorian People* (paperback edn., 1971), p. 51.
52. D. A. Hamer, *John Morley, Liberal Intellectual in Politics* (Oxford, 1968), p. 48.
53. J. S. Mill, *A System of Logic* (8th edn., 1941), p. 615.
54. *Why I Am A Liberal*, p. 93.
55. Quoted in Mosse, *Liberal Europe*, p. 81.

56. *Why I Am A Liberal*, pp. 119–23.
57. *Ibid.* p. 93.
58. *Morning Star*, 6 July 1865.
59. Arnold, *Culture and Anarchy*, p. 87.

Chapter 2: The Creed of the Up-and-Coming (*between pages 49 and 72*)

1. G. Meredith, *Beauchamp's Career* (Memorial edn., 1910), I, pp. 136–7.
2. R. W. Dale, *Liberalism. An Address to the Birmingham Junior Liberal Association* (1878), p. 6.
3. Quoted in G. W. E. Russell, *Collections and Recollections* (1898), p. 457.
4. *Westminster Review*, XXXII (1839), p. 486.
5. *The Complete Prose Works of Matthew Arnold*, ed. R. H. Super (Ann Arbor, Mich., 1965), V, p. 69.
6. *Westminster Review*, I (1824), pp. 68–9.
7. Quoted in *Pressure From Without in Early Victorian England*, ed. P. Hollis (1974), p. 184.
8. *Ibid.* p. 191.
9. *The Times*, 27 November 1849.
10. *Fortnightly Review*, new series, II (September 1867), pp. 367–8.
11. J. Vincent, *The Formation of the British Liberal Party 1857–1868* (paperback edn., 1972), pp. 41–2.
12. J. Morley, *The Life of Richard Cobden* (1881), II, p. 396; G. B. Smith, *The Life and Speeches of John Bright* (1881), II, p. 181.
13. Quoted in R. Boyson, *The Ashworth Cotton Enterprise* (Oxford, 1970), p. 88.
14. E. Hodder, *The Life of Samuel Morley* (1887), p. 451.
15. Morley, *Life of Cobden*, II, p. 397.
16. Quoted in D. Read, *Cobden and Bright: A Victorian Political Partnership* (1967), p. 96.
17. A. Briggs, *Victorian Cities* (paperback edn., 1968), p. 119.
18. *Pall Mall Gazette*, 11 July 1885.
19. Goldwin Smith, *Reminiscences* (New York, 1910), p. 363.
20. Quoted in C. Harvie, *The Lights of Liberalism* (1977), p. 84.
21. *Ibid.* p. 86.
22. W. Bagehot, *Biographical Studies* (1881), p. 89.
23. J. Morley, *The Life of William Ewart Gladstone* (2nd edn., 1905), I, p. 780.
24. E. Stead, *My Father* (1913), pp. 78–9.
25. Quoted in D. Fraser, 'Voluntaryism and West Riding Politics', *Northern History*, XIII (1977), p. 206.
26. Cobden to Baines, 12 October 1841, Baines MSS, Sheepscar Branch Library, Leeds.
27. Meredith, *Beauchamp's Career*, I, pp. 136, 139.
28. G. M. Trevelyan, *The Life of John Bright* (1925), p. 263.
29. Smith, *Life and Speeches of Bright*, I, p. 482.
30. Quoted in J. MacCunn, *Six Radical Thinkers* (1910), p. 92.
31. Quoted in Briggs, *Victorian Cities*, p. 199.
32. Read, *Cobden and Bright*, p. 68.

33. *The American Diaries of Richard Cobden*, ed. E. H. Cawley (Princeton, 1952), p. 73.
34. Boyson, *The Ashworth Cotton Enterprise*, p. 227.
35. *Fortnightly Review*, old series, VI (September 1866), p. 358.
36. *The Liberal Tradition from Fox to Keynes*, ed. A. Bullock and M. Shock (1966), p. 136.
37. W. H. G. Armytage, *A. J. Mundella, the Liberal Background to the Labour Movement* (1951), p. 86.
38. *The American Diaries of Cobden*, p. 71.
39. Smith, *Life and Speeches of Bright*, II, p. 93.
40. *Disraeli, Derby and the Conservative Party. Journals and Memoirs of Lord Stanley 1849–1869*, ed. J. Vincent (Hassocks, 1978), p. 252.
41. W. F. Monypenny and G. E. Buckle, *The Life of Benjamin Disraeli, Earl of Beaconsfield*, VI (1920), p. 535.
42. A. Trollope, *Phineas Finn* (Oxford edn., 1949), I, p. 163.
43. *Fortnightly Review*, new series, II (December 1867), p. 727.
44. Morley, *Life of Cobden*, I, p. 130.
45. Quoted in J. Ridley, *Lord Palmerston* (paperback edn., 1972), p. 707.
46. Quoted in R. H. Murray, *Studies in English Social and Political Thinkers of the Nineteenth Century* (1929), I, p. 409.
47. *Administrative Reform Association Official Paper No. 1* (May 1855), p. 1.
48. *The Letters of John Stuart Mill*, ed. H. S. R. Elliot (1910), I, p. 153.
49. *Parliamentary Papers*, 1854–5, XX, p. 92.
50. *Ibid.*
51. *Fortnightly Review*, new series, II (September 1867), pp. 366–7.
52. Morley, *Life of Gladstone*, I, p. 687.
53. P. Magnus, *Gladstone* (paperback edn., 1963), p. 149.
54. *Ibid.* p. 112.
55. *The Times*, 31 December 1859; G. Watson, *The English Ideology* (1973), p. 337.
56. *The Liberal Tradition from Fox to Keynes*, p. 220.
57. M. Arnold, *Culture and Anarchy*, ed. J. Dover Wilson (Cambridge paperback edn., 1971), pp. 195, 186.
58. J. Newman, *Apologia Pro Vita Sua*, ed. M. J. Svaglic (Oxford, 1967), p. 262.
59. Boyson, *The Ashworth Cotton Enterprise*, p. 159.
60. *Free Trade and other Fundamental Doctrines of the Manchester School*, ed. F. W. Hirst (1903), p. xii.
61. *Hansard*, 3rd series, LXXVI (1844), 629.
62. Hodder, *Life of Samuel Morley*, p. 448.
63. J. S. Mill, *Three Essays*, ed. R. Wollheim (Oxford paperback edn., 1975), p. 116.
64. C. Brinton, *English Political Thought in the Nineteenth Century* (1933), p. 112.
65. *Complete Prose Works of Matthew Arnold*, V, p. 46; *Culture and Anarchy*, pp. 186, 51.
66. G. W. E. Russell, *Portraits of the Seventies* (1916), p. 177.
67. A. Trollope, *Autobiography* (Oxford, 1929), p. 209.
68. Quoted in Brinton, *English Political Thought*, pp. 186–7.

Chapter 3: The Love of Liberty (*between pages 73 and 98*)

1. J. Morley, *The Life of William Ewart Gladstone* (2nd edn., 1905), I, p. 813.
2. J. Morley, *Recollections* (1918), II, p. 364.
3. J. S. Mill, *Autobiography*, ed. J. Stillinger (Oxford paperback edn., 1971), pp. 64–6.
4. Quoted in G. Watson, *The English Ideology* (1973), pp. 26, 203.
5. *The Amberley Papers*, ed. B. and P. Russell (1937), II, p. 375.
6. Watson, *The English Ideology*, pp. 207–8.
7. J. H. Newman, *Apologia Pro Vita Sua*, ed. M. J. Svaglic (Oxford, 1967), pp. 54, 233.
8. Undated MS scrap in Holyoake Collection, Co-Operative Union, Manchester. I owe this reference to Dr. Edward Royle.
9. L. E. Grugel, *George Jacob Holyoake* (1976), p. 89.
10. W. L. Courtney, *John Stuart Mill* (1889), p. 142; J. H. Morgan, *John, Viscount Morley, An Appreciation and Some Reminiscences* (1924), p. 37.
11. S. Butler, *The Way Of All Flesh* (Shrewsbury edn., 1925), p. 110.
12. *The Letters of J. S. Mill*, ed. H. S. R. Elliot (1910), II, p. 362.
13. J. Morley, *The Life of Richard Cobden* (1881), I, p. 120; Newman, *Apologia Pro Vita Sua*, p. 185.
14. Watson, *The English Ideology*, p. 33.
15. Morley, *Life of Gladstone*, I, p. 853.
16. *Ibid.* I, p. 745.
17. F. W. Knickerbocker, *Free Minds: John Morley and His Friends* (Cambridge, Mass., 1943), p. 163.
18. *Ibid.* p. 154.
19. Quoted in W. E. Mosse, *Liberal Europe: The Age of Bourgeois Realism* (paperback edn., 1974), p. 81.
20. Morley, *Life of Gladstone*, I, p. 758.
21. *Ibid.* I, p. 389.
22. P. Magnus, *Gladstone* (paperback edn., 1963), p. 99.
23. Morley, *Life of Gladstone*, I, p. 757.
24. D. P. Hughes, *The Life of Hugh Price Hughes* (4th edn., 1905), p. 82.
25. Morley, *Recollections*, I, p. 78.
26. *Ibid.* I, p. 20.
27. Quoted in R. H. Murray, *Studies in English Social and Political Thinkers of the Nineteenth Century* (1929), I, p. 416.
28. Lord Acton, *The History of Freedom* (1909), p. 3.
29. J. S. Mill, *Three Essays*, ed. R. Wollheim (Oxford paperback edn., 1975), pp. 14–15.
30. J. Morley, *On Compromise* (2nd edn., 1886), p. 250.
31. Mill, *Three Essays*, p. 13.
32. Newman, *Apologia Pro Vita Sua*, p. 256.
33. M. Arnold, *Culture and Anarchy*, ed. J. Dover Wilson (Cambridge paperback edn., 1971), p. 203.
34. Mill, *Three Essays*, pp. 133–5.
35. J. S. Mill, *Principles of Political Economy*, ed. W. J. Ashley (Oxford, 1920), p. 942.

36. Morley, *On Compromise*, p. 283.
37. Mill, *Three Essays*, p. 13.
38. *Ibid.* pp. 75–6.
39. *Ibid.* p. 108.
40. *Ibid.* p. 18.
41. Arnold, *Culture and Anarchy*, p. 74.
42. Mill, *Three Essays*, p. 87.
43. Quoted in G. E. Fasnacht, *Acton's Political Philosophy* (1952), p. 19.
44. *Ibid.* p. 39.
45. Morley, *Recollections*, I, p. 21.
46. Mill, *Three Essays*, p. 82.
47. Quoted in D. A. Hamer, *John Morley, Liberal Intellectual in Politics* (Oxford, 1968), p. 40.
48. *Ibid.* p. 183.
49. J. F. Stephen, *Liberty, Equality, Fraternity*, ed. R. J. White (Cambridge, 1967), p. 11.
50. *Ibid.* pp. 72, 81.
51. W. E. Gladstone, *Midlothian Speeches, 1879* (Reprint, Leicester, 1971), p. 117.
52. Mill, *Autobiography*, p. 177.
53. J. L. Garvin, *The Life of Joseph Chamberlain*, I (1932), p. 152.
54. J. Morley, *Miscellanies, Fourth Series* (1908), p. 167.
55. C. Harris, *Islington* (1974), p. 112.
56. Quoted in R. Evans, *The Feminists* (1977), p. 20.
57. *The Complete Prose Works of Matthew Arnold*, ed. R. H. Soper (Ann Arbor, Mich., 1965), V, p. 318.
58. *Fortnightly Review*, new series, XIV (August 1873), p. 149; *ibid.* (September 1873), p. 314.

Chapter 4: The Nonconformist Conscience (*between pages 99 and 122*)

1. W. E. Gladstone, *Gleanings of Past Years* (1879), I, p. 158.
2. *Nonconformity and Politics by a Nonconformist Minister* (1909), p. 111.
3. Quoted in J. Roach, 'Liberalism and the Victorian Intelligentsia', *Cambridge Historical Journal*, XIII (1957), p. 70.
4. M. Arnold, *Mixed Essays* (1879), p. 136.
5. A. Lunn, *Come What May* (1940), p. 117.
6. Quoted in S. Koss, *Nonconformity in Modern British Politics* (1975), p. 22.
7. D. P. Hughes, *The Life of Hugh Price Hughes* (4th edn., 1905), p. 120.
8. *The Complete Prose Works of Matthew Arnold*, ed. R. H. Super (Ann Arbor, Mich., 1965), V, p. 71.
9. G. Eliot, *Felix Holt the Radical* (Illustrated copyright edn., n.d.), I, p. 261.
10. Quoted in J. F. Glaser, 'Nonconformity and the Decline of Liberalism', *American Historical Review*, LXIII (1958), p. 354.
11. M. Arnold, *Culture and Anarchy*, ed. J. Dover Wilson (Cambridge paperback edn., 1971), p. 58.
12. Quoted in R. G. Cowherd, *The Politics of English Dissent* (New York, 1956), p. 157.
13. R. W. Dale, *Churchmen and Dissenters* (1862), p. 24.
14. *Ibid.* p. 22.

15. G. M. Trevelyan, *The Life of John Bright* (1925), p. 40.
16. Quoted in R. Masheder, *Dissent and Democracy* (1864), p. 101.
17. Trevelyan, *Life of Bright*, p. 19.
18. J. W. Robertson-Scott, *The Life and Death of a Newspaper* (1952), p. 242.
19. J. MacCunn, *Six Radical Thinkers* (1910), p. 221.
20. J. Morley, *On Compromise* (2nd edn., 1886), p. 113.
21. C. Binfield, *So Down to Prayers: Studies in English Nonconformity 1780–1920* (1977), p. 104.
22. E. F. Rathbone, *William Rathbone, A Memoir* (1905), p. 142.
23. *Nonconformity and Politics*, p. 171.
24. *Nonconformist*, 1 January 1880.
25. Hughes, *Life of Hugh Price Hughes*, p. 119.
26. E. Hodder, *The Life of Samuel Morley* (1887), p. 246.
27. *Baptist Year Book* (1880), p. 3.
28. *Nonconformist*, 4 June 1885.
29. A. W. W. Dale, *The Life of R. W. Dale* (1898), p. 286.
30. Quoted in M. Barker, *Gladstone and Radicalism: The Reconstruction of Liberal Policy in Britain 1885–1894* (Hassocks, 1975), p. 30.
31. *Hansard*, 3rd series, CCXVI (1873), 24.
32. Quoted in letter from Edward Baines to John Andrew, 21 December 1874, Baines MSS 45/20.
33. H. C. Colman, *Jeremiah James Colman, A Memoir* (1905), p. 260.
34. Baines to John Andrew, 21 December 1874, Baines MSS 45/20.
35. Quoted in D. A. Hamer, *John Morley, Liberal Intellectual in Politics* (Oxford, 1968), p. 110.
36. J. Amery, *The Life of Joseph Chamberlain* (1951), IV, pp. 511–12.
37. J. G. Rogers, *Autobiography* (1903), p. 215.
38. *Congregationalist*, VIII (October 1879), p. 862.
39. A. W. W. Dale, *Life of R. W. Dale*, p. 420.
40. *The Times*, 28 November 1890.
41. *The Times*, 9 September 1879.
42. Quoted in G. Watson, *The English Ideology* (1973), p. 193.
43. G. Eliot, *Felix Holt the Radical*, II, p. 173.
44. *Nineteenth Century*, L (September 1901), p. 370.
45. *Speeches of Richard Cobden on Questions of Public Policy*, ed. J. Bright and J. E. T. Rogers (1870), I, p. 68.
46. Quoted in A. Briggs, *Victorian People* (paperback edn., 1971), p. 211.
47. D. Read, *Cobden and Bright: A Victorian Political Partnership* (1967), p. 89.
48. Quoted in Cowherd, *Politics of English Dissent*, p. 132.
49. Read, *Cobden and Bright*, p. 32.
50. J. Morley, *The Life of Richard Cobden* (1881), I, p. 201.
51. Hughes, *Life of Hugh Price Hughes*, p. 79.
52. Quoted in Briggs, *Victorian People*, p. 211.
53. W. E. H. Lecky, *A History of England in the Eighteenth Century* (1899), VII, p. 384.
54. F. Whyte, *The Life of W. T. Stead* (1925), I, p. 21.
55. *Westminster Review*, XXV (April 1836), p. 17.
56. E. Stead, *My Father* (1913), p. 92.

57. Whyte, *Life of W. T. Stead*, I, p. 71.
58. *Ibid.* I, p. 237.
59. *Ibid.* I, p. 71.
60. Robertson-Scott, *Life and Death of a Newspaper*, p. 108.
61. *Ibid.* p. 141.
62. *Ibid.* p. 152.
63. Morley, *Life of Cobden*, II, p. 59.
64. B. Harrison, *Drink and the Victorians* (1971), p. 162.
65. *Ibid.* p. 270.
66. The Revd. W. Arthur to Edward Baines, 9 February 1874, Baines MSS 63/12; L. T. Baines to Edward Baines, 7 February 1874, Baines MSS 63/20.
67. A. G. Gardiner, *The Life of Sir William Harcourt* (1923), II, p. 232.
68. *The New Liberal Programme*, ed. A. Reid (1886), p. 82.
69. Quoted in Peter Clarke's review, 'Liberals and Faddists', *Times Literary Supplement*, 10 February 1978, p. 164.
70. Harrison, *Drink and the Victorians*, p. 287.
71. Rathbone, *William Rathbone*, p. 270.
72. Gardiner, *Life of Sir William Harcourt*, II, p. 105.
73. Quoted in Barker, *Gladstone and Radicalism*, p. 208.
74. Harrison, *Drink and the Victorians*, p. 207.
75. R. L. Nettleship, *Memoir of T. H. Green* (1906), p. 55.
76. *The Political Correspondence of Mr. Gladstone and Lord Granville 1868–1886*, ed. A. Ramm (Oxford, 1962), I, p. 3.
77. P. Magnus, *Gladstone* (paperback edn., 1963), p. 242.
78. H. Broadhurst, *The Story of His Life* (1901), p. 88.
79. I owe this reference to Mr. Desmond Fitzpatrick. It is quoted in his unpublished study of G. W. E. Russell, Chapter Five, p. 8.
80. Robertson-Scott, *Life and Death of a Newspaper*, p. 104.
81. *Congregationalist*, VIII (October 1879), p. 862.
82. Whyte, *Life of W. T. Stead*, I, p. 52.

Chapter 5: Non-Intervention and Self-Determination (*between pages 123 and 148*)

1. *The Political Writings of Richard Cobden* (1867), I, p. 1.
2. Cobden to Baines, 1 March 1848, Baines MSS.
3. *Political Writings of Cobden*, I, p. 25.
4. *The Times*, 27 October 1879.
5. R. Cobden, *England, Ireland and America* (1835), p. 42.
6. *The Speeches of John Bright*, ed. J. E. T. Rogers (1883), II, p. 382.
7. J. Morley, *The Life of Richard Cobden* (1881), II, p. 440.
8. R. Kelley, *The Transatlantic Persuasion: The Liberal–Democratic Mind in the Age of Gladstone* (New York, 1969), p. 224.
9. Morley, *Life of Cobden*, II, p. 10.
10. A. Tennyson, 'The Third of February, 1852', lines 43–7.
11. G. M. Trevelyan, *The Life of John Bright* (1925), p. 256.
12. *Political Writings of Cobden*, I, p. 492.

13. F. W. Knickerbocker, *Free Minds: John Morley and His Friends* (Cambridge, Mass., 1943), p. 257.
14. D. Read, *Cobden and Bright: A Victorian Political Partnership* (1967), pp. 206–207; Morley, *Life of Cobden*, II, p. 361.
15. *The Times*, 4 January 1878.
16. Quoted in J. Ridley, *Lord Palmerston* (paperback edn., 1972), p. 631.
17. *Ibid.* p. 349.
18. *Ibid.* p. 630.
19. G. Meredith, *Beauchamp's Career* (Memorial edn., 1910), I, p. 151.
20. J. Bryce, *Studies in Contemporary Biography* (1903), pp. 97–8.
21. L. A. Tollemache, *Talks with Mr. Gladstone* (1901), p. 180.
22. Trevelyan, *Life of Bright*, p. 249.
23. *Hansard*, 3rd series, CXXXVI (1855), 1761.
24. A. Tennyson, 'Maud', Book X, lines 37–43.
25. *Political Writings of Cobden*, I, pp. 282–3.
26. F. Whyte, *The Life of W. T. Stead* (1925), I, p. 155.
27. J. L. Sturgis, *John Bright and the Empire* (1969), pp. 107–8.
28. Morley, *Life of Cobden*, I, p. 230.
29. Cobden, *England, Ireland and America*, p. 45.
30. Morley, *Life of Cobden*, I, p. 410.
31. Ridley, *Palmerston*, p. 791.
32. Quoted in D. M. Schreuder, *Gladstone and Kruger, The Liberal Government and Home Rule 1880–85* (1969), p. 44.
33. *Political Writings of Cobden*, I, p. 490.
34. J. L. and B. Hammond, *James Stansfeld* (1932), pp. 22–3.
35. J. S. Mill, *Dissertations and Discussions, Political, Philosophical and Historical* (1859), II, p. 381.
36. J. S. Mill, *Three Essays*, ed. R. Wollheim (Oxford paperback edn., 1975), p. 411.
37. W. E. Gladstone, *Midlothian Speeches 1879* (reprint, Leicester, 1971), pp. 115–17.
38. W. Bagehot, *Biographical Studies* (1881), p. 93.
39. J. Morley, *The Life of William Ewart Gladstone* (2nd edn., 1905), I, p. 656.
40. Trevelyan, *Life of Bright*, p. 293.
41. Tollemache, *Talks with Mr. Gladstone*, p. 88.
42. *Ibid.*
43. Quoted in J. L. Hammond, *Gladstone and the Irish Nation* (1938), p. 64.
44. Quoted in P. Knaplund, *Gladstone and Imperial Policy* (1927), pp. 193, 202, 204.
45. Quoted in R. Blake, *The Conservative Party from Peel to Churchill* (paperback edn., 1972), pp. 126–7.
46. *Nineteenth Century*, IV (September 1878), p. 569.
47. *Hansard*, 3rd series, CCXII (1872), 217.
48. *Hansard*, 3rd series, CCCIV (1886), 1081.
49. Quoted in Hammond, *Gladstone and the Irish Nation*, pp. 684–5.
50. Quoted in P. Knaplund, *Gladstone's Foreign Policy* (new edn., 1970), p. 56.
51. *Hansard*, 3rd series, CCXXXIV (1877), 426.
52. *Contemporary Review*, LIII (March 1888), pp. 334–5.

53. Quoted in K. O. Morgan, 'Gladstone and Wales', *Welsh Historical Review*, I (1960), p. 82.
54. Mill, *Three Essays*, p. 384.
55. Quoted in G. E. Fasnacht, *Acton's Political Philosophy* (1952), p. 130.
56. *The Correspondence of Lord Acton*, ed. J. N. Figgis and R. V. Laurence (1917), p. 185.
57. *Hansard*, 3rd series, CCXXXII (1877), 726.
58. *Hansard*, 3rd series, CCXXXI (1876), 184.
59. Quoted in P. Magnus, *Gladstone* (paperback edn., 1963), p. 175.
60. *The Political Correspondence of Mr. Gladstone and Lord Granville 1868–1886*, ed. A. Ramm (Oxford, 1962), I, p. 140; *Hansard*, 3rd series, CXXXIX (1855), 1810–11.
61. W. E. Gladstone, *Gleanings of Past Years* (1879), IV, p. 249.
62. *Ibid.* IV, p. 256.
63. Knaplund, *Gladstone's Foreign Policy*, p. 57.
64. Whyte, *Life of Stead*, I, p. 156.
65. Quoted in R. Shannon, *The Crisis of Imperialism 1865–1915* (paperback edn., 1976), p. 149.
66. Knickerbocker, *Free Minds*, p. 258.
67. Sturgis, *John Bright and the Empire*, p. 108.
68. Whyte, *Life of Stead*, I, p. 156.
69. *Ibid.* II, pp. 326–7.

Chapter 6: Trust the People (*between pages 149 and 168*)

1. W. E. Gladstone, *Speeches and Addresses Delivered at the Election of 1865* (1865), p. 47.
2. J. Bryce, *Studies in Contemporary Biography* (1903), p. 97.
3. *Why I Am A Liberal*, ed. A. Reid (1885), p. 43.
4. *Letters of John Stuart Mill*, ed. H. S. R. Elliot (1910), II, p. 45.
5. *Fortnightly Review*, new series, VIII (November 1870), p. 590.
6. Quoted in A. J. P. Taylor, *The Troublemakers* (1957), p. 69.
7. J. S. Mill, *The State of Society in America* (1836).
8. Address by Edward Baines, Baines MSS 60/13.
9. J. Morley, *The Life of William Ewart Gladstone* (2nd edn., 1905), I, p. 759.
10. *Hansard*, 3rd series, CLXXXII (1866), 37–8.
11. G. M. Trevelyan, *The Life of John Bright* (1925), p. 151.
12. J. MacCabe, *The Life and Letters of G. J. Holyoake* (1908), I, p. 150.
13. *Ibid.* II, p. 162.
14. G. J. Holyoake, *The Liberal Situation* (1865), p. 23.
15. *Hansard*, 3rd series, CLXXXIII (1866), 148–9.
16. *Essays on Reform* (1867), pp. 29–31.
17. E. Baines, *Household Suffrage and Equal Electoral Districts* (1841), pp. 7, 8.
18. *Hansard*, 3rd series, CLXXV (1864), 293, 298–9.
19. *Hansard*, 3rd series, CLXXV (1864), 324–5.
20. *Hansard*, 3rd series, CLXXXII (1866), 8.
21. R. Masheder, *Dissent and Democracy* (1864), p. 252.
22. J. Morley, *The Life of Richard Cobden* (1881), II, p. 98.

23. Trevelyan, *Life of Bright*, p. 393.
24. Morley, *Life of Cobden*, II, p. 365.
25. Trevelyan, *Life of Bright*, p. 368.
26. *Ibid.* p. 367.
27. M. Arnold, *Culture and Anarchy*, ed. J. Dover Wilson (Cambridge paperback edn., 1971), p. 64.
28. *Ibid.* p. 104.
29. Edward Baines to Alexander Ritchie, 12 May 1865. Baines MSS 45/15.
30. Arnold, *Culture and Anarchy*, p. 64.
31. *The Works of Thomas Hill Green*, ed. R. L. Nettleship (1888), III, p. cxviii,
32. J. S. Mill, *Three Essays*, ed. R. Wollheim (Oxford paperback edn., 1975). p. 304.
33. *Ibid.* p. 197.
34. Quoted in E. S. Pankhurst, *The Suffragette Movement* (1931), p. 46.
35. P. Magnus, *Gladstone* (paperback edn., 1963), p. 383.
36. Mill, *Three Essays*, p. 278.
37. *Ibid.* pp. 284, 286.
38. *Ibid.* pp. 247, 254.
39. *Ibid.* p. 265.
40. D. Wiltshire, *The Social and Political Thought of Herbert Spencer* (Oxford, 1978), p. 113.
41. Holyoake, *The Liberal Situation*, pp. 9, 14.
42. A. P. Martin, *The Life and Letters of Viscount Sherbrooke* (1893), II, p. 263.
43. *Hansard*, 3rd series, CLXXXIII (1866), 152.
44. Morley, *Life of Cobden*, II, p. 53.
45. *Fortnightly Review*, new series, II (September 1867), p. 363.
46. *Tory Democrat—Two Famous Disraeli Speeches*, ed. E. Boyle (1950), p. 26.
47. R. T. Shannon, *Gladstone and the Bulgarian Agitation* (1963), p. 136.
48. W. E. Gladstone, *Gleanings of Past Years* (1879), I, pp. 198, 201.
49. Quoted in R. Kelley, 'Midlothian', *Victorian Studies*, IV (December 1960), p. 132.
50. *Ibid.* p. 136.
51. E. Stead, *My Father* (1913), p. 80.
52. B. Harrison, *Drink and the Victorians* (1971), p. 270.
53. *National Liberal Federation Report* (1887), p. 30.
54. F. Whyte, *The Life of W. T. Stead* (1925), I, p. 112.
55. J. L. Garvin, *Life of Chamberlain*, II (1933), pp. 84–5.
56. *The Times*, 22 May 1886.
57. J. F. Stephen, *Liberty, Equality, Fraternity*, ed. R. J. White (Cambridge, 1967), p. 212.
58. Quoted in T. J. Spinner, *George Joachim Goschen, The Transformation of a Victorian Liberal* (Cambridge, 1973), p. 95.
59. Mill, *Three Essays*, p. 245.
60. Lord Acton, *The History of Freedom* (1909), p. 54.
61. G. Meredith, *Collected Letters*, ed. C. Cline (Oxford, 1970), III, p. 1475; Martin, *Viscount Sherbrooke*, II, p. 445.
62. D. A. Hamer, *John Morley, Liberal Intellectual in Politics* (Oxford, 1968), p. 253.

63. *The Public Letters of John Bright*, ed. H. J. Leech (reprint, 1969), p. 234.

Chapter 7: Lib–Labism (*between pages 169 and 181*)

1. J. L. Garvin, *The Life of Joseph Chamberlain*, II, (1933), p. 143.
2. J. Arch, *The Story of His Life* (1898), p. 380.
3. J. Morley, *The Life of Richard Cobden* (1881), I, p. 467.
4. J. M. Baernreither, *English Associations of Working Men* (1889), p. 6.
5. J. L. MacCabe, *The Life and Letters of G. J. Holyoake* (1908), II, p. 98.
6. J. S. Mill, *Principles of Political Economy*, ed. W. J. Ashley (Oxford, 1920), p. 699.
7. *Ibid*. pp. 760, 764.
8. J. S. Mill, *Autobiography*, ed. J. Stillinger (Oxford paperback edn., 1975), p. 138.
9. Quoted in P. N. Backstrom, *Christian Socialism and Co-Operation in Victorian England* (1974), p. 65.
10. Mill, *Principles of Political Economy*, p. 792.
11. *The Public Letters of John Bright*, ed. H. J. Leech (reprint, 1969), p. 245.
12. *The Public Addresses of John Bright*, ed. J. E. T. Rogers (1879), p. 343.
13. Morley, *Life of Cobden*, I, p. 299.
14. E. Hodder, *The Life of Samuel Morley* (1887), p. 251.
15. Quoted in R. Boyson, *The Ashworth Cotton Enterprise* (Oxford, 1970), p. 153.
16. Quoted in W. H. G. Armytage, *A. J. Mundella, the Liberal Background to the Labour Movement* (1951), p. 320.
17. Quoted in A. V. Dicey, *Lectures on Law and Public Opinion* (1914), p. 199.
18. Quoted in A. Briggs, *Victorian People* (paperback edn., 1971), p. 257.
19. Armytage, *A. J. Mundella*, p. 70.
20. Quoted in D. A. Hamer, *Liberal Politics in the Age of Gladstone and Rosebery* (Oxford, 1972), p. 16.
21. Quoted in M. Barker, *Gladstone and Radicalism: The Reconstruction of Liberal Policy in Britain 1885–1894* (Hassocks, 1975), p. 91.
22. Quoted in F. M. Leventhal, *Respectable Radical: George Howell and Victorian Working Class Politics* (1971), p. 199.
23. *Tory Democrat—Two Famous Disraeli Speeches*, ed. E. Boyle (1950), p. 48.
24. MSS Reminiscences of T. H. Green by C. A. Fyffe, fols. 3, 4, in Balliol College Library, Oxford.
25. Goldwin Smith, *Reminiscences* (New York, 1910), p. 363.
26. *Essays on Reform* (1867), pp. 36, 40.
27. J. L. MacCabe, *G. J. Holyoake*, II, pp. 40–41.

Chapter 8: The Voluntary Principle (*between pages 182 and 199*)

1. J. Morley, *The Life of William Ewart Gladstone* (2nd edn., 1905), II, p. 825.
2. *The Works of Thomas Hill Green*, ed. R. L. Nettleship (1888), II, pp. 39–40.
3. E. Miall, *Views of the Voluntary Principle* (1845), p. 145.
4. J. S. Mill, *Principles of Political Economy*, ed. W. J. Ashley (Oxford, 1920), pp. 948–9.

5. *Nonconformist*, 20 July 1842, p. 497.
6. *Parliamentary Papers*, 1871, XIX (Reports from Commissioners), p. 729.
7. Quoted in B. Harrison, *Drink and the Victorians* (1971), pp. 208, 210.
8. A. Trollope, *Autobiography* (Oxford, 1929), p. 215.
9. E. Baines, *Education Best Promoted By Perfect Freedom* (1854), p. 28.
10. J. S. Mill, *Three Essays*, ed. R. Wollheim (Oxford paperback edn., 1975), p. 193.
11. Quoted in J. Morley, *Miscellanies, Fourth Series* (1908), pp. 152–3.
12. E. Miall, *The Nonconformist's Sketchbook* (1842), p. 249.
13. E. Hodder, *The Life of Samuel Morley* (1887), p. 455.
14. E. Baines, *Letters to Lord John Russell on State Education* (1847), p. 41.
15. *Ibid.* p. 3.
16. *Ibid.* p. 4; E. Baines, *On the Lancashire Plan of Secular Education* (1848), p. 8.
17. Baines, *Letters to Lord John Russell*, p. 42.
18. *Nonconformist*, 18 February 1852, p. 117.
19. E. Baines, *Remark on as Speech and Plan of Lord John Russell* (1856), p. 15.
20. Baines, *Letters to Lord John Russell*, p. 42.
21. *Nonconformist*, 20 July 1842, p. 497.
22. E. Baines, *An Alarm to the Nation on the Unjust, Unconstitutional and Dangerous Measure of State Education Proposed by the Government* (1847), p. 15.
23. Baines, *Letters to Lord John Russell*, p. 112.
24. E. Baines, *The Social, Educational and Religious State of the Manufacturing Districts* (1843), p. 1.
25. J. S. Mill, *Dissertations and Discussions, Political, Philosophical and Historical* (1859), I, p. 32.
26. Baines, *Letters to Lord John Russell*, p. 41.
27. Baines, *On the Lancashire Plan*, p. 11.
28. E. F. Rathbone, *William Rathbone, A Memoir* (1905), p. 368.
29. *Charity Organisation Society 5th Annual Report* (1875), pp. 5–6.
30. E. Miall, *The Politics of Christianity* (1863), p. 41.
31. Quoted in H. F. L. Cocks, *The Nonconformist Conscience* (1943), p. 30.
32. Quoted in M. Richter, *The Politics of Conscience, T. H. Green and His Age* (1964), p. 327.
33. T. H. Green, *Lectures on the Principles of Political Obligation* (2nd edn., 1948), p. 39.
34. Goldwin Smith, *Reminiscences* (New York, 1910), p. 230.
35. Mill, *Principles of Political Economy*, p. 978.
36. *Ibid.* p. 942.
37. *The Speeches of W. E. Gladstone* (1892), X, p. 132.
38. Edward Baines to James Kay-Shuttleworth, 19 October 1867. Baines MSS 52/11.
39. Quoted in N. Longmate, *The Hungry Mills* (1978), p. 134.
40. Mill, *Principles of Political Economy*, p. 950.
41. *Ibid.* p. 953.
42. *Ibid.* p. 958.
43. *Ibid.* p. 977.
44. *Ibid.* p. 978.

45. *The Long Debate On Poverty*, ed. A. Seldon (1972), p. 117.
46. C. L. Mowat, *The Charity Organisation Society 1869–1913* (1961), p. 133.
47. *Hansard*, 3rd series, CCLXXX (1883), 986.

Chapter 9: The Passion for Improvement (*between pages 200 and 221*)

1. J. Morley, *The Life of William Ewart Gladstone* (2nd edn., 1905), I, p. 757.
2. *Fortnightly Review*, new series, XVI (October 1874), p. 414.
3. T. H. Green, *Lectures on the Principles of Political Obligation* (2nd edn., 1948), pp. 227–8.
4. *The New Liberal Programme*, ed. A. Reid (1886), p. 111.
5. H. Fawcett, *The Economic Position of the English Labourer* (1865), p. 43.
6. Quoted in G. M. Trevelyan, *The Life of John Bright* (1925), p. 165.
7. *The Times*, 31 October 1866, p. 12.
8. *Hansard*, 3rd series, CCLX (1881), 60.
9. *The New Liberal Programme*, p. 11.
10. The phrase was originally used by the 7th Earl of Shaftesbury.
11. *Hansard*, 3rd series, CLXXXVIII (1867), 1549.
12. Quoted in *Pressure From Without in Early Victorian England*, ed. P. Hollis (1974), p. 305.
13. E. Hodder, *The Life of Samuel Morley* (1887), p. 419.
14. Quoted in E. P. Hennock, *Fit and Proper Persons* (1973), p. 140.
15. Quoted in W. F. Monypenny and G. E. Buckle, *The Life of Benjamin Disraeli, Earl of Beaconsfield*, V (1920), p. 194.
16. Hennock, *Fit and Proper Persons*, p. 75.
17. *Ibid.* p. 75.
18. R. W. Dale, 'The Perils and Uses of Rich Men', *Weekday Sermons* (1867), pp. 175–6.
19. A. W. W. Dale, *Life of R. W. Dale* (1898), p. 402.
20. Quoted in H. M. Lynd, *England in the 1880s* (Oxford, 1945), p. 167.
21. Quoted in Hennock, *Fit and Proper Persons*, p. 143.
22. Quoted in E. E. Gulley, *Joseph Chamberlain and English Social Politics* (1926), p. 86.
23. *The Times*, 21 September 1885.
24. R. W. Dale, *Liberalism, An Address to Birmingham Junior Liberal Association* (1878), p. 12.
25. B. Webb, *My Apprenticeship* (2nd edn., 1946), p. 159.
26. A. V. Dicey, *Lectures on the Relation between the Laws and Public Opinion* (1914), p. 64.
27. J. L. Garvin, *The Life of Joseph Chamberlain*, I (1932), pp. 384–5.
28. Quoted in P. Clarke, *Liberals and Social Democrats* (Cambridge, 1978), p. 137.
29. J. L. Hammond, *Gladstone and the Irish Nation* (1938), pp. 710–11.
30. *Hansard*, 3rd series, CLXXIII (1864), 1553–4.
31. Lynd, *England in the 1880s*, p. 150.
32. Hodder, *Life of Samuel Morley*, p. 452.
33. *Methodist Times*, 4 November 1886.
34. Garvin, *Life of Chamberlain*, II, pp. 56–7.

35. *Ibid.* II, p. 57.
36. *Ibid.* II, p. 61.
37. *Ibid.* II, p. 78.
38. *Ibid.* II, p. 78.
39. Quoted in D. A. Hamer, *Liberal Politics in the Age of Gladstone and Rosebery* (Oxford, 1972), p. 97.
40. P. Fraser, *Joseph Chamberlain, Radicalism and Empire, 1868–1914* (1966), p. 82.
41. *The Works of Thomas Hill Green*, ed. R. L. Nettleship (1888), III, p. 370.
42. *Ibid.* pp. 371–4.
43. *Ibid.* p. 375.
44. *Ibid.* pp. 383–4.
45. A. Toynbee, *Lectures on the Industrial Revolution in England* (1884), p. 219.
46. *The Works of T. H. Green*, III, p. 367.
47. *Ibid.* p. 386.
48. F. Whyte, *The Life of W. T. Stead* (1925), I, p. 113.

Chapter 10: The Waning of Optimism (*between pages 222 and 260*)

1. A. W. W. Dale, *The Life of R. W. Dale* (1898), p. 634.
2. *The New Liberal Programme*, ed. A. Reid (1886), p. 172.
3. W. Bagehot, *The English Constitution* (new edn., 1963), p. 277.
4. G. E. Fasnacht, *Acton's Political Philosophy* (1952), p. 18; *The Queen and Mr. Gladstone*, ed. P. Guedella (1933), p. 380.
5. T. J. Spinner, *George Joachim Goschen: The Transformation of a Victorian Liberal* (Cambridge, 1973), p. 92.
6. H. M. Lynd, *England in the 1880s* (Oxford, 1945), p. 73.
7. *Ibid.* p. 84.
8. T. Mackay, *Public Relief of the Poor* (1901), p. 92.
9. H. Spencer, *The Man Versus the State* (8th thousand, 1885), pp. 1, 4.
10. *Fortnightly Review*, new series, XXXVIII (October 1885), pp. 465–7.
11. J. Roach, 'Liberalism and the Victorian Intelligentsia', *Cambridge Historical Journal*, XIII (1957), p. 60.
12. H. Spencer, *Man Versus the State*, p. 7.
13. Roach, *art. cit.*, p. 71.
14. *Ibid.* p. 80.
15. *Fortnightly Review*, new series, XXXVIII (October 1885), p. 474.
16. *The Times*, 23 April 1885.
17. W. E. H. Lecky, *Democracy and Liberty* (1896), I, p. 229.
18. *Ibid.* I, p. 227.
19. M. Arnold, *Culture and Anarchy*, ed. J. Dover Wilson (Cambridge paperback edn., 1971), pp. 35–6.
20. J. L. Garvin, *The Life of Joseph Chamberlain*, I (1932), p. 159.
21. F. Montague, *The Limits of Individual Liberty* (1885), p. 2.
22. *The Queen and Mr. Gladstone*, p. 382.
23. *The Times*, 18 July 1977.
24. *Nineteenth Century*, XXVI (August 1889), p. 186.

25. Quoted in D. A. Hamer, *Liberal Politics in the Age of Gladstone and Rosebery* (Oxford, 1972), p. 147.
26. *Nineteenth Century*, XXVI (August 1889), p. 186.
27. W. S. Churchill, *Lord Randolph Churchill* (1906), I, p. 268.
28. *Nineteenth Century*, XXVI (August 1889), p. 187.
29. Churchill, *Lord Randolph Churchill*, I, p. 268.
30. *Nineteenth Century*, XXVI (September 1889), p. 498.
31. Quoted in S. Yeo, *Religion and Voluntary Organisations in Crisis* (1976), p. 261.
32. *Nineteenth Century*, L (September 1901), p. 369.
33. Quoted in F. M. Leventhal, *Respectable Radical: George Howell and Victorian Working Class Politics*, p. 53.
34. A. G. Gardiner, *The Life of Sir William Harcourt* (1923), I, p. 90.
35. H. Hyndman and W. Morris, *A Summary of the Principles of Socialism* (1884), p. 4.
36. A. Trollope, *The Prime Minister* (Oxford, 1952), II, p. 265.
37. Quoted in G. Watson, *The English Ideology* (1973), p. 167; P. Magnus, *Gladstone* (paperback edn., 1963), p. 257.
38. Quoted in Lynd, *England in the 1880s*, p. 292.
39. E. Hodder, *The Life of Samuel Morley* (1887), p. 397.
40. Quoted in letter of the Revd. George Murphy to *Daily News*, 7 September 1886.
41. Quoted in M. Barker, *Gladstone and Radicalism: The Reconstruction of Liberal Policy in Britain 1885–1894* (Hassocks, 1975), p. 150.
42. Quoted in D. A. Hamer, *John Morley, Liberal Intellectual in Politics* (Oxford, 1968), p. 305.
43. L. T. Hobhouse, *Liberalism* (1942), p. 214.
44. I owe these references to Dr. Edward Royle.
45. A. W. W. Dale, *Life of R. W. Dale*, p. 649.
46. B. Webb, *Our Partnership* (1948), pp. 162–3.
47. *Manchester Guardian*, 17 October 1900.
48. *Fortnightly Review*, new series, XV (March 1874), p. 305.
49. *Nonconformist*, 17 December 1879.
50. Goldwin Smith, *Reminiscences* (New York, 1910), p. 364.
51. Quoted in Barker, *Gladstone and Radicalism*, p. 129.
52. Quoted in J. Morley, *Miscellanies, Fourth Series* (1908), p. 278.
53. Quoted in R. Shannon, *The Crisis of Imperialism 1865–1915* (paperback edn., 1976), p. 149.
54. A. Tennyson, *Locksley Hall Sixty Years After* (1886), lines 73–8.
55. Hamer, *John Morley*, p. 142.
56. J. Morley, *On Compromise* (2nd edn., 1886), pp. 20, 21, 37.
57. *Ibid.* p. 126.
58. *The Times*, 5 April 1888, p. 7.
59. J. Morley, *The Life of William Ewart Gladstone* (2nd edn., 1905), II, p. 779.
60. *Ibid.* II, p. 461.
61. *The Correspondence of Lord Acton*, ed. J. N. Figgis and R. V. Laurence (1917), pp. 239–40.

62. *The New Liberal Programme*, p. xiv.
63. Quoted in Hamer, *Liberal Politics in the Age of Gladstone and Rosebery*, p. 170.
64. Morley, *Life of Gladstone*, II, p. 711.
65. Quoted in Lynd, *England in the 1880s*, p. 183.
66. *The Times*, 20 November 1889, p. 10.
67. *The Times*, 23 April 1889, p. 8.
68. R. H. Murray, *Studies in English Social and Political Thinkers of the Nineteenth Century* (1929), I, p. 404.
69. *Hansard*, 3rd series, CCCXXV (1888), 1132.
70. *The Times*, 23 April 1889, p. 8; *Ibid.* 20 November 1889, p. 10.
71. Quoted in E. Feuchtwanger, *Gladstone* (paperback edn., 1975), p. 262.
72. *The Speeches of W. E. Gladstone* (1892), X, p. 132.
73. Barker, *Gladstone and Radicalism*, p. 146.
74. *Ibid.* p. 147.
75. *Fabian Essays* (6th edn., 1962), pp. 246-7.
76. Barker, *Gladstone and Radicalism*, p. 92.
77. *The Times*, 12 December 1891; *Hansard*, 4th series, II (1892), 1711.
78. *Hansard*, 4th series, XI (1893), 1857.
79. *A Plea for Liberty*, ed. T. Mackay (1891), p. 141.
80. Quoted in H. V. Emy, *Liberals, Radicals and Social Politics, 1892-1914* (Cambridge, 1973), p. 10.
81. Gardiner, *Life of Harcourt*, II, p. 231.
82. *Commonweal*, 7 January 1888.
83. *Correspondence of Lord Acton*, p. 235; Hamer, *Liberal Politics in the Age of Gladstone and Rosebery*, p. 141.
84. Quoted in Magnus, *Gladstone*, p. 146.
85. Quoted in P. Stansky, *Ambitions and Strategies: The Struggle for the Leadership of the Liberal Party in the 1890s* (Oxford, 1964), p. 35.
86. Quoted in P. Knaplund, *Gladstone's Foreign Policy* (new edn., 1970), pp. 266-7.
87. Letter to J. Cowan, 17 March 1894, quoted in Morley, *Life of Gladstone*, II, p. 775; remarks to Stead quoted in J. W. Robertson-Scott, *The Life and Death of a Newspaper* (1952), p. 170; letter to a friend quoted in *The Collapse of the British Liberal Party*, ed. J. A. Thompson (Lexington, Mass., 1969), p. 12.
88. Morley, *Life of Gladstone*, II, p. 776.
89. Quoted in D. Read, *The English Provinces 1760-1960* (1964), p. 165.
90. Webb, *Our Partnership*, p. 124.
91. L. E. Elliott-Binns, *Religion in the Victorian Era* (1936), p. 407.
92. Quoted in A. F. Havighurst, *Radical Journalist: H. W. Massingham* (1974), p. 77.
93. Quoted in Hamer, *Liberal Politics in the Age of Gladstone and Rosebery*, p. 223.
94. *Essays in Liberalism by Six Oxford Men* (1897), p. 3.
95. *Ibid.* p. 4.
96. *Ibid.* p. 95.

97. *Ibid.* pp. 272, 269.
98. J. Arch, *The Story of His Life* (1898), p. 404.
99. Quoted in Magnus, *Gladstone*, p. 432.
100. G. W. E. Russell, *Sir Wilfrid Lawson: A Memoir* (1909), p. 315.
101. The phrase was first used by L. A. Atherley-Jones in an article in the *Nineteenth Century* in 1889.
102. *Progressive Review*, I (October 1896), p. 3.
103. *Progressive Review*, I (November 1896), p. 138.
104. Webb, *Our Partnership*, p. 109.
105. *The Liberal Tradition from Fox to Keynes*, ed. A. Bullock and M. Shock (1966), p. 212.
106. K. Nott, *The Good Want Power: Essays in the Psychological Possibilities of Liberalism* (1977), p. 2.
107. Gardiner, *Life of Harcourt*, II, p. 479.
108. Morley, *Life of Gladstone*, II, p. 715.
109. Quoted in Hamer, *John Morley*, p. 354.
110. J. H. Morgan, *John, Viscount Morley* (1924), p. 99.
111. *The Holmes–Laski Letters*, ed. M. D. Howe (1953), I, p. 278.
112. J. Morley, *Politics and History* (1923), p. 75.
113. Quoted in P. F. Clarke, *Liberals and Social Democrats* (Cambridge, 1978), p. 215.
114. N. M. Butler, *The Faith of a Liberal* (New York, 1924), p. 4.

Index

Numbers in bold type indicate the location of biographical notes about individual Liberals mentioned in the text.

Aberdeen, Lord, 30, 103, 129

Acland, A. D., 250, 251, **265**

Acton, Lord, 12, 32, 36, 41, 43, 63, 73, 79, 84, 85–91, 144, 167–8, 245, 252, 260, **265**

Administrative Reform Association, 29, 64

America, United States of, 36, 60–3, 68, 77, 88, 123–4, 135–6, 162, 256

American Civil War, 36–7, 120, 136, 153–4

Anti-Corn Law League, 25–6, 57–8, 151, 152, 155, 241

Applegarth, Robert, 176

Arbitration, 130, 135–6, 174–6

Arch, Joseph, 169, 176, 179, 255, **265**

Argyll, 8th Duke of, 65, 140, 204, 224, 245, **265**

Arnold, Matthew, 12, 14, 17, 44, 59, 71, 72, 78, 91, 96, 99, 105, 107, 110, 114, 157, 158, 166, 194, 198

Culture and Anarchy, 40, 48, 69, 71, 86–7, 88, 101, 229

Friendship's Garland, 50, 100

Ashworth, Henry, 54, 60, 61, 131, 178, **265**

Asquith, H. H., 107, 220, 221, 243, 250, 251, 257, 258, 259, 260

Atherley-Jones, L. A., 232

Attwood, Thomas, 58

Bagehot, Walter, 33, 56, 72, 111, 143, 223, 224, **265**

Baines, Edward, the elder, 20, 25, 31

Baines, Edward, the younger, 23, 25, 28, 30, 31, 34, 37, 38, 52, 54, 55, 57, 71, 99, 106, 108, 116, 117, 124, 150, 154–5, 158, 184, 185–9, 194, 198, **266**

Baring, Francis, 18

Bass, M. T., 54, 169, 174, 178, **266**

Beales, Edmund, 38, **266**

Becker, Lydia, 159

Belgium, 18, 36, 82, 123, 142, 147, 242

Belloc, Hilaire, 114, 254, 255, 260

Benn, Ernest, 231

Benn, John, 213

Benn, William Wedgwood, 231

Bentham, Jeremy, 19, 26, 61, 73, 74, 200

Beveridge, William, 256, 260

Birmingham, 25, 30, 32, 57, 58–9, 77, 93, 100, 106, 110, 113, 124, 165, 180, 185, 208–10, 213, 215, 242

Bismarck, Otto Van, 36, 242

Blanc, Louis, 84

Bosanquet, Bernard, 220

Bowring, John, 25

Bradford, 31, 55, 57, 113, 153, 235

Bradlaugh, Charles, 76–7, 94, 98, 110, 127, 204, 205, 247, **266**

Bramwell, Baron, 225

Briggs, Henry, 171

Bright, Jacob, 159, **266**

Bright, John, 12, 17, 24, 26–9, 30, 31, 34, 36–7, 45, 46, 50–1, 52, 53, 55, 57, 58–9, 61, 62, 66, 69–71, 93, 115, 117, 152, 153, 155, 159, 170, 176, 178, 180, 182, 203, 205, 208, 222, 233, 235, 237, 244, 247, 255, 260, **266**

and foreign affairs, 120, 123–31, 134, 139–40, 143

and Nonconformity, 100, 102, 103, 111–13

and Parliamentary reform, 38, 151, 156–8, 160, 167, 168, 172–4

Broadhurst, Henry, 122, 169, 234, **266**
Brodrick, G. C., 33, 38, 56, **266**
Brougham, Henry, 200
Browning, Robert, 73, 82
Bruce, H. A., 53, 116, 206, **267**
Bryce, James, 33, 35, 38, 56, 60, 82, 85, 92, 128, 149, 153, 250, 251, **267**
Buckle, Henry, 44
Bulgarian atrocities, the, 105, 109, 114, 121–2, 142–3, 146, 164
Buller, Charles, 19
Burns, John, 234, 249
Burt, Thomas, 169, 178, 234, 235, 249, **267**
Butler, Josephine, 95, 119
Butler, Montague, 227, 228
Byron, Lord, 11, 84, 92

Cadbury, George, 260
Caine, W. S., 116, 200, **267**
Campbell, Sir George, 140, **267**
Campbell-Bannerman, Henry, 68, 250, 259, **267**
Canada, 36
Cardwell, Edward, 53, 55, 64, 65, **267**
Carlyle, Thomas, 35, 37, 44, 59, 69, 75, 91, 94, 194, 198
Carnegie, Andrew, 248
Cattell, Charles, 76, 93
Cavour, Camillo, 35, 82–3
Chadwick, Edwin, 200, 208
Chamberlain, Joseph, 43, 59, 62, 65, 93, 99, 100, 101, 106, 108–9, 117, 159, 165–6, 169, 180, 201, 205, 206, 207, 209–11, 213, 215–17, 221, 222, 224, 229, 230, 236, 242, 246, **267**
Charity Organisation Society, 189–90, 193, 198, 199, 220
Chartism, 22–3, 25, 41, 76, 151, 152, 170
Childers, H. C. E., 53, 65, **268**
Churchill, Lord Randolph, 232
Church rates, 24, 100, 101, 102
Cleveland, Grover, 68
Clifford, John, 110, 239, **268**

Cobden, Richard, 12, 20–1, 22, 24, 26–9, 30, 31, 34, 36, 37, 40, 50–1, 52, 53, 54, 57, 58, 59, 60–3, 66, 68, 69–71, 78, 82, 111–12, 116, 120, 123–38, 152, 155, 156, 163, 170, 176, 178, 182, 186, 202, 205, 208, 218, 219, 233, 255, 260, **268**
Collings, Jesse, 60, 205, 231, **268**
Collins, John, 25
Colman, J. J., 54, 108, 110, **268**
Complete Suffrage Union, 25, 151
Comte, Auguste, 80
Constant, Henri, 18, 81, 160
Contagious Diseases Acts, 95, 119, 199, 200
Co-operative movement, 150, 170–2
Corn laws, repeal of, 26, 27, 111–12
Cowen, Joseph, 92, 235, **268**
Crimean War, 29, 67, 129–30, 133, 145
Crosskey, H. W., 100, 106
Crossley, Francis, 31, 54, 171, **268**

Daily News, the, 30, 124, 155
Daily Telegraph, the, 30, 50
Dale, R. W., 49, 59, 71, 100, 101, 106–7, 108, 109, 110, 112, 113, 208, 211, 222, 239, 240, 244, 253, **268**
Dawson, George, 100, 208–9, **268**
Derby, Lord, 31, 37, 83
De Tocqueville, Alexis, 81, 160
Devey, George, 12
Dicey, A. V., 33, 38, 133, 138, 143, 195, 211, 226, 227, 228, **269**
Dickens, Charles, 29, 30, 59
Dilke, Charles, 93, 110, 165, 230, **269**
Disestablishment, 24, 107–10
Disraeli, Benjamin, 17, 26, 38, 39, 49, 62, 78, 94, 100, 120, 121, 125, 128, 136, 137–8, 145, 163, 164, 177, 179, 208
Don Pacifico, 127, 128
Doulton, Henry, 54, **269**
Durham, Earl of, 23

Economist, the, 26, 33
Edinburgh Review, the, 18, 73

Education, 105–7, 185–8, 205–6
Education Act (1870), 60, 106, 122, 194, 206
Egypt, 138–40
Eliot, George, 33
    Felix Holt the Radical, 45, 47, 100, 111
Ellis, Tom, 141
Escott, T. H., 215
Eyre, Governor, 37, 120

Fabian Society, 229, 231, 243, 249
Fawcett, Henry, 33, 37, 93, 116, 127, 142, 149, 153, 159, 171, 192, 202, **269**
Fawcett, Millicent, 149
Fife, Earl of, 140
Fisher, H. A. L., 260
Foote, G. W., 76, 77
Forster, W. E., 55, 57, 60, 106, 143, 206, 222, **269**
Fortnightly Review, the, 33, 34, 42, 43, 52, 61, 77, 109, 150, 229
Fowler, H. H., 250
Fox, Charles James, 18
Fox, W. J., 76, 77, 97, **269**
France, 17, 18, 26, 28, 31, 35, 79–81, 129–30, 134–5, 145, 242
Freeman, E. A., 34, **269**
Free trade, 19, 62, 67–9, 130–1, 233–4
Froebel, J., 41

Gambetta, Leon, 35
Gardiner, A. G., 114
Garibaldi, Giuseppe, 35, 38, 79, 82, 92, 154
George, Henry, 203
Germany, 31, 81–2, 85, 197, 234, 242, 256
Gervinus, George, 47, 82
Gibson, Thomas Milner, 30, **269**
Gilbert and Sullivan, 11, 96
Gladstone, W. E., 12, 13, 26, 30, 31, 32, 35, 36, 39, 40, 53, 55, 56, 59, 63, 65, 73, 77, 79, 81, 83, 84, 91, 93, 94, 95, 96, 116, 118, 119, 149,
    150, 169, 170, 179, 201, 218, 232, 237, 246, 252, 253, 255, 256, 258, 260, **270**
    and economy, 66–8, 252
    foreign policy, 123, 125, 128, 129–31, 133–48
    and Ireland, 115, 140, 203–4, 222–3, 230, 245–6
    Midlothian campaigns, 92, 131, 133, 138, 164–5, 166, 168
    and Nonconformists, 99, 104–5, 107, 109–10, 112, 121–2
    and Parliamentary reform, 38, 151, 152–5, 166
    popular appeal of, 163–8, 236
    and social reform, 206, 213–16, 221, 249–51
    and trade unions, 177
    views of others on, 14–15, 200, 224, 225, 227–30
    voluntaryist sympathies of, 182, 191–3, 198, 247–9
Glynn, C. G., 173
Gordon, General George, 115, 139
Goschen, G. J., 53, 65, 167, 193, 214, 224, 225, 228, **270**
Granville, 2nd Earl, 53, 65, 121, **270**
Greece, 82, 92
Green, T. H., 34, 35, 55, 73, 77, 81, 85, 103, 117, 120, 128, 133, 149, 158, 179, 182, 189, 191, 199, 202, 207, 215, 217–20, 244, 256, **270**
Grey, 2nd Earl, 19
Grey, Edward, 147, 243, 257, 258
Grote, George, 19, 78
Guizot, Francis, 18, 81

Habsburg Empire, 27, 36, 144, 242
Haldane, R. B., 243, 257
Hammond, J. L., 114, 147, 254
Harcourt, W. V., 32, 39, 117, 118, 119, 184, 199, 207, 237, 249, 251, 270
Hardie, Keir, 249
Hardy, Thomas, 243
Harmsworth, Alfred, 114
Harrison, Frederic, 33, 38, 81, 176, 240, **270**

Hartington, Lord, 222, 228
Hegel, Georg, 81, 85, 90
Henderson, Arthur, 249
Herbert, Auberon, 93, 116, 204, **270**
Herzin, Alexander, 84
Hirst, F. W., 147, 254, 255, 259
Hobhouse, L. T., 114, 147, 220, 239, 242, 257
Hobson, J. A., 147, 213, 220, 221, 257
Holyoake, George, 76–7, 84, 92, 93, 97, 152, 162, 163, 170, 171, 180, **270**
Howell, George, 39, 93, 97, 118, 142, 152, 154, 169, 173, 178, 179, 180, 202, 234, 235, 237, 251, **271**
Hughes, Hugh Price, 83, 100, 105, 110, 112, 120, 215, 220, 221, 239, **271**
Hughes, Thomas, 32, 36, 37, 45, 169, 170, 171, 176, 177, **271**
Hugo, Victor, 84, 126
Humboldt, Wilhelm von, 82
Hume, Joseph, 19, 27, 28, 174
Hunt, Leigh, 28, 75
Huskisson, William, 67
Hutton, Richard, 153, 180, **271**
Hyndman, Henry, 180, 237

Illingworth, Alfred, 235, **271**
Income tax, 67, 110
India, 91, 126–7, 136, 138
Ireland:
   Home Rule for, 39, 107, 109, 115, 140–1, 165, 221, 222–3, 227, 230–2, 245
   land reform in, 203–4, 224
Italy, 18, 27, 35, 79, 82–4, 132, 134

Jackson, Andrew, 36, 61
James, Henry, 66, **271**
James, William, 12
Johnson, Paul, 226
Jones, Ernest, 174, 232
Jowett, Benjamin, 34, 143

Kant, Immanuel, 81
Keynes, J. M., 256, 260
Kinglake, Alexander, 32

Kingsley, Charles, 12, 37
Kossuth, Lajos, 84, 133

Labouchere, Henry, 205, **271**
Laffite, Jacques, 18
Laissez-faire, 195–7, 199, 211, 214, 223, 224, 225
Landor, W. S., 82
Land reform, 201–5
Lansbury, George, 248
Laski, Harold, 259
Lawson, Wilfrid, 111, 116, 118, 200, 256, **271**
Leader, Robert, 31
League of Nations, 147
Lecky, William, 228
Leeds, 20, 25, 30, 31, 32, 38, 51, 55, 57, 113, 117, 150, 156
Leeman, George, 210
Lever, William Hesketh, 171, 260
Liberal Imperialists, 12, 243, 257
Liberal Unionists, 12, 230–1, 254
Liberation Society, 102, 108, 109, 241
Liberty and Property Defence League, 224–5
Lichfield, 2nd Earl of, 189, 193, **271–2**
Lincoln, Abraham, 37, 62
Liverpool, 30, 53, 55, 189, 240, 255
Lloyd George, David, 100, 118, 141, 203, 258
Loch, Charles, 189, 198, **272**
Locke, John, 73, 75, 168
Lovett, William, 25, 151
Lowe, Robert, 65, 162, 163, 168, 206, 223, **272**
Lowery, Robert, 151
Lubbock, John, 178, 200, 247, **272**
Lunn, Henry, 41, 99

Macaulay, T. B., 20, 43
MacDonald, Alexander, 178
MacDonald, Ramsay, 249, 257
MacDonnell, P. J., 254
Mackay, Thomas, 225
Maine, Henry, 226–7, 228, 243, 256
Manchester, 26, 32, 36, 38, 55, 56, 57–9, 66, 71, 72, 106, 124, 126, 155, 187, 208

Manchester Guardian, the, 30, 35, 114, 240, 257
Manchester Party, 26, 27, 32, 76, 123, 124, 125, 129, 130, 131, 176
Manchester School, 28, 30, 50, 58, 131, 133, 135, 200, 205, 217, 219
Mann, Thomas, 234, 235, 257
Manning, Henry, 103, 250
Marx, Karl, 173
Massingham, Henry, 114, 147, 220, 259
Masterman, Charles, 114
Mather, William, 251, **272**
Maxse, F. A., 189
Mazzini, Giuseppe, 18, 69, 82–4, 92, 144
Mearns, Andrew, 213
Melbourne, Viscount, 19, 24
Meredith, George, 12, 33, 49, 62, 73, 82, 168, **272**
   Beauchamp's Career, 26, 33, 39, 47, 58, 128, 189
Miall, Arthur, 104
Miall, Edward, 24, 25, 28, 34, 37, 57, 99, 101, 106, 107–8, 116, 120, 126, 158, 183, 185–8, 190, 194, 198, 243, **272**
Mill, James, 21, 51
Mill, John Stuart, 12, 20, 21–4, 29, 32, 34, 35, 36–7, 40, 41–2, 45, 46, 47, 49, 51, 54, 64, 70, 74, 75, 77–82, 84, 93, 94, 95, 96, 97, 113, 117, 132, 136, 142, 144, 150, 169, 172, 183–4, 188, 200, 201, 217, 219, 260, **272**
   On Liberty, 73, 82, 85–91, 223
   On Representative Government, 65, 144, 158–62, 167
   Principles of Political Economy, 63, 171, 183, 191, 195–7, 203
Molesworth, William, 19
Montague, F. C., 230
Morel, E. D., 125
Morley, John, 33, 34, 35, 36, 42, 43, 44–5, 46, 52, 55, 57, 60, 62, 65, 73, 77–90, 94, 97, 103, 108–9, 113, 114, 117, 119, 120, 126, 143, 147, 150, 159, 163, 168, 174, 202,

209, 222, 238, 244–8, 251, 252, 254, 255, 258–60, **272–3**
Morley, Samuel, 29, 30, 34, 37, 38, 43, 51, 54, 70, 71, 95, 99, 101, 105, 108, 109, 116, 169, 173–7, 180, 185, 194, 198, 207, 214, 235, 238, 244, 260, **273**
Morris, William, 41, 142, 229, 237, 252
Mundella, A. J., 57, 60, 61, 165, 169, 170, 174–8, 206, 210, 239, 244, 249, 251, 252, **273**
Murray, Gilbert, 260

National Liberal Federation, 62, 118, 165–6, 167, 206, 231, 232, 235, 242, 246, 248, 250, 254
Neale, E. V., 172
Newcastle, 57, 92, 152, 247, 248
New Liberalism, 12, 213, 215, 220–1, 231, 233, 246, 251, 257–8
Newman, J. H., 11, 44, 69, 75, 78, 86, 91
Newnes, George, 114
Nietzsche, Friedrich, 243
Nonconformist, the, 24, 25, 101, 102, 104, 105, 185
Northern Echo, the, 55, 113–15, 121
Nott, Kathleen, 258

O'Brien, Bronterre, 25
O'Connor, Feargus, 22, 25
Old Mortality Society, 34, 82, 133
Olivier, Sydney, 257
O'Neill, Arthur, 25
Owen, Robert, 23

Paine, Thomas, 75
Pall Mall Gazette, the, 95, 103, 113–15, 119, 148, 166, 221
Palmer, George, 54, 235, **273**
Palmerston, Viscount, 24, 27, 28–9, 31, 32, 37, 38, 63, 93, 113, 120, 123, 124, 127, 128–9, 130, 131, 132, 145, 152, 153, 155, 163
Pankhurst, Emmeline, 95
Pankhurst, Richard, 95
Parnell, Charles, 110–11

Peace Society, 120, 126, 129, 130
Peel, Sir Robert, 24, 26, 31, 64
Perks, R. W., 109
Phillimore, J. S., 254, 255
Philosophic Radicals, the, 19–21, 23, 29, 74, 127
Place, Francis, 27, 60, 200
Pochin, H. D., 224, 225, **273**
Poerio, Carlo, 83
Positivism, 80–1, 84
Potter, George, 173
Progressive Review, the, 257
Proportional representation, 161–2
Prostitution, 119
Pulszky, Francis, 84

Radical Programme, 109, 205, 215–16, 221, 230
Rainbow Circle, 257
Rathbone, William, 54, 55, 65, 104, 116, 118, 172, 189, 200, **273**
Reform Acts:
  1832, 14, 17, 18, 35, 54, 73, 202
  1867, 38–9, 158, 163, 206
  1884, 166–7, 216, 226, 238
Reform Bills:
  1864 (Baines's), 38, 154–5, 158, 162
  1866 (Gladstone's), 163
Reform League, 38, 76, 154, 156, 169, 173
Reid, Andrew, 47, 222, 223
Reid, R. T., 238, **273**
Reid, Thomas Wemyss, 31, **273**
Rendel, Stuart, 141, **274**
Republicanism, 93
Richard, Henry, 25, 27, 126, 130, 188, **274**
Ripon, Marquess of, 138, 246, 251, **274**
Ritchie, D. G., 219
Robertson, J. M., 239, 257
Rochdale, 24, 55, 57, 61, 100, 102, 150, 151, 170, 173, 205
Roebuck, J. A., 19, 27, 28
Rogers, J. G., 109, 110, 122, **274**
Rogers, J. T., 34, 38, 202, 204, **274**
Rogier, Charles, 36, 77

Romilly, Samuel, 200
Rosebery, Earl of, 107, 140, 166, 232, 243, 251, 253, 254
Rossetti, Gabriele, 84
Roundell, C. S., 190, **274**
Rowntree, Seebohm, 171, 260
Ruskin, John, 44, 237
Russell, G. W. E., 122, 233, 244
Russell, Lord John, 32, 38, 97, 155
Russia, 35, 129–30, 136–45, 234, 256
Rylands, Peter, 65, **274**

Salisbury, Lord, 14, 145, 206
Salt, Titus, 31, 37, 54, 55, 57, 71, 173, 174, 178, 207–8, 260, **274**
Samuel, Herbert, 220, 254, 257
Scarr, Archie, 51
Scotland, 54, 57, 107, 140–1
Scott, C. P., 114
Scott, Sir Walter, 17
Secularist movement, 75–8, 96–8
Seeley, Sir John, 242
Selborne, Lord, 65, **274**
Shaftesbury, 7th Earl of, 69, 186
Shaw, G. B., 241
Sheffield, 31, 57, 113, 175, 206, 239
Shelley, P. B., 75, 84
Sidgwick, Henry, 33
Simon, J. A., 254, 255, 257
Smith, Adam, 73–4, 124
Smith, Goldwin, 34, 37, 38, 56, 69, 93, 124, 167, 178, 179, 191, 241, **274–5**
Smith, Southwood, 200
Southey, Robert, 17
Spain, 17
Spectator, the, 33, 153
Spencer, Herbert, 26, 37, 70, 77, 80, 114, 162, 185, 199, 225–6, 256, **275**
Spender, J. A., 114
Standring, George, 239
Stanley, Lord, 61
Stansfeld, James, 31, 46, 47, 82, 84, 85, 93, 96, 119, 132, 133, 142, 173, 194, 200, **275**
Stead, F. H., 199

Stead, W. T., 55, 57, 95, 99, 103, 110, 113–15, 119–20, 121–2, 130, 146, 147–8, 165, 166, 220, 221, 255–6, **275**
Stephen, James Fitzjames, 33, 41, 91, 99, 127, 143, 167, 224, 226, 227, 228, **275**
Stephen, Leslie, 33, 38, 77, **275**
Sturge, Joseph, 25
Swinburne, A. C., 82

Taylor, J. E., 54
Taylor, Peter, 93, 184, 198, **275**
Temperance, 115–19, 120, 184, 206–7, 212
Tennyson, Alfred, Lord, 43, 92, 125, 129, 143, 227, 243, 245
Thackeray, W. M., 12, 29, 47, **275**
Thiers, Adolphe, 18, 35
Thomas, Alfred, 141, **275–6**
Thomas, Hugh, 226
Thomasson, Thomas, 241
Tillett, Ben, 234, 235, 257
Times, The, 37, 68, 71, 96, 111, 127, 155, 246
Toynbee, Arnold, 219
Trade unions, 169, 175, 176–7, 234–5, 256

Trevelyan, Charles, the elder, 63, 189, **276**
Trevelyan, Charles, the younger, 257
Trevelyan, G. M., 14, 260
Trevelyan, G. O., 33, 116, 142, 165, 166, 231, 257, **276**
Trollope, Anthony, 12, 32–3, 44, 47, 53, 66, 72, 142, 184, **276**
Phineas Finn, 62
Phineas Redux, 40
The Prime Minister, 43, 237
The Duke's Children, 224
Tupper, Martin, 44

Vandervelde, Émile, 242
Victoria, Queen, 20, 38, 39, 93, 224
Vincent, Henry, 25, 120, 126, 152

Wales, 54, 57, 107, 117, 140–1, 143–4
Watson, R. S., 175, 251, **276**
Webb, Beatrice, 211, 229, 240, 253
Webb, Sidney, 111, 229, 236, 248, 257
Whiggism, 12, 18–20, 39–41, 73, 76, 102, 163
Williams, J. C., 240–1, **276**
Women, emancipation of, 95–6, 115, 159
Wordsworth, William, 74